To

Barry ~

DEAL

ALL IN THE DOWNS

Good wishes,

Gregory Holyoake

Gregory Holyoake

S.B. Publications

for
Judy Wilson
who loves Walmer

Companion Volume:
DEAL: Sad Smuggling Town

First published in 2008 by S. B. Publications
Tel: 01323 893498
Email: sbpublications@tiscali.co.uk

ISBN 978-185770-3429

Cover design: Ian Fuggle
Special photography: Ian Giles
Front cover picture: 'Off Deal' by JMW Turner, courtesy The Walker Gallery, Liverpool
Back cover picture: Queen Elizabeth the Queen Mother, Lord Warden of the Cinque Ports, leaving St. Mary's Church, Walmer
Title page: Goss Souvenir china of a Deal bathing machine

Designed and Typeset by EH Graphics (01273) 515527

All in the Downs the fleet was moor'd,
The streamers waving in the wind,
When black-eyed Susan came on board,
Oh! Where shall I my true love find?

John Gay

Pollock's toy theatre production of 'Black Ey'd Susan'.

The Royal Thames Yacht Club Ocean Match from Nore to Dover in June 1874 © British Library.

CONTENTS

THE GREAT DOWNS

'A Forest of Masts'

THE GREAT DOWNS off Deal encompasses that part of the English Channel which lies between the Kent Coast and the Goodwin Sands. The Sands act as a natural breakwater against easterly winds while, with the wind in the west, the land forms a protective weather shore for ships seeking shelter from winter storms. Indeed, Gattie in 'Memorials of the Goodwin Sands' (1904) asserts that the name derives from the Saxon 'duna', meaning protective dunes or sandbanks. And because of its unique position the Downs has been known to mariners worldwide and is, indisputably, the most famous anchorage in the world.

The Downs provides a safe anchorage of around fifty square miles which in times of conflict was able to accommodate the entire British Fleet. (The shallower north end is known as the 'Small Downs' and lies inside the sandbank known as the 'Brake') There, in the days of sail, with good holding ground in a depth of from 10 to 20 metres, fleets of several hundred vessels could lie at anchor for weeks. Pritchard states in his 'History of Deal' (1864) "From seventy to eighty pennants we have seen at one time flying from the mast-head, and three Admirals commanding three fleets rendezvousing in the Downs at one and the same time."Formerly, there might be four hundred large ships at anchor while a convoy of one hundred merchantmen left for a world voyage, smaller vessels tagging along for safety.

Bayley presents the Anchorage in his authorative 'Seamen of the Downs' (1929) as "A strategical point of infinite value in war, commanding as it does the shortest passage to and from the Continent." Indeed, the Downs has been closely identified with the Royal Navy for centuries and has witnessed numerous notable battles.

The Downs was the scene of the invasion by Julius Caesar who made his initial assault on Kent in 55 BC. His fleet of eighty transports plus war galleys conveying 10,000 men sailed directly across the English Channel from conquered Gaul (France) to Dover where they were repelled by Celts hurling missiles from the soaring cliffs. The Roman navy then sailed eight miles, hugging the coast until they came to "low, lying land" (Saxon: 'dylle') from which Deal's name derives. Warring Britons, their naked bodies daubed with woad, their wild hair stiffened with lime, relentlessly rode their sleek chariots into battle and drove the Romans from the shore.

Spurred on by the bravery of the standard bearer of the Tenth Legion Caesar's troops effected a landing and they established a fortified ship camp stretching the length of the foreshore. Sudden storms, aided by a high spring tide, wrecked this encampment and Caesar was forced to sue for peace before returning with his battered fleet to the Continent. Next summer Caesar returned with a vengeance conveying his vast army in specially adapted ships with greater beam, in order to give them more capacity for carrying, and lower freeboards, to ensure speedier embarkation of troops. Additionally, they were designed to be propelled by oars as well as sail so that they had better manoeuvrability in the treacherous Channel waters.

Caesar's new fleet consisted of eight hundred warships carrying five legions and two thousand cavalry. This time his point of landing was further northwards in the vicinity of modern Sandwich. The Britons, fearing the size and strength of the invaders, discreetly retired inland. Caesar marched his troops across Kent to pursue the fleeing natives to the banks of the River Thames. Principal tribe was the Cantii from which the county's name, 'Kent', derives. Triumphantly Caesar returned that winter to Rome where he was hailed as the conqueror of the Empire's most northerly territory. He made a pompous display of offering British pearls at the Shrine of Venus, from whom it was believed he descended.

A third Roman invasion came one hundred years later. Aulus Plautius sailed for Britain in 43 AD and landed unchallenged on the Kentish coast. He encamped at Rutupiea (Richborough) then an island at the approach to the wide Wantsum Channel that divided the Isle of Thanet from the mainland. Emperor Claudius travelled from

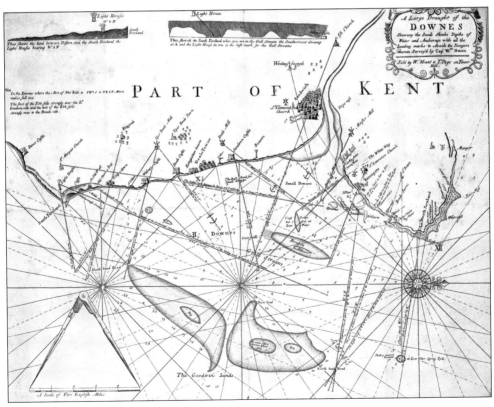

A large Draught of the Downs by Captain William Nunn circa 1750.
© National Maritime Museum.

Rome to claim the victory and entered through a triumphal arch riding an elephant, proclaiming himself Conqueror of Britain. Richborough, Dover, Lympne and Pevensey were established as ports for the Classus Britannica (British Fleet) which protected merchant ships from marauders while passing through the Straits of Dover. Twin lighthouses were built on the cliffs at Dover to guide vessels into harbour during hours of darkness. One Roman Pharos remains - Britain's oldest standing building - within the precincts of the Norman Castle. This time the Roman occupation was more permanent and it lasted for four hundred years.

First naval engagement between England and France - conducted in open waters by ships under canvas - took place in the Downs during the reign of Henry III. In 1215, an armada was prepared by Philip Augustus, King of France, abetted by Pope Innocent III, for the invasion of England. The French fleet was opposed north of Deal by thirty-six ships commanded by Hubert de Burgh, Lord Warden of the Cinque Ports. Archers, skilful with longbows, began their formidable attack, paving the way for the English to board the French ships. The French, vastly superior in numbers of ships and men, fought bravely but were unable to resist the sudden onslaught. It was said that upwards of one hundred knights, rather than be taken prisoners, leapt into the sea clad in full armour.

A further determined assault by the French on the Kent coast took place two years later. Eustace the Monk assembled a fleet of eighty warships with which to cross the Channel, round the North Foreland and lead an assault on London. Hugh de Burgh commanded a smaller fleet which, although outnumbered, demonstrated superior seamanship. This meeting of the rival fleets took place south of the Goodwins. The English, the wind in their favour, adopted the ploy of steering down upon the enemy's ships, ramming and sinking them. Cunningly the decks of the English warships had been sprinkled with quicklime to prevent the French boarding. The wind, being high, blew the quicklime into the enemy's faces and blinded them. Eustace was slain and his army annihilated. This is the first recorded instance of chemical warfare.

Sandwich was recognised as England's premier port in medieval times since its harbour could accommodate massive fleets. It served as both the landing place for travellers to London and pilgrims to Canterbury. It was the first naval base and the main port of departure for the Continent. This thriving Cinque Port owed its unique status to its wide harbour at the head of the Wantsum Channel which at that time separated the mainland from Thanet and thus rendered it, effectively, an island. It was the only port that led directly into the Downs and from thence both merchant and warships had safe access to the narrowest point of the Channel, then known as 'The English Sea'.

From the Norman Conquest onwards there is a constant record of illustrious personages landing at Sandwich or sailing from its vast harbour.

Thomas Becket, after his quarrel with Henry II, sailed secretly with "two brisk mass-brothers to make him fellowship" into exile from Sandwich in 1164. King Richard I received a tumultuous welcome as he sailed into the Downs after his release from captivity by Leopold, Duke of Austria, on 31 March 1194. Edward III assembled a grand fleet to oppose our "ancient enemy" across the Channel, punish the French for aiding the Scots and enforce his claim to the throne of France in 1340. Yet another colourful occasion was when Edward, the Black Prince, returned victorious from Poitiers with his prisoner, King John of France, to Sandwich in 1357.

Exactly a century later, in 1457, Sandwich was invaded by the French. A tremendous army from Honfleur made a surprise attack in which the Mayor, John Drury, was killed. Ever since, the Mayor of Sandwich wears a black robe with black bows attached to his chain of office in mourning for this cowardly deed. Deal, as a former Corporate Member of Sandwich, adopts a black robe but with gold trimmings to indicate half-mourning. (Cinque Port Mayors all wear scarlet robes)

Perkin Warbeck, the personator of Richard, younger son of Edward IV, one of the two princes presumed murdered in the Tower of London, arrived with his army in the Small Downs on 3 July 1495. The Pretender, promoted as 'The White Rose of England', intended rousing the support of the Kentishmen in his claim to the throne as Richard IV. Warbeck had sailed from Vlissingen on 2 July, confident that the men of Kent - Yorkist in their inclination - would support him against the Lancastrian king, Henry VII. Instead the Kentishmen hotly defended their country from these presumptuous invaders.

Trained bands from Sandwich ambushed Warbeck's army in the Sandhills and captured most of the leaders who were then tried in London. Afterwards they were executed and hung in chains "for seamarks or lighthouses" along the coast. Henry VII commended his loyal subjects and commanded beacons to be built in celebration across Kent. Warbeck, meanwhile, had watched the defeat of his army from a safe distance and then, cowardly, slipped away to Ireland.

At the beginning of the 16th century Sandwich Haven began to silt up and the sea slowly receded. According to Leland's 'Itinerary' (1535): "Sandwich be not celebrated by cawse of Goodwine Sandes, and the decay of the haven". The inhabitants struggled to save their harbour and appealed constantly for help from the crown. But it was the construction of the Henrican castles at Deal to defend the Downs that signalled the end of the town's prosperity.

Henry VIII, after his quarrel with the Pope over his intended divorce of Catherine of Aragon, feared invasion from Catholic countries - France and Spain - on the Continent. Loot from dissolved monasteries filled his coffers and enabled him to defend this vulnerable coastline. Henry built a trio of castles - Walmer, Deal and Sandown - and the Barbican Gate at Sandwich. Further he increased the strength of the Royal Navy which frequently assembled in the Downs. When Henry ascended the throne in 1509, the country's fleet consisted of only five warships but at his demise forty years later he had more then fifty armed warships at his personal disposal. Moreover, he set up the Admiralty and Navy Board specifically to control them. Henry toured the Kent coast on more than one occasion to inspect both defences and warships although records are ambiguous concerning these informal visits.

Henry VIII throughout his reign traversed the English Channel on state visits or military campaigns when the pomp and pageantry of his sea progresses might be observed from the clifftops between Deal and Dover. The young, athletic Henry crossed from Dover to Calais with six hundred archers in four hundred ships to invade France in June 1513. On that beautifully calm afternoon his convoy resembled a spectacle "such as Neptune never saw". The elderly, corpulent King again sailed from Dover with a prodigious fleet - his own ships sported cloth of gold - to lay siege to Boulogne in 1544. Undoubtedly, the most spectacular event of the reign was a grand parade of ships transporting five thousand statesmen, tents and pavilions, plate, glasses, cutlery and cooking untensils plus a vast amount of food and wine for the summit meeting between the two rival monarchs - Henry VIII and Francis I of France - at the Field of the Cloth of Gold in 1540.

A painting "after Holbein" depicts Henry standing exuberantly amidships on his flagship, 'Henry Grace God', as he embarks from Dover. This scene employs a great deal of artistic licence since the 'Great Harry' - she carried 72 guns and 700 men - was far too cumbersome to enter either Dover or Calais Harbours because of her excessive draught. Laker, however, affirms that this first two-decker came into the Downs to shelter when she lost both her bowsprit and main-topmast in June 1522. It must be remembered that from the reigns of Edward III until Mary Tudor, Calais, which lies directly opposite Deal, was an important English territory. It was a garrison town and military supplies were ferried across the Channel from Dover, Deal and Sandwich. There was also a regular trade in fish - required by Roman Catholics for religious observation on fast days - and Downs boatmen jealously guarded this lucrative cross-Channel trade.

When Elizabeth I made her own royal progress through Kent in 1573 she lodged for three days at Sandwich where she was entertained lavishly. The authorities seized the opportunity to present Her Majesty with a petition for the restoration of Sandwich Haven. Graciously she agreed to consider their proposals and handed the supplication to William Cecil, Lord Burghley, Secretary of State. He consulted and annotated a map drawn up twenty-five years earlier depicting the walled town of 'Sandewhiche', the silted mouth of the haven leading into 'The downis' and the 'Ile of Tennet'. The purpose of this anonymous map was to show the route of a projected 'Newe cutte' leading eastwards from the port diagonally across the Sandhills to a jetty alongside the halfway beacon. This, like later plans, was shelved because the government became interested in developing Dover Harbour. Sandwich Haven, from this time onward, was abandoned as the premier Cinque Port while Deal, its 'limb', rose to prosperity.

Thomas a Becket landing at Sandwich from the Queen Mary Psalter
© British Museum.

Increase in trade in Tudor times tempted pirates who terrorised the Narrow Seas. In October 1536, four Flemish ships headed by 'The Admiral of Sluys' entered the Downs, landed and plundered local boats of their "herrings, hogbushes, arrows and beer". A few days later these ships robbed a Deal fishing boat of its entire catch but then sent a pinnace ashore on St. Leonard's Day (6 November) to cut the cable of Captain Rychardson's boat and tow it away. The pirates were later trounced by Sir John Dudley who captured their flagship while his own sister ships, 'Lion' and 'Sweepstake', pursued them to the French coast. Rychardson's inventory of his losses - two long bows, sheaves of arrows, barrels of beer, bread, candles, boots, bonnets - reveals the equipment of a typical Channel fishing boat of that period.

Henry VIII and Elizabeth I both dealt harshly with pirates. In 1536 Henry passed a law making piracy a common offence and punishable, in extreme cases, by death. Most troublesome pirate during his reign was Andrew Barton whose favourite hunting ground was the Downs. This Scottish privateer held a "letter of marque" from James IV to exercise his fiendish acts upon the Flemings but he extended his plundering indiscriminately to ships of all nations, including England.

Henry VIII ordered a naval campaign against this "proud Scot that roves over the sea" in the summer of 1511. He entrusted the task of capturing the scoundrel to Admiral Sir Edward Howard, and his brother, Thomas, later Duke of Norfolk. They were paid a phenomenal sum for fitting out and victualling two hired vessels 'Barbara' and 'Mary Barking', which were put at their disposal. When these ships were seaworthy, Sir Edward Howard laid a trap. He ordered an escort to conduct English merchantmen safely in convoy (the current term was "wafting") to Zealand. The plan was to tempt Barton into attacking this tempting target and his own ship would then be ambushed.

Howard's tiny flotilla caught sight of Barton by accident as he lurked in the vicinity of the Thames Estuary waiting for just such a profitable cargo ship to emerge. Previously, the Howards and their ships had been riding out a storm in the Downs but as they left the two brothers became separated. And it was Thomas who espied Barton first while crashing through the same storm with two ships of his own - 'Lion', loaded with "eighteen pieces of Ordinence" and a pinnace, 'Jennet Pyrwin', carrying "ninescore men and fifteen cannons on each side", stolen from King Hans of Denmark. These were huge ships with tremendous armament for the times.

According to Edward Hall's 'Chronicles' (1548):

"The lord Howard, lying in the Downs, perceived where Andrew was making towards Scotland, and so fast the said lord chased him that he overtook him; and there was a sore battle: the Englishmen were fierce, and the Scots defended them manfully, and Andrew ever blew his whistle to encourage his men yet, for all that, the lord Howard and his men by clean strength entered the main deck. Then the Englishmen entered on all sides and the Scots fought sore on the hatches but in conclusion Andrew was taken, which was so sore wounded that he died there. Then all the remnants of the Scots were taken with their ship called 'Lion'."

Meanwhile Sir Edward chased the smaller bark, 'Jenny Pyrwin', round the North Foreland and - firing his cannon, arquebuses and crossbows - captured her crew and paraded them through London. All the pirate ships were impounded and added to the Tudor fleet. James IV bitterly protested about the harsh treatment of his protegé and Henry, uncharacteristically, showed magnanimity by releasing his prisoners since he did not wish to risk open warfare between the two nations. Sir Edward Howard was appointed Admiral of England, Ireland and Aquitaine for successfully demonstrating Bluff King Hal's dominance of the Narrow Seas. The captured 'Lion' was borne as a trophy into the Thames and became the second largest warship in the English Navy.

Elizabeth I, who earned a dubious reputation as 'The Pirate Queen' was, in her turn, plagued by pirates. The Downs was now the domain of a new spate of bold buccaneers - French, Flemish, Portuguese and English - which spurred Elizabeth into action. She instituted the convoy system to safeguard merchantmen from marauders and there were severe penalties for masters of solitary ships who spurned this protection. They shall be "punished at their return", she declared, "for their contempt in putting in danger the Queen's people and the shipping of the realm."

The English Channel, which had become the highway of commercial Europe, was infested with pirates. In 1568 Elizabeth ordered three of her sturdy warships 'Antelope', 'Swallow' and 'Aid' - manned by 500 sailors under the command of Captain William Holstock, Commander of the Navy, to cruise with the express intention of ridding the Downs of piracy. Yet these vigilantes themselves turned pirates and captured Flemish and Portuguese hoys laden with plate, spices, salt and wine. The Queen's wrath was terrifying when she learned that pirates had pillaged the ship in which her ambassador, Lord William Somerset, was sailing across the English Channel as her representative at the baptism of Charles IX's daughter in January 1573. Pirates attacked the ship, killing several of the crew and stealing the baggage in which was concealed a magnificent gold font, Elizabeth's personal christening gift for the royal infant.

Holstock was phenomenally successful in capturing pirates of several nationalities and their plunder was despatched to London. In one month alone, he apprehended thirty-five rogue ships and around one thousand prisoners were sent ashore at Deal. Twelve pirates who had been involved in stealing the Queen's chalice were hanged in chains along the foreshore. After fulfilling his mission Holstock blatantly turned pirate and he swiftly captured fifteen merchant ships laden with treasure. . .

But soon there was an even greater threat to the security of the nation. . .

King Philip II of Spain challenged Elizabeth's sovereignty over Protestant England and despatched his "invincible Armada" to invade England in the late summer of 1588. This consisted of 130 galleons and 20 caravels commanded by the Duke of Medina Sidonia. On board were approximately 20,000 soldiers, 9,000 sailors and 2,000 slaves plus noblemen, gentlemen and their retinue with over 3,000 pieces of ordnance. The plan was to sail along the English Channel and rendezvous in the Straits of Dover with the Spanish forces - 'The Army of Flanders' - stationed in the Netherlands. The soldiers would then be transported across the Channel in specially prepared craft to make a landing at Sandwich Bay under the direction of Philip's nephew, The Duke of Parma.

Philip's Grand Fleet, whose progress had been impeded by storms, arrived off the Lizard on 19 July. Forewarned they were met by the English Navy consisting, initially, of a medley of about 150 ships commanded by the Lord High Admiral of England, Lord Howard of Effingham, assisted by the more experienced Vice Admirals Drake,

Hawkins and Frobisher. Huge Spanish "sea-castles" sailed in a stately crescent formation eastwards through the Channel hotly pursued by the tenacious Admirals who - conserving their powder and shot - shadowed the invaders without engaging them. Flying Tudor white and green colours from their masts these smaller, lighter, faster ships sailed "low and snug" in the water. Eventually the opposing fleets were becalmed off the South Goodwins where the Spanish ships were driven by the spring tides towards the French coast.

Elizabeth I had less than three dozen of her own warships to command and therefore relied upon the Cinque Ports to supplement her own Navy. The Lord Warden of the Cinque Ports duly issued a proclamation that "no ship, bark, or other vessel should pass the seas, whose voyage or absence may be above six weeks out of England." His inventory of the ships available at that time for combatting the invasions reveals that Sandwich had forty-three vessels, Deal six and Walmer five. As the threat continued the Cinque Ports increased their required complement by an additional six vessels, each attended by a thirty ton pinnace, at a tremendous cost. True to form Cinque Ports sailors were ready to defend the realm. . .

17th century playing card showing the fireships sent against the Armada © British Museum.

At Deal the Tudor castles were garrisoned by a brigade of halberdiers, a battalion of musketeers and a troop of horse. Artillery had also been placed upon the shore - culverins, sakers and cannons royal - and the thunder of gunfire was stupendous. It drew crowds who watched the sea battle from the clifftops between Deal and Dover. According to Chapman's 'The Invader's Shore' (1937): "The conflict had then been raging for close upon five days as the belligerents slowly stemmed the waters of the Channel before a south-westerly breeze, and now they lay under the loom of the Foreland in the greatest disorder, almost motionless, and plying one another with great fury."

At dusk on 7 August, Lord Howard, aboard his flagship, 'Ark Royal', anchored off Dover, ordered fireships to be launched against the Armada. Eight ships, covered with pitch, tar and rosin, were packed with brimstone, saltpetre and other combustibles while their cannons were loaded with double shot so that they would discharge spontaneously when the heat became intense. Conditions were perfect. A sharp wind was blowing and a stiff sea running. It was calculated that these "hellburners" - hissing and crackling - would drift swiftly and surely towards the towering galleons crowded together in Calais Roads.

13

Two fireships were intercepted by the Duke of Medina Sidonia - an act of sheer heroism by the Spanish crews - but six careered towards the midst of the anchored Armada. The resulting inferno, fanned by high winds, spread alarm and confusion among the proud and haughty Spaniards. In their panic they cut their cables to escape the path of the floating timebombs which came careering towards them and, in consequence, several galleasses, including the Spanish Admiral's, were driven ashore. Propaganda playing cards printed in the 17th century describe them as "weighing anchors, cutting Cables and betakeing themselves to flight".

The English admirals were now joined by Lord Henry Seymour and Sir William Winter who had both been stationed with the reserve squadron of the Queen's warships in the Downs. The combined fleets now numbered almost two hundred ships of all types which together presented a formidable force. They sailed in a direct line across the Straits and fell mercilessly upon the dispersed Armada. After a final assault near Gravelines the Duke of Medina Sidonia ordered a retreat northwards through some of the most treacherous waters of Britain. The Spanish Grand Fleet escaped complete destruction by the English admirals by sailing a tortuous route through the North Sea and round by the coasts of Scotland and Ireland before limping back to Spain. "God's blew with His winds," announced a commemorative medal, "and they were scattered."

This "Protestant wind" dealt just as harshly with the remainder of the English fleet who had anchored in the Downs to allow their victorious crews to be paid off before they were demobilised and dispersed. An infection, caused by "sour beer", disabled the crews. Unfortunately a gale blew for several days making it impossible for urgent supplies - food and medicine - to be transported from the shore to the stranded warships. The crew, without pay, turned mutinous. Slowly boats managed to land thousands of sick and wounded seamen who then lined the beaches, "dying where they lay", at Deal, Sandwich, Margate and Dover. Sir John Hawkins, Treasurer of the Navy, a fighting seaman and hardened adventurer, wrote to Lord Burghley: "It would grieve any man's heart to see them that have served so valiantly to die so miserably."

When James I ascended the throne in 1601 he terminated the war with Spain and waived the traditional salute by foreign ships in English waters. (Merchantmen, as well as warships, were required to lower their top-gallants in respect of Britain's superiority at sea or risk being fired upon and forced to pay for both powder and shot) But it was a sadly depleted Navy that he bequeathed to his son, Charles I, and early in the new reign its total strength went down to below thirty ships. Charles revived the unpopular levy called "ship money" to enable him to increase his shipbuilding by tenfold. During the Commonwealth the number of warships had dramatically increased and by the end of Charles II's reign England had 173 warships whose maintenance was paid for by the nation. This was the beginning of the modern Royal Navy. Pride of the Stuart fighting fleet was 'Sovereign of the Seas' although this showpiece was cut down from three decks to two because she was too unwieldy. Still she had an active life, first fighting the Dutch under the Commonwealth with the 'Royal' lopped off her title and later, under Charles II, as 'Royal Sovereign'.

Foreign ships were forbidden to engage in warfare in the Downs. Charles I was placed in a predicament when Holland and Spain fought a fierce battle off Deal. Charles, supposedly neutral, made a secret pact with Philip of Spain to provide a safe passage for his troops travelling by sea to fight in the Netherlands. Kentish folk did not

Engraving by Visscher of 'The Battle of the Downs' in 1639.
Courtesy: Dutch Maritime Museum.

share his Catholic sympathies and supported the Protestant Dutch. Tension between the two warring countries increased alarmingly and there was an obvious threat to national security when their warships encroached upon the English Channel.

In the autumn of 1639 the Spanish sailed in a Grand Armada to protect their possessions in the Low Countries from constant attacks by the Dutch. By chance a fleet of Hollanders, under the leadership of the infamous Admiral Martin van Tromp, fell in with the Spaniards in the English Channel. A tremendous battle took place in the Straits of Dover. Tromp deployed his flotilla in a line-of-battle formation in a leeward position which was the first documented case of such tactics in history. Despite the fact that the Dutch were outnumbered the Spaniards took flight. They rounded the South Foreland and anchored in a line which stretched along the shore from Sandown to Walmer Castle.

When van Tromp's fleet received reinforcements from the Continent the Dutch pursued the Spanish ships - burning and sinking - into the Downs. Defiantly their navy, which exceeded one hundred warships, anchored northwards and hemmed in the Spanish galleons. This was a complicated situation for Sir John Pennington, Captain of Sandown Castle and Admiral of the Narrow Seas. (Captain Pennington was famous for building a modest fleet of pinnaces - 'The Ten Lions' Whelps' - to fight the French in the Downs) At that time he had only thirty-four small ships at his disposal and yet he was charged with keeping the peace and protecting the Downs, then referred to as the 'King's Chamber'.

Sir John consulted King Charles who was anxious to prevent a conflict in the Downs. He expressed his concern that "if any ships miscarry and be sunk there, it

Before the Battle of the Downs by Reinier Nooms. Courtesy: National Maritime Museum.

would be the ruin of the best harbour in the Kingdom." Duplicitously the King provided the Spaniards with men and ammunition while the Lord Warden arranged to victual them while stranded at Deal. The Dutch arrived at the moment the English were transferring gunpowder on board the Spanish ships. Captain Pennington nobly informed his men that they should attack any ship which fired the first shot.

Inevitably, on 31 October, a bloody battle began. Captain Pennington, aboard the 'Unicorn', considered, in the confusion of the early morning mist, that the Dutch Admiral was the aggressor since he had suddenly weighed anchor and bore down with his fleet upon the Spaniards. Van Tromp claimed it was just his response to the Spaniards firing on his own barge as it was rowing him around his warships. The puny English fleet, that had hoped to remain neutral, tacked away to the north and when the fog lifted began to fire upon the Hollanders and drove them beyond the South Foreland. The Lord Warden, the Earl of Suffolk, watched intently from the ramparts of Dover Castle as the warring ships sailed westwards into the Straits. He then ordered his lieutenant, Sir John Manwood, to take charge of the situation since a vast number of Spanish warships had either been sunk in the Downs, crippled on the Goodwins or stranded along the coast. Casualties included a magnificent Portuguese galleon of fifty-two brass guns which had been driven ashore at Deal.

Two Hollanders had also faltered between Deal and Walmer Castles but, although the English cannons were turned against them, they resisted returning the fire. Surprisingly the town sustained only moderate damage. Trained bands from Sandwich were ordered to stop the boatmen from looting and also to prevent the despised Spanish sailors from being molested. Defiantly, van Tromp returned to the Downs, struck his topsail to England and fired a salute of nineteen guns. The Spanish fleet had been annihilated and their sea power never recovered from this devastating defeat. Moreover, the Battle of the Downs, which was a flagrant violation of English neutrality within sight of the Kent coast where the Navy was reluctant to intervene, brought humiliation to England.

During the Civil War the confusion nationally was reflected locally when the three castles and the fleet riding in the Downs passed alternately between Royalist and Roundhead control. At the Kentish Rising of 1648 a large number of county folk defected to the Royalists and this had a terrific impact on Deal. The fleet resented the appointment of landsmen to naval commands which they complained, reasonably, was "contrary to the customs and orders of the sea". Shrewdly, Lord General Fairfax sent the wives of recalcitrant seamen aboard warships to return to the Parliamentarian side. Further, he commanded Colonel Nathaniel Rich to besiege the castles after they had been taken by Royalists.

Six royalist warships appeared in the Downs with thirty Flemish ships to present a threatening force under the direction of the exiled Prince Charles assisted by Prince James and Prince Rupert. Audaciously they seized several merchant ships and confiscated their treasures to fund their loyal crews. Meanwhile Col. Rich, who had subdued Walmer Castle, stationed troops in the Sandhills near the Halfway Houses although the main body of his men were billeted at Upper Deal. He knew the fleet could not remain in home waters for long without coming ashore for fresh water or provisions. Timorous Deal folk, sensing trouble, escaped to the countryside. . .

There were several minor skirmishes involving the 'Sea Royalists' but the most serious incident occurred on 13 August when an army comprising 500 soldiers, 250 sailors plus a few London apprentices landed under the cover of darkness and the protection of their ships' guns. They marched secretly in a wide arc across country to surprise the Parliamentary forces entrenched at Deal Castle. The invaders reached their desired position without discovery but a deserter from one of the ships warned Col. Rich of an imminent attack from the rear. Swiftly, Rich despatched 300 musketeers and 100 cavalry to repel the Royalist soldiers who retreated to marshland where they could not be pursued on horseback.

The Parliamentary forces pretended to retreat, thus drawing the Royalists from their safe terrain into an ambush by musketeers. They were, themselves, pursued to the drawbridge of Sandown Castle where they were rounded up, killed or captured. The king's son, realising his rebellion had miserably failed, retreated to Holland. And the subsequent fall of Sandown Castle marked the end of this Great Kentish Rising.

The might and strength of Lord Protector, Oliver Cromwell, was expressed in his magnificent Navy which was, reluctantly, acknowledged abroad. He realised its potential as a powerful force in defending his new regime and repelling foreign champions of the exiled Stuarts. Lord Clarendon, royalist statesman, once declared that Cromwell's enormous power at home was as "nothing compared with his greatness abroad". Astutely Cromwell appointed loyal and experienced leaders to command his warships. The Earl of Warwick was duly created Lord High Admiral in charge of the Channel Fleet and his base became Walmer Castle. Cromwell, it appears, took a great interest in Kent's sea defences and made his own inspection tour of coastal batteries.

The First Dutch War (1652 - 4) occurred shortly after the overthrow of the English Monarchy when the enmity between the navies of England and Holland heightened. (William of Orange was Charles I's son-in-law and therefore opposed to Cromwell's Protectorate) Initially hostilities focused upon the revived tradition that foreign ships were compelled to strike their flags and topsails whilst passing through the Narrow Seas. Commodore Young fell in with a handful of Dutch warships convoying merchantmen in the Downs early in May 1652. When the braggart Dutchmen refused to lower their colours, they were assailed with such ferocity that they soon felt humbly obliged to salute the English flag.

A few days later the Dutch retaliated. Major Bourne was riding with his ships close under Deal Castle when a larger fleet commanded by Admiral Martin van Tromp sailed into the Downs and promptly anchored. Trouble brewed. The Dutchmen pretended that they were sheltering from adverse weather conditions but General Blake in 'Assurance' insisted the Dutch still dipped their flags. He fired three warning shots, the third struck Tromp's ship and the Admiral replied with an aggressive shot from his flagship,'Brederode'. A five hour battle ensued in which both fleets were damaged but the Dutch fleet withdrew under cover of darkness. The Battle of Goodwin Sands fought on 29 May 1652 was the first engagement of the prolonged Anglo-Dutch Wars.

Admiral van Tromp continued to harry English warships but with such little success that he was relieved of his command. He was replaced by Admirals de Ruyter and de Witte who jointly commanded a hostile fleet which assembled off the North Foreland on 28 September 1652. General Blake accompanied by Vice Admiral Penn and Rear Admiral Bourne joined forces to drive the Dutch warships to the back of the Goodwin Sands and then pursued them to the coast of Holland. Although victorious the English losses were vast for this particular encounter. Three Dutch men-o'-war were sunk and one more blown up but the victory cost the English three hundred dead and the same number wounded.

Chastened by their own disaster the Dutch reinstated van Tromp who immediately sailed into the Downs with seventy-seven warships to avenge his honour. On 28 November he located Blake in his flagship, 'Triumph', riding ahead of his depleted fleet, which included 'Victory' and 'Vanguard', off Deal. A storm was imminent which meant that neither side could attack and they remained at deadlock. When the weather improved both fleets weighed and a bloody battle took place. The English ships were outnumbered and, despite Blake's heroism, his losses were, once more, great. The Dutch captured the English 'Bonaventure' and 'Garland' and sank three more warships. Blake renewed his attack but the fight was unequal and he retired honourably to the River Thames. Haughtily van Tromp, who also lost a fearful number of men, claimed this imperial victory. He hoisted a broom at his masthead as a sign that he would sweep the English from the seas.

Blake responded to the insult the following year by harassing the Dutch with increasing intensity. He fastened a whip to his own masthead as an indication that he was visibly driving them from our shores. Clearly this was a game that two could play.

The conclusion of this First Dutch War was fought off Deal in 1653. A fleet of almost one hundred English vessels jointly commanded by Monk, Dean and Penn, encountered a Dutch fleet of identical numbers, jointly commanded by van Tromp and de Ruyter. The squadrons engaged. For two days a battle raged with terrible losses on both sides a little to the north of the Goodwin Sands. Blake's timely arrival, however, ensured the Dutch were routed. Thirteen of their ships were destroyed, two thousand men were killed or wounded and over one thousand five hundred were taken prisoner. The remnant of the Dutch fleet was ambushed in the River Texel by General Monk and van Tromp was finally killed. A condition of the Peace Treaty was that the Dutch would in future strike their flags "in such manner as hath been at any time heretofore practised under any form of Government."

Diarist, Samuel Pepys (1633 - 1703) sailed through the Downs upon his promotion as Secretary to his cousin and patron, Edward Montagu, prior to the Restoration of the Monarchy in 1660. Cromwell had personally appointed Montagu joint General-at-Sea but later during the Commonwealth he had been promoted to sole Commander of the English fleet. Pepys gives a breezy

There is a tradition that one of the captains of the local warships sent to fight the Armada lured a Spanish galleass onto the Goodwins. When she became stranded she was fired upon repeatedly and set on fire.

During the Commonwealth 'Major' and 'General' were naval as well as military ranks. Charles II reintroduced the term 'Admiral' to replace the former favoured 'General-at-Sea'. Previously 'Admiral' was a semi-marine address for a dignitary employed exclusively by the Cinque Ports.

Bodies of seamen recovered from battleships during the Dutch Wars were still dressed in their Sunday best clothes which they had been wearing when they had been impressed into service from the streets of Deal.

In 1711 the first ship belonging to the South Sea Company passed through the Downs on her voyage to the Pacific.

account of shipboard life in his 'Diary'. From the porthole of his snug cabin aboard 'Swiftsure' he spied through a borrowed telescope a bevy of pretty women aboard a nearby East Indiaman. He relished the drama of rattling guns and billowing smoke that enveloped the anchored fleet when allied ships exchanged salutes with the three coastal forts. He dined off a barrel of pickled oysters, paced the deck to adjust to the rocking of the ship, familiarised himself with sailors' terms, enjoyed his first glimpse of the French coast, caroused at taverns in the "pitiful" port, discoursed with the tiresome chaplain, Edward Ibbott (afterwards Rector of Deal) - all before retiring at nightfall to play the "viallin".

Montagu, sensing a royalist revival, took it upon himself to sail over to Holland in 'Naseby' to escort the exiled Prince of Wales back across the English Channel. Pepys accompanied his master and was entrusted with carrying the royal pet dog (which had not been housetrained) when His Majesty stepped ashore at Dover where he was proclaimed King Charles II. His elation at Charles' restoration soon turned to contempt for the new king and his licentious court which is revealed in the secret scribblings in his 'Diary'. Afterwards Montagu remained in the Downs, savouring his triumph but he was soon rewarded for his loyalty by being created First Earl of Sandwich. At Deal jubilant townsfolk lit bonfires, set up maypoles and knelt in the herb-strewn streets to drink the health of the Merry Monarch.

After the Restoration there was a flurry of activity in the Downs as Charles' aunt, the Queen of Bohemia, was escorted over from Holland. Another time the Duke of York's infant daughter, Mary, was taken over to Dieppe to learn french while staying with a nobleman's family. Frequently the royal brothers, Charles and James, returned to these waters purely for recreation. Charles had discovered the pleasure of sailing during his exile in Holland and in the early part of his reign he was often to be seen sailing in either 'Henrietta' or 'Katherine' in the Downs. Great interest was aroused when he commissioned his own yacht - the first to be built for the sovereign's own pleasure - and the royal 'Greyhound' was anchored off Sandown Castle in June 1675.

Such healthy pursuits were interrupted by the Second Dutch War (1664 - 7) the battles of which were almost exclusively fought in the Downs. The rupture was occasioned by the old sore of saluting the English flag within the Narrow Seas. The Dutch had been compelled to dip to the colours of the Commonwealth but they firmly refused to show that same mark of respect to ships of the Restoration. England and Holland's commercial and maritime rivalry had by that time intensified to such a degree that war, once more, was inevitable.

Command of the English fleet was divided between James, Duke of York, as Lord High Admiral, and Prince Rupert and the Earl of Sandwich who were appointed Joint Generals-at-Sea. The Dutch fleet was placed under the competent control of young Cornelius van Tromp who amply demonstrated he had inherited his father's capabilities of seamanship. The theatre of war constantly shifted between the Dutch coast and the Downs where several engagements took place in the vicinity of the North Foreland and the Goodwin Sands. There smaller craft, when under attack, could make for the protection of the guns of the three castle whose walls were netted with turf as camouflage. Yet the Dutchmen might not have given up the chase so easily if they had realised that the armament of the Great Castle consisted merely of "fower old Dismall Honey-combd Gunns which every time they were shot of more endangered the gunners than them." Further, captains of warships were hampered by being unable to send ashore for fresh water or provisions since the plague was rife at Deal. Despite the risk the newly formed Duke of York and Albany's Maritime Regiment, forerunner of the Royal Marines, was marched to Deal in their smart yellow uniforms and placed under the direction of Silius Titus, Keeper of Deal Castle.

The Great Fire of London, the Plague and the Dutch Wars had crippled Stuart resources. Undoubtedly victories by the fleet had quelled any serious continuation of hostilities with Holland. Conditions for termination of war were negotiated and the 'Treaty of Breda' was signed on 11 July 1667. News of peace was proclaimed at Deal by guns and trumpets, accompanied by parades and bonfires. Unfortunately English avarice in intercepting a rich merchant fleet passing in convoy through the Channel precipitated a Third Dutch War (1672 - 4) Action, this time, focused upon the North Sea and culminated in the Battle of Sole Bay in which the Earl of Sandwich was killed aboard his flagship, 'Royal James'.

Lord Nelson by Lemuel Abbott
© National Maritime Museum.

After the Glorious Revolution William III unwisely gave Captain William Kidd a "letter of marque" permitting him to attack enemy shipping. Specifically for this purpose, Kidd fitted out a hybrid rowing/sailing ship, 'Adventure Galley', which anchored in the Downs on 10 April 1696. Soon after Kidd sailed upon the High Seas and began those nefarious practices which earned him his dubious reputation as a buccaneer. Captain Kidd was finally apprehended, tried at the Old Bailey and sentenced to death. His body, along with his accomplices, was hung in chains to be washed by three tides at Execution Dock in 1699.

On 1 May 1707 a convoy of thirty-five West Indiamen - loaded with cargo valued at two million pounds sterling - sailed from the Downs. They were escorted by three men-o'-war, 'Royal Oak' (74 guns) 'Hampton Court' (70 guns) and 'Grafton' (70 guns) through the English Channel. At Beachy Head they were surprised by the buccaneer, Claude de Forbin, and attacked by his French squadron that captured twenty-one merchant ships. Valiantly, the escort ships dashed into their midst with their colours flying and opened fire. Captain Acton was killed and 'Grafton' taken; Captain Clements was killed and 'Hampton Court' was made to strike; Captain Wylde survived but his ship, 'Royal Oak', was holed and forced to retreat to Dungeness where she grounded. She was floated upon the flood tide and brought for repairs to the Navy Yard at Deal.

The following summer a fleet of warships assembled in the Downs with the express purpose of crossing to France and blockading the port of Dunkirk. The plan was to prevent the tyranny of Forbin and his fellow pirates - Dugay, Tronin and du Bart - but the expedition was thwarted by a storm. When the commanders finally negotiated the Channel they were informed by the master of a passing galliot that a squadron had left Dunkirk intent upon invading England. It had just rounded the North Foreland with Prince Charles Stuart, the 'Old Pretender', and his supporters on board. The British Squadron, commanded by Sir George Byng and Vice Admiral Lord Dursely, abandoned their initial project and gave chase assisted by a contingent of foot soldiers from Deal.

An inexplicable calamity occurred on 19 September 1700. One of Admiral Sir George Rooke's squadron, H.M.S. 'Carlisle', a fourth rate man-o'-war, was riding at anchor off Deal with 128 officers and crew aboard when she suddenly exploded. She sank within seconds, leaving little more than twisted masts and the submerged stern castle to mark her presence. Death toll might have been greater but her captain, surgeon, purser, carpenter and gunner (whose presence might have averted the catastrophe) had gone ashore on business. The subsequent court martial failed to establish the cause of the disaster - accident or arson - although it was assumed a member of the crew had been stealing gunpowder from the magazine. Among the victims was Charles, brother of Admiral Sir Basil Beaumont, who later lost his life in the Downs during the Great Storm of 1703. The Admiralty requested Trinity House to survey the site with a view to dispersing the wreck but the exact spot eludes modern divers who are anxious to chart its precise location.

In September 1742 the crew of the Indiaman, 'King William', kept the boat's crew of two men-o'-war - 'Shrewsbury', frigate, and 'Shark', sloop - at bay for almost twenty-four hours in the Downs. The boatmen had been sent to press the crew of the returning Indiamen into service in the regular Navy. Artfully, 'King William', when confronted, took refuge close to the Goodwin Sands out of range of the frigate's guns. Here, "the tide being spent and the wind veering ahead", she was obliged to anchor and the warship's boats were at once despatched with pressmen to board her.

Pandemonium erupted. The enraged ship's crew - primed with alcohol - assailed the boats with missiles, including broken bottles, seriously wounding the mate of 'Shrewsbury'. Tactfully the pressmen retreated. At night the crew of 'King William' confined their master and broke open the arms chest so that when the boats made two further attempts to board at dawn they were repulsed with pistols and musket fire. Finally the 'Shark' frigate ran down upon the Indiamen, fired broadshots repeatedly onto her deck and compelled the entire crew to submit to impressment.

In 1755 two Indiamen, 'Triton' and 'Norfolk', appeared simultaneously in the Downs. They were immediately confronted by the 'Falmouth' man-o'-war whose captain ordered a boat to press the returning sailors. The crew of 'Triton' dropped shot into the boat in an attempt to sink her while hoisting sail and, aided by a southerly wind, swept swiftly away. The pressmen then turned their attention to her sister ship, 'Norfolk', whose crew "attacked them with hatchets, cutlasses and treenails, made sail and obliged them to quit the ship." For once the press gang afloat had suffered a defeat. A rare occurrence.

Another regrettable incident at sea occurred on 3 January 1773. A stiff breeze was blowing as the Deal cutter packet, 'Express', sailed from the Downs to Calais. By the time she reached midway it had increased to a hard gale. Her counterpart, the packet, 'Union', loaded with mail, was stranded by the same strong winds in Calais Harbour. Her mate, Mr. Pascall, a native of Deal, decided to transfer the mail and, accordingly, departed in a skiff rowed by seven Frenchmen. Unfortunately the cutter was carried along too fast to stop and she shot past the little boat which was struggling against the immense waves. The occupants were cast into the water but only the mate managed to cling to the upturned boat. Yet hostilities between the two countries were then at such a peak that the French guard watching from the shore declined to launch a rescue boat to save the Englishman. That same day all eight bodies plus the mailbag were washed up on Goodwin Sands.

The Great Mutiny of the Fleet in 1797 was most serious at Spithead and the Nore but there were reverberations in the Downs. Seamen took control of 'Beaulieu' after sending all their senior officers ashore although their example was not followed by nearby vessels including the 'Fairy'. When the mutineers attempted to blow up their ship, a few loyal members of the crew "went below with lights, drove these desperadoes to their hammocks, battened down the scuttle to the magazine and placed a guard upon it." ('Kentish Gazette' 24 June) At the subsequent court martial the ringleaders were sentenced to be hanged from the yard-arm and their bodies were buried in the grounds of the Naval Hospital.

Vice Admiral Lord Nelson, victor of the battles of the Nile, Copenhagen and Trafalgar, suffered his only defeat at Deal. He was first stationed in the Downs when Captain of 'Albermarle' in the bleak winter of 1782. Captain Nelson's first impression of the port was not favourable and he pronounced the Downs Station "a horrid bad one". He confided in his 'Journal': "Going on well for a month have I been laying here, and driving from one end of the Downs to the other. Such weather I never saw in my life as has been for this month past, nothing but wrecks all over the coast." (25 January)

Next morning Captain Nelson made a brief visit ashore when a sudden storm arose at sea. An East Indiaman, 'Brilliant', parted her riding cable and was on a collision course with 'Albermarle'. Nelson raced to the beach but not even the skilled Deal boatmen would risk returning him to his ship. Eventually some of the more daring boatmen offered to make the trial for fifteen guineas and to the astonishment of bystanders

'Dorothea' destroyed by torpedo in the Downs.

Nelson was seen struggling with a mountainous surf to reach his ship. He managed to board 'Albermarle' which had already lost her bowsprit, foremast and figurehead, and steer her to safety away from the Goodwins.

Napoleon Bonaparte was assembling a flotilla along the French coast in order to invade England in the summer of 1801. Vice Admiral Lord Nelson was commanded to check this vast fleet. He hoisted his flag aboard the 'Medusa', a thirty-two gun frigate, which was attended by a swarm of gunboats and bombships in the Downs. He organised a midnight commando raid on enemy shipping. His plan was to secretly tow the enemy ships away from their moorings and then either sink them or set them alight. In the event the raid went horribly wrong - Napoleon had chained his warships together - and many of Nelson's gallant seamen were killed. Among the casualties was his close companion, Captain Edward Thornbridge Parker, who subsequently died of his wounds. His funeral procession left from the Naval Yard for burial with full honours in St. George's Churchyard.

Nelson's mistress, Emma, and her accommodating husband, Sir William Hamilton, arrived in Deal to comfort the injured sailors. For this purpose they hired a suite of rooms above the boathouse at 'The Three Kings' Hotel' (now 'The Royal') Nelson employed this hotel as his shorebase. He landed there daily at its jetty to study since he was constantly seasick, wracked with toothache and suffered from a cold. Whilst Sir William went fishing in the company of Yawkins, a "reformed" smuggler, Nelson and Emma explored the countryside in their carriage, visited the local gentry and swam from a hired bathing machine. When Emma returned to Merton to set up home for this strange 'menage à trois', Nelson was truly desolate at being left "thumping in the Downs". He was not sorry to leave Deal since he pronounced it "The coldest place in England, most assuredly". (20 October)

After the Battle of Trafalgar the battered flagship, 'H.M.S. Victory', with Nelson's

The Downs off Deal

24

body aboard - preserved in a barrel of brandy - limped into the Downs under jury mast on 16 December 1805. Flags on the buildings of the King's Navy Yard, the Port Admiral's Office and the Customs House flew at half-mast while all the fishing boats lowered their pennants and ensigns on their mizzen masts. Delayed by a violent gale 'H.M.S. Victory' lay anchored off Deal for three days before proceeding on its mournful journey along the Thames towards Chatham escorted by a Dover pilot, Edward Sherlock. Victory celebrations were naturally muted in Deal and Walmer.

Nelson's triumph curtailed Government sponsorship of an early form of torpedo which would have been a tremendous benefit for warfare at sea. In October 1805 an American engineer, Robert Fulton, travelled to Walmer to convince Prime Minister William Pitt of the importance of his revolutionary invention. Fulton's secret weapon was simply a catamaran loaded with explosives and fitted with a fuse which would destroy enemy ships remotely. He described his successful attempt to blow up a Danish brig, 'Dorothea', anchored in the Downs in his manual, 'Torpedo Warfare and Submarine Explosions' (1810):

> "I filled one of the Torpedoes with one hundred and eighty pounds of powder, and set its clockwork to eighteen minutes. . . At forty minutes past four the boats rowed towards the brig, and the Torpedoes were thrown into the water; the tide carried them under the bottom of the brig, where, at the expiration of eighteen minutes, the explosion appeared to raise her bodily about six feet; she separated in the middle, and the two ends went down; in twenty seconds, nothing was to be seen of her except floating fragments. . ."

H.M.S. Niger sunk by German submarine, 11th November 1914.
Courtesy: David Chamberlain.

In the Downs

War leaders gave a mixed response to the demonstration: Earl St. Vincent expressed his opinion that "Pitt was the greatest fool that ever existed, to encourage a mode of war which they who commanded the sea did not want" while Lord Castlereagh thought that "the success of Mr. Fulton's experiment gives me great confidence in our means of annoying the enemy in their own parts with very little comparative risk to ourselves." Whatever their views, Fulton received more positive encouragement for his inventions by the American Government.

That same year, when Napoleon Bonaparte marched to combat the united forces of Austria and Russia, the Government resolved to create a favourable diversion by sending an auxiliary army into Northern Germany in an attempt to reconquer Hanover (of which the monarchs from George I to William IV were also king). A considerable force of 13,000 men was assembled in the Downs under the command of Lord Cathcart in the closing months of that year and set sail under the temporary orders of General Don. Major-General Sir Arthur Wellesley (later Duke of Wellington) was appointed to the command of a brigade in this army and he embarked from Deal in late December. Three times he attempted to sail but he was driven back by storms, each time losing two or three hundred men by shipwreck on Goodwin Sands.

Sir Arthur returned to Walmer to command his first expedition to Portugal in 1808. About the same time as her husband became entangled with the wars with Spain and Portugal, Kitty Wellesley brought their two young sons for a holiday to Broadstairs. Her visit coincided with the ill-conceived Walcheren expedition which set sail from the Downs during the summer of 1809. The object of the mission was an attack upon the low-lying island of Walcheren, Flushing and nearby arsenals in Holland. Efficiently organised and equipped the expedition, alas, suffered from the doubtful leadership of Pitt's elder brother, the Earl of Chatham.

The assault was of great magnitude. A massive fleet composed of two hundred warships and four hundred transports were assembled under the command of Sir Richard Strachan. Boatbuilders were commissioned to prepare flat-bottomed boats that would penetrate the marshy approach to the River Schelde. Six hundred boatmen were employed for weeks ferrying 40,000 troops from the beach to their warships. Independent of these ships engaged in the outfit of aggression were numerous ships at anchor detained for want of convoys. The whole of the Downs between the Forelands was one great mass of shipping so that, according to the correspondent for the 'Kentish Gazette' (16 July): "The Downs exhibits a forest of masts. . ."

Thousands of soldiers and sailors stood at the water's edge waiting for boats to convey them to their ships while scores of their women crowded on the shore to take a final leave of their menfolk before they sailed into battle. Local boatmen reaped a rich reward, their boats requisitioned as transports, while the inns thrived by accommodating strangers who had arrived from all parts of the kingdom. Initially the expedition was regarded as a holiday, particularly by the gentry who gathered on the beach to watch the colourful sight presented by shipping in the Downs. On 21 July Kitty Wellesley travelled over to Deal to join the throng. "A more magnificent (sight) cannot be conceived than that of the Fleet now in the Downs, above 500 sail of transports including 50 men-of-war," she confided in her diary. "God Almighty protect our brave Men, success attend them."

Lady Wellesley, in company with most of the gentry, was not around to witness the appalling sight of soldiers suffering from marsh disease returning in cramped boatloads to the beaches at Deal and Walmer that autumn. There, devoid of hope and care, they were left to die in their hundreds, few people willing or able to offer them shelter or sustenance. . .

During the early days of the First World War recruits encamped at Walmer were formed into the Royal Naval Division and ferried across the English Channel. They were landed at Dunkirk to join a Royal Marine Brigade in Antwerp in an attempt to strengthen the Belgian Army's resistance against the advancing German army. Later these raw recruits returned to form part of the the Dover Patrol which was instituted under the command of Rear Admiral Hood on 12 October 1914. The urgent problem was to prevent German submarines from attacking ships carrying precious cargoes of foodstuffs urgently required to sustain the British Public.

This auxiliary patrol in the Downs examined all merchant ships - British, Allied or Neutral - before allowing them to proceed in convoy through the Dover Straits. A phenomenal task. At peak periods 120 ships were examined each day. In all 121,707 ships were investigated between 1915 and 1917. Hundreds of vessels lay at anchor overnight protected from enemy raiding craft by cruisers and destroyers from Harwich or Dover. The Royal Navy employed a variety of local pleasure boats as boarding vessels for their Downs Boarding Flotilla.

Surprisingly German U-boats took little advantage of all these targets and one of the few examples of torpedoing inside the Goodwins is that of the minesweeper, H.M.S. 'Niger', on 11 November 1914. Actually she was a torpedo gunboat built in 1892 that had been stationed in the Downs for several months of the war. Around midday H.M.S. 'Niger' was struck by a torpedo fired by the veteran Kapitanleutnant Walther Forstmann, from his U-12 submarine. At that time H.M.S. 'Niger' was engaged in boarding duties for contraband control purposes and was anchored for most of the time in the Downs, totally unprotected, about a mile from Deal Pier. A tempting target for a submarine ace!

People of Deal and Walmer, watching from the shore, received an intimation that something was amiss with the gunboat when a cloud of black smoke belched from her engines. Through binoculars her crew could be seen mustering on deck as the vessel visibly sank lower in the water. Just after noon she capitulated. She turned keel uppermost, her masts bending under the strain, and then, bow first, she slid gracefully under the water. Deal and Kingsdown lifeboats, plus numerous shore craft, promptly launched to her assistance. There was a strong westerly breeze but with the wind aft it did not take long for the rescuers to arrive at the scene, just outside the Bank Buoy. Although most of the boats were overcrowded - the galley, 'Hope', picked up 44 men - all the officers plus 77 crew were rescued. For the remainder of the war a 'Wreck' lightship was positioned to define the site of the sunken vessel.

Throughout the war members of the Dover Patrol removed 426 enemy prisoners or suspects from vessels in the Downs. On 12 November 1914 a sailing ship, 'Kwanga', arrived, crewed mainly by German reservists, who "appeared surprised to hear of the declaration of war". That same autumn a spy was captured posing as a wounded Belgian sergeant and was admitted as a patient to the Grange War Hospital. When he recovered his wounds he was escorted to Calais by the Belgian Military Police where he was confronted with a soldier whose identity he had assumed. The bogus Belgian was convicted as a spy and shot.

The Dover Patrol, which involved tremendous risk, was manned mainly by Kentish fishermen. They were required to operate a vast fleet of trawlers, drifters and minesweepers whose duties involved fixing nets to limit access to the Straits of Dover, planting minefields to prohibit approaches inside the Goodwins and constantly patrolling to safeguard this section of the South East Coast. The fleet was concentrated day and night over a wide belt of deep mines that extended across the English Channel with the object of denying the passage of enemy submarines on the surface and forcing them to dive directly into the minefields below. To ensure that this anti-submarine measure was effective at night a blaze of light was maintained from shore to shore by means of huge magnesium flares. The challenge of this intense illumination invited attack, however, and in February 1918 a powerful force of enemy destroyers defied the Dover Patrol and raced eastwards through the minefield killing about seventy fishermen. Heroically the next night the patrol was renewed and continued in full strength until the termination of hostilities.

Admiral Sir Reginald Bacon, who was for three years the Admiral Commanding at Dover, wrote in his history of 'The Dover Patrol' (1919): "It is interesting to note how the historic anchorage of the Downs played so important a part in the war - another example of the way in which geographical positions retained their importance in spite of changes in war material and methods."

Captain David Bone penned a detailed account of the

British Merchant Service during the Great War in 'Merchantmen-At-Arms' (1919) He mentions the 'War Channel', a passage two hundred and eighty miles long, that had to be constantly swept for mines and cleared in advance of traffic through the English Channel.

Sailings were restricted to daylight since Allied vessels were required to make their protected anchorage before nightfall. Ships then grouped in large scattered convoys ready to proceed in safety through the Dover Straits. The spectacle they formed against the snow-clad mainland resembled a maritime pageant whose beauty rivalled any in peacetime:

"In all the story of the Downs, the great roadstead can rarely have presented a scene as when, on a chill winter morning, we lay at anchor awaiting passage. Overnight, we had come in under convoy from the westward, eighteen large ships, to swell the tonnage that had gathered from the Channel ports. From Kingsdown to the Gull, there was hardly water space to turn a wherry. Even in the doubtful holding ground of Trinity Bay, some large ships were anchored, and the fairway through the Roads was encroached upon by more than one of us - despite the summary signals from the Guardship. All types were represented in our assembly; we boasted a combination in dazzle paint to set us out, and our signal flags carried colour to the mastheads to complete the variegations of our camouflage. . .

"The teeth of the Goodwins had bared to a snarl of broken water that shewed the young flood making when movement began among the ships. Long experience had accustomed the pilots to the ways of the minesweepers, and when the clearing signal 'Vessels may proceed' was hoisted at the yardarm of the Guardship, there were few anchors still to be raised. Crowding out towards the northern gateway, we found ourselves in close formation. Variations of speeds rendered the apparent confusion difficult to steer through, but the action of a kindred masonry among the pilots seemed to clear the narrow sea-lane. There was little easing of speed; with only a few hours of winter daylight to work in, shipping was being driven at its utmost power to make the most of the precious time. "All out", stoking up and setting a stiff smoke screen over the seascape, we thinned out to a more comfortable formation, while the smaller craft, taking advantage of the rising tide, cut the inner angles of the channel to keep apace."

The signing of the Peace Treaty of Versailles was celebrated by gunfire in the late afternoon of 5 July 1919. A cacophony was made by simultaneous sounds of ships' sirens, railways whistles and church bells. One anti-aircraft gun, affectionately known as 'Peggy', fired a salute of twenty-one guns and pilot cutters, drifters and tugs in the Downs responded with a joyful noise on their sirens. Decorations were soon in evidence throughout the town and patriotic music was played by the band of the Royal Marines. Later a number of German steamers, including several large liners, anchored in the Downs after they had been handed over to Britain and France in accordance with terms of the Armistice.

At the commencement of World War Two the Downs was included in the Nore

Command whose Commander-in-Chief was Admiral Sir H. Brownrigg. A huge minefield was laid to block the outer reaches of the North Sea so that all seaborne traffic through the English Channel was directed into the Downs which was sealed at both ends by Guardships. There vessels of all nations were detained and searched, as in the last war, by the Royal Naval Contraband Control. When France fell to the Germans the Downs also became the refuge of warships of the Royal Netherlands Navy.

Ships were forbidden to communicate between themselves and the shore except via the examination tugs, hoisting flags in the International Code or, in foggy weather, by morse on sirens. All navigational lights and beacons were extinguished and the names of ships painted out. There were so many casualties resulting from collisions, torpedoes and floating magnetic or acoustic mines that this part of the great roadstead earned its nickname, 'The Hospital'.

The Coastguard developed a new role in assisting requisitioned tugs, trawlers and drifters of the Royal Naval Patrol Service. New duties included signalling, acting as sentries, transporting wounded sailors and rescuing airmen who had ditched into the sea. They also directed local boatmen when they organised their own transport service taking out urgent provisions, fuel and medicines. Extra staff were recruited and auxiliary stations were opened at Walmer and Sandwich. The Station Officer was supported by three retired Royal Navy servicemen at the main station along the Marina.

In May and June 1940 Deal boatmen formed part of the armada of "little ships" involved in the massive evacuation of Dunkirk. This legendary expedition, known as 'Operation Dynamo', was masterminded by Vice Admiral Betram Ramsay from the Admiralty's Headquarters in the secret tunnels within the cliffs below Dover Castle. The Germans had swiftly occupied Belgium and France and surrounded thousands of British, French and Belgian troops on the coast at Dunkirk where they were repeatedly machine-gunned and dive-bombed by enemy aircraft. Prime Minister Winston Churchill ordered all available south and eastern coastal craft to race to the rescue and ferry troops repeatedly from the beaches to awaiting transports anchored offshore. Convoys of ships - destroyers, corvettes, minesweepers, naval trawlers, pleasure steamers, Dutch skoots - carrying almost 400,000 troops then returned in abnormally calm seas via tortuous routes avoiding minefields to the refuge of Folkestone, Dover, Ramsgate and Margate harbours. Rapid onward transport was provided by the East Kent Road Car Company and Southern Railway.

Despite government censorship Deal folk realised the scale of the catastrophe. Black palls of smoke from raging fires could be seen, frequent pounding of artillery was heard and frantic movement of vessels was observed across the Dover Straits. The Rev. William Daniels held an impromptu service on the foreshore praying desperately for the safe return of the fishing vessels which had left from Deal beach. Eventually the signal was received, 'BEF evacuated', thus ending, after ten momentous days, "one of the great campaigns in the sea story of Britain."

After the Fall of France Calais came under the control of the German Army which installed cross-Channel guns rendering it impossible for Allied ships to anchor in the Downs. Convoys escorted by destroyers and airplanes were further protected by towing barrage balloons. They carefully picked their way through this narrow section of the English Channel which was studded with mines and masts of wrecks. Powerful

Pinnaces from the fleet in the Downs © Angus Neill

searchlights were installed at intervals along the coast so that no landing craft escaped their penetrating beams while 6-inch naval twin guns were concealed at intervals between Sandown and Kingsdown. All the same Deal came under constant bombardment from salvoes of shells fired from long range guns between Calais and Boulogne and later the deadly V1 pilotless bombs and V2 rockets.

At the start of the war Deal had been unwisely chosen as a reception area for evacuees from London and the Medway Towns. Once the danger of bombardment was realised local children joined the evacuees who were then evacuated to South Wales. The Central Schools were partly requisitioned by the Army and the remaining pupils were allocated half-time compulsory education. Evacuation escalated as the situation worsened and soon the former population of 23,000 was reduced to around 7,000. A period of deep depression followed.

Prime Minister Winston Churchill, who was also newly appointed Lord Warden of the Cinque Ports, paid fleeting visits to Walmer Castle in 1940 and 1942 to inspect coastal defences. He ordered the demolition of Deal's iron pier in order to prevent the coastal guns from having a clear line of fire. The Victorian pier had been breached by the Dutch motor boat, 'Nora', mined while awaiting her checks by Contraband Control in 1939. (After the war, in appreciation of his services, Churchill was awarded the Freedom of Deal)

The greatest seaborne assault in the world's history took place on 5 June 1944 known as 'D-day'. In the early hours of that morning, a fleet of mixed vessels sailed out from the mouth of the Thames and crossed the Channel en route for the beaches of Normandy. Convoys of steamers escorted by destroyers and curious craft towed by powerful tugs and corvettes swept through the Downs under cover of smoke screens concealing them from the enemy's batteries. A strange medley of ships - liners, tankers, cargo steamers, munitions barges, cattle boats and coasters - passed

31

in procession from the Gull Stream to the South Foreland. After the initial landing prefabricated sections of the 'Mulberry Harbour', secretly constructed at Richborough Port, were towed across and sunk in position. Once allied troops had established a firm position in enemy territory the laying of PLUTO (Pipe Line Under The Ocean) began in earnest. Vast quantities of oil were pumped over several months from the Isle of Grain direct to France. After the German garrison at Calais capitulated and the long range guns were finally silenced, the Downs once more became a place of safe anchorage.

When Victory in Europe was officially announced by Mr. Churchill there were muted celebrations in Deal and Walmer. Church bells rang out spasmodically and shops displayed flags and bunting. Residents sported favours - red, white and blue - in addition to their best clothes as they walked into town. Thanksgiving services were held in local churches and there were parades of servicemen. For a long time after the cessation of hostilities, however, the blackout on the coast was slow to lift because U-boats still lurked in home waters unaware that they had been called upon to surrender.

THE SMALL DOWNS

'England Afloat'

THE DOWNS was regarded as the most important waterway in Europe - if not the world - harbouring ships of every nation. It was the home base for both warships and merchantmen when either setting off or returning from an ocean voyage. The myriad craft - lightships, liners, freighters, ferries, cutters, coasters, trawlers, barges, pinks, snows, hookers and doggers - seen from the shore in the famous Anchorage gave rise to the description, 'England Afloat'.

The Small Downs is the shallow area with a depth of from 5 to 10 metres between the entrance to Sandwich Haven and the Port of Deal. The two towns vied with each other to supply commodities and consumables while the sheer volume of ships brought all the needs and problems attendant with a floating city. Over the centuries a microcosm of the world of shipping passed through these waters - convicts and cannibals, duellists and deserters, preachers and pirates, spies and smugglers, monarchs and mutineers. . .

The most splendid era of sea voyages arrived with the ascendancy of the East and West Indiamen. It began with the incorporation of the Honourable East India Company by a charter of James I in 1609. This company - familiarly known as 'John' Company - became, quite simply, the most magnificent and powerful corporation the world has ever seen. The main object was trading but to achieve that their ships needed to fight their way across the oceans of the world and, therefore, each Indiaman was heavily armed. According to Bayley in his definitive 'Seamen of the Downs' (1929) they were "stately, well-founded, comfortable vessels designed for carrying capacity and fighting qualities rather than general speed". Further, Indiamen were ably commanded and gave a good account of themselves when opposed by pirates, privateers or warships and they left a mark on the Far East which was not easily erased.

Lordly Indiamen were a familiar sight in the Downs. "Yesterday, if I could have enjoyed the sight," wrote Lord Nelson in 1801, "passed through the Downs 100 sail of West Indiamen." The East India Company employed its own agent at Deal to transact business incidental to the movements of so large a fleet outward and homeward bound. After the Indian Mutiny in 1858, the Crown commandeered the huge territories of this Company and its monopoly was abolished. A new type of sailing ship then evolved and its beautiful proportions were reflected in the waters of the Downs. . .

The China and Colonial tea clippers that superseded them were considered by

An Indiaman in full sail in the Downs.

Bayley to be among "the finest creations of the shipbuilder's, sailmaker's and rigger's art". Leading stars in this constellation were 'Lightning', 'Lothair', 'Hallowe'en', 'Pericles', 'Sir Lancelot', 'Norman Court', 'Miltiades', 'Cimba', 'Thermopyloe' and 'Cutty Sark', all of whom frequently swept gracefully through the Downs. "This was the culmination of the great epoch of sail", the author considered, "and the captains, officers and crews vied with one another in a sporting rivalry to achieve excellence."

During the middle of the 19th century these "majestic queens of sail" vied with each other to bring the new season's teas from China to London. They were so brilliantly navigated that, although they never sighted each other during their epic voyages, they habitually reached identical destinations with an interval of only a few hours. Bayley recalls a famous race where a trio of clippers left the Min River on the same tide and docked in the River Thames on the same tide in the summer of 1866. 'Ariel' entered the Downs at 8 a.m. on 6 September (after 99 days out) while 'Taiping' (again 99 days out) appeared - incredibly - just ten minutes later! 'Serica' (99 days out) arrived at noon the same day while 'Fiery Cross' (101 days out) followed her during the night of 7 September. Bayley, who had witnessed the culmination of this "titanic" race as a youth, never forgot the excitement: "It was a pretty sight to see these fine vessels with a fresh breeze and every stitch of canvas set racing through the Downs, straining every point to win the coveted blue ribbon of the ocean."

At this time there was a rapidly expanding Colonial trade when beautiful little barques, that worked the West Indian and Cape routes, and the yacht-like topsail schooners, which were employed in the fruit trade, used to thrash their way down Channel when other vessels did not dare to venture forth. . .

The Downs was the scene of the first recorded salvage diving operation in England. Jacob Johnson, who lived in Sandwich, employed a team of five intrepid "wrack men" in the early 17th century. Presumably they used a diving bell to recover cannon and anchors from local waters in their hoy, 'Charity'. Originally Johnson hailed from Enkhuizen, a seaport in Holland, where he had already established his recovery trade. He found a ready patron in King James I's favourite, George Villiers, Duke of Buckingham, who did not entirely trust him although he addressed one effusive letter: "To my Loving friend Mr. Jacob Johnson, the Dyver." (22 August 1628)

A marvellous account of a departure from the Downs for a hazardous voyage to the Barbary Coast appears in the 'Diary' of the Rev. Henry Teonge, chaplain aboard H.M. frigate, 'Assistance', in the early summer of 1675. This impoverished country parson scrounged "a little jug of ink" from a Deal landlady with which to pen - in poetry and prose - lively description of a sea voyage in Stuart times:

> "Claret and brandy, punch and good ale abound,
> Wishing us safety to the pleasant Downs."

Teonge conjures up evocative images of the pathos and humour of a sailor's life. Porpoises swimming alongside the ship as it rounds the North Foreland (taken to be the sign of bad weather ahead). . . a Dutch Squadron with its overexcited crew, firing and rejoicing, that they are sailing so close to home. . . clutching at pillars in the steerage as he preaches his Sunday sermon to the sailors during a storm at sea. . . first glimpse of the coast of France through a "prospective glass" as the sky slowly lightens at dawn. . . the captain's son rushing from gun to gun, putting his infant fingers in their breeches and shouting, 'Booh!'. . . laughter as he is carried ashore from a pinnace high on boatmen's shoulders and then picking his way through washing laid out to dry on Deal beach. . . pressing for men among the merchantmen which slyly steal away under cover of darkness. . . and the farewell salutes, 'God-speed', by six men-o'-war as 'Assistance' finally departs from the Downs. (It was a peculiar custom of the Navy to salute with an uneven number of guns: an even number was reserved for a funeral at sea)

The Downs was also a place for romance. The 17th century sailor, Edward Barlow, recalls his courtship of Mary Symons, a servant from London, who followed him by land down to Deal:

"And being come down she sent me word, and I going ashore, and being come together we soon concluded of the matter. And having some acquaintance in the ship, we agreed to send for a licence to Canterbury for our marriage together.

A 17th century sketch of the Downs by Edward Barlow.
© *National Maritime Museum.*

And having procured one, which cost me eighteen shillings, on the 21 January we were married in the parish church of Deal in Kent by the minister of the same, before some acquaintance and several witnesses.

And returning from the church, which was a small mile out of the town, at the King's Head in Deal we had our wedding dinner, being accompanied with several persons of good repute and credit, as the commander of His Majesty's ship, 'Assistance', Captain Wiltshire, and two or three more commanders, and our own commander, Captain Jones, and several of our merchants, which were going passengers with us, and a gentlewoman, also going for the island of Jamaica.

And being all very merry, having music and wine a-plenty, and good victuals enough, being willing to make one merry and joyful night of it, not knowing when I should have another; and it was to prove, I did hope, one of the best day's work as to my future happiness in this world, for I had met with a good wife, which every man doth at his first marriage. But it is an old saying, 'A good Jack makes a good Jill' and 'The proof of the pudding must be in the eating'." ('Journal' 1678)

Alas, the young couple's happiness was short lived for Barlow also records the subsequent parting when his West Indiaman, 'Guannaboe', sailed for Jamaica:

"So staying on shore at Deal after our marriage two days, it having cost me near ten pounds whilst I was ashore; and then a fair wind coming, and all ships preparing to sail, and then being to part with my wife, I could not without tears, but part we must, and taking my leave of all acquaintance ashore, and providing a horse to carry my wife to Canterbury, she got on, and taking me leave of my wife, she returned to London, from whence she came. . ."

Famous preachers have passed through the Downs. The great Quaker, George Fox (1624 - 1691) founder of the Society of Friends passed through the Downs on his way to America. He embarked with his companions at Gravesend and arrived early evening at the Anchorage. He lodged overnight at Deal where he had preached to a large assembly the previous year and rejoined his yacht the next day. According to his 'Journal' (1671):

"In the afternoon, the wind serving, I took leave of my wife and other Friends, and went on board. Before we could sail, there being two of the king's frigates riding in the Downs, the captain of one of them sent his press-master on board us, who took three of our seamen. This would certainly have delayed, if not wholly prevented, our voyage, had not the captain of the other frigate, being informed of the leakiness of our vessel, and the length of our voyage, in compassion and much civility, spared us two of his own men. Before this was over, a custom-house officer came on board to peruse packets and get fees; so that we were kept from sailing till about sunset; during which delay a very considerable number of merchantmen, outward-bound, were got several leagues before us. Being clear, we set sail in the evening, and the next morning overtook part of that fleet about the height of Dover."

Another Quaker, William Penn (1644 - 1718) left from the Downs for the New World and founded Pennsylvania. Penn obtained a special grant from Charles II and embarked in the 'Welcome', a 300-ton vessel, to cross the Atlantic on 1 September 1682. He took his servants, wardrobe, stores, provision, furniture and even carved doors and their frames with him on his journey. The large ship carried one hundred colonists on its smooth voyage which after two months entered calm water through the Capes of the Delaware. Unfortunately smallpox was also carried on board at Deal and thirty Friends expired before they reached America.

The Methodist preacher, George Whitefield (1714 - 70) came into the Downs on his way to America at the beginning of 1738. Then aged only twenty-four Whitefield was of a striking appearance. He was described as tall and handsome with piercing blue eyes but he also had a marked squint and he wore a fluffy white wig. Undoubtedly he was a powerful preacher - eloquent and melodious - since he elicited an emotional response from his congregation. His 'Journal' gives fascinating glimpses into the frustrations of travel by sea at this period.

Whitefield boarded his transport ship, 'Whitaker', at Gravesend and, in company with two other vessels, 'Amy' and 'Lightfoot', rounded the North Foreland and entered the Downs where it was becalmed for almost a month. He wasted no time in preaching to the soldiers aboard the trio of ships ("Mine are but little flocks") before obtaining permission from Captain Whiting to go ashore at Deal with his companion, James Habersham, a Yorkshire schoolmaster who later became President of Georgia.

He was welcomed by the Postmaster and preached at a lodging house where he was so successful that he was invited to preach at the three local churches - St. George's, St, Leonard's and St. Nicholas' at Sholden - in turn. Thousands flocked to hear this revolutionary preacher that the town was soon kindled into a "holy flame". At St. Leonard's people climbed onto the leads to peer into the upper windows to hear his sermon which lasted three hours! Open air services along the seashore gave Whitefield the chance to preach against smuggling which, he noted, was "a sin that does most easily beset the Deal people". The only sour note came from the intolerant Dr. Nicholas Carter, Perpetual Curate of St. George's Church, who wrote an impertinent letter to the Countess of Huntington, a renowned patron of Methodists, complaining of Whitefield's "mischief".

Ironically the south-westerly wind that prevented Whitefield's ship from sailing blew home a merchantman carrying another famous Methodist, John Wesley. He arrived in the Downs aboard 'Samuel' on 1 February after crossing the Atlantic from Georgia. It was fortuitous the two preachers never met since Wesley was depressed and discouraged after his disastrous expedition to America. Whitefield, ignoring his mentor's advice to return to London, sailed to Gibraltar on the first lap of his journey to the New World.

Explorers and travellers have ventured forth from the Downs. William Dampier

A lugger setting off to the aid of a ship in a gale by Henry Moses
© Deal Maritime and Local History Museum.

(1651 - 1715) explorer and buccaneer, habitually departed from the Downs when he was commissioned to investigate the coasts of Australia, New Guinea and New Britain for the British Government. Dampier was a sharp observer of natural phenomena - his ship's log records the earliest known sighting of a typhoon - and a pioneer of scientific exploration. Dampier's account of his early exploits, 'A New Voyage Round the World' (1697) ends with a description of his ship, 'Defence', returning in convoy to winter in England. "When we came as high as the South Foreland, we left them standing on their Course, keeping on the back of the Goodwin Sands; and we luft in for the Downs, where we anchored." (16 September 1691)

Daniel Defoe (1660 - 1731) regarded as the first English novelist, won worldwide fame with 'Robinson Crusoe' (1719). His exciting tale of a shipwrecked mariner stranded on a desert island in the Caribbean Sea was based upon the factual experiences of a Scottish sailor, Alexander Selkirk, whose memoirs Defoe probably consulted. Selkirk joined a later expedition financed by Dampier's as 'Sailing Master' in the galley 'Cinque Ports' which sailed from the Downs in May 1703. After a quarrel with her captain Selkirk was marooned on the rocky island of Juan Fernandez in the South Pacific Ocean. There he remained isolated for almost five years until rescued by another pirate ship, 'Duke', commanded by Captain Woodes Rogers. Ironically her pilot was the ubiquitous Dampier, who had first recommended Selkirk for the post of First Mate.

Defoe mentions Deal and the Downs in his monumental, 'Tour Thro' the Whole Island of Great Britain' (1724 - 6):

> "This place would be a very wild and dangerous road for ships, were it not for the South Foreland, a head of land, forming the east point of the Kentish shoar; and is called, the South, as its situation respects the North Foreland; and which breaks the sea off, which would otherwise come rowling up from the west, this and a flat, or the bank of sands, which for three leagues together, and at about a league, or league and a half distance run parallel with the shoar, and are dry at low water, these two I say, break-all the force of the sea, on the east and south, and south-west; so that the Downs is counted a very good road.
> And yet on some particular winds, and especially, if they overblow, the Downs provides a very wild road; ships are driven from their anchors, and often run on shoar, or are forced on the said sands. . and terrible havoc has been made in the Downs at such times."

Henry Fielding (1707 - 1754), author of 'Tom Jones', suffered from poor health towards the end of his life. The novelist was advised to recuperate by taking a trip on the Continent and, accordingly, he set sail in the ship, 'Queen of Portugal', in 1754. He recorded his journey in 'A Trip to Lisbon' (published posthumously in 1755). When his ship was becalmed in the Downs he was astounded by the avarice of the Deal boatmen. "At Deal a boat often brings more profit in a day than it can produce in London in a week, or perhaps a month," he bemoaned.

> "... about 3 o'clock, the wind being now full in our teeth, we came to anchor in the Downs, within two miles of Deal. My wife, having suffered intolerable

pain from her tooth, again renewed her resolution of having it drawn, and another surgeon was sent for from Deal, but with no better success than the former.

... my daughter and her companion were both retired seasick to bed; the other passengers were a rude schoolboy of fourteen years old, and an illiterate Portuguese friar, who understood no language but his own, in which I had not the least smattering. The captain was the only person left on whose conversation I might indulge myself; but unluckily, besides a total ignorance of everything in the world but a ship, he had the misfortune on being deaf. In this situation necessity and choice were one and the same thing; the captain and I sat down together to a small bowl of punch, over which we both soon fell asleep, and so concluded the evening." (Tuesday 2 July)

Next morning the captain resolved to continue their voyage and so weighed anchor and hoisted sails. It was not long, however, before the wind changed direction and the captain was obliged to return to his former station and once more cast anchor there. Reluctantly he launched his own boat to buy fresh provisions for his passengers who otherwise would have found the price of hiring a boatman for this purpose prohibitive.

"... we were incapable of procuring anything from Deal, but at a price too exorbitant, and beyond the reach of even modern luxury - the fare of a boat from Deal which lay at two miles' distance being at least three half crowns: and, if we had been in any distress for it, as many half guineas; for these good people consider the sea as a large common appendant to their manor, in which, when they find any of their fellow-creatures impounded, they conclude that they have a full right of making the pay at their own discretion for their deliverance." (Thursday 4 July)

The intrepid young explorer, William Hickey (1749 - 1830), was twice in the Downs. First time was in 1768 when he was sailing aboard 'Plassey', an East Indiaman bound for Madras, when it became windbound off North Foreland on Christmas Day. As he felt terribly seasick Hickey took the opportunity to go ashore to eat his dinner in comfort at Margate. Next day he travelled by post chaise to Deal where he put up at the 'Three Kings'. 'Plassey' followed him into the Downs where it sheltered for several days from the violent westerly winds. To pass the time Hickey was offered a round trip of thirty hours' duration by a smuggler about to depart for Boulogne!

Hickey's 'Memoirs' give an accurate account of the vagaries of sea voyages in the mid-18th century:

"We had passed a very merry day, and were just talking of going to bed when we heard a gun fired, and soon after several others from different ships in the Downs. A Deal man coming in told us the wind had suddenly gone to the north-east, and the fleet were getting under weigh. Instead, therefore, of retiring to our comfortable beds, we were obliged to prepare for embarking. In a few minutes the house was all hurry and confusion - paying bills, packing

40

trunks, etc. I had luckily a week before engaged with a boatman for one guinea to put me on board the 'Plassey' whenever a signal was made, be the weather what it might; for which some of my shipmates laughed at me as being more than was necessary, a crown being the usual price. I now found that I had acted wisely; for as it was a bleak night, blowing smartly, with snow, the boat people would not receive a soul under three guineas each, and some paid five." (4 January 1769)

A second voyage to Jamaica in 1775 again brought Hickey into the Downs where his ship, 'New Shoreham', anchored "amidst a fleet of near four hundred sail". These were mainly transports laden with naval and military stores, provisions and livestock to serve the British troops fighting in America. This time Hickey lodged at the 'Three Kings' although, in his opinion, "all the inns in Deal are wretched". Captain Surman, tempted by a light northerly breeze, set sail in the evening with the fleet but he soon regretted his decision. At daylight ten ships only were in sight - three were flying signals of distress - and 'New Shoreham' was veering dangerously close to the French coast.

Captain Surman returned to the Downs for essential repairs to his sails and longboat. Hickey was rowed ashore and checked in at the 'Hoop and Griffin' where he was made comfortable against a gale that was brewing. Later he learned that nine ships had parted from their anchors and had been driven ashore in a tempest between Deal and Sandwich. 'New Shoreham' had fared even worse by being blown in his absence towards the North Sea. When it next braved the Downs Hickey asked a boatman to ferry him to his ship. The charge for this service had now risen to ten guineas!

Captain James Cook (1728 - 1779) received a tremendous welcome when he arrived in the Downs on 12 June 1771. The Royal Society had organised an expedition to the Pacific to observe the transit of Venus and Cook had received a commission to command its ship, 'Endeavour', which sailed from Plymouth on 25 August 1768.

The (rising) flood tide runs from South to North and the (falling) ebb tide runs from North to South in the Downs. Unusually, the flood tide runs from approximately an hour before high tide to about three hours after.

In 1669 a shark about eight feet long swam about "two oars' length" from spectators on Deal beach. After a considerable time beating against the wash it "played about and then went to sea."

During the winter of 1689 the cold was so intense that the Thames was frozen over. Homeward bound ships anchored in the Downs rather than risk becoming ice bound in London's river.

Midshipman Paul Mace of Weymouth fell overboard from the 'Dublin' Indiaman anchored in the Downs in March 1788. His body lay buried in the Sandhills undiscovered for three weeks.

Concurrent with the tremendous noise of the creaking timbers as ships left the Downs was the haunting chant of the shanties sung by men on the decks as they unfurled the sails. Sailors often referred to them as "chanties" since the name derives from the French verb 'chanter' (to sing)

Working songs were confined to merchantmen since the Royal Navy was always a silent service where hands were piped to their duties by the boatswain's silver whistle.

After successfully observing the transit on 3 June at Tahiti, the 'Endeavour' made a pioneering voyage around the coast of New Zealand before touching upon Australia. On board were artists and botanists to record the geography of these unchartered shores. Cook's voyage, which lasted nearly three years, was universally acclaimed as a pioneering achievement.

A gruesome tale of cannibalism concerns a sailor, William Boys. The son of a nonconformist woollen draper, Boys was baptised on 26 June 1700 at the Independent Chapel, Deal. Distantly related to certain landed gentry in Kent, Boys seemed destined for the ministry but chose instead to go to sea in a merchantman commanded by a friend of his father.

After a brief spell in the Royal Navy Boys sailed as Second Mate in an ill-fated slaver, 'Luxborough Galley', which departed from the Downs on 21 October 1725 for the coast of West Africa. After exchanging negroes for cargo this "prime sailer" caught fire on its homeward bound journey from Jamaca. It was thought two black boys had mischievously set fire to a cask of rum and the powder room consequently exploded. Along with a handful of the ship's crew Boys jumped aboard its yawl, a boat built in Deal. They kept afloat for fourteen days - without food, drink, chart, compass, mast nor sail - until rescued by a fishing boat off Newfoundland. Boys was one of only seven sailors who survived by devouring the bodies of their shipmates. According to the 'Annual Register' (March 1774) Boys lived off the corpse of his fellow officer "while it remained sweet".

Captain Boys was so traumatised by this experience that for the remainder of his life he fasted for a fortnight commencing on the anniversary of his rescue. He commissioned a series of dramatic paintings by Cleveley to hang in his library and these are now displayed at the National Maritime Museum. His seal for letters showed a device of a ship on fire with the motto: 'From fire, water and famine, by Providence preserved'. Boys - he later lost his false teeth in a tornado - was renowned for his spartan regime. In 1761 he was made Lieutenant-Governor of the Royal Hospital, Greenwich. He died in 1774 and his monument surmounted by a stone urn remains conspicuous in the graveyard of the Congregational Church (now 'Landmark Centre'). His eldest son, William, was the renowned Sandwich surgeon, botanist and antiquarian.

The Downs was the venue for naval and scientific experiments. A Dutchman named Meisters invented a "machine-ship" which could be pointed at an enemy warship and made to explode remotely when it reached its target. The machinery was set in motion by the removal of a pin and the last man to leave the ship was ordered to bring this with him as he jumped into his boat. (For this unenviable task he received a small reward) Seventeen of these bomb vessels were moored off Deal in 1694 but they failed miserably in performance. An abortive attack on the forts of Dunkirk led to a quarrel among the sponsors and Meisters was charged with desertion.

A gentler experiment was performed aboard the frigate, 'Minerva', on 28 September 1759. A machine described as "a pensile chair by which the heavenly bodies may be observed at sea in the most boisterous weather" was invented by Christopher Irwin. Interest was generated because, should the instrument prove satisfactory, it would solve the problem of accurately determining longitudes while at sea. Dr. Blair, mathematical tutor to George II, travelled down expressly for the purpose of reporting on the success of this experiment. Indeed, the invention caused considerable excitement since it was found that, when an observation for the longitudes was taken one evening, the error "did not exceed seven or eight minutes". On a further trial of the marine chair an observation of Jupiter's satellites at night was "not subject to a greater error than three minutes of time".

Fishermen in the Thames caught a shark on 1 December 1787. The fish measured over nine feet long with "a seventeen inch yawl of a jaw embellished with five rows of teeth". The men hauled it aboard, opened it up and found its belly to contain a silver watch and chain, a cornelian seal and fragments of lace which they presumed were the earthly remains of the brute's last victim. The watch bore the name of its maker, 'Henry Watson, London'. He was contacted and from his records verified the fact that it had been commissioned by Ephraim Thompson of Whitechapel who had intended it as a good luck token for his son when he made his maiden voyage aboard the ship, 'Polly'. Later Captain Vane reported that 'Polly', had been rocked by a violent squall when she passed through the Downs two years earlier. Master Thompson, he said, had been washed overboard and drowned. And the shark? Old Thompson brought the carcass, had it stuffed and displayed it in his parlour as a grim reminder of his son's fate.

Jane Austen (1775 - 1817) stayed briefly with her brother, Edward, at Rowling, part of the estate of Goodnestone Park, in the summer of 1796. The budding author soon became familiar with this part of the country, dividing her time on subsequent travels between Rowling House and Edward's magnificent inherited estate, Godmersham Park, near Canterbury. Her letters written to her devoted sister, Cassandra, during this period contain numerous references to Deal, although it is not certain whether Jane actually visited the town.

Jane's faultless knowledge of seamanship evident in her mature novels, 'Mansfield Park', and 'Persuasion', derives from her two 'Sailor brothers' - Charles and Francis - whose distinguished naval careers culminated in their both becoming admirals. While awaiting commissions the brothers were regularly at Deal and on one occasion Jane expressed a desire to accompany Charles (recently promoted to Second Lieutenant) when he wished to join his frigate, 'Tamar', lying at anchor in the Downs. Jane wrote: ". . . he will proceed in one of the night coaches to Deal. I want to go with him, that I may explain the country to him properly between Canterbury and Rowling, but the unpleasantness of returning by myself deters me." (21 January 1799)

During the Napoleonic Wars Francis Austen was stationed at Ramsgate where he was employed in raising a body of 'Sea Fencibles' trained in artillery from among the fishermen that would protect this coastline in the event of an invasion. Captain Austen was responsible for the district lying between Sandown and the North Foreland while the Commander of the Deal district was Captain Coffin. One of his responsibilities was to keep boats of His Majesty's Navy trim and serviceable ready to meet the expected foe. It was for this reason that Captain Austen entered into correspondence with George Lawrence, Storekeeper of the Navy Yard at Deal, while aboard 'Leopard' in June 1804.

Napoleon, in the event, did not attempt a landing but Captain Austen remained a highly respected figure in Ramsgate. His devotion to religion was greatly admired and he was pointed out a "the officer who knelt in church". It was there that he met and fell in love with Mary Gibson whom he married in July 1806. 'Mrs. F.A'. proved to be a devoted wife and she dutifully followed her husband around the coast wherever he was expected to land and for this reason she was often at Deal where she seems to have "lodged in every house in the town". Indeed, their fourth child, George, was born here in October 1812.

Jane drew upon her sister-in-law's experiences when she was writing 'Persuasion', her last complete novel, published posthumously in 1818. In the novel kindly Mrs. Croft describes her feelings of loneliness and despair while her husband was away at sea: "The only time that I have ever really suffered in body or mind, the only time that I ever fancied myself unwell, or had any ideas of danger, was the winter that I passed by myself at Deal, when the Admiral (Captain Croft then) was in the North Sea. I lived in perpetual fright at the time, and had all manner of imaginary complaints from not knowing what to do with myself, or when I should hear from him next". (Chapter 8) Happily, the fictitious Mrs. Croft soon adjusted to her strange new surroundings for she later pronounced the town "snug".

Fanny Burney (1752 - 1840) daughter of the celebrated organist, Dr. Charles Burney, caused a sensation with the publication of her novel, 'Evelina', in 1778. Acclaimed by society, she was admitted into the Royal Household and given a position in attendance on Queen Charlotte at the time of King George III's madness. She relinquished her tedious courtly role as Second Keeper of the Robes in 1793 when she married (at the age of forty) General Count D'Arblay, a French refugee aristocrat exiled by the Revolution.

Life for Fanny was shattered when her emigré husband was recalled to France to reclaim his property in 1801. M. D'Arblay refused to take up arms against England during the French Wars yet - surprisingly - his principles were admired and his honour remained untarnished. Fanny and their sickly son, Alexander, eventually joined him in Paris during the brief Peace of Amiens. Unknown to them the couple were to remain in France for over a decade. . .

In the summer of 1812 Fanny was suddenly presented with an opportunity to leave France. She feared that her teenage son would be liable to conscription at a time when Napoleon was preparing to invade Russia so she used her father's infirmity and her own ill health (she had just undergone a mastectomy without anaesthetic) as excuses to return to England. Fanny and Alexander, with the aid of a sympathetic government official, secured a passage aboard a neutral ship, 'Mary

Jane Austen by her sister, Cassandra
© National Portrait Gallery.

Anne', ostensibly bound for New York but secretly sailing for Dover. After a nerve-wracking wait for six weeks at Dunkirk while the Captain attempted to recruit more passengers they set sail on 12 August. Soon after, their ship was becalmed under a scorching sun mid-Channel. All this time Fanny was confined to her hammock.

An extraordinary coincidence then took place which worked in the exiles' favour. Britain, already at war with France, also declared war on America. Immediately the Prince Regent ordered a general embargo on all vessels flying the American flag "within any part of His Majesty's dominions". The ship in which the D'Arblays were travelling - a lame duck stranded off the coast of Kent - was captured by a British sloop-of-war. 'The Times' reported the incident: "DEAL Aug 14th. The Ship, 'CASTILLIAN', has detained and sent into the Downs the American ship, 'MARY ANNE' from Dunkirk, with one hundred and one passengers on board."

Fanny Burney by E.F. Burney
© National Portrait Gallery.

The following morning when Fanny crawled up onto the deck she was recognised by Lieutenant Charles Harford. He handed her into his own boat and rowed her the short distance to Deal. Rapturously Fanny recorded her safe landing in her Journal:

> "We had anchored about half a mile, I imagine, from the shore; which I no sooner touched, than, drawing away my arm from Mr. Harford, I took up, on one knee, with irrepressible transport, the nearest bright pebble, to press to my lips, in grateful joy at touching again the land of my Nationality after an absence, nearly hopeless of more than 10 years."

Luck remained with Fanny. The new Port Admiral was Thomas Foley and Fanny was already acquainted with his wife. Lady Lucy welcomed her to Admiralty House and kindly lent her the use of her carriage. She paraded her around the neighbourhood but insisted that Fanny continued to wear her elaborate French hat. Fine fare there was in plenty: "Our first Dinner at Sir Thomas's was extremely amusing both to Alexander & myself. A large fillet of Veal, & a noble Sirloin of Beef were a sight that seemed to us, after the small and dainty French plats we had left, to demand a whole Garrison to devour." At one point during the meal, Fanny was puzzled by a plate decorated with a portrait of Lord Nelson and the word 'TRAFALGAR' emblazoned round the rim. Nelson's victory was explained to her and she apologised for her ignorance which was due to the effective news embargo in France.

False reports of a mutiny aboard a ship in the Downs appeared in the newspapers relating to the merciless treatment of Lieutenant Richard Gammage who was hanged for murder at the yardarm of the brig, 'Griffon', on Monday 23 November 1812. During the absence of Captain George Trollope, Lieutenant Gammage, who was a popular officer, assumed command of 'Griffon' whilst wintering off Deal. Once, during his distinctive career, he dived overboard in the darkness to rescue a marine who had fallen into the water from the deck of 'L'Eclair'. But then he became involved in a brawl aboard 'Griffon' which led to his downfall. On 20 October 1812 he intervened in a quarrel between Sergeant Lake of the Royal Marines and the ship's carpenter, who was his superior in rank. Lieutenant Gammage proposed a mild punishment for the Marine who obstinately protested. Gammage lost his temper, drew his sword and made a thrust at Sergeant Lake. Alas, this proved fatal.

Immediately Lieutenant Gammage handed over command to the Second Lieutenant and surrendered himself to justice. The Port Admiral, Thomas Foley, presided over the subsequent Court Martial which was held on board the ship in the Downs. Lieutenant Gammage represented himself at the trial but he did not offer a strong defence and he was sentenced to death with a recommendation for mercy. The Lords of the Admiralty deliberated the punishment at great length and the ship's company petitioned the Prince Regent for leniency. Despite all these efforts the verdict stood and the death warrant was signed.

On the day appointed for execution Lieutenant Gammage rose at dawn, dressed in black and spent several hours in his devotions. At nine o'clock a gun was fired and the signal for the punishment was hoisted at the fore-top-gallant masthead. After Captain Trollope read aloud the warrant, Lieutenant Gammage bravely walked to the top deck where he was saluted by the sentries. Then his arms were tied behind his back, a weight was attached to his feet, the noose was fastened around his neck and his face was covered with a black handkerchief. When a second gun was fired, Lieutenant Gammage was hoisted to the top of the yardarm in full view of the assembled fleet. Afterwards the body was carried ashore and buried in the cemetery behind the Naval Hospital.

An actual mutiny was resolved by Deal boatmen about 1820. The crew of 'Alexander' from Hamburg mutinied as their ship passed down Channel. They murdered the Captain and his son but the Second Mate was spared since he was the only one left alive who could navigate the ship. The mutineers ordered him to sail into the North Sea where they planned to plunder the cargo, kill the mate and sink the ship. Instead he purposely ran 'Alexander' onto the Goodwins where several Deal boats, including the local longboat crewed by seventeen men, launched to his aid. Assessing the true situation the canny boatmen alerted a nearby warship, 'Pioneer', whose Commander despatched an armed contingent to overwhelm the mutinous crew.

A truly dismal sight must have been the constant ferrying of shackled prisoners onto the chartered merchantmen waiting to transport them to penal colonies in the

New World. Transportation of felons halted abruptly with the American War of Independence and prisons became so overcrowded that, as a temporary measure, they were incarcerated in rotting hulks. These "oubliettes afloat" were condemned fighting ships moored - bow to stern - at the mouth of the River Medway. Pip in Dicken's 'Great Expectations' (1861) refers to them as "wicked Noah's arks".

From 1800 onwards the Government authorised scores of splendid frigate and sleek clippers to be adapted as convict ships, the expense for which was borne by the Treasury. Communal cells were provided below decks where male, female and juvenile prisoners were inhumanely confined in insanitary conditions for a tedious journey lasting five months to New South Wales, Australia, or Van Diemens Land (now Tasmania). Prisoners were attended by a naval surgeon and guarded by marines yet, undeniably, they suffered deprivation, disease and brutality.

First recorded convict ship to be lost on a passage to Australia was a triple masted barque, 'Amphitrite', blown by a gale onto Boulogne Sands on 31 August 1833. There was a tremendous loss of life among the 102 female prisoners and twelve children. Tragically, many of them might have been saved - the ship was close to harbour - but the master, John Hunter, rejected the aid of a pilot boat to direct her ashore since he considered his charges might abscond once they reached land. J.M.W. Turner attempted to convey the carnage in his unfinished painting, 'Disaster At Sea' (1835).

There were further tragedies and triumphs on these voyages. Five Newgate prisoners sentenced to be sold as slaves to Barbados escaped from their transportation ship in the Downs in November 1668. The felons managed to swim ashore but foolishly kept to the main road when they attempted to walk back to London and they were inevitably caught. In September 1783 fifty convicts wearing wrist and ankle irons escaped from 'Swift' after breaking out from their quarters, overpowering their officers and rowing ashore in stolen boats. They were all rounded up by nightfall and the next day the convicts - manacled in pairs - resumed their pathetic journey to Africa and Cape Colony in Nova Scotia.

A veritable zoo passed through the Downs. Ships bearing names of animals, birds and reptiles include 'Ferret', 'Antelope', 'Gazelle', 'Tiger', 'Panther', 'Elephant', 'Kangaroo', 'Viper', 'Scorpion', 'Crocodile', 'Alligator', 'Cygnet', 'Lark' and 'Nightingale'.

One of Dickens' characters, Tony Jobling alias 'Weevle' in 'Bleak House' refers to being "in the Downs" meaning a state of depression.

Bayley in 'Seamen of the Downs' mentions a record of 700 sailing ships - an exceptional occurrence - in the Downs. They had been forced to shelter for six weeks because of intermittent gales.

American forensic scientists have recently discovered that Dr. Crippen, the notorious wife murderer, who was recognised as he passed through the Downs, may have been innocent. The DNA of the woman found buried in the cellar of his Holloway house does not match that of the descendants of his wife, Cora, and the body is now thought to have been that of a man.

Seven members of the crew of a Lancaster bomber that had crashed into the sea boarded their rescue dinghy and landed on the Goodwins. They were rescued by the Walmer lifeboat, 'Charles Dibdin', in the early hours of 25 April 1944.

A Victorian music sheet showing S.S. 'Great Eastern'
© National Maritime Museum.

'George Third', which departed from the Downs on 12 September 1834, lost more than half her 220 prisoners when she struck an unchartered rock off the coast of Tasmania yet a certain amount of pride was taken in the fact that another veteran convict ship, 'Surrey', achieved a record speed of sailing from Deal to Australia in just over one hundred days on her tenth similar voyage in 1840. In 1857 Samuel Baker, landlord of 'The Ship Inn', was convicted of manslaughter and condemned to transportation. He was escorted aboard the ship, 'True Briton', bound for the West Indies. On the voyage several convicts planned to break into the magazine and blow up the ship but, instead, they opened casks of spirits, became intoxicated and were overpowered. Baker, however, ended his days as the prosperous proprietor of a country inn in New Zealand.

Deal has welcomed royalty. King George II, on his return from Hanover, landed here in 1740. His arrival was regarded as a great occasion and avidly reported in the 'Kentish Post':

"On Monday last (October 13th) about 10 o'clock His Majesty landed at Deale and as the Barge approached the Shore, Mr. Carr, Collector of Customs at that Place, attended with his four-wheeled open Chaise and caused it to be drove into the sea; so that the Barge was pulled close to it; when the said Mr. Carr assisted His Majesty whilst he stepped out of the Barge into the Chaise; which carried him to the House of Capt. Baker, a Member of Parliament, and after a short stay His Majesty proceeded in Capt. Baker's Chariot to Canterbury."

Captain Hercules Baker, M.P. for Hythe, resided at 'Beach House', a prominent building on the foreshore. It boasted an elevated platform from which Naval officers in residence could survey through telescopes a panorama of the Downs.

Princess Adelaide of Saxe-Coburg-Meinengen, who became the compliant wife of the Duke of Clarence (later William IV, the 'Sailor King') landed at Deal on 3 July 1818. Adelaide arrived from Calais in the yacht, 'Royal Sovereign', and was conveyed ashore in the Port Admiral's barge which was saluted by the frigate, 'Severn'. She landed on the beach opposite the Navy Yard and proceeded to the 'Three Kings Hotel' attended by a guard of honour furnished by the 10th Hussars. Next day two carriages transported Adelaide and her mother to London where, strangely, she was lodged in a hotel rather than a palace.

This shy princess never forgot the warm welcome she received at Deal and for that reason she always held the town in great affection. During the residency of the Earl of Liverpool the Duke and Duchess of Clarence spent a holiday at Walmer Castle in the summer of 1820. Later Queen Adelaide became a generous benefactor. She contributed towards the cost of constructing the Royal Adelaide Baths which were opened along Beach Street on her birthday in 1835 and she gave a donation towards the building of St. Andrew's Church in 1850. Today several houses in the Conservation Area still bear her name.

A truly magnificent site was when S.S. 'Great Eastern', designed by the engineer, Isambard Kingdom Brunel (1806 - 1859) passed through the Downs in the autumn of 1859. Built at Millwall this massive steamship (692 ft long) was launched sideways from her moorings into the Thames to begin her initial voyage around the coast to

Holyhead. She soon caught the imagination of the public and was represented by everything from children's alphabet books to music sheets for polkas and quadrilles.

Brunel's third and final 'Leviathan' was a masterpiece of design. The combination of two paddle wheels and a screw propeller allowed this giant passenger liner remarkable manoeuvrability while six masts and five funnels gave power to her tremendous longitudinal strength. The fittings and decor were superb so that her proposed four thousand passengers might travel in style - without stopping to refuel - to India, perhaps, or Australia.

Unfortunately, a series of accidents earned S.S. 'Great Eastern' the reputation of being an unlucky ship. On 8 September an explosion on board killed five sailors and injured several more as she steamed past Dungeness. Brunel never lived to see his "great babe" sail on her maiden voyage from Liverpool to New York in 1860 because he died after a short illness the previous year. And as a commercial ship S.S. 'Great Eastern' failed and never made those luxurious cruises to the Far East. Instead she ended her days ingloriously, laying cables under the Atlantic Ocean, before being broken up in 1888.

Notorious criminals have been associated with the Downs. Most famous was the Whitechapel murderer known as 'Jack the Ripper' who the American crime writer, Patricia Cornwell, identifies as the artist, Walter Sickert, in her study, 'Portrait of a Killer' (2002). A scrap of white feint lined paper torn from an account book with a cryptic note scribbled in pencil, purportedly from the Victorian mass murderer, was placed in a bottle and washed ashore between Deal and Sandwich.

The message read:

> "S.S. 'Northumbria Castle'. Left ship. Am on trail again. Jack the Ripper."

This missive, which was one of hundreds sent from all parts of the country to taunt the police, is dated "Sept. 2nd/89", which probably refers to when it was handed in to the police. Although it is regarded as a hoax the timing of the note corresponds with the murder of an unknown female whose torso was found in Pinchin Street, Whitechapel, on Tuesday 10 September 1889. Cornwell points out that Sickert was familiar with this part of the coast and often took a steamer from either Dover or Folkestone to France and is convinced he could have thrown this chilling message in a bottle overboard on one of his jaunts.

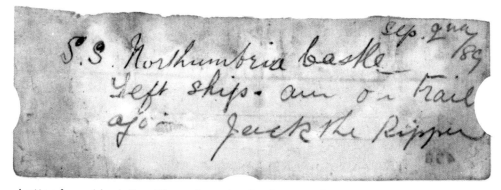

Letter from 'Jack the Ripper' washed ashore at Deal. © National Archives.

Criminal history was made when the notorious poisoner, Dr. Hawley Harvey Crippen, passed through the Downs on board S.S.'Montrose', travelling from Antwerp to Canada in July 1910. Allegedly the genial Dr. Crippen had buried the mutilated body of his wife, Cora, a blowsy musical artiste whose stage name was 'Bella Elmore', in the coal cellar of their house in Camden Town, North London. He then registered as 'Mr. Robinson' and eloped with his mistress, Ethel le Neve, feebly disguised as his son, on the Canadian Pacific Railway Company's luxurious steamer. The pair were recognised by Captain Kendall who radioed a message in morse code to Scotland Yard. His marconigram read:

"HAVE STRONG SUSPICIONS THAT CRIPPEN LONDON CELLAR MURDERER AND ACCOMPLICE ARE AMONGST SALOON PASSENGERS. MOUSTACHE SHAVED OFF, GROWING BEARD. ACCOMPLICE DRESSED AS BOY, VOICE MANNER AND BUILD UNDOUBTEDLY A GIRL."

Dr. Crippen © AKG-Images.

Chief Inspector Walter Drew caught a faster ship from Liverpool, the White Star liner, 'Laurentic', and, impersonating a pilot, secretly boarded S.S. 'Montrose' as she entered St. Lawrence River. He noticed that the saloon passenger pointed out to him as 'Mr. Robinson' had a mark on the bridge of his nose from recently wearing spectacles, had indeed shaved off his moustache and was now growing a beard. Unmasked, Dr. Crippen was arrested upon his arrival at Quebec and returned to London. After a sensational trial at which he strongly protested his innocence, Dr. Crippen was convicted upon circumstantial evidence of murder and hanged at Pentonville Prison. This was the first instance of Marconi's ship-to-shore wireless telegraphy being employed to trap a criminal and it demonstrated that, because of modern technology, future fugitives from justice had nowhere to hide.

S.S.'Montrose' was sold to the Admiralty in 1914. Stripped of her luxurious trappings she was filled with concrete and prepared for sinking to block the western approach to Dover Harbour. The intention was to prevent the entry of German U-boats into this vulnerable port. During a gale on 28 January 1915 she was torn from her moorings, drifted through anchored naval craft and out through the eastern entrance into the Downs. Volunteers from a tug boarded her in an attempt to bring this unmanageable vessel under control but they, themselves, needed to be rescued by the Deal lifeboat, 'Charles Dibdin'. Ironically, the four tugmen were drowned only a few days later when their vessel was in collision with an oil tanker. Another coincidence is that the last man who jumped from the deck of the ill-fated ship was named 'Crippin'!

On 6 September 1911 - thirty-six years after Captain Matthew Webb had swum the English Channel - Thomas William Burgess, a bluff Yorkshire businessman, also attempted the Big Swim. Burgess was accompanied by three local boatmen - Harry Pearson, Dick Mercer senior and Dick Mercer junior - who manfully rowed their own foresail mizzen punt after abandoning their motor boat, 'Elsie', because its engine disturbed the swimmer. Burgess smeared himself with lard to retain bodily heat and wore a pair of goggles and rubber trunks as protection against the elements.

The flood tide, sweeping eastwards, carried Burgess swiftly alongside the South Goodwin lightship until 1 p.m. when he rode the ebb tide for four hours back towards the Varne Sandbank. Employing his famous left-arm stroke, he managed to reach midway between Dover and Calais around midnight. He was constantly stung by jelly fish and he complained of heartburn and seasickness. Even when the coast of France was finally sighted at first light the tide drove the party back a full seven miles.

As dawn approached Burgess' spirits rose and he attacked the final lap with renewed vigour. Once more the tide repulsed him when only four hundred yards from the shore and he found himself drifting past the headland, Cap Gris Nez. Eventually, he reached shallow water and stumbled ashore - deliriously - at Le Chatelet. Total

The annual lifeboat race in Deal Regatta.

time was 22 hrs 35 mins with an average speed of $1^3/_4$ miles an hour. This amazing feat was applauded by a handful of French fishermen.

The Downs Regattas remain a highlight of the social calendar. They were instituted on 10 August 1826 by Captain Hugh Pigot as a laudable effort to ease the tension between the local boatmen and members of the Coastal Blockade. It was the first annual aquatic event of its kind and early patrons numbered the Duke of Clarence and Queen Victoria. Luggers and galleys from along the south coast competed in the rowing races while yachts entered the sailing contests from as far away as Cowes, Isle of Wight. One contest was the lifeboat race but the most eagerly anticipated was the Deal boatmen's race in which they competed in their eight-oared service galleys for a purse containing twenty-one sovereigns. The race was always offered up as 'A Challenge to the World' (the challenge was never taken up!). Festivities on Royal Regatta Day closed with a firework display and a grand ball at the Assembly Rooms. The regattas were discontinued at the start of the Great War but revived shortly afterwards and have continued their popularity right up to this present time.

Deal, Walmer and Kingsdown Amateur Rowing Club was founded by Sir Ernest Justice Charles, one of the town's great benefactors, in 1927. Sir Ernest was determined to ensure that local youths were kept purposely occupied and for that reason he also provided headquarters for the Boy Scouts and a sports ground for Deal Town Football Club. The generosity of this genial high court judge was unbounded. He provided a boathouse with a clubroom above and a fully equipped gymnasium supervised by Royal Marine P.T.I's. Later he added a second boathouse adjacent to the 'Forrester Inn' on land formerly owned by Walmer Brewery. Further, he presented a new racing four-oared regatta galley, 'Ernest Charles', plus a pairboat christened 'Bruce' (which was his middle name). As a tribute to his memory the rowing club still sport judicial colours: mauve and grey.

Since its formation Deal's Rowing Club has taken part annually in regattas organised by the Coast Amateur Rowing Association. Deal, Walmer and Kingsdown Regattas had been revived shortly after the First World War but suspended during World War Two. A popular postwar event was the race to extinguish a galley set alight at sea. At one time the Rowing Club was the proud possessor of two of their own service galleys: 'Saxon King', eventually sold to Walmer Sea Scouts, and 'Our Boys', lost during the world famous rescue race in 1959.

Over the centuries, the Downs have experienced extreme meteorological conditions. Earthquakes have been surprisingly numerous. According to Boys 'History of Sandwich' (1792) "a most fierce and terrible earthquake" rocked shipping in the Downs on 6 April 1578. It was accompanied by "a marvelouse greate noyse as thoughe the same had been the shotte of some great batterie, or a number of cannons shott off at one instante". In 1692 a summer storm culminated in a thunderbolt that dismasted and set on fire an Indiaman sheltering in the Downs. Even the massive walls of Deal Castle "shook and trembled" so violently it was feared the whole structure might collapse. On 24 March 1701 a waterspout, which suddenly appeared and agitated the waters, was observed by a chaplain aboard one of His Majesty's ships in the Downs and reported to 'The Royal Society'. A second waterspout was seen close to the Gull Stream where it damaged one of the Royal Navy ships about the year 1830.

A fearful storm was recorded on the afternoon of 18 February 1807. A West Indiaman was driven headlong onto the beach at St. Margaret's Bay; another large ship went down off Dover; two brigs went ashore, one at Kingsdown, the other at Sandown - all with great loss of life. Twenty-one ships were lost between the Forelands and to the disgrace of the inhabitants pillaging prevailed. Next year a storm caused great flooding which swamped the chambers of Sandown Castle, swept away timber quays and forced inhabitants to be rescued from their bedroom windows in the North End. Again, a destructive storm visited the Downs where four hundred ships were anchored on 29 November 1836. Hovelling luggers could not render assistance as they struggled themselves to keep afloat. Yet another storm occurred on 13 February 1870 when a north-east gale gradually increased in ferocity over a period of five days. Five merchant ships that had ignored the boatmen's warnings came ashore between Walmer Castle and Kingsdown Cliffs. Valuable cargo - rum, sugar, spices - were lost despite determined attempts to salvage.

Last century Deal experienced a terrible storm on 7 September 1952 when over four inches of rain fell coinciding with an exceptional high tide. The Fire Brigade was employed for thirteen hours pumping out water from cellars while four hundred telephones were put out of action. The southern end of the High Street was flooded so that shop girls had to be carried into work by men wading knee deep in water while negotiating floating furniture and abandoned cars. Undoubtedly it was Deal's noisiest night - with constant thunder and lightning - since the cessation of shelling in the Second World War.

Pritchard informed that the grampus - a breed of dolphin with a distinctive rounded blunt nose, tall dorsal fin and sickle shaped flippers - had been seen swimming in small shoals in the Downs. They appeared when the roadstead was free of shipping and the wind blowing in the east, "gamboling about and throwing up jets of water

Walmer Beach with East Barracks, Walmer Road Mill and Telegraph Station.

All aboard the 'Skylark'

into the air at considerable height". Possibly these playful mammals had been attracted by the abundant shoals of herrings which tempted them out of their latitude.

The carcass of a juvenile humpback whale was washed ashore at Kingsdown beach in April 2006. This was a rare occurrence since these mammals are generally found in the North Atlantic Ocean. The whale, which was an endangered species, measured twenty feet long and weighed ten tonnes. It was removed by volunteers from the British Divers Marine Life rescue and reportedly offered to the Queen. Traditionally whales, sturgeon, porpoises and dolphins, if washed ashore or caught in home waters, are deemed to belong to the sovereign since they are regarded as 'Fishes Royal'. When a whale was actually claimed by the monarch it was divided into three: the head for the king, the torso for the captor and the tail for the Queen to use in her corsetry (although, in fact, whalebone is only found in the head). On this occasion Her Majesty declined to accept the offer.

A beached whale at Pegwell Bay © Angus Neill

THREE WALMER CHURCHES

'Silent witnesses to heroic deeds'

AFTER THE NORMAN CONQUEST the victorious knights loyal to Duke William swept along the south east to subdue the shoreline. One influential family, the d'Aubervilles, settled at Walmer and built a handsome moated manor house and private chapel - Walmer Court and Old St. Mary's Church.

Duke William granted the manor of Walmer (valued at one knight's fee) to William d'Auberville, the son of Roger d'Auberville, who had been his loyal companion, and he held a barony in Essex and Suffolk. This powerful knight appears to have built the original house which would have been a simple timber stronghold on a strategic position, all traces of which have disappeared. Later his son, Hugh, replaced it with a permanent stone keep or castle. Over the centuries the manor house developed into a venerable mansion with towers built of bolder flints and ashlar stones prominently placed to command a view over the Downs.

Walmer Court, the ruins of which can still be inspected, was one of the few moated manor houses in Kent. It was a two-storeyed rectangular building with all its doors and windows - apart from a few embrasured arrow slits - on the first floor. The undercroft (which remains) was where wine, ale, wheat and provisions would be stored along with people and animals in times of danger. At the south-east corner are the remnants of a spiral staircase leading to the former solar where the Lord of the Manor resided. The house was never crenellated but its thick walls allowed for defence rather than offence.

Hugh d'Auberville probably built the Norman Church in the grounds of the Manor House. When he died in 1139 he left a widow and only son, William, who was a minor. Sir William (afterwards referred to as William d'Auberville Senior) married Maud, eldest daughter of Ralph de Glanville, Justiciary of the Kingdom from 1180 until the accession of Richard I in 1189. He was also Lord of the Manor of Westenhanger, a Justice of the County and a great benefactor of Christ Church, Canterbury. Sir William was most distinguished, however, by founding Langdon Abbey and granting Walmer Church "in pure and perpetual alms" as part of its endowment.

Neither his son, William, nor his daughter, Emma, survived him and, sadly, his second son, Hugh, died shortly after him. Hugh left a son, William, who was a minor and therefore known as Sir William d'Auberville, Junior. He was the last male heir and with his demise in 1245 expired the illustrious line of d'Auberville.

Sir William's daughter, Joan, married first Sir Henry de Sandwich of Dent-de-Lion, Thanet, but they had no children, and secondly, Sir Nicholas de Criol, Baron of the Exchequer and afterwards Lord Warden of the Cinque Ports and Sheriff of Kent. The de Criols (variously spelt 'Cryoll', 'Crioll', 'Cryel', 'Kriell', 'Kiriel' or 'Keriell') were valiant soldiers who fought in various wars against the Scots and Welsh. Sir Nicholas de Criol was the third son of Bertram de Criol, known as the 'Great Lord of Kent', and he, himself, through his marriage to Joan, became Lord of Westenhanger and later Lord Warden of the Cinque Ports. Successive members of this family were also Constables of Dover Castle, Lords Warden of the Cinque Ports and Sheriffs of Kent. Historians tend to confuse them since they bore identical names: Nicholas.

Sir Thomas, the last of this valiant line, was honoured for his victories in France. When the French retaliated by an audacious raid on the Kent coast in 1457, Sir Thomas repelled them. According to 'The English Chronicle': "This same year the xxviii day of August, on the Sunday in the morrow, the Frensshmen robbed and spoyled the toune of Sandewyche in Kent, abyding thereynne an hoole day, and at the last a knyght of the contre called sir Thomas Kyriel drove them back to the see, and kylde many of theym." Later, Sir Thomas became embroiled in the Wars of the Roses, fighting for the Yorkists, but he was eventually slain through treachery. Hasted declares that he was "against the law beheaded and murdered" in 1461. (In the churchyard several stone coffins were discovered and, lacking inscriptions, they were assumed to have belonged to the de Criols.)

Thereafter Walmer Court passed, generally by marriage through the female line, into a succession of notable Kentish families. These included the Fogges, the Ishams, the Hugissens and finally the Leiths who retain their interest in Walmer today.

Old St Mary's Church, situated within the area protected by the dry moat, was probably the private chapel of the d'Aubervilles. Throughout England the typical pattern was that a manorial estate often became an ecclesiastical parish with a church

Old St. Mary's, Walmer.

being built by the Lord of the Manor on a convenient site within his domain. At that time Upper Walmer was devoted to farming and therefore all the farmers and labourers from the village would attend the Norman Church, which like the Manor House, is thought to date from circa 1120. No mention of the church is made in the Domesday Book (A.D. 1085) since it formed part of the Manor of Folkestone.

There is evidence, however, that a Saxon Church was situated here or near this site. 'Domesday Monachorum', a twelfth century parchment (claimed to be a satellite of 'Domesday Book') which records payment owed by churches in Kent for "Chrysm money", is preserved at Canterbury Cathedral. Chrysm money was a fee paid by clergy in every parish when they received the sacred oil required for baptisms annually during Holy Week. Payments were arranged according to a customary assessment which was based upon a unit of seven denarios. Larger churches paid multiples of that sum but the most common fee was twenty-eight pence.

This cherished document was written by scholarly monks in three contrasting scripts. The book opens in a beautiful leisurely hand which dates to shortly after the death of Archbishop Lanfranc (1089 A.D.). Walmer Church appears early in this list - "De Wealemere xxviii d" - and this would suggest that it was established and flourishing soon after the Conquest. An original Saxon Church would have been built of timber and therefore no trace of it has survived.

Sir William d'Auberville Senior accompanied King Richard the Lionheart on one of the bloodiest crusades. When he returned from the Holy Land he gave thanks for his preservation by founding an Abbey at Langdon near Dover in 1192. This was served by Premonstratensian or White Canons who hailed from Leiston in Suffolk. The Abbey was dedicated to St. Mary the Virgin and St. Thomas the Martyr whose images appear on the extant seal. Sir William piously gave St. Mary's Church at Walmer, together with the churches of Oxney, Landon and Lydden, for the monks to say masses for his and his wife's souls.

Walmer Church was styled in ancient documents: "Ecclesia Beatea Mariae de Walmerre" (The Church of Blessed Mary of Walmer). Originally this typical Norman church consisted of a small nave and chancel with north and south doorways. Its exterior walls are built of rough flint with ashlar stone dressings which indicate an early construction. The grand semi-circular chancel arch, although plain on the east side, is richly embellished on the west with sunk lozenge, flat billet and chevron mouldings. This indicates an approximate date for the construction of the church as 1120 A.D. Only one of the Norman windows remains high on the north wall. Above the chancel arch are impenetrable fragments of a medieval wall painting while low down on the south wall are the remains of a 'lychnoscope', a window supposed to have been intended for lepers to view the service.

The High Altar was dedicated to the Holy Trinity and before it three lights were constantly kept burning. Benefactors - John Lotte, John Schepey and Edna Oyn - left money in their wills to maintain them. Bequests ranged from a bushel of barley to a wether (castrated ram). The Rood rested on its beam which spanned the chancel arch. A statue of Our Lady adorned the chancel and stood on the bracket that remains on the north wall. Altars dedicated to Saint John the Baptist and Saint Nicholas, each adorned with its own light, were probably placed on either side of the chancel arch in the nave.

An outer portico was built on the south side in 1835. Although sympathetic with the building it conceals a lofty Norman doorway. Its weathered semi-circular arch also boasts a variety of chiselled chevron, double billet and sunk lozenge carving. The keystone had an ornament and doubtless there was a tympanum filling the arch. On the stones of the doorway there can be found the traces of three medieval Mass dials.

Originally there was a tiny belfry surmounting the west gable. It contained two bells, one of which bore the inscription: "ioseph hatch made me, 1635". Joseph was the son of Thomas Hatch who founded the famous bell foundry at Ulcombe, near Ashford, about 1599. In 1888 the larger bell was removed to the tower of New St. Mary's Church and it was the first to ring there. A replacement wooden bellcote bore a clock presented in memory of Major General Eaton Monins, an officer who had fought at Waterloo and who died at Wellesley House in 1861.

Walmer Church was ministered to for centuries by the monks of Langdon Abbey. "Frater Willielmus Waynflete", Abbot of Langdon, was alluded to as "vicarius de Walmere" about 1482 in the Visitation Book of Bishop Redman, Visitor General of the Premonstratensian Order. This association with the Abbey - records of which are now lost - accounts for the fact that no complete list of incumbents can be compiled prior to the Reformation. Afterwards Walmer Church was served by Perpetual Curates - the first was Christopher Burton in 1560 - but during the incumbency of Rev. John Branfill Harrison the living was constituted a vicarage in 1866. Its value was so small, however, that several of the incumbents held other preferments in surrounding villages: Goodnestone, Ash, Chislet, Ripple and Great Mongeham.

At the Reformation when Henry VIII assumed the position 'Supreme Head of the Church of England' he appointed Thomas Cromwell his 'Viceregent'. Cromwell, invested with this new spiritual power, ordered the suppression of all religious houses of less value than £200 per annum in the summer of 1535. Two of the principal commissioners appointed to this distasteful task were Doctors Legh and Leyton (or Layton) whose youth and impetuosity were "likely to execute their work rather thoroughly than delicately". This particular region lying so close to the Continent attracted their attention and they paid a visit to Langdon (in addition to Dover and Folkestone) at the very outset of their labours.

Dr. Richard Layton was instantly put in a foul mood after his long journey on horseback since he reported spending "a goode space knokying at theabbottes dore faste lokked" which illicited no response apart from "theabbottes litle doge that. . . bayede and barkede". He bashed down the door with a poleaxe and surprised the abbot's mistress who, after examination, was clapped in a cell at Dover. The abbot, "a dangerous and desperate knave", was also escorted under armed guard to Canterbury where he was thrown into gaol.

Langdon, the commissioners reported, was "sore in decaye" while the abbot appeared "a veray un thrifte yvell housband, and of yll rule, and his convent veraye ignorant and poore". Naturally this damning report hastened the dissolution of the abbey and the abbot, William Sayer, together with his ten brethren, reluctantly surrendered his religious house, including the valuable church plate, to the king on 13 November 1535. Langdon Abbey was the first monastery to be suppressed.

Only fragments remain of the vast abbey at Langdon where once Edward II lodged in grand style. A map dated 1882 shows the extent of the original buildings which encompassed the vast church with its side chapel, an infirmary, cloisters opening onto a square lawn and a long dormitory over the chapter house and refectory. Most of the

St. Mary's Church, Walmer.

stone was transported to Deal for the construction of Henry's three castles. The abbey farm survived and a fine red brick house was built for the bailiff. The cellars of this 16th century building incorporate remnants of the abbey walls - chalk blocks bodged with flint - and beneath one of the corbels of the former undercroft is carved a monk's grimacing face. A magnificent tithe barn remains and there are traces of the site of the abbey mill and fish ponds. The Tudor farm buildings were adapted in Victorian times and the sprawling stables and outhouses today form a complex used by traditional craftsmen including a blacksmith and a woodturner.

Walmer Church passed into the hands of Henry VIII. It survived solely through the efforts of his friend, Thomas Cranmer, Archbishop of Canterbury. Cranmer considered the church to be of little value, however, since he reported: "The parish of Walmer is destitute of a perpetual Vicar; the endowment of the Vicarage is not sufficient for a priest's living. The priest and clerk have taken down the few images in the church but have not abused and burnt them." Laker notes that Walmer Rectory and Grange were subsequently leased first to William Killigrew and then to Falk Boughton, who was probably a relative of William Boughton, Captain of Walmer Castle. St. Mary's Church, considerably rebuilt, remained from that time onwards in the patronage of successive Archbishops of Canterbury.

During the reign of Elizabeth I, when the Reformation was firmly established in England, the first Anglican priest, Rev. Christopher Burton, was installed at Walmer. In 1575 Queen Elizabeth ordered an enquiry into the number of communicants in each parish and it was revealed that there were eighty-one - probably the entire population

- at Walmer. At the Commonwealth the Puritan Parliament required all English churchgoers to sign the 'Solemn League and Covenant' which attacked all forms of Catholicism in 1643. This daunting document was read "distinctly and audibly" from the pulpit by the tractable "minister", Rev. Anthony Bromstone, after which his congregation of fifty-nine parishioners either signed their name or made their mark, which at least ensured their Curate retained his living. At the Restoration Charles II encouraged the reversal of church doctrine and the Book of Common Prayer was reinstated by the Act of Uniformity which was passed in 1662. The new curate, Rev. William Stanley, found no difficulty in complying with the Act and so he, too, retained his benefice until his demise in 1680.

Even the fabric of the little church has had a chequered history. Towards the end of the 18th century there was a massive increase in the population of Walmer and so the church was enlarged to accommodate the expanding congregation. Sadly, the alterations showed a distinct lack of sympathy towards this historic building. Galleries had already been added along the north and west walls early in the nineteenth century but even these did not provide sufficient seating. In 1816 an additional aisle consisting of a brick building measuring 36 feet by 20 feet wide was erected on the north side of the church. Materials from the demolished Deal Barracks in Queen Street were donated by its owner, Mr. Leith. Alas, this improvement destroyed the Norman doorway. (The incumbent was Rev. Thomas George Clare, M.A.)

Ten years later a further enlargement was deemed necessary but in this instance there was some opposition. Mr. Leith, Lord of the Manor, pointed out that "there is now a chaplain appointed to do duty to the Blockade men, and which will supply the wants of the lower part of the Parish as the service is performed in the Hospital." A meeting of the newly formed Church Improvement Committee at 'The Drum' alehouse resulted in funds being raised for another extension of the north side which, in effect, threw the building out of proportion. A square block of plain brickwork, approached by a short ascent of four steps, with slated roof and wooden windows was built on the north side. This was filled with seats, above which was a cumbersome gallery on three sides, reached via a separate entrance from the exterior. The congregation faced southwards towards the three-decker pulpit which was moved first from the south-east corner to a position in the north part of the nave and finally in its present position against the south wall. Few of the congregation had a view of the altar. A hook in the ceiling for the sounding board indicates the original position of the pulpit. (The incumbent then was Rev. Edward Owen, M.A.)

Inside the church there are several treasures. The font which stands proud of the porch has an ancient bowl with a pyramidical deal cover bearing the date '1664' on its knop. High on the north wall of the chancel hang the royal arms of George I. There is a stand displaying a volume of 'Certain Sermons or Homilies of Famous Memories' printed in 1713. The windows are enlivened with a number of stained-glass saints: St. Nicholas appears in his dual role of patron of sailors and children; St. Cecilia is accompanied by angels playing musical instruments; St. Elizabeth of Hungary gathers roses in her apron while St. George stands triumphantly over a dragon, quaintly described in the guide book as "beautiful but dead". The east window presents the Virgin and Child seated on a garden bench surrounded by English roses.

There are myriad monuments which Elvin calls "silent witnesses to heroic deeds on land and sea". Most prominent are memorials to the Harvey family including Sir

Formerly, the Vicar and congregation of Old St. Mary's have joined in the ceremony of 'Beating the Bounds' to establish the extent of the parish boundaries. This involved small boys scrambling through the narrow porter's window of Deal Castle since the boundary of Deal and Walmer passes through the Tudor fortress.

The Countess of Liverpool presented a barrel organ which served Old St. Mary's Church for a quarter of a century. Later, a proper organ was presented by Mrs. Twopenny and this remained until 1888.

A curious inscription on a tombstone adjacent to the porch mentions Elizabeth Mary "of the other side". This refers, not to the fact that she has passed over to the other world, but that her epitaph appears on the reverse of the tombstone.

Upon the demise of successive monarchs and Lords Warden it was customary to drape the pulpit, reading desk and principal pews with black crape in mourning.

Henry Harvey (died 1810), Knight of the Bath, Admiral of the White Squadron who, after distinguishing himself in the memorable victory of the First of June 1794, was appointed Commander-in-Chief of the prestigious Leeward Island Station where, enviably "he acquired a Fortune by subduing the Enemies of King and Country". Also remembered are his young sons Henry (died 1788), Acting Lieutenant in H.M.S. 'Rose' drowned off Newfoundland and Richard (died 1794), Lieutenant of H.M.S. 'Ardent', destroyed by fire in the Mediterranean. Also his grandsons William (died 1842) and Richard (died 1843) who both died of yellow fever in the West Indies.

The memorial tablets generally have maritime or military connections: Lieutenant Colonel Robert Gordon (died 1853) who served the Honourable East India Company in Bombay until he transferred to the Indian Army, and Lieutenant William Henry Royse R.N. (1861) of H.M.S. 'Snake' who died of fever at Ningpo, China. The tablet to the memory of Captain Richard Budd Vincent (died 1831) includes a representation of a sinking ship, supposed to be H.M. sloop, 'Arrow'. Vincent was made a Companion of the Honourable Military Order of the Bath for his gallant conduct in defending a valuable convoy in the Mediterranean in 1805. Most of his crew were either killed or wounded and Vincent was compelled to strike his own colours after ensuring the safety of the convoy only moments before his own ship, 'Arrow', sank.

There are memorials recalling two Captains of Sandown Castle who fought in the Napoleonic Wars: Sir John Hill, K.T. (died 1854), Rear Admiral of the White, who took part in the Battle of the Nile, and William Willmot Henderson (died 1854), Rear Admiral of the White who was present at Trafalgar. (His monument is embellished with anchors, flags and cannon) More humbly, there are tablets to Robert Huggins (died 1770), Pilot of Deal and Captain Peter Fisher R.N. (died 1844), Superintendent of H.M. Dockyard, Sheerness.

The oldest monument is a handsome alabaster wall tablet, high on the north wall of the chancel, honouring the brothers William and Edmund L'Isle, who both died in 1637, placed their by their surviving brother, Nicholas. Edmund was a personal friend of Queen Elizabeth I and Captain of Walmer Castle for twenty-one years. Both brothers were equerries to the first two Stuart sovereigns, James I and Charles I. Their coat of arms includes a boar's head, running colts and a crest of a millstone.

Lord Warden, the Duke of Wellington, was a most

punctilious attender of Old St. Mary's when he was in residence each autumn at Walmer Castle (1829 - 1852). Every Sunday he rode over to the church, a great Bible tucked under his arm, where he tied his horse to the ancient yew nearest the porch. He would curl up in one corner of his private pew immediately under the triple-decker pulpit and fall asleep during the long sermon, snoring loudly...

The Duke's old-fashioned rented square pew was in a dilapidated state according to Benjamin Hayden, the artist, who accompanied the Duke to church one Sunday while staying at the castle to paint his portrait: "From the bare wainscot, the absence of curtains, the dirty green footstools, and common chairs, I feared I was in the wrong pew. . ." All the same, it must have been a thrilling sight for the congregation of this country church to have among them the greatest figure in the land.

The story is told that one Sunday a certain pew was occupied by a group of ladies who were strangers to the village. They had been ushered there by mistake upon entering by the churchwarden who had concluded that, since he was late, the usual occupier had no intention of attending service that morning. Presently this pompous parishioner arrived and, without hesitation, turned the whole party out into the aisle. There they stood, all eyes gazing upon them, deeply confused and acutely embarrassed. Promptly, the Duke rose from his seat, opened the door of his own pew and politely invited them inside.

It was said that the Duke would have wished to be buried in this humble village church rather than in the full pomp and splendour of St. Paul's Cathedral. "Where the tree falls, there let it lie," was his stated opinion. By custom the Duke's hatchment (a pictorial lozenge-shaped board displaying his armorial bearings or "achievements") was carried in front of his funeral procession when he died in 1852. It now hangs high on the north wall over the site of the Duke's pew which stood in the annexe, since demolished. Curiously, the hatchment displays only one of his innumerable orders - the Order of the Garter - although, in truth, the Duke's orders were said at the time to have exceeded in number and importance anything of the kind ever possessed by a single person.

Elizabeth I, in the first year of her reign, commanded that every "parson, vicar or curat" should "kepe one book or register, wherin they shall write the daye and yere of everye wedding, christening and burial." Walmer parish registers commenced in 1560/1 although only a parchment copy remains down to 1598. During the Civil War the parish registers were neglected. The Puritan Parliament forbade the clergy to resort to the holy offices of the church: baptism of infants was neglected, marriage became a civil contract and burials were performed without any religious ceremony. In 1653, an Act of Parliament directed that a registrar should be appointed in every parish charged with keeping of a Register Book and to enter all publications of banns, marriages, births and burials but there is no indication of any such appointment at Walmer. At first, the registers of births, marriages and deaths appeared in the same book but in 1753 a separate book was required to record all marriages and in 1812 baptisms and burials were also recorded in different books.

The Register of Burials commences: "The names of them yt were buryed in the Phshe church of Walmr in ye year of lour lorde god 1560 ao 3 Elizabeth regine." The date of the first entry is "ye xi februarye 1560". It makes gruesome reading:

1638 Two flemish mariners out of a ship cast away upon the Goodwin

October 8

1639 Martha Leake infant drowned in a well July 30

1649 Richard Mons hanged him self the 23 of June

1735 Mr David Denn Grocer of Deal who perished in the flames or in the fall of his house was Buried August 27th

1814 24th December a woman called Ragged Kitty Died from the inclemency of the weather.

There are a number of anonymous sailors drowned at sea:

A Body washed ashore at Walmer (20 April 1818)

John Matwell, brought onshoer from a West Indiaman passing through the Downs, age not known (9 December 1826)

Body of a boy, name unknown, found on the beach (29 December 1830)

John Peter Allan From a ship in the Downs (8 January 1818)

There are twenty-one burials recorded from H.M.S. 'Medusa' and three from H.M.S. 'Leyden' beginning from 17 August 1801. These were both flagships of Lord Nelson while stationed in the Downs and the burials are evidence of his abortive Battle of Boulogne.

There are several burials listed of miserable prisoners aboard convict ships passing through the Downs being transported to Australia: Charles Whitworth and Henry Thompson (both 19 January 1818) from 'Tottenham'; Frances Smith (3 December 1821) from 'Richmond' and William Simpkins (14 July 1835) from 'Mary Ann'. Also recorded is the burial of Private William Rowe of the 20th Regiment Infantry who died on 13 November 1824 aboard 'Lady East'. The Journal of the Surgeon Superintendent of this convict ship exists and reveals the infinite care taken of this fever-ridden soldier who had been hospitalised from the moment he had boarded at Chatham.

Various entries date from 1815 to 1830 and refer to prisoners, marines, sailors, their wives and children from aboard H.M.S. 'Severn' (a fourth-rate frigate) and H.M.S. 'Ramillies' (a third-rate sloop) which were the floating headquarters of the Coastal Blockade led by Captain William McCulloch, contemptuously known as 'Flogging Joey'. Later burials relate to H.M.S. 'Talavera', a stationary depot ship belonging to the Coastguard that replaced the Coast Blockade.

In addition to the burials in the churchyard the register contains a record of the interments of the Burial Ground attached to the Royal Naval Hospital as well as those in the Military Ground at the North Barracks. This is not a complete list of burials since it is reported by Rev Charles Fielding, Curate in Charge of Walmer from 1812 to 1822 that "between the years 1817 and 1829 about 30 burials took place there by the Chaplain to the Severn Guard Ship lying in the Downs of Sailors who died on board and those of the preventive service."

Extracts from this book:

August 1st 1797 Thomas Hunter, mutineer executed on board the Beaulieu.

December 27th 1803 A seaman thrown up on the Beach by the Royal Hospital.

April 12th 1804 A midshipman found on the beach, unknown.

Among the registers appears a Memorandum Book where for some time baptisms and burials were entered by the parish clerk, with his erratic spelling, until they found their way into the regular records.

> 1760 Joel Wellard drown'd June 20th his body not found.
> 1761 Eliz: Church Spinster Drounded in the Sea, a Lunetick, Buried 13th Sepbr.
> 1768 Bearid Ann the Dauter of ualinton upton January:3
> 1775 John the son of the widow watson Exerdentley drounded in the Sea was buried march 16th.

Also there are several notes of 'Tax Paid' after certain burials pointing to the infringement and subsequent fine of wealthy parishioners buried in linen rather than wool. The 'Act for Burying in Woollen' came into force in 1679 for the purpose of "lessening the importance of the importation of linen from beyond the seas, and the encouragement of the woollen and paper manufactures of this kingdom". This curious Act, which was not repealed until 1814, required an affidavit to be signed within eight days testifying that the deceased was not buried in linen under a penalty of £5.

Elvin describes the Norman Church as "prettily situated on rising ground near the north-westerly boundary of Upper Walmer". Originally, the sloping churchyard was small, encompassing half an acre, but it was expanded over the years as the population of the village increased. The churchyard once boasted two venerable yews. It was a common practice by the clergy to plant pairs of yews - male and female - after the Norman Conquest. They were at that time the only evergreen trees in England and they were regarded as a symbol of everlasting life. These sacred trees were generally planted along the pathway leading to the principal entrance to the church. Traditionally, the vicar waited by the yew furthest from the porch (and not the lychgate) to greet the coffin before it continued its sad procession through the churchyard.

There are several assumptions why yew trees are often located in churchyards. First, they may have provided bows for men to practice archery. Edward II ordained that every man should possess a bow of his own height and that every town should provide butts for them to practise their skills in archery on high days and holidays. Secondly, berries were poisonous to cattle and yews were therefore confined within a walled churchyard. Thirdly, bows of yews were carried in procession on Palm Sunday which in Wales was called 'Yew Sunday'.

The Conservation Foundation Country Living Tree Campaign authenticated the one remaining (female) yew to 1400. This is not, however, unusually old and dispels the tradition that it supplied Richard I with a bow for his Third Crusade. (This story possibly originates from the fact that one of the owners of the Manor House, William D'Auberville Senior, accompanied the Lionheart to the Holy Land in 1189) The male tree died around 1880 and although the present yew was damaged it survived the hurricane of 1987. At one time animals were carved inside its hollow trunk.

The churchyard was the burial ground for the parish from Norman times onwards and therefore contains several notable burials. Oldest tombstone lies immediately opposite the south porch and commemorates 'John Bassett (died 1680), one of the gunners of His Majesty's Castle of Walmer'. To the right of the path leading to the extended churchyard is the grave of Daniel Bishop (died 1846), a Bow Street Runner who arrested Thistlewood, ringleader of the Cato Street Conspiracy. To the north-east of the church is a curious monument of a young naval surgeon, Jeremiah Ryan (died 1808). A doubtful tradition persists that he was killed by the cannon ball which surmounts his memorial. Also to be found is the grave of Duncan McArthur (died 1855), one of the physicians to Nelson's fleet while in the Downs and Physician to the Royal Naval Hospital at Walmer. He attended the Duke of Wellington at his demise at Walmer Castle in 1852. Nearby is the grave of John Kale (died 1840), from the 71st Regiment who fought at Waterloo. Hidden beside an avenue of yews is an oval plaque on a granite cross depicting World War One soldiers firing a machine gun. This recalls Brigadier General Henry Cecil Montague Hill (died 1931), late of the Buffs, who raised the Machine Gun Corps.

One humble memorial recalls the widow, Sarah Smith, Mistress of the Sunday School (died 1839). Sarah had travelled with her six children from the North of England and she became a much respected woman when she settled in the parish. Another respected woman buried there is Elizabeth Norman (died 1842), housekeeper to the Duke of Wellington. There is also the tombstone of Charlotte Baugh (died 1842), widow of Isaac Baugh, secretary to Warren Hastings, Governor General of India. Perhaps the most pathetic inscription appears on the tombstone of Isabella Netherville Watkins located close to the ruins of the Manor House. "The deceased was descended from a long line of ancestry, having been a member of the Most Ancient Noble, but decayed house of the Nethervilles, a family not unknown to fame ere their arrival in this country with the Conqueror."

At one time the concerns of the Vestry of Walmer were dual - church and civic - and the minute book records relevant duties, charities and transactions. It considered the supply of gas for the village, made arrangements for the disposal of sewage, organised the building of new roads, protested about the proposed railway lines by three rival companies, fought off plans to annexe the parish to Deal and even organised a cricket match on Goodwin Sands.

Walmer Vestry was also concerned with upholding law and order in the village. It employed a succession of constables whose duties ranged from searching for vagrants to apprehending murderers. Accounts are extant from 1813 until 1830 which show the quarterly invoices submitted by various police constables for their services which ranged from 'Taking up a Soldier for a breach of the Peace' (1s 0d) to 'Quelling a Riot' (1s 0d). Constable William Clayton was paid two shillings for "Apprehending two Men armed with Pistoles" (30 July 1816), while Constable Douglas Morrison was paid one guinea for "Taking into Custody John Hornsbey of Clapton by Order of the Rev. M. Pennington, J.P., in the House of Mr. Daws, King's Head, Walmer, on the Charge of Murder" (7 October 1819). Constable Joseph Flowers was paid one shilling for putting Thomas Pearson in the "Stocks" and a further shilling for "taking three boys to the Magistrates for taking a boat from the beach belonging to Mr. Pack" (27 January 1828).

In 1833 Walmer Vestry also appointed two parish beadles - James Bocannon and Edward Hall - who were each paid nine shillings per week and provided with uniforms consisting of a blue coat with a red collar, hat and staff. Two years later it resolved to have a more efficient Constabulary Force. In 1846 James Parsons was recruited from the Metropolitan Police Force. He was charged with keeping the peace in the parish and was required to report personally to the Vicar every Monday morning. Although he was amply paid eighteen shillings per week, the P.C. Parsons proved unsatisfactory and was dismissed.

When it was decided towards the end of the nineteenth century to replace the church with a more commodious building Old St. Mary's forlornly became a mortuary chapel. Today, happily, services are occasionally conducted in this historic church when the same cracked bell that summoned the Duke of Wellington calls present parishioners to divine worship.

A large increase in the population of boatmen at Lower Walmer in the early part of the 19th century meant that it became necessary to erect a "chapel-of-ease" along the Strand. First active steps were taken by Rev. Henry William Wilberforce, M.A., during his brief incumbency at Old St. Mary's (1841 - 3). Henry was the youngest son of William Wilberforce whose persistent campaigning resulted in the Parliamentary Bill abolishing the slave trade.

When Queen Victoria and Prince Albert with their two young children spent an autumn holiday at Walmer Castle, Rev. Henry Wilberforce was invited to preach at divine service on Sunday 13 November 1842. He chose an apt sermon - "For as the lightning cometh out of the east. . . so shall the Son of Man be" (Matthew 24 v 27) - considering the gathering storm viewed through the castle windows overlooking the Downs.

This fervent young curate had already introduced a daily service at Old St. Mary's and an evening service at the Navy Hospital. He was emphatic that the spiritual life of the seafarers at Walmer should not be neglected which is why he proposed that a church should be built closer to the seashore. He readily persuaded the Duke of Wellington as Lord Warden to be among the first subscribers since Walmer Castle was in the parish. (The Iron Duke had earlier made a donation towards the opening of a school in Cambridge Road in 1838)

St. Saviour's Church showing its bell tower and steeple.

Sadly, Rev. Henry Wilberforce had left by the time sufficient funds had been raised for the building of the new church to commence. On 15 August 1848 the foundation stone was laid by Mrs. Harriet Bridges, mother of the poet, Robert Bridges, who lived at 'Roselands', Upper Walmer. The following year (2 July 1849) the church was consecrated by the Most Reverend John Bird, Lord Archbishop of Canterbury. It was dedicated to the Holy Saviour and the first incumbent was Rev. William Buckston Holland. The architect was John Johnson of London, the builder was William Denne of Deal and the total cost was £1,530.

St. Saviour's is built in the Decorated style and it originally consisted only of a nave, south aisle and small chancel. (The north aisle was added in 1896) The walls are of Hassock stone, externally faced with blue Ragstone, and these rest on flint foundations with Caen stone dressings. There are west and south doorways, the latter boasts a wooden porch on a masonry basement.

The church was intended to accommodate 380 people (229 pews were reserved for poor folk) but by the time the church was opened the number of boatmen had greatly dwindled. A huge stove heated the church although it was found that "it can never be used in cold wintry weather with northerly winds, without imminent risk of suffocating with its noxious fumes both priest and people."

The east end, originally whitewashed, was later brightly painted with exotic fruit and gold stars. There is a plain deal roof. The English altar has gilded eagles on each of the four riddel posts. A flamboyant east window has three principal lights showing scenes of the crucifixion. The topmost light shows Christ in Majesty. A hidden sliding door in the oak panelling conceals the reserved sacrament. The organ which stands on the north side of the nave was moved from the gallery while a brass eagle replaces the plain deal lectern. The original stone mural pulpit - now oak - is placed in a most peculiar position against the south abutment of the chancel arch. Entrance is contrived by means of a small archway reached via three stone steps in the south wall of the chancel. The preacher appears to leave the church and re-enter for his sermon!

At the west end is an octagonal stair turret leading to the steep tiered pews in the childrens' gallery. There are narrow timber treads through which the bell rope passes and a slender handrail.

Surmounting the west gable was a small wooden spirelet covered with shingles and housing a single bell. A heavy gale carried away the weathercock from atop the spire in January 1884. During a severe thunderstorm on the early morning of Sunday 10 August 1890 the church was struck by lightning which destroyed the belfry. The boy whose duty it was to ring the bell for services had only just left his post in the gallery. Eventually, the spire, which had been undermined, was removed for safety. In the churchyard is a granite memorial with a crucifix commemorating the men of Lower Walmer who fell in the Great War.

Dark war clouds were again gathering over Europe during 1939 and by September of that year the church was fitted with black curtains and shutters to allow essential services to continue. At that time the congregations were small because three quarters of the population of Deal and Walmer had been evacuated. Fortunately, the church was vacated when a fragment of shell pierced one of the three main stained-glass windows. It narrowly missed the figure of Christ bearing His cross but scored the choir stalls before falling in the aisle. Harold and Vivien Lyons who kept a nearby drapery-cum-grocery shop (although they had little to sell) looked after the lonely church. Wintertime was most frightening - "the empty streets, the empty beach, where danger could erupt out of the night"- owing to its exposed position. In gratitude, the meeting hall which occupies the south aisle was named the 'Lyons Room'.

An hotel, 'Royal Standard', in Lower Walmer was converted into a private residence, 'The Grange', to serve as a temporary Vicarage. The first true Vicarage, secured through the efforts of Rev Henry Wilberforce, was 'Glebe House' atop Drum Hill. This is an imposing yellow brick building with tall twisting chimneys, a brick porch and a pair of deep bays. (Apparently, it was also the residence at one time of a former Lord Chancellor) It was later replaced by 'Clare Cottage' on the opposite side of the road adjacent to 'Gothic House'.

Alterations to the old parish church were considered to have ruined its character and plans were mooted for its replacement. There was a particular desire for a more harmonious building whose appearance would be truly sympathetic towards its divine purpose. A subscription list was opened and parishioners proved generous but progress in building a church was inordinately slow. Lord Warden, Earl Granville, K.G., proved a worthy benefactor and a site was obtained atop Constitution Hill overlooking The Glen. Eventually, on 13 April 1887, the foundation stone, located under the east window, was laid by Countess Granville.

During the excavations for the foundations of the new church labourers revealed the existence of an ancient trench which extended obliquely across the hill from east to west. The soil in this trench contained a large quantity of mammalian bones. Two human skeletons, buried for centuries, were decapitated by the workmen's spades. A

New St. Mary's Church in the snow.

69

single piece of Upchurch pottery marked with a cross lay nearby. It was assumed this was the burial place of a Christian convert. (Elvin suggests that 'Walmer' derives from 'gwal' meaning a site near a Roman fortification and 'mer' meaning sea = "The Roman fortification by the sea".)

On 5 April 1888 Dr. Edward White Benson, Archbishop of Canterbury, conducted a service of consecration in the new church which was dedicated to Saint Mary. After the ceremony His Grace was conveyed in grand style by Earl Granville's personal carriage for a reception at Walmer Castle. New St. Mary's was officially constituted the parish church of Walmer.

New St. Mary's was built of Kentish ragstone with Bath stone dressings at a cost of £8,000 from designs by Sir Arthur Blomfield. It is in the Early English style and consists of a lofty, wide and spacious nave with arcades of five arches opening to its two small north and south aisles, a chancel with north and south transepts, and a baptistry. But it does not have a correct orientation since the altar actually faces north-east. It accommodates six hundred worshippers. A later Vicar, Rev. Canon Bruce Hawkins, commented that the new church "smacks of Victorian triumphalism".

The interior is impressive. A handsome reredos before the High Altar is formed of 'opus sectile', which is a type of mosaic employing large fragments of glass. The subject is the Nativity. The east wall of the reredos is decorated in the same style of mosaic and includes figures of the Four Evangelists. The low chancel screen is alabaster and at the foot of the steps is a brass eagle lectern. There is a Caen stone circular pulpit relieved by Purbeck marble and a Caen stone font. The original organ was built by the local firm, F.H. Browne. There are commodious vestries for clergy and choir and a hammer beam roof.

Choir stalls, prayer desk and font cover are made of rare sequoia wood. Sequoia or Colossal Redwood is a Californian tree whose timber is described in Rhind's 'Vegetable Kingdom' as of "a fine red colour, close-grained, but light and brittle". This is the first known instance of wood from this tree being used in England. Its warm hue, redder than cedar, gives the church an extremely rich appearance.

Chief glory is the stained-glass windows. The east window is a triplet and depicts the Ascension. In the lower part appear the apostles with the Virgin Mary

William Pitt, while Lord Warden only once attended divine service at Old St. Mary's. Clearly, he was not a churchgoing man.

Pitt had been visited by William Wilberforce, the ardent campaigner for the abolition of slavery, at Walmer Castle in 1792. Their conversation revolved safely around politics.

The original contract specified that St. Saviour's was to be built "on the east side of the High Road leading from Walmer to Deal." If the builder had carried out his instructions to the letter the new church would have been built on Walmer Green.

Services at St. Saviour's were often disrupted when boatmen were called out to man the lifeboat. An annual lifeboat service is still held at this church.

Among the subscribers to New St. Mary's were the food manufacturers Crosse and Blackwell and Huntley & Palmer.

distinguished by her white coiffure and gold drapery. The west window shows marine scenes from the New Testament. Three small lower windows were given by John Lewis Roget, famous for his 'Sketches of Deal, Walmer and Sandwich' (1911) and the only son of Dr. Peter Mark Roget, originator of 'Roget's Thesaurus of English Words and Phrases'. Windows in the War Memorial Chapel feature three warrior saints - St. George, St. Alban and St. Martin - while windows in the north and south aisles depict the Patriarchs, the Prophets and the Twelve Apostles. The animals and birds depicted there are remarkably fine.

Blomfield's bell tower was completed in 1893 as a memorial to the late Earl Granville and dedicated by Archbishop Benson. Amongst the contributors to the cost, surprisingly, were some of his political opponents. However, the funds were not sufficient to provide both tower and spire owing to a national memorial inaugurated in London. The single bell from the old church was replaced by a peal of eight bells hung in 1893.

The Victorian vicarage stands atop the grandly named Constitution Hill. It is approached via an exceedingly long, dark tradesmen's tunnel whose roof was reinforced with concrete as a surface shelter in the Second World War. The Rev. Peter Hammond wrote a book, 'The Parson and the Victorian Parish' (1977) while in residence. A new vicarage was built in the grounds facing St. Mary's Road in 1986. Nearby, 'Elizabeth House', which incorporates church offices and meeting rooms, was officially opened by Queen Elizabeth, the Queen Mother, in 1991.

The centenary of New St. Mary's in 1888 was also celebrated by a visit from Queen Elizabeth, the Queen Mother, Lord Warden of the Cinque Ports, who was at that time staying on board H.M.S. 'Britannia' anchored in the Downs. On this occasion Rev. Canon Bruce Hawkins preached the address and he wittily remarked that on 100th

Interior of St. Mary's Church.

71

birthdays the normal custom was to receive a telegram from the Queen. "Today we are honoured with a royal presence," he quipped. Every other year from that time onwards until her demise, Her Majesty made private visits to St. Mary's Church which were always occasions for celebration.

Old St. Mary's Church, Walmer.

THE GOODWIN SANDS

'The Shippe-Swallower'

THE GOODWIN SANDS is a perilous sandbank concealed beneath the waves stretching roughly between the North and South Forelands. They are, in reality, composed of two distinct sandbanks - North and South Goodwins - bisected by a channel known as 'Kellet Gut'. Situated four miles east of Deal, they measure approximately twelve miles long from the North Sand Head to the South Sand Head and five miles diagonally across from east to west across the Kellet Gut. Lying in the Strait of Dover, which forms the narrowest part of the world's busiest highway, the English Channel, they present an obstacle to shipping. Over the centuries they have gained an evil reputation for devouring ships and are, therefore, known as the 'widow maker' or 'shippe swallower'.

This comparatively small area of the Narrow Seas has been responsible for more wrecks and the consequent loss of more lives than any other stretch of water around Britain. Richard Larn, compiler of the authoritative 'Shipwreck Index of Great Britain', categorically states: "Of the countless thousands of natural obstacles which represent a hazard to shipping in the western world, there is no single headland, island, rock, sandbank or bar which has earned such infamy or been more feared by seamen than the Goodwin Sands". Paradoxically, when the wind is in a certain quarter, this "small archipelago of islands" have acted as a massive breakwater by holding back the tremendous waves encountered in the English Channel. It is claimed that they have saved a thousand ships for every one they have devoured and, indeed, the town of Deal owes its protection to their existence.

Studying charts of the Goodwin Sands the impression is given of a lobster with a huge claw extending in a south-westerly direction, the tips of which are divided into the North and South Callipers. (The 'Callipers' may take their name from their resemblance to the curved dividers used by navigators for measuring distances on their charts) The South Calliper reaches towards a sharp point known as South Sand Head, notorious for mountainous green seas. The curve in the body of this imaginary 'lobster' on the south-west edge is Trinity Bay, formerly known to God-fearing boatmen as 'Abraham's bosom'.

At the opposite end of the Goodwin Sands is the North Sand Head - once known by smugglers as 'Jamaica Land' - with, at the highest point, the great bank of the Goodwin Knoll. On the north-west side of the North Goodwins, from opposite Ramsgate to almost opposite Deal, is the Gull Stream which was the route taken by most medium-sized ships passing from the Thames Estuary inside the Goodwins to the English Channel. The Brake is another mound at the western edge of the Gull Stream while the changeable Kellet Gut, sometimes navigable, divides the two halves of the Goodwin Sands. Westwards is the world-famous anchorage divided into the Great and Small Downs.

During a low spring tide, around twelve miles of the North and ten miles of the South Sands are exposed, but at low neap tides nothing at all is revealed. Bayley describes the features of the dry sands:"... their characteristics comprise promontories, knolls, bays, spits, gullies, "foxfalls" and "swatchways", the latter being considerable waterways through which the prevailing tidal currents rush with great force, creating difficult and often dangerous eddies and whirlpools, thus adding seriously to the normal danger in reaching wrecked vessels. Foxfalls are pits like wells, some of them twenty feet deep, and difficult holes to get out of in case of accident."

The changing shape of the Goodwin Sands has rendered them difficult to chart. At first, they were marked as a shapeless sandbank on primitive charts but over the centuries experienced navigators began to record their treacherous features.

Earliest chart which shows the Goodwins on a scale sufficiently detailed for navigational purposes was drawn by a Dutch pilot, Lucas Janszoon Waghenaer, in

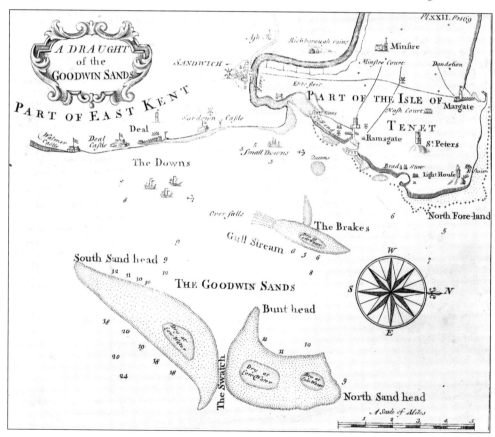

A Draught of the Goodwin Sands c. 1750 © National Maritime Museum.

1583. His hand coloured"sea-atlas", enlivened with drawings of sailing ships and sea monsters, was copied by Anthony Ashley five years later and was published in the 'Mariners' Mirrour'. This English version was commissioned by Queen Elizabeth I's Privy Council to assist in the repulsion of the Spanish Armada. Waghenaer's charts, considered accurate at the time, were perused privately in libraries rather than consulted aboard ships and subsequent collections of marine atlases were commonly called"waggoners". Sketched from seawards, they show panoramic views of foreign coastlines reported by sea captains and customs officials although their observations were far from perfect. The single sandbank marked"ye Goodwyne"is a most curious shape - almost a straight line facing the English Channel but undulating towards the Kent coast and ending in a sharp point at the southern tip.

A 'Coastal Chart of South-East England' by William Borough, an Elizabethan seaman who commanded 'Bonavolia' that sailed against the Armada, was compiled in 1596. The chart was commissioned by the Queen's councillors in the aftermath of the Spanish Armada. It shows an impossibly long, slender strip marked 'Goodwynde Sand' stretching from Foreland to Foreland and lying opposite the 'Downes Roads'. The first known chart to show the Goodwins as two distinct broad sandbanks bisected by a narrow channel was produced by Robert Jager in 1629. His purpose was to convince Charles I of the necessity of building a new harbour to replace Sandwich Haven. This deep swatchway, splitting an oval sandbank in half, is confirmed in a marine atlas produced by the Dutch cartographer, Pieter Goos, in 1666, and a chart by Joseph Ross, Trinity House pilot, in 1779.

A later chart made by Charles Labelye, engineer and former 'Teacher of the Mathematicks in the Royal Navy', in 1736 presents "the True Shape and Situation of the Coast between the North and South Forelands and of the adjacent sands together with the Soundings at Low Water, Places of Anchorage, & All the necessary Leading Marks."The South Goodwins is shown twice as long as the North Sandbank and there is a wide swatchway drawn between the two unequal halves. This swatchway is the elusive Kellet Gut, an open channel navigable by ships of deep draught, later noted during a survey by H.M.S. 'Kellet' in 1926. (Mysteriously, it appears on some charts but not on others since it closes up completely for several years at a time) First systematic survey of the Goodwin Sands, however, was undertaken by Graeme Spence on behalf of the Admiralty in 1794/5.

After decades of meticulous recording, it is now possible for surveyors to discern a predictable pattern in the movement of the Goodwin Sands. Nevertheless, despite modern scientific aids to navigation, the Goodwins are potentially a risk to ships that strike them. Deep water lies close along the eastern edge and vessels that ground in this vicinity are in immediate danger of breaking their back as the tide falls (eighteen feet at Spring tides) leaving her bows fast in the Sands with her stern unsupported. A vessel running fully onto the sandbank will fare no better since the tides will sweep the sand from under her bow and stern to leave her stranded amidships and liable to snap in two. Time passes and the wrecks slowly corrode and either 'swaddle down' into the Sands or slip off the edge into deeper water as the tides alter the shape of the edges and the waves pound at the hulks. . .

The origin of Goodwin Sands is steeped in mystery. References in ancient manuscripts indicate that there were three islands in the vicinity of the Roman 'Portus Rutupinus' at the head of the Wantsum Channel. The northern island was 'Tanatus'

(Thanet); the southern island was Rutupiae' (Richborough) and the third which lay to the south-east was known as 'Infera Insula' ('Low Island' or 'Lomea'). Earliest mention of Lomea in print appears in 'De Rebus Albionicis Britannicus', written by John Twyne (1501 - 81) schoolmaster and antiquarian from Canterbury. The author is the sole authority that century for the transformation of a fertile island into the treacherous sandbank:

"Of Lomea, or as it is now called Goodwin Sands . . this isle was very fruitful and had much pasture; it was situated lower than Thanet from which there was a passage by boat of about three or four miles. This island in an unusual tempest of winds and rain and in a very high rage of the sea was drowned, overwhelmed with sand, and irrecoverably converted into a nature between that of land and sea. . . sometimes it floats, while at low water, people may walk upon it."

Inexorably, the Sands are associated with the Saxon statesman and warrior, Earl Godwin, father of Harold II. Apparently he was an early Lord Warden and, according to Philpot's Roll (1627) he was also "constable of the Castell of Dover". He became the most powerful man in the realm and amassed vast wealth and gained great lands. Earl Godwin, who frequently sailed from Sandwich, is supposed to have anchored his ships in a natural harbour on the Sands although, in reality, he was more likely to have sheltered them in the Downs.

One improbable story relates how Earl Godwin while returning home at the head of his fleet was wrecked and drowned on the sandbank - and the name 'Goodwin Sands' perpetuates his memory - but, truth to tell, he suffered a stroke while dining with his son-in-law, Edward the Confessor, at Winchester, Easter 1053. He was buried in the Old Minster - a Benedictine Monastery - but his remains were swallowed up in the building of Winchester Cathedral in 1079.

Apparently Earl Godwin, of "unhallowed memory", made a predatory excursion into the Weald of Kent, which at that time was thinly populated but heavily wooded. There he was surrounded by a superior army and, while lying in concealment, made a sacred vow that, should his life be spared, he would construct a steeple atop Tenterden Church to the honour of the Holy Saints. Earl Godwin, after returning home in safety, neglected to fulfil his promise and his sea-girt domains were swamped as a divine punishment. An alternative version relates that Earl Godwin was so diligent in fulfilling his pledge that he actually spent all his funds in building this church steeple. Consequently he neglected to maintain the wooden walls of his island estate which was overwhelmed at the next tempest. Unsurprisingly there is not a shred of geological nor historical evidence to support such fanciful tales.

There are yet more conflicting details. Apparently, after the Norman Conquest, William the Conqueror presented Godwin's estates including his island to the Abbot of St. Augustine's Abbey at Canterbury. Improvidently, the Abbot declined to repair its seawall with material already collected for that purpose but diverted the stone to build the church at Tenterden. The sea broke in during a storm and engulfed Lomea so that it was transformed into a treacherous sandbank.

One verifiable fact is that there were two great storms: one occurred in 1014 when Godwin was alive and the other in 1099 when he was long since dead. Each of these storms was followed by an inundation of the sea resulting in appalling loss of life, land and property. The Saxon Chronicle describes the second catastrophe: "... in the year 1099, on the festival of St. Martin, the sea-flood sprang up such a height, and did so much harm as no man remembered it ever did before, and this was the first day of the new moon." Huge waves wrought havoc with the seascape and the coastline changed forever. Powerful tides and currents, rips and races may have formed this vast sandbank "of uncertain behaviour and ill-defined dimensions" mid-Channel.

William Lambard, the antiquarian and topographer, in 'Perambulations of Kent' (1570) ascribes the latter storm to divine retribution for Earl Godwin's crimes. He tells how, as punishment for his numerous sins, Godwin's island in Kent was overwhelmed and "sonke sodainly into the Sea." In the brief reign of William II (1087 - 1100): "... there was a sudden and mighty imundation of the sea, by which a great part of Flanders was utterly destroyed and lost, whilst at the same time various places both in England and Scotland also suffered most dreadfully, but especially the Estates of Godwyn, Earl of Kent, which were first covered with a fine light sand, and afterwards overwhelmed by the waves and so destroyed." And he concludes his account that Godwin's island "not onely remaineth covered (by the waters), but it is become withall a most dreadfull gulphe and the Shippe Swallower."

Yet another tradition connects the silting up of Sandwich Haven and the formation of the Goodwins with the building of the steeple atop St. Mildred's Church at Tenterden. An ancient proverb asserts:

> "Of many people it hath been said,
> That Tenterden steeple
> Sandwich Haven hath decayed"

Sir Thomas More, Henry VIII's Chancellor, made his own enquiries into how this 'shelfe' of sand was formed. In his 'Dialogue Concerning Heresies' (1529) he mentions that "divers men of worshippe" were sent into Kent to discover the cause of both the silting up of Sandwich Haven and the emergence of the Goodwin Sands. An elderly inhabitant gave a strange reply:

> "There start vp one good olde father and sayd ye masters saye euery manne what he wyll cha marked this matter well as some other. And by god I wote howe it waxed nought well ynoughe. For I knewe it good and haue marked so chaue when it began to wax worse. And what hathe hurte it good father quod these gentyll men? By my faythe maysters quod he yonder same tenterden stepell and nothyng ellys that by the masse cholde twere a fayre fysshe pole. Why hath the stepell hurte the hauen good father quod they? Naye byr lady masters quod he ych can not tell you well why but chote well it hath. For by god I knwe it a good hauen tyll that stepell was bylded. And by ye mary masse cha marked it well it neuer throue synce."

Sir Thomas scoffed at the idea but included it in one of his sermons as a demonstration of how heresies arise through false information. Bishop Hugh Latimer repeated this ridiculous tale as a "merry toy" to enliven one of his own sermons preached before King Edward VI in London. There cannot be any possible link between the steeple, the sands nor the harbour - St. Mildred's Church at Tenterden acquired a tower but not a steeple in 1476 - although the name 'Tenterden' supposes a connection with Thanet since it denotes "the swine pastures of the people of Thanet". Yet it merely indicates that the land was once owned by the religious order at Minster-in-Thanet where St. Mildred was the first Abbess.

The Goodwin Sands were excavated extensively throughout the 19th century by experienced engineers who separately determined that they are simply a mass of clean sand deposited on a bed of chalk.

In 1843 James Walker, a civil engineer, concluded that: "I consider the Sands as the natural consequence of the peculiar formation of the place, and of the cross tidal currents upon it, just as any other sands may be formed." And that conclusion is generally accepted today. According to the United Kingdom Hydrographic Office, the last time the Sands were comprehensively surveyed was in 2000 but "surveys of parts of the Goodwins are rendered almost on an annual basis, either by the Royal Navy, Trinity House or commercial companies." The Goodwin Sands are, therefore, a densely surveyed area and at no time has there been the slightest indication that they were ever cultivated.

The Goodwin Sands has been celebrated in literature. William Shakespeare weaves a story around the loss of a valuable cargo ship on the Goodwins in his dark comedy, 'The Merchant of Venice' (c1596). Antonio, a rich merchant, borrows three thousand ducats from Shylock, the Jewish moneylender. Shylock, who hates all Christians, offers the loan free of interest for three months but mischievously suggests a "merry bond". Should Antonio default in his repayment, he must forfeit a pound of his own flesh! Foolishly Antonio agrees to this preposterous contract while awaiting the arrival of his merchandise by sea. Alas, his homeward bound ship runs into difficulty as it passes through the English Channel. The disaster is related by two close friends:

> SOLANIO: Now what news on the Rialto?
> SALERIO: Why, yet it lives there unchecked that Antonio hath a ship of rich lading wracked on the narrow seas, the Goodwins I think they call the place, a very dangerous flat, and fatal, where the carcasses of many a tall ship lie buried, as they say, if my gossip Report be an honest woman of her word. (Act 3 Scene 1)

First proposal to construct a lighthouse to warn mariners of the dangers of the Goodwin Sands was made by an Elizabethan entrepreneur, Gawen Smith, around 1580. Ostensibly, his scheme was for the benefit of seafarers but, in reality, it was intended for his own wealth:

> "Whereas I haue ben downe vppon the Goodwyn Sandes, and vppon sundry places thereof, as towchinge the beacon which I haue pertely promysed. And fyndinge the place verye dangerowse, yett am I resolved to goe forwarde with provision this wynter tyme and frame the woorcke agaynste the latter end of Maye so that I may haue your Lordship's furtheraunce to assure vnto me and my heires theis demaundes followinge.
> I demaunde ijd of every ton for every shipp and vessell beinge above v ton and vnder a houndred that pases by and of every one

above one houndred jd of the ton; ffurther I demaunde for every person that shalbe saved by meanes of that beacon which haue suffred shipwrecke or suche like to haue of them ijs vjd le peece.

And for this I undertake to make the foresaid beacon fyrme and staide vppon the foresaid Goodwyn Sandes xx or xxx foote above the highe water marke which shalbe able to receyve and preserve xxx or xl persons at the leaste, which beacon shale shewe his fyre xx or xxx myles by nighte and xx daye by suffycyenyt markes.

And he humblie cravethe of her Majestie for the further encoraginge of the said woorckes a sute worthe one thowsand powndes when he shall delyver her Majestie grasse, hearbes or flowers growinge natuarally in that place (all deceipte set a parte).

Also he cravethe of her Majestie a sute worthe two thowsand powndes when he shall plante or place anie peeces of ordynance howe great soeuer, gyvinge her Majestie good and suffycyent securytie for the saffetye of them which maye serue in that place for defence."

Over the centuries, there have been several more practical attempts at lighting the Goodwins by erecting fixed beacons on the actual sandbank. One proposal came from William Bush, a civil engineer from Deptford, in 1836. He claimed to be the inventor of both a beacon and a lighthouse which could be built on shoals or sandbanks for the preservation of life at a cost of £100,000. Trinity House approved his plans but artfully delayed any construction.

Captain (later Admiral) Frederick Bullock R.N. put forward an alternative proposal for a beacon that would double as a refuge for "shipwrecked mariners of all nations". Trinity House adopted his plan which consisted of an upright mast, formed from the jib boom of a frigate (40 feet in height and 12 inches in diameter) with a single

Captain Bullock's safety beacon of 1840.

platform or "crosstree". This refuge beacon was constructed with the assistance of Captain Boys, Superintendent of the Navy Yard at Deal. It was floated out to the Goodwins on 10 September 1840 aboard H.M.S. 'Boxer' and firmly fixed in a position described vaguely as "seven miles from Deal". (This was probably at the North Sand Head or even the most easterly part of the South Goodwins)

At the summit of Captain Bullock's beacon was an hexagonal trelliswork gallery which could accommodate "twenty people in comfort or thirty people crowded together". Beneath this gallery appeared a second shelter which might hold a further twenty people. Instructions in eight languages told the survivors to hoist a blue flag, kept in a canvas bag, on the light top mast. There was a fresh supply of bread and a barrel of water with a small supply of spirits for their sustenance. The mast was sunk in the sand through a stout oak frame in the form of a cross secured by four iron bars weighted with ballast. It was supported by eight chain stays, or "shrouds", in pairs attached to iron piles seventeen feet long driven into the sand. A rope ladder in addition to iron cleats enabled the mast to be climbed while a large basket chair could be lowered to assist injured survivors to reach the top. Finally, the sides of the gallery were fitted with a sail cloth which could be unrolled and fastened to the flagstaff to form a shelter.

Captain Bullock explained the true practicality of his proposal: "As the Goodwins are partly dry at low water to a great extent, and as vessels which strike them seldom go to pieces in a single tide, the probability is that some of the wrecked crew would be enabled to reach the sand during the interval, and the safety beacon would then become their only refuge." Captain Boys was the first man to climb the beacon, amid loud cheers, and wave a Union Jack and give three cheers for Queen Victoria.

Bullock's beacon was inspected by Prince Albert on Wednesday 30 November 1842 while he was on holiday with Queen Victoria at Walmer Castle. Leaving the beach about noon on a calm day in the four-oared gig belonging to the steamship, 'Fearless', the Prince was conveyed to Trinity Bay. Unfortunately, the state of the tide would not allow an examination of the beacon at close quarters and so Captain Bullock merely explained the method of its construction. Cheap and simple to construct, Captain Bullock's beacon survived almost four years until it was run down by a Dutch galliot on 5 August 1844. It was replaced one month later but this second beacon was swept away in a gale on 23 October 1847.

Bush came up with another project which was to convert the entire sandbank into a 'Harbour of Refuge'. The bold venture was to have been achieved by sinking a series of cofferdams linked together to form a continuous seawall. His masterpiece, however, was his 'Light for all Nations'. This spirited design involved building a massive column in three sections with two galleries reached by an internal staircase leading to a forty-foot lantern. At the summit was to be a lifesize cast-iron statue of Queen Victoria (although this was later changed to a patriotic figure of Britannia).

Bush managed to secure sponsorship from the Duke of Wellington who was, at that time, Lord Warden of the Cinque Ports. (The Duke, himself, had laid before Parliament his own plan to fortify the Goodwins against the French in 1843 but his preposterous proposal was spurned by Parliament)

In 1840, an order was placed with Thorncliffe Ironworks, near Rotherham, Yorkshire, for construction of the huge 120-ton caisson on which the lighthouse was to stand. It was shipped in sections to Deal where it was assembled at the Navy Yard. The Duke and several distinguished gentlemen duly gathered on the foreshore on 18 September 1841. They had been invited to watch an experiment to sink the caisson in shallow water near the old wooden pier north of the 'Royal Hotel'.

On 22 October the steamer, 'Monkey', towed the caisson further out to sea but the vessel ran aground and it was cast adrift. Another steamer, 'Shearwater', rescued the device and returned it to the beach where it promptly sank. There it remained in the vicinity of Sandown Castle, an obstacle to boatmen and an embarrassment to Bush.

After repair it was refloated and towed to the Sands on 28 July 1842. It reached its location safely on the North Calliper where it settled - leaning slightly - on the sandbank. Over the next few months it was buffeted by a succession of storms and sank much further than planned. Finally, on 15 October, it was struck by an American timber ship, 'Nancy', which overturned the caisson before disintegrating with the loss of her entire crew.

Undaunted, Bush tried to salvage the caisson and rebuild his structure on a more modest scale in the middle of the Sands. After a third attempt a modified version of his lighthouse began to take shape. Indeed, it looked so promising that the designer and his friends dined on roast beef and plum pudding in the living quarters fifty feet above the waves on 19 January 1845. By July the lighthouse was so close to completion that Bush and his family slept for several nights on one of the chambers beneath the lantern room.

Trinity House then informed the triumphant designer that his lighthouse was placed in such a dangerous position that it risked luring vessels actually onto the sandbank and they ordered its demolition. Bush's structure had cost £12,000 (the expense had been shared by Bush and Wellington) and taken five years hard labour. Gattie informs that the wreck of Bush's lighthouse remained on the Sands, marked by a flagpole, for a long period.

There were further attempts at lighting the actual sandbank. Early in the 19th century Lieutenant Benjamin Worthington from Dover proposed a triangular structure that would support a light, lifeboat, gun and bell. A civil engineer named Steward positioned a single pile beacon on the eastern edge of the Goodwins (or the southern side of the Kellet Gut) in September 1844. It promptly collapsed. After a second unsuccessful attempt, Steward's project was abandoned. James Walker built a more stable construction on 6 July 1844 and this lasted for six years until it shifted alarmingly and was ordered to be removed by Trinity House. In 1849 Trinity House erected its own beacon on the Sands which, amazingly, remained in position for thirty years until it was destroyed in a storm.

There were scores of proposals for building on the Goodwin Sands in the mid-19th century. The most sensible were for lighthouses. John Martin, a venerated painter of religious scenes, designed an ingenious suspended lighthouse; Thomas Stevenson proposed to construct his lighthouse atop a mound of rubble. Sir John Rennie and Captain Vetch forwarded similar ideas to form an island that would act as a breakwater protecting the mainland. Among the more bizarre suggestions for their development, however, were an artesian well, an asylum and even a chapel for shipwrecked mariners!

Perhaps, though, the most ambitious project was to turn the Goodwin Sands into London's third airport. The serious proposal which would have "minimum environmental impact" plus "a high degree of security" was projected by European Transport Interchange Ltd. in 2002. This site was first suggested as an alternative to Foulness near Southend thirty years previously, according to the 'Daily Telegraph' (15 May 1969). The subsequent Review expanded the idea: "The airport is conceived as a 24hr passenger and freight hub, located 7.5km due east of Deal on sandbanks at the southern end of the Goodwins." There were to be four runways on two islands with a road bridge connected to the mainland east of Dover supported by a fast rail link to London. The Ministry of Transport turned down the scheme as it was not financially viable. The cost: £9 billion.

The Sands shelve dramatically in the vicinity of the East Goodwin lightship - a deadly trap for shipping - and it is here that the majority of wrecks occur. And, although the outer edge of the Goodwins is well lighted and buoyed, visibility in fog or snow is practically nil. The eastern edge of the sandbank is composed of extremely hard sand and many vessels, after striking, are holed and rebound or sink in deep water. Fewer vessels come to grief on the northern part of the Sands because the tide runs at three knots whereas it runs at five knots on the southern swatch.

More than once it has been suggested that the dangerous location of the Sands might prove advantageous to the protection of the realm. 'Naval Tracts', published in the reign of Charles I, suggested that the Goodwins could be employed to ensnare invaders:

> "A ship riding at The Downs and fearing a surprise attack from an enemy in the night, with a southerly wind, by placing two boats with lights on either side of the Brake will direct one how to pass the Channel and around the Sands which being done and the lights taken away, the ship that pursues them will run upon their death if they follow."

Indeed, such tactics may have been employed during the invasion of the Spanish Armada. Gattie states that the commander of one of the six ships provided by the Cinque Ports came from Deal. Being familiar with the banks and shoals of home waters, he lured one of the great galleasses onto the Goodwins where she stranded and became an easy target. Ultimately she was burned and her captain and crew either killed, drowned or taken prisoner.

The appellation, "shippe-swallower", is apt since the Goodwins demonstrate a voracious appetite for swallowing ships whole. George Goldsmith-Carter in 'The Goodwin Sands' (1953) offers one explanation for the phenomenon: "Frequently, a vessel becomes stranded on the sands, often across a ridge. On which, after the tide has fallen and left her unsupported, she breaks her back. The broken vessel then starts to 'swaddle herself down' or, in other words, to make a grave for herself. Swift tides pile sands over her, the tremendous surf smashes away masts, funnels and superstructure and what is left is soon buried."

D. P. Capper in his 'Moat Defensive' (1963) pictures the "vast and varied company" of ships that have ended their days on these 'Sands of Death': "Below them are buried the bones of countless vessels from crude early craft to Roman galley and from medieval cog and fully-rigged ship to yesterday's steamer." Speculation over the total number of losses, it seems, has been wildly exaggerated. Richard Larn in 'Shipwrecks of the Goodwin Sands' (1995) includes a comprehensive list of over one thousand shipwrecks. "This", he propounds, "represents only some two-thirds of the probable total", an estimate based upon his own researches covering the period from 1298 until 1975.

Larn has discovered that the first known reference to a shipwreck in the Downs is mentioned in the Calendar of Patent Rolls during the reign of Edward I. Neither the name of the ship nor its location is recorded apart from the vague indication that it was "near Sandwich". Her owner, William Martyn, informed the King on 7 June 1298 that his ship had been cast away whilst returning from Flanders. Ominously, he appealed for a jury to investigate his complaint that his cargo of armour had been plundered by local boatmen.

Edward Barlow, who served in the Royal and Mercantile Navies during the early Stuart period, left a rare account of being shipwrecked on Goodwin Sands. He records in his 'Journal' how he was "raked and cast away in a pretty ship" when returning from a fishing expedition to Norway on the night of 23 October 1675. The master of 'Florentine', Captain John Rolloit, attributed his misfortune to witchcraft and suspected a curse placed on his ship by the landladies of Bergen because several members of his crew had neglected to settle their bills. His suspicions were compounded after the discovery of a stray black cat aboard!

"... And it being very dark and blowing pretty hard, we turned four hours as well as we could, sometimes standing one way and sometimes another, but we were fearful of the Goodwin Sands, for neither our master nor mate nor any in the ship were very well acquainted with them: yet we hoped we should get to windward of them and carry clear into the Downs, for we saw the lighthouse very fair upon the South Foreland, and the land showing as it were not half a mile from us, but it was very dark.

So standing to the southward a pretty while, we tacked again and stood to the northward, hoping that tack to get into the Downs, but it pleased God it proved

A wreck on the Goodwins

otherwise to our great misfortune, for sounding, at last we came into eighteen fathom water, yet did not understand how we should have the lights kept, they being set for marks; yet indeed the land deceived us most, for it showed to us so near that we hoped we should carry it clear of all. But the next sounding we had but five fathom, so in great haste putting our ship"a-stayes", the other way, before she could get about, we were in three fathom water; and then in great haste we let fall our anchor with all sails standing, for the tide of flood being come, we judged ourselves upon the South Sand Head, which is the southernmost part of the Goodwin Sands; and that, being a little come on the first part of the sands, at high water weighing our anchors, the tide of ebb would help us off again. . . But before the ship"thwarted", or we could hope to get our anchor up, it blowing very hard, our ship struck on the sand to our great astonishment and fear.

And our master ordered me presently to fire a gun, for I was then gunner aboard, so I fired one, which was to have some boats to come from Deal or Dover to our assistance, our ship striking several times very hard. And I fired two guns more, but it blowing hard and very dark, and about eleven or twelve of the clock in the night, we could expect no help or assistance from anybody, but must make what shift we could for ourselves.

And the ship beating extremely, so that all expectations were lost in hopes of saving the ship and goods, how to save our lives was the first expedient, for of that we were in great danger.

So getting out our boats, our master did desire us to make what shift we could to save our lives. So I running down to my chest, having this book there and hoping to save it, and unlocking my chest, took it out with about five pounds in English money and Spanish gold and silver, leaving the key in my chest and coming away without taking a rag of clothes more than what I had on my back, leaving behind me three or four suits: and climbing upon the deck in all haste, our master with eight or nine men more, were going from the ship in the smallest of our boats, and I leaping into her in all haste before she put from the ship, away we came before the wind, sometimes edging a little towards the shore when the sea would suffer us, for it ran extremely high upon the sands, and broke many times up into our boat; and we were in more danger of our lives in the boat than whilst we were in the ship, and were forced to keep one of us always throwing out water as it came in; yet through the mercy of God, we got safe of the Sands. . ."

At dawn Barlow and the crew rowed towards the shore. The Admiral of the Downs sent his pinnace and longboat from his frigate, 'Garland', to offer them assistance. Safely landed, Captain Rolloit commissioned several Deal boatmen to board the stricken ship and salvage anything of value, including Barlow's chest and clothes, before the ship broke up. But the weather worsened and Barlow and his companions watched in dismay as 'Florentine' disappeared from the horizon. And to add to his misery, the boatmen spirited away most of his possessions, leaving him and his companions destitute.

During the Victorian era many famous ships were wrecked on the Goodwins:

The celebrated China tea clipper, 'Cutty Sark', had a brush with disaster on the Goodwin Sands between 10 and 12 November 1877. At that time, 'Cutty Sark', considered to be the fastest clipper in the world, had been modified for employment in the Australian wool trade. Early that month she cleared from London and Sydney with a crew of twenty-eight hands and immediately encountered a strong wind with thick rain and a falling glass as she rounded the North Foreland. Captain Tiptaft thought it expedient to ride out the storm in the Downs rather than continue the voyage into the English Channel.

For a time 'Cutty Sark' lay quietly at anchor while the promised storm brewed. But by Sunday 11 November it was blowing a vicious south-westerly gale. Already there were sixty sailing ships, besides several large steamers, taking shelter in the Downs. Channel ports from Margate to the Lizard were reporting winds of hurricane force and lifeboat crews were constantly called out along the length of the south coast.

Pandemonium reigned in the Downs. Blue lights, flares and rockets showed in every direction as cables parted and ships strayed. Five tall ships came ashore at Pegwell Bay. . . Margate was full of dismasted coasters. . . a large barque sank off Broadstairs. . . and a second barque struck the Goodwins. Deal galleys launched through the boiling surf to take spare anchors and chains to ships rolling helplessly on the tempestuous seas. All through the night there were collisions in the crowded roads with drifting ships crashing into stationary vessels, dragging them from their moorings. Ships ground together until their spars came tumbling down upon their petrified crews. Men leapt from ship to ship in their terror so that several vessels came ashore carrying foreigners who had sprung aboard them in their panic.

By Monday the hurricane was at its height. 'Cutty Sark' parted both her cables but before she could be brought under control a brig collided with her port side. The two ships ground together momentarily and then parted in the darkness. There was a further crash. This time it was a vessel to starboard. Captain Tiptaft began to fire distress rockets and burn blue lights to summon urgent assistance as this noble clipper was driven helplessly through the Gull Stream.

The tugboat, 'Macgregor', lying some distance south-west of the Kentish Knock, was alerted. It took the tug an hour's steaming at top speed to reach 'Cutty Sark' which by then was drifting perilously close to the Sands. A rope was thrown aboard the clipper and the steamer started to tow her. A second tug, 'Benachie', arrived and the pair, working in tandem, were able to nudge the clipper through the Princes Channel to an anchorage off Greenhithe. Next morning she was towed to London and moored in East India Dock. The clipper's narrow escape enhanced her reputation among crewmen as a lucky ship.

'Shannon', a large collier brig from Shields, has the distinction of being wrecked three times on the Goodwins in a single night.

First, she went aground on the steep bank near the East Goodwin lightship on 5 February 1880. She drifted off into deep water but unfortunately, from the violence of the wind and waves, she was driven back onto the sandbank but once more she managed to float off. Her crew were congratulating themselves at their extraordinary good luck when 'Shannon' was again blown back onto the sandbank with extreme force. This time she became a total wreck, broke up and disappeared altogether. Fortunately the Deal lifeboat succeeded in taking her crew off although all the cargo was lost.

A remarkable coincidence occurred in the early years of the twentieth century when two ships - both named 'Mahratta' and owned by the same shipping company - were wrecked on the Goodwins less than one mile distant from each other. The first 'Mahratta' was, at the time, the largest ship claimed by the Sands. She was on the last

SS 'Mahratta' wrecked on the Goodwins in 1909.

lap of her voyage from Calcutta to London and Dundee with passengers plus a general cargo. On 9 April 1909, this Brocklebank Line ship went aground in Trinity Bay close to the Fork Spit. A stiff breeze was blowing although it was a fine day and so the accident must be attributed to a navigational error. Despite assistance from eight tugs and three lifeboats, she failed to refloat and inevitably split in two.

Coxswain William Adams attended with the North Deal lifeboat, 'Charles Dibdin', and stood by for a total of fifty hours. Gradually, Captain Ellery, his crew and passengers consisting of ninety souls were lifted from the wreck but tragically the Chief Engineer committed suicide. A fleet of local luggers and galleys arrived on the scene to salvage the diverse cargo but the rascally boatmen filched most of the crates of tea. The police were alerted and searched local homes where they found that many drains were blocked and cellars flooded with swollen tealeaves!

At the commencement of the Second World War, a sister ship, 'Mahratta II', carrying a similar cargo and travelling an identical route, ran aground on the Goodwin Sands while homeward bound from India. On 6 October 1939 this ship was waiting in the Downs to be checked by Contraband Control but, impatient to continue his journey, Captain Hill, unwisely, decided to proceed without the aid of a competent pilot. 'Mahratta II' also stranded on the Fork Spit and this time six harbour tugs and two Admiralty lighters were summoned to attempt to refloat the buckled vessel. Two motor boats - 'Lady Haig' and 'Skipjack' - ferried the Indian crew to the safety of the tugs while local boats helped to offload the cargo. Once again the crates of tea proved too much of a temptation to the wily wartime boatmen.

During the First World War, three German submarines were sunk by British warships close to the Goodwin Sands. In 1917 the UC - 46 was rammed by the destroyer, H.M.S. 'Liberty'; the British submarine torpedoed the UC - 63 and the destroyer, H.M.S. 'Gipsy', aided by armed drifters, shelled the U - 48 which ran aground on the North Sands Head on 24 November 1917.

Further details of the demise of the piratical Underseeboot 48 can be gleaned from 'Dive Kent' (1994). Commanded by Kapitanleutnant Carl Edeling with a crew of 36, the 725-ton German submarine left Wilhelmshaven on 21 November 1917 to attack shipping in the Western Approaches. She could achieve over 15 knots on the surface but was sighted 60 miles off Dover and bombed, but not hit, by a seaplane. Edeling dived and waited for dark to begin his run through the Straits. His compass failed and the strong westerly tide carried him onto nets off the North Goodwins which tangled his propellers and the submarine stranded. Despite jettisoning oil fuel, fresh water, gun ammunition and three torpedoes, he failed to free his submarine from the sandbank.

At dawn, U - 48 was spotted by the trawler, 'Meror', and three drifters, 'Majesty', 'Paramount' and 'Present Help' but soon three more drifters, 'Acceptable', 'Feasible' and 'Claud Hamilton' appeared on the scene. A fierce gun battle was cut short when the destroyer, HMS 'Gipsy', joined in the affray. Although the submarine had the superior armament, she was unable to employ it effectively since she was outnumbered by the lesser armed fighting ships. When the submarine caught fire, Captain Edeling ordered her to be scuttled rather than be captured by the British. The explosion, marking the end of the submarine's mischievous career, was greeted with cheers from onshore spectators. Periodically, subsequent changes in the shape of the sandbank causes the intact submarine to emerge for brief periods when she inevitably becomes the target of sport divers hunting for souvenirs.

Occasionally aeroplanes have been claimed by the Sands. On 18 October 1923 a Focker monoplane, belonging to the Royal Dutch Air Mail Service, was being flown

Goodwin Sands German submarine U-48.
Courtesy: Richard Larn, Shipwrecks UK Ltd.

from Amsterdam to London by a Russian, Captain Ivan Smirnoff. The engine overheated owing to adverse weather and the pilot made a forced landing on the Sands. He brought his plane down at a mere 35 mph and it slewed to a halt on the soft surface in about 20 yards. A remarkable piece of flying! The crew of the East Goodwin lightship raised the alarm and the pilot plus his three passengers were rescued although the plane, lacking a radio, was lost, along with mail and luggage, to the waves.

A more dramatic event took place on 9 July 1940 when Spitfires from No. 54 Squadron forced a German Heinkel HE 59 seaplane (D - ASUO) to land on Goodwin Sands. At the time the seaplane was serving as an air ambulance rescuing aircrew from the sea after they had ditched. Four members of its crew were themselves rescued from the water by the Gravesend tug, 'Vincia', which was based at Ramsgate after having completed two round trips to Dunkirk. The seaplane was towed off by the Walmer lifeboat and beached at Deal before being escorted into Dover Harbour.

In the immediate postwar period the English Channel was exceptionally busy with the transportation of food, supplies and equipment to Europe by the American Liberty ships. Liberty ships were built in large numbers in order to beat the wolf pack attack of the convoys by the German Navy. This was made possible by the refinement in welding techniques that replaced former tortuous riveting. Victory ships were slightly larger than Liberty ships and were more sophisticated in that they were equipped with additional cargo handling gear such as derricks and Samson posts. There was great rivalry between the American shipyards to assemble prefabricated cargo ships in the least amount of time. (The record was for four and a half days!)

Unwisely, administrators of the American Navy declined to employ pilots to navigate these heavy freighters since they regarded the additional expense as not being cost-effective. "Employment of pilots for such waters is considered unnecessary; the navigational requirements are regarded as lying well within the professional capacity of competent shipmasters," arrogantly stated the official document. "The subject waters are of wide expanse and relatively free of dangers. . ." The inevitable result was that an enormous amount of accidents occurred which earned this section of the coast the pseudonym, 'Calamity Corner'.

On 30 January 1946 'Luray Victory' (9,000 tons) bound from Baltimore to Bremerhaven with a cargo consisting mainly of cereals, steamed up the Channel at maximum speed oblivious to an impending storm. Consequently she struck the South Calliper with such force that she immediately became a total wreck. Freddy Upton, the new Coxswain of 'Charles Dibdin Civil Service No 32', launched in the darkness to her assistance. At dawn the Walmer lifeboat transferred wire hawsers from the stranded ship to waiting tugs but, despite every effort, 'Luray Victory' refused to shift. The lifeboat itself was in danger of being stranded as the Sands began to dry with the ebb tide.

Tenaciously Walmer lifeboat stood by the stricken vessel throughout the next day and night - although her crew had to return to base to refuel - until it became obvious the ship was breaking up. Reluctantly the Captain signalled that he had ordered his men to abandon ship. The whole complement of 49 men duly scrambled down the ship's side on rope ladders and into the safety of the lifeboat. Finally the heavily laden lifeboat rounded the South Goodwin lightship and, braving tempestuous seas, headed hard for home.

*The two halves of SS 'Agen' wrecked on the Goodwins on
13th January 1952. Courtesy: David Chamberlain.*

On 13 September 1946, a beautifully calm day, the American Liberty ship, 'Helena Modjeska' (7,000 tons) was observed progressing slowly on the west side of the Sands. She was carrying a cargo of foodstuffs, military vehicles and high explosives from Marseilles to Bremerhaven. Captain William Curran refused the assistance of a pilot and attempted to cut through Trinity Bay. He seemed confused by the warning maroons fired by the Coastguard and - clearly lost - his ship foundered on the Goodwins.

Coxswain Freddie Upton launched the reserved lifeboat, 'Langham', to the steamship's assistance but, once on board, his expert advice was curtly dismissed by Captain Curran. Instead, he made a futile attempt to drive his ship - her engines racing and her propellers thrashing - across the sandbank although it was obvious that she was firmly grounded. Eight tugs arrived and attempted to release the ship but, with the rise and fall of the tide, she was doomed.

Eventually Captain Curran capitulated and begged the assistance of the expert lifeboatmen. Valuable military vehicles were then discharged onto lighters which was a dangerous task considering the presence of the explosives! The crew were transferred to the lifeboat while the tugs towed the stranded ship clear of the Sands. At this moment a couple of stowaways - German prisoners-of-war - were discovered cowering in a crate. In the middle of the night, a gale erupted and the ship split in two, the two halves drifting wide apart... The aft section of the hull was refloated and beached at Sandwich Bay while the fore part was moored off Deal. Eventually both bow and stern were towed into the River Blackwater where they were sold for scrap.

On Christmas Eve 1946 another Liberty ship, 'North Eastern Victory' (7,617 tons) bound from New Orleans for Antwerp with a cargo of flour, rice and grapefruit, confidently steamed up Channel. Foolishly ignoring the warning guns fired by the South Goodwin lightship, she ran into shallow water at the South Sand Head. The impact of the crash damaged her wireless aerials while thick fog rendered it pointless to fire distress flares. Luckily the warning guns had alerted Joe Mercer, retired Coxswain of Walmer lifeboat, who launched his motor boat, 'Rose-Marie', curious to know the cause. When he arrived at the scene he found the American steamship - high and dry - on the sandbank and, boarding her, he advised her captain she would soon break her back.

Joe Mercer doubled back to notify Coxswain Upton that a vessel was aground near the East Goodwin lightship. Subsequently Walmer lifeboat launched but when she arrived it was clear the freighter had already broken her back. Her crew of 36 men were transferred to the lifeboat although the captain and six officers remained to salvage the cargo. At dawn on Christmas Day the lifeboatmen returned and ate cold turkey, drank rum and sang carols while they waited to take the remaining officers off the ship which was listing alarmingly and starting to disintegrate. For a long time the tilting foremast and Samson posts of the sunken steamship remained above the water to testify that, once again, victory had gone to the sea...

Three American vessels leaving their skeletons on the sandbank within a single year led the American War Shipping Administration to reconsider their churlish commands.

More recently, during the early hours of 20 November 1991, 'Ross Revenge', which served as the pirate radio ship, 'Radio Caroline', snapped her anchor chain and drifted fifteen miles towards the Goodwins. Her caretaker crew slept soundly as she grounded on the Sands but when they awoke to their predicament they raised the alarm on their VHF transmitter. Ramsgate lifeboat was the first to respond to the calamity as she ran aground on the sandbank. A RAF rescue helicopter from Manston also attended and winched the nervous crew - including disc jockeys - to safety. Dover Harbour tugs, 'Dextrous' and 'Deft', also arrived and, once the seas became calmer, managed to secure a cable to the ship's stern and tow her through the Kellet Gut into Trinity Bay. For a time 'Radio Caroline' was considered a curiosity while she was berthed in Dover Harbour. Eventually she was towed along the Thames Estuary into Chatham Dockyard where she resumed broadcasting popular music to the mainland.

Curiously, there have been two cases of burials on Goodwin Sands.

One was an eccentric relative of John Evelyn who recorded in his Diary:

> April 12th 1702: This night died my B. in Law Glanvill after a tedious sicknesse: in the 84th yeare of his Age; & Willed his Body to be wrapt in Leade, and carried downe to Greenewich, where it was put aboard in a yaght, and Buried in the Sea, between Dover and Calais about Godwin-Sands: which was don the Tuesday or Wednesday after, which made much discourse; hed having no relation at all to the Sea.

A second temporary burial in this most singular graveyard is recorded in 'London Evening Post' (16 May 1751):

"We have an Account from Hambourg that on the 16th April last, about six Leagues off the North Foreland, Capr. Wyrck Pietersen, Commander of a Ship call'd the Johannes, took up a Coffin, made in the English Manner, with the following Inscription upon a Silver Plate, 'Mr. Francis Humphrey Merryditch, died March 25, 1751, aged 51', which Coffin the said Captain carried to Hambourg, and then open'd it, in which was inclosed a Leaden one, and the Body of an elderly Man embalm'd and dress'd in fine Linnen - This is the Corpse that was buried in the Goodwin-Sands a few Weeks ago, according to the Will of the Deceas'd."

Edward Hasted in his 'History and Topographical Survey of the County of Kent' (1800) noted: "When the water is off these sands become exceeding hard and firm insomuch that many people land and stay hours on them for pleasure in summer but when the tide begins to cover them they become soft and so float to and fro with the waves and when they retire settle the same as before."

Foolhardy folk have for the last two centuries ventured out to the sands on warm summer evenings to play a variety of sports including football, tennis, croquet, athletics and even boules on this sandy stadium. Picnics and jaunts have been held there and a carriage recovered during the last century testifies to the fact that young gallants once attempted to drive a coach and horses across the Goodwins.

Not all expeditions to the Sands have ended happily, however.

In August 1884 a party of excursionists from Ramsgate had landed on the Goodwins and by an oversight the tide was allowed to rise before the group could be reassembled. Crossing the shivering sands in a small boat to an awaiting cutter became a task of considerable risk and danger.

Charles Bowbyes and his three young companions (Edward Obree, George Buttress and William Erridge) were far less fortunate when they sailed out to the Sands towards the end of the nineteenth century. They had spotted a collier stranded on the sandbank and launched their galley punt, 'Hope', in an endeavour to salvage its cargo of coal. There was, after all, a calm sea with an off-shore breeze - ideal weather conditions for a trip to the Goodwins.

Leisurely, the men landed and began to explore the collier which was already swaddling herself into the sands. They loaded sacks of coal into their boat confident that they had plenty of time before the turn of the tide. It was with dismay that when they decided to return to the shore they found their boat was full of water. It seems the weight of the coal had sprung the ancient timbers in the bottom of 'Hope'. Frantically, the friends attempted to jettison the heavy sacks in the hope that their boat might yet still float. Already the flooding tide was rippling through the crumbling gullies, linking them to a changing pattern of shallow waterways.

The men hailed a passing barge, waving frantically, but the skipper assumed the men were skylarking and sailed on leaving them to a slow and agonising death. . .

Most frequent game which has been played on this most precarious pitch is cricket. (Prudish Victorians criticised such sporting events as "a wicked blasphemy" against all those unfortunate victims of the rapacious Sands) Mention of the first recorded match which took place on 13 August 1813 appears in F.J. Harvey Darton's 'A Parcel of Kent' (1924). On that occasion Mr. Thomas Elgar of Ramsgate and four gentlemen of that town challenged Mr. George Witherden of Bethersden and four gentlemen of the Isle of Thanet. The latter team won by a single run: 22 to 21. After the match winners and losers both drank the health of George III "three times three".

A second valiant team of cricketers set sail from Ramsgate in the summer of 1824 under the leadership of Captain Kennet Beacham Martin, Harbour Master. Risking high tide and quicksand these intrepid sportsmen enjoyed a serious game in which all the rules were strictly observed. Fielding on the waterlogged pitch proved to be a problem and the ball was repeatedly lost in pools and gullies. (Aware of these hazards the captain had brought a plentiful supply) One gentleman seemed to find conditions conducive because he scored a total of sixty-seven runs. Play over, corks were drawn and the loyal toast was drunk to King George IV.

A third match played in 1839 almost ended in disaster for the intrepid Deal youths who ventured forth in an open boat to the Goodwins. Their game was hugely enjoyed and refreshments followed from a well-stocked hamper. Meanwhile, storm clouds darkened the summer sky and the wind strengthened with alarming speed but no one seemed to care. Unwisely the youths ignored the warnings of the experienced boatmen to make for the shore. Eventually the party boarded their small boat but, before traversing half a mile, rough waves forced them to return to the Sands. Fortunately friends on the mainland raised the alarm and the terrified pranksters were rescued by a hovelling lugger.

Two elevens from Margate competed on this extraordinary ground in August, 1844. The exact site for this fourth attempt was adjacent to Captain Bullock's Beacon, recently damaged by a Dutch galliot.

Ten years later, on 10 August 1854, a fifth match was arranged by two Walmer worthies - Messrs. Thompson and Hammond. Twenty-four players were recruited. They included Captain Pearson and the crew of 'Spartan', one of the finest luggers on the foreshore. Rev Peter C. Hammond, Vicar of Walmer, mentions that the parish vestry organised a cricket match on Goodwin Sands in his book, 'The Parson and the Victorian Parish' (1997). Presumably this is the one. The teams were landed on the Sands around five o'clock in the afternoon and, after walking for a quarter of a mile, a spot sufficiently high and dry was found for the game to begin in earnest. Play lasted until sunset, the winning team scored fifty-seven runs and the party returned to the shore by bright moonlight.

This event was reported in the 'Illustrated London News' (26 August 1854)

"The Goodwins, which have been from time immemorial associated with peril and destruction, have just been the scene of exhilarating sport. It appears that on the 10th inst. A party - got up by Mr. Morris Thompson, Mr. Hammond, and others at Walmer - visited the sands for the purpose of playing a game of cricket. Captain Pearson and a picked crew of the 'Spartan', one of the finest luggers on Deal Beach, were selected for the occasion. The day was beautifully calm, and the party (twenty-four in number) arrived, and were safely landed on the sands at five in the evening. After walking about a quarter of a mile a place sufficiently high and dry was found; when the match commenced and continued until nearly sunset, the winning party obtaining fifty-seven runs. The sands were intersected in every direction with narrow but deep gullies or, as they are termed by the sailors, 'swatches', with swift running streams into which it was dangerous to step. A sad association of ideas crowded the mind on looking over this awfully melancholy place. Here thousands of gallant fellows have been entombed - here millions of property have been engulfed; and here was a picture contrasting vividly with present scenes of pastime.

The party returned home safely about ten at night. The evening was fine and ripples on the surface of the sea as the lugger ploughed homeward were most beautifully illuminated with phosphorescent light."

A watercolour of a cricket match by W.H. Macklin hangs in the Chiesman Pavilion at the St. Lawrence Ground owned by Kent County Cricket Club. Rich in detail, it shows a lively game in progress with the ball impossibly high and the umpire in top hat, shirt and waistcoat, signalling: 'Out!' Despite its attribution to 'circa 1840', the painting seems to record the latter match.

Three foolhardy cyclists from London rode round the Goodwins on 31 August 1887. They were rowed out to the Sands by an obliging Deal boatman. There they must have presented a strange spectacle as they alighted from their boat, bicycles on backs, wading knee-deep in water! Keeping close to the edge, they jauntily cycled round wrecks and only dismounted when wheels sank into soft sand. One member managed a mile in three and a half minutes flat!

Veteran boatman, Joe Mercer, a stalwart member of Walmer Lifeboat crew, ferried out an elegant female cyclist in his galley punt on 7 August 1906. This adventurous young lady, smartly dressed in blouse, tie, cycling skirt and straw hat, certainly managed to retain her poise as she cycled along the hard, undulating surface.

A game of bowls was successfully played on the Goodwins on 13 July 1913. A faded, foxed photograph bears witness to the event when pipe-smoking, cloth-capped men played this gentle sport close to the remains of a partially submerged wreck.

Deal boatmen have often played an impromptu game of football on the Goodwins.

A cricket match on the Goodwin Sands in 1854.

Deal residents can recall the occasion when the All Blacks rugby touring side played their exciting match on Boxing Day, 1921. The team had been taking a midwinter break in the vicinity when they decided on the spur of the moment to venture out to the Sands. They were taken out in the only three motor boats then beached at Deal: 'Golden Spray', 'Skipjack' and 'Moss Rose'. Two of the skippers were Tommy Upton and Harry Meakins. "It was a brilliant, sunny day," recollects one elderly inhabitant. "The teams returned to New Zealand with tales of the day they threw a ball about in the English Channel."

Four golfers, members of the Royal Cinque Ports Club at Deal, headed by the amateur champion, W.I. Hunter, played a round on the shoals on 19 July the following year.

The first time an organised cricket match was played on Goodwin Sands during the twentieth century was in June 1959. Alderman Eddie Butcher, Mayor of Ramsgate, captained one team while his Chaplain, Rev. J.C.F. White, led the opposition. This event celebrated the bicentenary of the construction of Ramsgate's Royal Harbour and the 75th Anniversary of the Incorporation of the Borough. Play lasted only half an hour and inquisitive seals watched the Mayor's team win by four runs.

The tradition was again revived on 3 July 1975 when the crews of the Royal Navy Survey Ships, 'Echo', 'Enterprise' and 'Egeria', having spent months charting the area, took time off to play cricket with a soft ball on the sandbank. Dressed in mock period costume - top hats, flapping shirts and knee length trousers - the crews enjoyed a vigorous game which lasted a full hour. The self styled 'W.G. Grace's XI' scored 68 runs in twelve overs but then their opponents, 'Sir Len Hutton's XI', knocked up 76 runs in nine overs. Returning to the safety of their ships the sportsmen left the stumps to sink beneath the Channel waters.

Two summers later (5 July 1977) a crew of Royal Marines from Walmer also endeavoured to play cricket on the Goodwins. Her Majesty's rowing boat, 'Hannah Snell' (named in honour of the legendary eighteenth century female recruit) slipped silently from the shore conveying a contingent of Royal Marines Commandos steeled for an amphibious assault on the Sands. After the Captain had traced out a line twenty-two yards long with his boot, play commenced supervised by an umpire garbed in 'foulies' and rubber waders. Tea interval was fixed for five o'clock but in the absence of a pavilion the players adjoined to a nearby puddle where they drank the loyal toast to Queen Elizabeth II.

Kent cricketers made a surprise expedition to the Goodwins on Monday 1 July 1985. A fleet of thirteen small fishing boats transported about one hundred spectators to the sandbank in idyllic weather conditions. They were greeted by a group of seals basking in the warm sunshine. Kent XI challenged a Select XI composed of members from various clubs in Thanet. The novel event had been organised to raise funds for a grandstand at the St. Lawrence Ground, Canterbury.

'Silly point' took on a new meaning as umpire Peter Turner from RAF Manston admitted difficulty in judging leg before wicket. Captain of the Kent team, Chris Cowdrey, opened the batting equipped with snorkel and flippers but Derek Underwood, normally a deadly bowler, had little joy with his delivery. The original idea of ten overs per side was drastically reduced by the numerous photocalls since the match attracted coverage by radio, television and the national press.

A temporary postbox was erected on the shoals and special covers featuring the rival teams were issued to coincide with 'Safety at Sea' stamp issues. A commemorative tie was also produced to mark the occasion - maroon with a design of the rearing white horse of Kent above three stumps and a wreck on a stretch of golden sand. Stumps were drawn around 7 p.m. with a surprising win for the Select team by three wickets. (This may have been a biased result since the scorer was the daughter of the organiser and the sister of the skipper who was celebrating his birthday) Afterwards, the party headed back towards the mainland for a champagne reception at Deal Castle.

In recent years there have been several trips by hovercraft to raise money for local charities. The world's largest hovercrafts - 'Princess Anne' and 'Princess Margaret' - have transported hundreds of holidaymakers to the northern extremity of Goodwin Sands. Among the more bizarre exploits have been wine tasting, strawberry teas, fancy dress competitions, musical concerts, kite flying, handbell ringing, tap dancing, tug-of-war contests, aerobic demonstrations, miniature hovercraft rides, amateur radio and live television broadcasts. A Bell 206 Jet Ranger helicopter from Manston Airport landed and its crew alighted to join the revellers during one expedition in June 1992. Deal Striders organised a one mile race with certificates signed by Sir Roger Bannister awarded to the winners in May 1993. Mayors of the Cinque Ports joined in a combined Anglo-French service of reconciliation which happened to coincide with the V.E. Day Anniversary in June 1995. On this occasion the band of the 5th Battalion of the Princess of Wales Royal Regiment from Canterbury proudly marched past and played.

These frivolities came to an end when the fleet of hovercraft were retired in favour of the car-carrying high speed catamaran, SeaCat.

In the high summer of 2006 cricket played on the sands brought risk to the players. B.B.C. programme, 'Coast', recorded a match as a background to its presenter explaining the Kent coastline. Just as the tide began to

Few artefacts have been recovered from the Goodwins but items that have surfaced number Roman amphorae, ancient weapons, bronze cannon, ships' bells and anchors.

Unimaginable wealth - gold, silver, precious metals and valuable jewellery - lie buried under the Sands. "Great treasure", laments Richard Larn, "has been entombed forever."

Among the curiosities dredged up from the Goodwins are two antique chamber guns - one of iron and the other brass - possibly relics from the Spanish Armada.

Also uncovered are a magnificent Chinese Ch'ing Dynasty vase with seahorse handles now displayed at Sandwich Guildhall, the wooden torso of a Dutch doll now displayed at Whitstable Museum and a post chaise - "wheels and all".

During the Second World War, the shipwrecked 'Mahratta' on the Goodwin Sands was used by R.A.F. bombers for target practice.

Mahogany furniture from the passengers' cabins of the sunken 'Mahratta' still graces the elegant rooms of local homes.

When the Belgian steamer, 'Flanders', sank in the Downs in February 1940, the ship's mascot was rescued from the water. It was a pig called 'Adolf'.

turn, it was thought wise for the film crew and cricketers to leave but as they loaded their inflatable dinghy with camera and sound equipment it stuck hard in the mud. When the players themselves boarded they found that there was more water inside their boat than outside! Rescue services were alerted and the Ramsgate lifeboat eventually brought everyone safely ashore. The cricketers were praised for being "stoical". Perhaps they had not realised the extreme danger they had been in on Goodwin Sands.

A summer picnic on the Sands.

LIGHTHOUSES AND LIGHTSHIPS

'Sentinels of the Strait'

THE SHOALS AND SANDBANKS of the Goodwins are so perilous they were at one time marked by two lighthouses, four lightships and ten buoys. These aids to navigation started mainly as private or commercial ventures but eventually came under the control of Trinity House.

The Corporation of Trinity House evolved from a Guild of Mariners, a charitable institution founded in the 13th century by Archbishop Stephen Langton. Henry VIII granted the Brotherhood its royal charter in 1514 under the grand title: "Master and Wardens of the Guild, Fraternity and Brotherhood of the Most Glorious and Undivided Trinity and of Saint Clement in the Parish of Deptford Stronde in Kent". Traditionally, the Corporation was committed to the safety of shipping and welfare of seafarers but over the centuries Trinity House assumed general maritime roles - navigating coastlines, erecting beacons, providing lights, laying buoys, superintending shipbuilding, granting certificates to pilots, masters and mates of the Mercantile Marine and recommending qualified seamen as sailing masters for the former Royal Navy.

In 1565 Elizabeth I awarded the Corporation the powers to ". . . erect beacons, marks and signs of the sea. . . hereby the Dangers shall be avoided and escaped and Ships the better come into their Ports without Peril." In 1604, James I conferred on Trinity House the compulsory pilotage of shipping and the exclusive right to license pilots. In 1836 William IV extended the authority of the Brethren further and empowered them to purchase all private nautical lights around the coast. Thus a uniform system was created whereby this historic brotherhood assumed responsibility for all such marker beacons throughout England and Wales. Today, Trinity House, as the General Lighthouse Authority for England and Wales, the Channel Islands and Gibraltar, provides the key navigation aids consisting of lighthouses, lightships, buoys and radio navigation systems. Their Headquarters is an imposing building, originally designed by Samuel Wyatt, on Tower Hill and the present Master is HRH Prince Philip, the Duke of Edinburgh.

Primitive lights to warn of the dangers around the English coast appear to have been manned fitfully through the exertions of monks from their own sense of religious duty during the Middle Ages. One early light to warn of the perils of the coastal headland was placed in a sheltered hollow of the cliffs at St. Margaret's Bay by a hermit, Brother Nicholas, in 1367. He was commended by Archbishop Langham for his Christian piety in aiding ships to navigate the offshore sandbanks. It is thought that the grand mansion west of the bay, formerly known as 'The Hermitage', commemorates this humane anchorite. The Reformation, which swept away the monasteries, terminated these invaluable voluntary beacons.

The North Foreland lighthouse, standing proudly atop the perpendicular cliffs of the Isle of Thanet, is the oldest established lighthouse in England. A deed of 1499 mentions "ye beacon that lyith at ye hedd of ye cliffe at Beecon Hill". It consisted of an iron basket with a wood fire fixed to a tall, stout pole and its purpose was almost certainly to warn of pirates or invaders rather than as a true aid to navigation.

The primitive structure was replaced by a lighthouse constructed of chalk blocks surmounted by a brazier in

The North Foreland lighthouse.

1581. Its purpose was to mark the northern tip of the Goodwins and to guide shipping safely around the exposed promontory into the mouth of the Thames Estuary. After his pursuit of the Spanish Armada, Sir Henry Seymour wrote of his relief at sighting "ye tower beacon of ye Foreland" which directed his warship, 'Rainbow', into the shelter of Margate Harbour.

First practical lighthouse, however, was erected there by Sir John Meldrum, a soldier-cum-speculator, in 1635. He proposed collecting dues from passing ships (one penny per ton from British vessels and two pennies per ton from foreigners) in order to maintain his private venture. Charles I granted Meldrum a licence in 1635 to build a two-storeyed octagonal timber tower to correspond with two lighthouses he also planned to build on the South Foreland. Illumination came initially from two dozen candles held in a chandelier hoisted aloft at dusk but the apparatus was later replaced by a coal fire. Unsurprisingly, this first 'Light House' constructed of timber, lathe and plaster was destroyed by fire in 1683.

Foundations of the present North Foreland lighthouse were laid by Robert Osbolston in 1691. This was a brick, stone and flint octagonal two-storey tower, forty feet high, served by an internal spiral staircase and surmounted by an open coal fire burning in an iron grate and fanned by the wind. This bulky fuel was an expensive, yet inefficient, form of lighting for it is recorded that the lighthouse used 100 tons of coal in a single year. A letter of instruction written by the new owner of the lighthouse to his agent at Deal exhorts him to "be diligent in keeping good fires this rumbustious weather".

About 1732 the fire was encased in a lantern to prevent it being extinguished by the rain but this meant it had to be laboriously blown by bellows by lightmen working throughout the night. Another problem was that now smoke and soot constantly obscured the light through the numerous sash windows. Thomas Baskerville, writing a description of the Downs Anchorage in the late 1600s, mentions the fact that: ".. when foreigners cast anchor here they must pay something towards the maintaining of the lights, constantly kept burning in the night to give warning to ships of the dangerous places." Early in the 18th century, tolls levied on ships benefiting from Broadstairs' conspicuous" light were donated to the Royal Naval Hospital, Greenwich.

The Admiralty appreciated the benefits of the lighthouses on the Forelands and, being concerned about the safety of ships in the Downs Anchorage, persuaded the hospital trustees to heighten the structure. Around 1790 a further two brick and stone storeys were added to the Broadstairs lighthouse, raising the tower to its present height of eight-four feet. At the same time the coal fire was replaced by eighteen Argand oil lamps with reflectors and lenses placed in the seaward windows encased in a decagonal, copper, glazed, fireproof dome.

Trinity House assumed control of both the North and South Foreland lighthouses, regarded as 'Sentinels of the Strait', in 1832. Immediately, their Chief Engineer, James Walker, was commissioned to modernise the design of the North Foreland lighthouse. The intermediate floors within the tower were demolished, most of the windows were removed and the exterior was painted white. A new lantern with a multi-wick burner and a first order catadioptric fixed lens was fitted in a lantern room built atop the tower to accommodate the light in 1890. The two adjacent keepers' cottages were also constructed. Basically, this is how the lighthouse and its apparatus appear today.

In 1860 an occulting light was installed but this was changed to its present flashing character when it was converted to electricity in 1920. (If the light duration is shorter than the following dark interval then it is termed 'flashing' but if the light endures longer than, or is equal to, the following dark interval then the light is termed 'occulting') This involved a 240V 3000W lamp with a code signal of five red and white flashes every twenty seconds which remains its characteristic today. The extreme range of its powerful lamp is nearly twenty miles. The height of the tower, including lantern house, is eighty-three feet, reached internally by over one hundred winding stone steps.

A radio beacon transmitting morse code was established that enabled ships - and aircraft - to take a bearing when navigating the dangerous promontory in fog. This became defunct at the end of the 20th century when the Differential Global Positioning Scheme (by which ships fitted with a special receiver are able to determine their position with astonishing accuracy from a constellation of artificial satellites in space) reduced all alternative systems of navigation to secondary status.

In November 1998 the North Foreland became the last lighthouse in England to be de-manned. Its mechanism is now triggered by a solar sensitising clock and is operated automatically between sunset and sunrise. The light is computer controlled and monitored by telemetry from Trinity House Operations and Planning Centre at Harwich in Essex. Immaculately painted white and green, standing in the centre of a pair of keepers' cottages on a trim lawn, North Foreland lighthouse is a listed building.

Sir John Meldrum headed a petition supported by masters of ships calling for a lighthouse at the South Foreland, near Dover, to mark the southern tip of the Goodwin Sands in 1634. Predictably, Trinity House opposed this laudable project. Their objection was threefold: the expense would be prohibitive, wreckers might show false lights and privateers would be directed into the Downs.

Further objections came from lodesmen who dismissed lighthouses as "costly follies". At the Court of Lodemanage in Dover these influential pilots protested: "We at sea have always marks more certain and sure than lights, high land and soundings that we trust more than lights. . . the Goodwins are no more dangerous now than time out of mind they were, and lighthouses would never lull tempests, the real cause of shipwrecks."

Sir John persisted and quickly built, at his own expense, twin towers on the clifftop at St. Margaret's Bay. These two white 'Light Houses' with beacon fires would distinguish them from his single lighthouse displayed at Broadstairs. At the South Foreland, one light was higher than the other so that their transit would lead vessels clear of the southern limit of the sandbanks. Once more, Sir John proposed recouping his expenses by levying tolls upon passing ships that would benefit from his edifices.

South Foreland lighthouse.

In 1690 the lights with their attendant fees were acquired by Robert Osbolston and in 1705 they passed into the care of his son, also named Robert. The lighthouse keepers they employed were lax in their duties and the coal fires were not always visible. Sir John Byng complained to the Admiralty in 1707 that he could "scarecely see the light all night long". Around this time the South Foreland lighthouses were bequeathed, along with the North Foreland lighthouse, to Greenwich Hospital.

Improvements were made to the lighthouses by the trustees in 1793. The Upper lighthouse was rebuilt with three storeys while the Lower lighthouse was restyled with only two storeys. Catoptric reflectors, revolving frames and magnifying lenses were introduced to intensify and direct the lights horizontally across the Dover Straits while the lights progressed from open coal fires in cauldrons to arcane lamps, burning first sperm then vegetable oil.

Trinity House acquired the two lighthouses in 1832 and completely rebuilt them in 1843. The Upper lighthouse was now encased in a square tower with a castellated parapet and comfortable cottages were provided for its keepers. All were enclosed in a masonry stone wall. The Lower lighthouse was also rebuilt as an octagonal stone structure in 1846. The quality of these lights were greatly improved when dioptric white lamps enhanced by silvered reflectors were installed in 1852.

Michael Faraday, the physicist, advised Trinity House to experiment with electricity in these lighthouses the following year. Accordingly, generators were housed in an engine room and the resulting intense light was visible from the gallery of a lighthouse twenty-seven miles distant on the French coast. Doubt was expressed, however, whether this blue/white light would penetrate fog as effectively as the yellow light produced by the oil lamps. Further experiments with gas lighting were not successful. Eventually the South Foreland lighthouse became the first to be permanently lit by electricity in England.

The South Foreland Upper lighthouse was involved with early experiments in ship-to-shore wireless telegraphy. Communication was established between the lighthouse and the East Goodwin lightship twelve miles distant in 1898. Trinity House gave permission for the Italian inventor, Guglielmo Marconi, to install his equipment on behalf of the 'Wireless Telegraph and Signal Company' at the South Foreland. This was the first time wireless was used at a British lighthouse.

Marconi dispatched his assistant, George Kemp, to direct the installation of an antenna, transmitter and receiver aboard the lightship. Kemp chronicled his subsequent ordeal in his pocket diary. On 17 December he was rowed out with his fragile equipment by Harry Pearson in the Walmer lifeboat galley which Kemp noted was "the quickest Life Boat known for beating to windward". This preliminary journey took three and a half hours but at last he reached the lightship which he found "pitching and rolling" in the open sea. Aided by the crew Kemp managed to erect a tall extension to one of the lightship's masts, allowing the antenna to rise ninety feet above the deck, before returning to shore that same afternoon. "This was rough experience in an open boat," he lamented.

Kemp returned to the lightship with provisions for one week on 19 December. He completed installation of the radio equipment despite huge waves crashing over the deck of the lightship which was held broadsides to the mountainous waves. While he was there the lightship was visited by the Rev. Thomas Treanor, Chaplain to the Missions to Seamen, who held a service below deck. On Christmas Eve Kemp aboard the lightship exchanged a message of seasonal greetings with Marconi at the lighthouse using a spark gap transmitter. On Christmas Day a south-westerly gale necessitated the crew easing out their mooring chain cable but the lightship began to plunge alarmingly making eating the traditional dinner unbearable.

Kemp, who was violently seasick, was marooned on the lightship until early in the new year because of boisterous weather. "Every steamer that approached the East Goodwin lightship", he noted, "turned and went back to anchor near the Downs." During that time he taught the lightshipmen "the Morse Code, how to manage the aerial and the leading-in wire, and how to manipulate the transmitter and receiver." They became proficient at sending wireless messages - at the rate of fifteen words per minute - to the mainland despite inclement weather. Kemp, though, was forced to borrow provisions from the crew until his own supplies arrived. He was so overjoyed at receiving them that he listed every item:". . . some mutton, a fowl, 2 bottles of Claret, 2 loaves, potatoes, a cabbage, sprouts and fruit". After over three weeks, Signor Marconi appeared with Harry Pearson in the Walmer lifeboat to take Kemp back to shore and tea at 'The Black Horse' inn.

Overall, the experiment was successful and the result was that vessels in trouble could receive immediate assistance in future.

Indeed, four months later the East Goodwin lightship's new wireless technology proved invaluable in communicating a disaster to the shore. In April S.S. 'R.F. Mathews' - literally carrying coal to Newcastle - rammed the lightship in dense fog. The crew employed Marconi's wireless transmitter to summon assistance from the shore. Inexplicably, Trinity House exercised caution about installing wireless telegraphy in their lightships and preferred to wait until radio telephones were available in the 1920s.

During the Second World War the South Foreland lighthouse came under the control of the Admiralty although it was still manned by Trinity House. The light was extinguished but rekindled - dimly and briefly - whenever a convoy passed through Dover Straits. After the Fall of France the North and South Foreland lighthouses were equipped with secret transmitters to jam German radar installations across the Channel. That same year the lantern and lens of the Upper light was shattered after being hit by shellfire from a long range gun on the French coast.

The Lower lighthouse had been dismantled in 1904. Probably this was

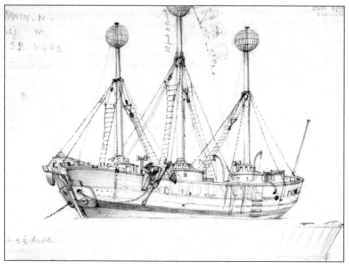

The Goodwin lightship sketched by E. W. Cooke.
© National Maritime Museum

because of cliff erosion but, in any case, the southerly drift meant that the transit line of the two lighthouses no longer indicated a safe passage through the Goodwins. Its tower was converted into a luxury home with the redundant lantern room proving an ideal sun lounge overlooking the sea.

The Upper lighthouse underwent various modifications - it was electrified in 1922, converted to unwatched in 1959 and modernised in 1969 - and remained operational for a long time after the war. Its single revolving second order dioptric light had been acquired from St. Catherine, Isle of Wight. Automation was introduced and the intense light produced was equal to one million candlepower visible for twenty-six miles in clear weather. Its characteristic was "white group flashing three times every twenty seconds". When it became redundant on 30 September 1988 this majestic structure was acquired by the National Trust. It can be visited although it is no longer illuminated.

Trinity House is responsible for the eight remaining unmanned, solar-powered lightships around the coastal waters of England and Wales. Formerly, the four original lightships marking each of the main compass points of the Goodwin Sands were regarded as indispensable to the safety of shipping since the sandbanks lie in the middle of the world's busiest shipping lane. Even today, the greatest concentration of lightships - Channel, Foxtrot 3, East Goodwin, Greenwich, Sandettie, Sevenstones, Sunk and Varne - occurs in this narrow portion of the English Channel although only one of the four light vessels which formed a "circle of light" marking the fickle sandbank survives.

During the 17th century Robert Hamblin, a Norfolk barber, and David Avery, a London businessman, raised a petition to anchor a ship burning candles in a lantern as a warning to navigators of the dangers of the Goodwin Sands. The Brethren of Trinity House ridiculed their proposal - one problem was mooring a vessel employing only hemp ropes since chain cables were not then available; a second objection was that candlelight would be totally ineffective while a third difficulty might be finding a robust crew. Shipowners disagreed, however, and backed their speculative venture. Accordingly the two business partners secured a Royal patent to establish the first lightship in English waters although they actually placed it at the Nore, at the entrance to the Thames Estuary, in 1732.

This Nore lightship was a conversion of a wooden-hulled merchant vessel. It showed two lights, consisted of half a dozen tallow candles in a conventional ship's lantern, suspended from each end of a yard on a single mast. Bridle iron chains of immense strength with weighty 'mushroom' anchors held the sturdy vessel to its difficult mooring but sails were kept at the ready should the vessel break adrift. This audacious private venture was the start of the trend to use unpowered, anchored lightships to indicate offshore hazards around the British coast.

About this time Captain Henry Taylor, a master mariner from Shields, devised a plan for a "floating light" to mark the Goodwin Sands. He complained to Trinity House that the Forelands lighthouses were inefficient. Apparently, ships were known to anchor and fire signal guns to wake up sleeping lighthouse keepers to rake up their fires! "We know one person who, while he lay in the Downs, saw thirty ships lost on the Goodwins... through mistaking one Foreland light for another," Taylor elaborated, "a case that often happens and is often attended with fatal consequences but which the floating light will effectively prevent." Grudgingly, Trinity House offered Taylor a substantial grant yet prevaricated over his suggestion.

The Napoleonic Wars resulted in fleets of warships entering and leaving the Port of London and anchoring in the Downs. This movement of troopships precipitated Trinity House's involvement in marking sandbanks around the Kent coast and Thames Estuary. Accordingly Hamblin and Avery's primitive lightship was replaced with an official vessel, which resembled a large herring buss, at the Nore in 1796. Two permanent lights were maintained until 1825 when a single light was substituted and this was replaced by a revolving light in 1855. The Nore lightship (LV 14) which came on station in 1839, served for just over a century. Like all Trinity House lightships, she was painted red with her name, NORE , in huge white letters emblazoned on her broadsides. Today, the shoals are marked by a buoy.

Trinity House at last made the marking of the Goodwin Sands a priority and sought advice from the Committee on Shipwreck regarding appropriate positions for their lightships. They commissioned Messrs. Randall and Brent of Blackwall to build a wooden vessel of 150 tons which was towed out to its position at the North Sand Head in 1795. This new lightship permanently displayed three spherical wicker 'daymarks' at each of its three mastheads which were supplemented by three Argand oil lamps hoisted from the deckhouse at sunset. These were provided by a certain Mr. Robinson who also supplied the vessel with copper lanterns, oil lamps, plate glass and an iron hearth. The lightship was manned by an experienced master, William Grice (formerly in charge of the Owers lightship at Spithead), his mate and ten crew. It was one of only half a dozen lightships at the start of the 19th century that marked the hazards around the coast of Britain.

Trinity House minutes for 1794 record this laudable intention:"Resolved, also, that three distinct lights be exhibited in this vessel, to distinguish them from the North and South Foreland Lights, and that a large bell be fix'd in the vessel, to be constantly rung in hazy and thick weather to warn ships as they approach the Goodwin Sands." (A chart by Laurie and Whittle contained in 'The Complete East India Pilot' Vol I published in 1796 reveals that this first lightship had been moved closer to the North Sand Head within its first year)

The threat of invasion from the Continent was so serious at this time that the Admiralty expressly ordered commanders of cruisers to assist and protect the North Sand Head lightship. Members of the lightship's crew were provided with two light four-pounder guns, six brace of pistols, twelve muskets and twelve long pikes "in case they be molested". This armament obviously proved an effective deterrent since there are no records of interference of the lightship by the enemy.

Eventually this early vessel was replaced by an 184-ton triple-masted iron vessel specially built at Blackwall at a cost of £5,587. This had a fixed light on each mast and its hull was painted bright red with the name, NORTH SAND HEAD, picked out in white letters. In 1877 her three fixed lights were replaced by a larger single lamp permanently held aloft and rotated by clockwork on a central mast. The character was changed to a single flashing white light, showing three times in rapid succession every minute, and visible for ten miles. There was also a Chinese gong for striking in fog. This primitive device was replaced by a siren when the lightship was renamed NORTH GOODWIN. (Lightvessels frequently lie on direct shipping routes and therefore it became the practice of installing sound warning devices for their own protection against collision by passing ships in foul weather)

In 1926 the North Goodwin lightship (LV 81), a red light vessel with her new name in large white letters on her hullsides, was the first to be built completely of steel. Furthermore, she was the first to be equipped with an electric light so that her dioptric lenses gave three 12,000-candlepower flashes every twenty seconds. (Dioptric is a term used to state the refractive power of the lens whereas catoptric, which is the opposite, refers to its reflective properties) Another development was the thick tubular tower amidships giving safe internal access via a vertical ladder to the lantern. Consequently, her light was far more powerful than any of her predecessors. This lightship was also equipped with a diaphone fog horn giving three blasts every minute when required. Improvements were gradually made to this type of vessel, providing the crew with cabins furnished with bunks instead of hammocks, a galley, mess and washrooms in an enlarged deckhouse amidship. Eventually LV 81 was retired to Greece.

The North Goodwin lightship (LV 20), one of the last and most powerful vessels built for Trinity House by Philip and Son of Dartmouth, served the North Goodwin station between 1976 and 1983. Her features included the retention of the central tubular column supporting the lantern, the diaphone positioned aft away from the roof of the lookout shelter and a forward landing stage for helicopters. Additional improvements were also made to the crew's quarters to ensure that each member had his own cabin. Regrettably only five of these superior vessels were built. Currently she serves the Channel station.

The majority of ships entered the Downs via the northern channel of the Gull Stream and this busy fairway was, therefore, an obvious place for Trinity House to position a second light. In 1809 the Gull lightship was moored on the western edge of the Goodwin Sands to mark the inside passage of the Gull Stream. It was a purpose-built 158-ton wooden vessel at a cost of £4,197 with the word GULL painted in large white letters on the sides of her hull. Two fixed lights shone from a yard on a single mast. A Chinese gong was provided to be beaten during fog but this was later replaced by a reed horn.

North Goodwin lightship © Angus Neill.

In 1825 the Gull lightship was given two masts, each having a pair of lights. In 1856 an American ship crashed into this vessel, temporarily extinguishing her candle lanterns. In 1860 the lightship became one of the first to show a revolving light and this was operated by clockwork. Its characteristic was one flashing white light every twenty seconds, visible for ten miles.

Fog in the English Channel was so dense throughout February and March, 1929, that the noise of lightships' sirens, horns and maroons made it virtually impossible for the inhabitants of Deal and Walmer to sleep. That spring the original Gull lightship was withdrawn for a complete haul and a replacement lightship (LV 38) was towed out to serve the station temporarily. Her service was brief. During the night of 18 March this replacement ship was struck by the Ellerman liner, S.S. 'City of York', making her way tentatively in thick fog up Channel to the port of London. The lightship was badly holed. Her master, Captain Williams, was trapped in his cabin amidship on the port side where the collision occurred and he was drowned. The watchman and crew of six, who were asleep at the time, were cast into the murky water. The 'City of York' anchored and sounded an SOS on her siren while her lifeboats attempted to rescue the stricken crew.

The Gull lightship was salvaged with lifting gear and beached at Deal for immediate repairs before being towed to Ramsgate where she was once more made seaworthy. Since the location could not remain unmarked, a local motorboat, 'Lady Beatty', was employed to warn ships of the danger. Her skipper, Harry Meakins, and his valiant crew's only method of signalling was waving a red flag and ringing a muffin handbell! Four days later a marker buoy was in position until the lightship, raised and refitted, could return to station in 1930. Her name was then changed to BRAKE to reflect her new position which, owing to dramatic changes in the sandbank, was now in closer proximity to the Brake Sand.

During the early part of the Second World War the Brake lightship was fully manned only if required by coastal convoys. On 16 January 1940, when visibility was reduced by snow flurries, an Italian steamer, 'Ernani', broke adrift from her anchor in the Downs and rammed the Brake lightship, holing her just above the waterline. The crew abandoned ship and, after rowing in their lifeboat for an hour in icy conditions, were fortunately rescued. Her master, Mr. J. Beet, was suffering from frostbite. Soon afterwards this lightship was withdrawn from service and replaced permanently by a light buoy in the Gull Stream. This lightvessel (LV 38) went on to serve at the Mouse Station in the Thames Estuary and was later sold to Thurrock Yacht Club as their floating headquarters in 1947. Today she lies derelict on the banks of the Thames at Grays in Essex.

The third vessel to mark the Goodwins was the South Sand Head lightship positioned in 1832. She was moored at the extreme southern end of the Goodwins, about four miles east of Dover and practically opposite St. Margaret's Bay. She was specially built at a cost of £3,212 by the Blackwall yard, famed for the building of Indiamen. A wooden vessel of 184 tons, her three masts were surmounted by red balls serving as 'daymarks' and a hoisting lantern which was lowered to the deckhouse during daylight. Her broadsides were painted red with SOUTH SAND HEAD picked out in white letters. When Captain Bullock RN surveyed the Downs in 1846 for Trinity House he included miniature sketches of all three light vessels with their appropriate daymarks and flashing codes at night.

The Brake lightship. Courtesy: Alan Major.

A more modern lightship, renamed SOUTH GOODWIN , replaced her in 1875. Among her refinements were a fog siren which blasted twice every minute and this device replaced the handbell rung by a crew member to warn of danger during poor visibility. In 1884 this same lightship received a permanent lantern giving two rapid white flashes every half minute, visible for ten miles. A steadying sail was retained on the after mast which generally flew the ensign, although storm warnings were sometimes flown.

"It seems almost a paradox," remarks Gattie, "that, of all vessels in the world, a lightship, carrying a brilliant light at her mast-head, should ever be run down."And yet in 1885 this same lightship was struck by an unknown vessel, resulting in one side being stove in and the lantern shattered. In December 1899 the South Sand Head lightship parted from her moorings and she drifted towards the edge of the sandbank. Because of the ferocity of the gales lifeboats found it impossible to rescue her stranded crew for three whole days. Undamaged, she was later towed back to her moorings by a Trinity House tender and the crew reboarded.

A new iron vessel (LV 71) built by John Crown of Sutherland, came on station at the South Goodwins in 1903. The next year another collision occurred which damaged her lantern. In 1914 she broke from her moorings and swept past the South Sand Head while her men exhausted all their supply of rockets to summon aid. The crew of the Deal lifeboat, 'Charles Dibdin', watched helplessly as she drifted into the open sea which, being wartime, was heavily mined and where rescue boats were forbidden to venture. Incredibly, she passed through the minefield unscathed and was eventually towed back to her station. Again, on 24 March 1929, the German steamer, 'Olivia', collided with the same lightship in thick fog but did not cause great damage. Finally, the American merchant ship,'Westaginaw', collided with this ill-fated lightship in 1930.

Immediately after the Second World War a new vessel (LV 90), built in 1937 by Philip and Son of Dartmouth, arrived from the Tongue station to become the new South Goodwins lightship. Her powerful dioptric electric light displayed in a latticed tower gave two 600,000-candlepower flashes every thirty seconds. In addition, there was a diaphone fog horn emitting two blasts - high and low notes - per minute in thick weather.

After the north, south and west (or inner) sides of the Goodwins were carefully lighted, Trinity House thought it prudent to place a fourth light on the east (or outer) side of the sandbank. This would assist navigators of ships passing outside the Goodwins or approaching from northern Continental ports. Accordingly a wooden vessel of 163 tons named EAST GOODWIN was moored there in 1874. She carried one revolving light showing every fifteen seconds visible for ten miles. The peculiarity of the light was that it was green which effectively warned navigators to "keep to the east" when passing along the 'Back of the Sands'. The lightship was also provided with a fog gong but this was later changed to a reed horn.

On 1 December 1903 the East Goodwin lightship was struck by the Cardiff cargo ship, 'Hazelmere', which necessitated considerable repairs. A new lightship (LV 87) replaced her in 1932 and remained on station, equipped with a radio beacon, until the Second World War. Another lightship (LV 93) came on station in 1947 and stayed until she was removed to the Galloper station in 1953. Built in 1938 this vessel exhibited an electric biform catoptric light of 300,000 candlepower giving one flash every fifteen seconds plus a diaphone fog horn blasting once every thirty seconds. She was one of the first lightships to be automated and converted to solar power. In 2005 LV 93 was sold out of service and converted into a photographic studio at Trinity Buoy Wharf, East London.

The development of lightships over the centuries reflects the rapid advance in technology. Early lightships had fixed lights. Later, revolving apparatus was invented with oil wick burners, focused in copper reflectors, and individual flashing characteristics were introduced. The circular lantern was positioned atop a central mast and supported by a stout chain so that it could be lowered by day for refilling the lamps, trimming the wicks and cleaning the glass ready for hoisting aloft at dusk to exhibit the light. Later lanterns were permanently fixed at their correct height and electrically lit, the power being supplied by diesel generators. This meant that the lamplighter had to climb the wires and enter the lantern by a narrow door - a precarious venture when the ship was heavily rolling.

Numbers of the crew were identical for all Goodwin Sands lightships. Originally, each crew consisted of eleven men. The Master and his Mate were on board alternately - one month at a time - together with six seamen plus a skilled carpenter. Three lampmen were required to attend the lanterns throughout the night. The crew spent two months on a ship and one month ashore where they were then expected to repaint buoys in the workyards and ferry out provisions in the tenders. Gradually, crews were reduced to seven men. . . then five. . . and their duties ranged from maintaining the lamps to driving fog signals. Crews were taken out to sea first by tender and later by helicopter from RAF Manston.

Accommodation for the crew was in the forepart of the lower deck. Initially, there was a relative amount of space in the early wooden vessels. There would be a coal fire stove for cooking and heating, a large refectory table, a well-stocked pantry, numerous lockers, washing facilities and rows of hammocks. The Master's cabin was furnished with several bunks (necessary to accommodate frequent visitors) a desk, bookcases, lockers, a table and an armchair. He could enjoy his own private washing facilities and a stove for warmth. Crew members slept in hammocks until they were provided with comfortable bunk beds after the Second World War.

Herbert Clark Russell recorded life aboard the 'Gull' lightship in his novel, 'The Longshoreman' (1896):

> "He led me below into a tolerably roomy but low pitched interior, shaped to the curve of the vessel's bows. Half a dozen hammocks were slung close up against the deck beams, and one had to stoop one's head to walk about under them. A large wooden table stood amidships, cleated to the floor, a row of lockers, designed to serve the purpose of seats, ran along the vessel's side on either hand; and a big globe-shaped lamp swung from the ceiling; here and there stood a sea chest or a tarpaulin kit bag, against the bulkhead hung a copper speaking trumpet, a telescope and a glazed printed card of rules and signals; and this, with a few odds and ends of oilskins and other nautical garments hanging from pegs, about completed the furniture of the forecastles. Such daylight as gained admission found its way through small squares of glass let into the sides of the scuttle or hatch, and the place was in a sort of semi-twilight." (Chapter XI)

The men were left to their own devices for leisure periods. Pursuits before the advent of television included painting, carving, marquetry, knitting, weaving, photography, playing cards and board games plus the inevitable constructing model ships in bottles. More practical occupations were making workboxes, woollen rugs and shoes for the family ashore. Bread was baked fresh daily but water was rationed. Fishing from the deck was a natural way of stocking the larder and the local catch would include dogfish, huss, roker and, at the short period of slack water, whiting. There were books, journals and periodicals in abundance. Passing yachts collected letters from a dip net while steamers threw on board yesterday's newspapers. Trinity House insisted that their vessels remained dry so alcohol was smuggled aboard in innocuous bottles. Tobacco was plentiful.

Lightshipmen had a secondary responsibility. After the formation of the National Lifeboat Institution in 1824, the crew were required to keep a constant watch for ships in distress and to alert the Coastguard. Indeed, lifeboats on the south-east coast came to depend heavily upon specific directions from the lightships - always their first port of call - for precise location of stricken vessels on the Goodwin Sands. This was often a tortuous route involving a detour of several miles and sometimes even involved crossing the sandbank or navigating its swatchways.

Lightships were provided with a pair of guns for firing rockets and a supply of distress maroons before the days of telegraphy and telephone. Carronades were positioned on the port and starboard quarters so that, in the event of a ship "standing in danger", the leeward gun would be loaded with a charge of one pound of black powder and fired at regular intervals. Semaphore was also employed to communicate with ships in the Channel.

Trinity House issued an order regarding the code of signals in case of shipwrecks on the Goodwin Sands: "If a vessel is on shore to the northward, a white rocket is to be discharged, in a northerly direction, fired at an angle of 45 degrees. If to the southward, a red rocket is to be fired in a southerly direction, at an angle of 45 degrees. If to the eastward, a blue rocket is to be fired in a perpendicular direction." (8 November 1832) Carronades only became obsolete towards the end of the Second World War when electrically-fired flash sound and trace rockets were provided in modern lightships.

Modern lightships were twin-masted with the lantern mounted amidships on a steel lattice tower support. The optic was an assembly of specially designed mirrors and with filament electric lamps adjusted to the type of flash unique to each vessel. The fog signal and horn were situated above the deckhouse clear of obstructions which might deaden the sound. Communication with the shore improved with wireless telegraphy and radio telephone.

A lively description of life aboard a lightship was penned by George Goldsmith-Carter in 'Looming Lights' (1947). After a spell in the Royal Navy this burly, young, Suffolk boatman was detailed as an "extraman" aboard the ancient wooden-hulled Nore Lightship. He lists his rations, clothing, toiletries and personal possessions he was allowed to take on board. "It is a sombre prospect to leave one's family and the sameness of everyday life, for an existence in a tiny everyday vessel, sometimes reeling in tremendous seas, in the company of six other men, who may not always prove congenial company," he remarked.

Shortly afterwards, George was transferred to the North Goodwin Lightship (LV 64) where he penned an account - graphic and gruesome - of his service in a "fog-ship" during the early years of the Second World War. At that time, the lightship was manned only intermittently to aid allied convoys for the duration of hostilities. Otherwise the lantern was extinguished and the name obliterated. The Relief Tender bringing tanks

East Goodwin lightship.

110

of water, oil, coal, stores and mail, was now armed. A twelve-pounder gun was positioned on her after-deck while machine guns were placed on the wings of the bridge. Decoy buoys were set to confuse the enemies entering into home waters. Ships of all non-belligerent countries at that time - Norway, Denmark, Sweden, Italy, Holland, Belgium, Greece, Spain, Ireland, Panama, America and Japan - were all thoroughly searched for contraband and escorted by a Guard Ship before they streamed through the English Channel.

And there were fresh hazards. Most feared were the sea mines - floating, magnetic and acoustic - one of which passed underneath the lightship's bow. The crew donned life jackets and held their breath as a strong current drove it harmlessly away. It became common for the lightship to be ringed by drifting mines which occasionally exploded at a distance and covered the deck with fine spray. Once George watched in horror as a vessel was struck by an enemy mine on the dim grey horizon. In seconds the ship reared violently from the water, reeled on her side and then disappeared beneath the waves with loss of all hands.

Clearly, the North Goodwin lightship was uncomfortably close to hostilities. After the Fall of France the British Expeditionary Force fought its way back to the coast and made a tactical retreat from Dunkirk. A fleet of small craft - everything from a motor launch to a paddle steamer - passed nearby to ferry troops from the beaches under fire to allied ships anchored offshore. During the Battle of Britain the lightshipmen watched dogfights in the sky overhead from the shelter of their deckhouse. Convoys of merchant ships steamed defiantly northwards - colliers, tankers, coasters and mailboats - painted a sombre grey as they crossed the bleak horizon. The seas were littered with abandoned cargo - chests of

Cigarette card showing South Goodwin lightship.

The Pharos on the eastern cliff of Dover is regarded as Britain's oldest standing structure. It was one of a pair of Roman lighthouses that guided ships safely into harbour.

The Venerable Bede referred to the Isle of Thanet as 'Tanatos' meaning 'Fire island'. Possibly, this indicates the vast number of beacons blazing on the island.

The Commonwealth Parliament ordered the North and South Foreland lights to be extinguished in the event of an invasion. It was thought that enemy ships would inevitably founder on Goodwin Sands.

The North Foreland lighthouse gave Wilkie Collins the title for his famous ghost story. One evening at dusk he was walking with Charles Dickens and came across the lighthouse which appeared out of the mist like... 'A Woman in White'.

When Charles Dickens wrote to the Earl of Carlisle to invite him to 'Bleak House' at Broadstairs, he promised him "a night-light in the room we shall give you". He was referring to the beams from the North Foreland lighthouse.

Marquetry box showing fully-rigged ship passing 'Gull' lightship.

In March 1899 Marconi sent the first wireless message across the English Channel from Wimereux, near Boulogne, to the South Foreland lighthouse. The reel of ticker tape - an undeciphered sequence of dots and dashes - is lodged with the Bodleian Library, Oxford.

There was a proposal at one time to install a lighthouse atop Deal Castle.

Experiments were made to improve contact between lightships and the shore by means of carrier pigeons. This proved unreliable since in high winds the birds returned to the nearest lightship for shelter.

Lanterns aboard lightvessels were commonly called 'moon boxes'.

Crews of lightships were dependent upon local boats to deliver their mail. Recipients of a letter would reward the nautical postman by placing coins in a bucket hauled over the side.

tea, crates of tomatoes and bunches of bananas - but more alarmingly the bloated bodies of drowned airmen. Dressed in watch-coat, sea-boots and warm woollies with his lifebelt around his waist, George could only watch from the deck in despair. He, like his companions, took comfort in the fact that no foe would intentionally sink a lightship. . .

The attack by enemy aircraft, then, took the lightshipmen by surprise.

When a nearby convoy was pursued by four dive bombers they included the lightship in their prey:

"The air was suddenly saturated by the swishing whistle of bombs. The watch below leapt to the deck, without stopping to dress. A succession of giant hammer blows shook our sides. Giant black and grey spouts, with fire in their hearts, leapt across our bow and quarter, only a matter of yards distant. Pieces of bomb casing rained down. The air was full of the stench of burnt explosive."

Another time twenty-five Dornier bombers crossed the Channel and one broke formation to attack the defenceless North Goodwin lightship.

"The air was filled with the swishing roar of bombs. Then came the thunder of water-deadened explosions. The ship reeled. Soot rolled in clouds from the galley and cabin funnels. Black stinking water deluged our decks. The drone of attackers died away. The smoke cleared. . . we looked around. . . we were still afloat."

On 18 July 1940 the East Goodwin lightship (LV 54) was sunk by German bombers. In October that same year the old composite South Goodwin lightship (LV 69) broke adrift on a rough night after being struck by a floating mine. Luckily the lightship was unmanned and there were no casualties. In October that same year the North Goodwin lightship - also unmanned - broke away from her moorings and drove ashore amid the beach defences at Walmer.

Eventually it dawned on Trinity House that Luftwaffe pilots, in their folly, were, indeed, targeting defenceless lightships and consequently ordered that all their vessels on the south and east coasts were to be de-manned. Their experienced crews were released for valuable service in the Naval Reserve or Mercantile Marine. A trawler patrol vessel came alongside the North Goodwin lightship with orders for the crew to abandon ship. George hurled his few belongings into a kit bag and jumped aboard the trawler where he joined his fellow men sipping hot tea laced with rum in the cabin as they sped away to relative safety under the cover of darkness. Buoys marked the boundaries of the dreaded shoals for the duration of the war.

After the cessation of hostilities lightships around the coast of Britain gradually returned to normal and crews were again permitted to man the light vessels marking the Goodwin Sands. This was thought to be the ideal vocation by ex-merchant navy and deep sea fishermen. Trinity House, however, insisted in reduced manpower and put into effect a programme of automation. Postwar conditions for lightship crews were vastly improved: hot water was available for washing, refrigerators kept food fresh while televisions provided welcome entertainment. Yet there was still the ever present risk of danger. . .

Worst postwar disaster occurred when the South Goodwin lightship (LV 90) parted from her riding cable and drifted from her moorings during a severe gale on the night of 26th November 1954. (The high southerly wind had increased from Gale Force 10

The South Goodwin lightship lost on the sands in 1954 © Fotofile.

Marquetry box with a design showing 'Gull' lightship.

First whistling buoy - whereby a whistle would be blown by air forced through it by the pressure of the waves and the ceaseless motion of the buoy - was placed as an experiment on the North East Goodwin in 1880 by Trinity House.

During the First World War lightshipmen were provided with rifles in case of enemy attack.

Entertainer, Hughie Green, visited the North Goodwin lightship in his yacht and Hattie Jaques, who lived at Margate, also climbed aboard.

One of the most popular construction kits made by Revell was a detailed model of the South Goodwins lightship.

When the North Goodwin lightship was presented with a turkey by friends from the mainland one Christmas in the 1960s, one of the crew made a model galleon out of the carcass and presented it to his seasonal visitors.

to Storm Force 11) The lightship was swept rapidly north-eastwards and struck the sandbank just south of the Kellet Gut. There she capsized and lay on her starboard side, gripped by the Goodwins, with mountainous seas and a falling tide.

The crew of the East Goodwin lightship noticed that the light from the South Goodwin had ceased flashing and alerted the Coastguard. Lifeboats from Ramsgate, Dover and Walmer swiftly attended but none were able to approach the stricken vessel. The Chief Superintendent at Trinity House Headquarters, Harwich, ordered the launch of the tender THV 'Vestal', later relieved by THV 'Patricia', but even these sturdy vessels were rendered helpless because of the maelstrom.

An American Army Air Force helicopter of the Air Rescue Squadron set off from RAF Manston. Its crew spotted a sole survivor clinging to the light tower despite heavy waves washing the deck. Captain Curtis Parkin flew his helicopter perilously low to winch up the exhausted civilian. He was a young scientist, Ronald Murton, who had been engaged in monitoring migratory bird numbers for the Ministry of Agriculture and Fisheries. Murton later gave his faltering evidence to the Trinity House Board of Enquiry:

"The ship lurched. . . She had a heavy list. . . The next instant we went over completely right onto her side. . . Water was coming through the hatch, filling (everything) up in seconds. In consequence, we were out of our depth in water. As water came in everyone was knocked about but I cannot visualise this very clearly. . . The water was rising rapidly. . . I realised I had to get out and made for the skylight. There was a heavy swell. Water gushing in the galley door and absolutely fantastic conditions. . . it took me about ten minutes to get to the skylight."

This was one of the first air-sea rescues to take place and the pilot received a silver medal for his bravery by the R.N.L.I. The next day the Royal Navy ship, H.M.S. 'Ramola', sent divers to locate any further survivors trapped inside the capsized vessel. They found that all the cabins and companionways were blocked with sand and, indeed, within a week every trace of the lightship had disappeared. All seven of her crew - comprising her Master (Horace 'Tom' Skipp), two lamplighters, two fog signal drivers and two seamen - drowned.

An old lightship (LV 65) temporarily marked the position of the South Goodwin lightship. In January 1955 a modern lightship (LV 17), actually intended for Seven Stones station, was hastily repainted and rushed to replace her permanently. This new vessel was later converted with a helipad so that crews might, in future, be relieved by helicopter. At the same time her red and white paintwork was abandoned in favour of an universal Post Office red. Another lightvessel (LV 5), completed in 1947, also served at the South Goodwin in 1963 until she removed to the Tongue station in 1972.

Trinity House, as a result of the tragedy, began a programme of replacing manned lightships with automated substitutes around the British coast. Automated vessels were gradually converted to solar power because the need for powerful lights dwindled as shipboard navigational equipment improved. Many former lightships were then discontinued or downgraded to increasingly sophisticated solar-powered buoys.

In December 1947 the North Sand Head lightship was replaced by an older vessel (LV 81) which had served at the Kentish Knock. This wooden hulled ship built in 1924 had the great improvement of an electric lamp with dioptric lenses reached by a vertical ladder inside its tubular tower. It now displayed three flashes every twenty seconds. In 1974 LV 81 was removed and sold to Greece after being replaced by a newer steel lightship (LV 16) which was also fitted with a helipad. This was the last manned ship to serve the North Goodwin. In August 1985 an automated light vessel (LV 5A), which had previously served at both the South Goodwin and Tongue stations, was moored into position at the North Goodwin. Her light and fog signal were operated remotely from the North Foreland lighthouse. Progress continued. In April 1988 the North Goodwin lightship was completely withdrawn from service and replaced by a High Focal Plane Buoy (1S7) marked 'N E Goodwin'.

In 1998 a further lightship (LV 95), originally built in 1939 and modernised in 1995, had come on station at the South Goodwin. She was the first vessel to be equipped with ninety solar panels to provide power for her 65W lamp. In addition, she was fitted with an electric fog signal having a two mile range. Yet another lightvessel (LV 6), completed in 1948, converted first to automation and then solar power, was placed at the South Goodwins station during 2000 and 2001. Lastly, an earlier lightship (LV 17) was fitted with solar panels at Ramsgate Royal Harbour and again took up her position at the South Goodwins in 2003. In 2006 the South Goodwins became the second light vessel to be replaced by a tall powerful solarised buoy (1S9) supplying additional Aids to Navigation.

Today, Trinity House regards its most important station as the East Goodwin. After the war numerous vessels have taken up their position on the outer edge of the Goodwins. The last lightship (LV 21) to be built by Philip's for Trinity House was placed at the East Goodwins in 1963 and remained there until 1976. She returned, fully automated, to the same station and served between 1997 and 2001. Meanwhile, a fully automated lightship (LV 22) had taken her place in 1995. Built by Richards Ltd., Lowestoft shipbuilders, she was the last vessel to be commissioned by Trinity House. Another light vessel (LV 19), built in Philip's yard, was placed at the East Goodwin station in 1995.

Since 2005 the former South Goodwin Lightship (LV 17) was removed to the East Goodwin station. This fully automated and solarised vessel is monitored and controlled by the Operational Control Centre at Harwich. She is a red lightship with her name, EAST GOODWIN , brazenly painted in white letters on her hull. Moored about one mile eastward of the sandbank, the sweep of her light which flashes every fifteen seconds is visible for twenty-three nautical miles. She has both a fog horn, which blasts twice every minute when required, and a transmitting radio beacon. Currently, she is the only remaining lightship to mark the rapacious Goodwin Sands.

THE PORT OF DEAL

'Victualling the Fleet'

AFTER THE DECLINE of Sandwich, Deal developed from a garrison town into a premier port whose main concern was victualling the home fleets of the Royal Navy. At the commencement of the 18th century Deal was regarded, after London, as one of the "four great ports" of England ranking with Plymouth, Portsmouth and Rochester (the old name for Chatham).

Ancient Britons had settled on high ground at Upper Deal to form a farming community which developed around the Norman church dedicated to Saint Leonard. Mentioned cursorily in 'Domesday Book' (1085) where it is listed among the possessions of the Canons of St. Martin's Priory, Dover, Deal's name is Latinised as 'Addelam' (meaning "at Dela"). Alternative titles that appear in early documents are Dola, Dale, Dele, Deyll, Deyle, Deele and Deale. Lambarde in his 'Perambulation of Kent' (1570) conjectures that the name derives from the Saxon word, 'dylle', meaning "low, lying land or a plain".

For centuries Deal was overshadowed by Sandwich which possessed a magnificent harbour approximately two miles wide. Regarded throughout the medieval period as England's premier port, it was originally called 'Lundenwic' since it lay at the entrance to the port of London. There was a phenomenal trade with the Continent and a popular phrase was: "Wine in, wool out". Gradually, the harbour mouth began to silt up and it became completely blocked after a Spanish ship owned by Pope Paul IV sank in 1461. Leland quaintly informs: "the caryke that was sunk in the haven in Pope Paulus' tyme, did much hurt to the haven and gathered a great bank." Monarchs who frequently embarked from Sandwich were constantly petitioned to help preserve the harbour but all these pleas were ignored. Instead, as the coastline changed, Deal rose to importance, despite the fact it lacked its own proper harbour. Laker puts it succinctly: ". . . as Sandwich sunk, so Deal arose."

From the reign of Edward the Confessor, shortly before the Norman Conquest, a group of ports along the south-east coast began to take responsibility for the defence of this vulnerable part of the English Channel. They evolved into the Confederation of Cinque Ports (pronounced 'sink' after the Norman word for five) - Sandwich, Dover, Hythe and Romney in Kent and Hastings in Sussex - to which two further ports - Rye and Winchelsea - were added later as 'Antient Towns'. It cannot have been coincidence that several of these selected ports were opposite the Downs with its easily accessible rallying point for warships and with their natural escape routes

117

north and south of the Goodwins. 'Limbs' were also added to assist with supplying ships and men and Deal (along with Ramsgate, Sarre and Fordwich in Kent and Brightlingsea in Essex) was attached to Sandwich with a Deputy appointed to act in the interest of the Town Mayor.

The Confederation of the Cinque Ports in medieval times supplied the main defence of England. Effectively they formed the nucleus of the royal fleet awaiting the command of their king. The Cinque Ports were charged with the duty of supplying the monarch with a huge armada totalling fifty-seven ships, each crewed by twenty men plus a ship's boy (called a 'grommet') under a rector or master. Ships and their crews were liable to service for fifteen days annually at the Port's expense after which time the expense was borne by the Crown. These terms of service remained unchanged until the beginning of the fourteenth century when the number of vessels was reduced to twenty-seven because, by then, the ships had grown in size, but their crews' compliment remained the same.

Their status was unique. In exchange for this important 'ship service', Edward I confirmed and extended their powers and privileges by a Royal Charter of 1278. Portsmen had the right to hold the canopy over the sovereign at the Coronation (this custom terminated with William IV), the men carrying it being created Barons. Fishermen were allowed to land their valuable catch of herring and sell it at Great Yarmouth, which led to open hostility between that town and the south-coast ports. Most importantly, they were able to administer their own justice at the Court of Shepway which was independent of the sovereign. The power of the Cinque ports was astronomical. It only ceased when Henry VIII took charge of the defence of the coastline and laid the foundation of his own Royal Navy.

Deal rose to great importance when Walmer Castle became the official residence of the Lord Warden of the Cinque Ports. The Lord Warden - a royal appointment - took precedence over the Lord High Admiral of England. The office of Lord Warden was created in the reign of Edward I (1272 - 1397) and was later combined with Constable of Dover Castle. He was responsible, not only for the defence of the south-east coast, but to enquire into prize money, piracy and shipwreck. Wrecks caused a problem. The Lord Warden claimed jurisdiction over the Narrow Seas with entitlement to a share of the spoils of local wrecks but his authority was constantly challenged by the Lord High Admiral. He contended that the authority of the Lord Warden was confined to the shore or only so far into the sea as a horseman could extend his lance.

The Lord Warden presided over the Court of Chancery which sat regularly in Saint James' Church, Dover. It took cognizance of all civil causes arising within the liberty of the Cinque Ports. The only appeal was to the Warden's Court of Shepway. The Court of Chancery fell into disuse during the reign of George I but the Lord Warden, shorn of this responsibility, still presided over the Court of Admiralty which dealt solely with maritime concerns.

He appointed Commissioners in salvage cases as arbitrators of disputes but stubbornly claimed his own right to "flotsam, jetsam and lagan, or floating, cast up and submerged wreckage". He also held a Court of Lodemanage by which all appointments and regulations regarding the Cinque Ports pilots (or 'lodesmen') were made although this body was transferred to the control of Trinity House in 1853. Further, the Lord Warden was responsible for "divers castles and forts" along the south-east coast.

This coastline was defended from earliest times. Leland, Henry VIII's librarian, in his 'Itinerary of Kent' (1540) mentions "a fosse or a great bank, artficial betwixt the town and se" and he surmises that it was intended as a first line of defence at Deal. "Surely the fosse was made to kepe owte ennemeyes ther or to defend the rage of the se or by the casting up beche or pible." Local legend asserted that this rampire was cast by Caesar's legions and referred to it as 'Rome's work'. The Sea Valley - natural or artificial - disappeared long ago but it appears to have been a long shingle bank between Deal and Walmer which swept down steeply from the seashore to the present High Street (formerly 'Lower Street') causing a deep depression that habitually filled with water. A deed dated 1582 mentions "the Sea bunke".

After Henry VIII's quarrel with the Pope about his intended divorce of Catherine of Aragon he risked invasion by both France and Spain. He proceeded to strengthen the coastline by building a string of fortifications which included the 'three castles that keep the Downs' - Deal, Walmer and Sandown. Their construction was swift and, despite one of the earliest strikes on record, they were finished in just eighteen months. Deal Castle was so far completed that it welcomed Henry's luckless fourth bride, Anne of Cleves, who was escorted across the Channel by a grand fleet commanded by the Duke of Southampton in December 1539.

These Henrican fortresses represented the last stage in castle construction. Their revolutionary design accidentally reflected the emblem of the Tudor rose, with Deal, "the great castle", having four 'petals' or lunettes while Walmer and Sandown each had four. The castles were built for the age of gunpowder and their rounded bastions provided a full 360 degrees range for their cannons. This curious circular construction would deflect enemy cannon balls while their low, squat elevation made it difficult for

Sandown Castle and Mill by Henry Moses
© Deal Maritime and Local History Museum.

enemy ships to target should they invade the Downs. Traditional features which were retained included a deep well housed in the central drum, a drawbridge over a dry moat plus an iron-studded doorway, protected by a portcullis and murder holes, positioned safely on the landward side. Ironically, the strength of these castles was not tested until the Civil War.

Henry VIII, who may have personally inspected progress of the building works, placed the castles under the control of the Lord Warden. First resident Lord Warden was Lionel Sackville, Duke of Dorset, who set about domesticating the stark building when the honour was bestowed upon him early in the 18th century. Prime Minister, William Pitt, made the castle his home and his niece, Lady Hester Stanhope, claimed responsibility for the planting of the celebrated gardens. Pitt, who was given the Freedom of Sandwich in 1795, made several excursions to review the Downs fleet in the Admiralty Yacht which lay offshore during his occupancy. Later Lord Wardens were Sir Winston Churchill and Queen Elizabeth the Queen Mother. Present Lord Warden is First Sea Lord, Admiral Lord Boyce, who was installed in 2005.

Most celebrated Lord Warden was Sir Arthur Wellesley, the Duke of Wellington. He resided at the castle every autumn from the time of his appointment in 1829 until his death there in 1852. A small museum at the castle displays personal relics including his Lord Warden's uniform, death mask and a pair of the famous boots. 'Wellington' boots were personally adapted from military boots by the Iron Duke. Originally, they were made so that the front of the boot covered and protected the front of the knee. The back of the boot was cut away to make it easier for a rider to bend the legs while in the saddle. After 1818, however, the name was attached to shorter boots made of plain black leather intended to be worn under trousers.

The Duke gave precise instructions for a new pair to his shoemaker, Hoby, of St.James, London:

Walmer Castle October 8 1839

Mr Mitchell,

I beg that you will make for me two pair of Boots of the usual form only four (or the thin of an hand) lines longer in the foot than usual. Send with the new false shoes that will fit this new size. If needed make them broader. If these boots should suit me I will send another (pair) of galoshes if I fit them; and (a pair) of shoes of the same size. I beg to have these boots as soon as possible, as I am Pained by those which I Wear at present.

Your obedient Servant,
Wellington.

Sandown Castle became the prison of the regicide, Colonel John Hutchinson, who had been one of the signatories of the death warrant of Charles I. An account of his incarceration was penned by his widow, Lucy, who was forced to lodge in the 'cut-throat town' of Deal. The castle succumbed to the encroachment of the sea - it may have had a meadow in front of it - and now only a fraction of the west bastion survives.

A survey into the state of decay of all three castles in 1616 revealed that Sandown was already in a ruinous condition: "Item, the mote walle next the sea being almost eaten through by reason of the rage of the sea in so much that the sea soketh into the mote or dich every spring tyde. . ." Indeed, around 1785, the sea broke through the outer wall of the moat of Sandown Castle which rendered it "barely habitable". During the French Wars it was patched up, but the decline was only halted temporarily. Later it served as a Coastguard Station and then a Military Hospital. Its last captain was Sir John Hill but his appointment in 1851 was merely honorary. Stones from demolished Sandown Castle appeared in the most unlikely places - the abutment to Deal Pier, the tower of Walmer Castle, the foundations of the Wesleyan Chapel and the Boatmen's Rooms. The garrison canteen became 'The Good Intent' and later 'The Castle Inn'.

The building of the three castles tempted inhabitants down from the hillside community at Upper Deal to the seashore. At first progress was slow. Chapman informs, "Not far from the Castle, upon the brow of the beach, were built a little group of houses tenanted mainly by fishermen" while Elvin includes a sketchy 'Mappe of Walmer Castle' showing "a little stage for fisher boates". Jetties and capstans were accompanied by temporary shelters erected by boatmen and pilots on the Sea Valley. But development began to speed up. . .

Captain Byng, Governor of Deal Castle, was annoyed that these makeshift dwellings obstructed his field of fire. He complained in 1627 that "the cottages which are built betwixt Deale castle and the bulwarke, which the survey adjudg most fitt to bee demolisht doe daily increase, yea and they continue building in the very trenches, and although they bee daily forbid, yet they persist." Parliament responded by ordering the demolition of these "noisome" buildings on the beach. Their inhabitants then appealed to Sir Edward Boys, the Deputy Lieutenants and Commissioners for Kent in 1645: "The major part of the petitioners have for about 30 years been employed in the service of His Majesty's castles for the good of the King and Parliament, they have erected

Looking northwards along the Esplanade.

several houses and cottages upon a place called Sea Valley. . . next the sea, bordering upon the Downs where His Majesty's navy ride. . . They were induced to erect such habitations so that they might be near at hand for service and the more ready at His Majesty's and the Parliament's command..."

Parliament was at that time embroiled in the Civil War and lost interest in the dispute. It continued at a local level, however, because the Deal Pilots submitted their own petition to Generals Blake and Montagu in 1656. "We have erected at our own cost houses on the beach waste ground, not worth 2s a acre, that we might serve the Navy and merchant ships" they argued reasonably. Eventually, petitions by these 'Tenants of the Waste' were successful and the Archbishop of Canterbury, who owned all the land reaching to the foreshore, began leasing plots for building on this Sea Valley. Public wharfs with patches of houses and stores were built so close to the sea that their walls were washed by every spring tide.

The Downs had always been a place of rendezvous for the fleet of the Royal Navy begun by Henry VIII and expanded by successive Tudor and Stuart monarchs. Wenceslaus Hollar etched a panorama of the Downs (circa 1649) with Calais in the distance, the castles on the seashore and a tremendous number of sailing ships.

The port of Deal sprang up to cater for the demands of both merchant and warships becalmed in the Downs. At first, the responsibility of victualling the fleet lay with the captains of the castles but this lucrative industry became the concern of local butchers, bakers, brewers, grocers and greengrocers. Related trades developed and the port was soon alive with boat builders, sail makers, rope makers, blacksmiths, tinsmiths, tanners, gunsmiths, candle makers, coal porters, barbers, shoemakers, tailors. . .

Water for both mariners and townsfolk was initially supplied by numerous wells. In 1689 a licence was obtained by Edward Burdett to construct a reservoir to supply Deal with fresh water. Land was excavated and a single well - known as 'Peggy Wraite's' - was dug. Ten years later permission was granted to draw water from the North Stream which criss-crossed the Sandhills. A pumping mill was constructed and water was conveyed across the marshes via a wooden conduit to a reservoir in Water Street. Later, an additional reservoir was built closer to the foreshore and a pumping mill was erected near to the gasworks at North Wall. But the best water was reckoned to be drawn from the 'Bear's Well' adjacent to the Town Hall and St. George's Church. (Waterworks at Upper Deal were not constructed until 1836)

Deal had a large number of windmills - seven - to supply flour to shipping in the Downs. Unscrupulous millers formed themselves into a cartel so that they could charge high prices to ships taking on stores. Their excessive prices were also sorely felt by inhabitants who risked starvation. The situation was resolved by Thomas Oakley, a humanitarian banker and shipping agent, who built a mill on the beach adjacent to Sandown Castle in 1797. Painted white, it was clearly visible to captains of ships who were encouraged to send ashore for supplies. His company sold flour at reasonable rates which created competition so that rival millers were soon forced to lower their exorbitant prices.

Eventually, there were four breweries - Hight's at the top of North Street, Hayman's at the bottom of Farrier Street, Hill's along the High Street and Thompson's atop Dover Road, Walmer. Hill's (formerly Oakley's then Iggulden's) also comprised three grand dwellings with hothouse, vinery, walled fruit and kitchen gardens. Local legend asserts that Thompson's - the last to survive - was financed by wreckers who lured a Spanish galleon onto the Goodwin Sands in the early 1800s. Edmund Thompson was reputed to have spent ransom money for the captured crew in setting up his prosperous brewery, Thompson and Son.

As the port prospered inhabitants deserted their timber shacks on the shingle and built durable properties in brick and stone. A simple street plan began to emerge in Lower Deal: Beach Street followed the line of the seashore, Middle Street linked the Castles while Lower Street developed into the commercial centre and changed its name to High Street. Myriad streets, lanes and alleys linked these winding thoroughfares and houses and cottages were built on plots leased by the 'Arch bishopp' who was Lord of the Manors of Court Ash, Deal Prebend and, prior to the Reformation, Chamberlain's Fee.

Substantial Georgian houses remain in abundance which testify to the affluence of former residents whose livelihood depended upon the sea. Authentic architectural features - doors, windows, chimneys, fanlights - attracted artists and writers to Kent's first Conservation Area. Many buildings reflect the influence of Dutch immigrants to East Kent. Domestic dwellings are frequently furnished with Dutch tiles uncovered behind fireplaces, around sinks, lining cupboards or "necessary houses". 'Dutch Corner', at the junction of Griffin Street and Middle Street, exhibits ornate Dutch gables but there are at least forty similar concealed among the roofscapes. The distinctive curvilinear type of Dutch gable became so indicative of the locality that it often appears in architectural manuals as the 'Deal Gable'.

There are few survivals from the Tudor period in Deal and Walmer. 'Court Lodge' at Middle Deal was probably built for successive Stewards of Deal Castle. It is a grand red brick dwelling on a flint base entered via an iron-studded doorway. Inside, there is a wealth of original fireplaces, beams and archways. An ancient timber door leads down to a large cellar built of scored stones acquired from dissolved monasteries. Just inside the porch is an intriguing wall cupboard with a lock which indicates that this building was once commercial premises. 'Court Lodge' has been in continual habitation since Tudor times and it has benefited from sensitive improvements in the 18th century.

Formerly, the grandest dwelling was the Manor House at Upper Deal. Constructed by Captain Joshua Coppin, first Mayor of Deal, it was restyled in Cromwellian times and sadly demolished in 1965. This imposing red brick mansion boasted a magnificent oak staircase and a remarkable bedroom furnished like an officer's cabin on a warship by a retired admiral. Latterly, it had been the residence of John Gaunt about whose family there is a romantic tale. According to legend they were outwardly respectable gentlefolk but in reality they masterminded smuggling operations along this coast. Signals could be exchanged from the rooftops with ships in the Downs and signatures were scratched on windows in the cabin with diamonds smuggled from Amsterdam.

The Great Plague which ravished London also raged at Deal. The register of St. Leonard's Church records 210 victims in 1665; 333 in 1666. A Royal Navy Hospital ship landed with hundreds of sick soldiers and sailors but townsfolk refused them shelter. Bubonic plague, it was thought, was brought to this port by ships from North Africa. Richard Watts, Surveyor of Customs and Excise, recorded the effects of this virulent disease in his diary from the comparative safety of Walmer Castle. "The North part is so much infected that they go one amongst another, but it is not above three houses at the South, where the richer and more moderate people live." Britain was then at war with Holland but the fleet anchored in the Downs were not mobilised

The Esplanade and Iron Pier.

since "the trained bands of Deal and Walmer cannot be in arms because of the infection." At the height of the pestilence one third of the population died and the town was sealed off until the plague abated. Victims were buried in open pits in the Sandhills and one gruesome discovery of a mass grave occurred at the beginning of the 19th century.

During the protracted wars with Holland, France and America the problem of dealing with the number of wounded seamen landed at the port became paramount. In 1664 the Commissioners for the Care of Sick and Wounded Seamen chose Deal as one of their designated "places of reception". They approved "a physician... chirurgeon, nurses, fire, candle, linen, medicaments, and all things necessary" but stipulated that these must be provided in "as husbandly and thrifty manner as possible". Shamefully, the Admiralty were tardy in paying the wages of medical staff and their expenses for patients nursed in lodgings around the town.

At the time of the French Revolutionary War there existed a large General Military Hospital in West Street which also served as a prison-cum-barracks for cavalry. Later, two naval surgeons - Packe and Leith - were contracted by the Admiralty to victual and render medical aid to the sick and wounded. This proved to be both an humane and a lucrative venture because George Leith earned seven shillings per week for every patient. By 1793 the Admiralty had constructed their own Royal Naval Hospital with a Lieutenant in charge. It is assumed this was on the site of the present grand edifice along The Strand. Completely rebuilt in 1812, it became the headquarters of the Royal Marines School of Music in 1950.

124

Deal became the starting point for sea voyages across the world.

The sailing route from the Port of London - navigating the Thames Estuary, following the North Kent coast and rounding the North Foreland - was tortuous. Passengers avoided the tedium and danger involved by travelling overland by stage coach from London across Kent and embarking from Deal. Once arrived, they might still wait a whole month for a suitable wind to carry their ships down Channel and so their stay in the port was often prolonged. Inns and hostelries sprang up to cater for weary travellers' need for accommodation. When the wind was in the east the port would fill up with homeward bound craft and their exhausted passengers also sought shelter and sustenance in the town. Landlords' charges were exorbitant but the revenue greatly added to the port's prosperity.

Most prominent was 'The Three Kings Inn' (now 'The Royal') which is now the only building to stand on the foreshore. Records are extant from the latter quarter of the 17th century when its facilities included stables, coach house, a capstan and a boat to ferry customers to their ships waiting in the Downs. Its list of distinguished visitors number Lord Nelson, Princess Adelaide and Sir Winston Churchill. Notable seafront hostelries include 'The Hoop and Griffin', which stood in Griffin Street, on the site of the Mary Hougham Almshouses, and 'The Royal Exchange Hotel', at the top of Exchange Street, now converted into flats.

From earliest times there was a myriad of smaller inns and public houses to cater for seafaring folk. Curiously, the Admiralty discouraged landlords from harbouring any of their sailors unless they arrived sick or "wet ashore". Several inns, since demolished, stood immediately on the foreshore to attract the custom of seafarers: 'Rodney', which stood on the beach between Oak Street and Brewer Street; 'India Arms', at the top of King Street; 'The Crown', a haunt of pilots, and 'The Fountain', which was the scene of a brutal murder at the start of the 20th century. Two notorious inns - 'Noah's Ark' and 'Jolly Sailor' - lay at the back of the town and were receiving centres for contraband. Most of our historic inns, however, have been converted into private dwellings - 'The Lifeboat', 'Albion', 'Mermaid', 'Tally Ho', 'Deal Lugger', 'Pelican', 'North Star', 'Globe', 'Yarmouth Packet', 'Scarborough Cat'. . . Elvin says the oldest inn at Walmer was the 'True Briton' on The Strand.

Towards the end of the 17th century Deal had expanded so rapidly that its population had far exceeded Sandwich. The inhabitants, naturally, resented the fact that they were still subject to the 'Custumal' (laws, customs and privileges of the ancient port) and resolved to improve their own town's status. One of the most active dignitaries in this matter was Thomas Powell, later Mayor of Deal and fervent Puritanical reformer. Accordingly, the Jurats met in the Vestry of St. Leonard's Church in the winter of 1698 to make plans for an application to Parliament for a charter which would convert Deal into an independent 'Borough and Market Town'. Deal would then be free to appoint its own Mayor and Council and make its own by-laws.

Deal's petition for a Charter gives a terrific insight into the state of the port at that period:

"Whereas the Town of Deale hath not been built above 70 years, and the greatest part of it within 20 years past, and hath now about three thousand Inhabitants and daily increasing, a Considerable place of Trade by shipping from most parts of the world; and very useful to the King's ships as well as merchants which are supplied here with Pilots, Anchors, Cables, Provisions, are all necessarys to the great accommodation of Navigation in General. And though but a Member of Sandwich lying five miles distant, pays more Taxes than Sandwich; furnish'd His Majesties Navy with 400 Seamen Annually, and entertain'd more Sick and wounded in time of War than all the Cinque Ports together. And if under the Government of a Magistracy within themselves will be better enabled to defend the Coast, there, from the attempts of a Foreign Enemy. The King's Customs will be better Collected and improved, the transporting of Wooll, and Exporting and importing prohibited Goods in these parts much better prevented: The Public Peace Preserved. All Riots, Tumults, Murders, Vice and Immorality, (which frequently happens where such members of People of all Nations Resort) suppressed and punished, Ships in danger, better Assisted. Wrecks, which are now for the most part violently taken and carried away by an unruly Multitude would then be preserved, which now cannot possibly be. Ships would then be furnished at most reasonable Rates, and all frauds in Selling of bread, Beer etc prevented. The Poor which are numerous better provided for and set at Work. Its not the least desired to Infringe the Rights of the Cinque Ports, but to enjoy the same privileges as Folkstone, Fordidge, Feversham and Tenterden, who are Corporations and yet Limbs or Members of the Cinque Ports as Well as we, many more advantages will therby rebound to the Publick and the better enable the Inhabitants at all times to contribute to His Majesties Service and the Defence and Welfare of the Kingdom."

Despite fierce opposition from Sandwich, the 'Charter of Incorporation' was duly obtained and signed by King William III. A deputation headed by Valentine Bowles was appointed to travel to London to collect the precious document. He carried it as far as Canterbury where the newly elected Mayor of Deal, Captain Joshua Coppin, received it and brought it to Deal in triumph. The charter with the borough seal was secured in an iron chest with three keys held by the Mayor, a Jurat and a member of the communality. Immediately, the new Town Council set about making their own laws. These concerned the public sale of fish, the fixed rate for beach ballast (3d per ton for Englishmen; 8d to foreigners) and strict rules for trading at fairs and markets.

The most important assertion by the independent town was its prerogative to press men into the Royal Navy in times of war. (Oddly, this right of forcibly seizing law-abiding subjects for the sovereign's service was denied the Army) Pressing was a blot on the Navy since the formation of the Cinque Ports up until the middle of the 19th century although the 'Press Act' remains - unrepealed - on the Statute Book. Bounties were occasionally offered by the Admiralty as an incitement to enlist and this would consist of several weeks pay depending on the rating of the warship.

Five boats with fifty men and fifteen officers regularly patrolled for pressing between Deal, Dover and Folkestone. They were grouped under a Regulating Officer, either a captain or a lieutenant, who was accompanied by a surgeon, usually a local practitioner. This officer was paid a fee of one pound per day plus a five shillings subsistence. His men's pay varied. In 1743 a gangsman received "ten shillings for every good seaman procured, in full for his trouble and the hire of his boat". There were strict regulations regarding impressment (bachelors were retained but householders were released) but with such generous remuneration there were often abuses, particularly in the thriving port of Deal. "If their Lordships would give me authority to press here, I could frequently pick up good seamen ashore," Lieutenant Oakley boasted to the Admiralty in 1743.

Armed with hangers and cudgels the press men would operate both at land and sea. Generally, it was reckoned "the darker the night, the dirtier the weather" the greater the haul of potential sailors who were caught unawares. Captain Dent of the 'Shrewbury' man-o'-war gloated that he returned with "six very good seamen, natives and inhabitants and five of them good bachelors" after only a few hours spent pressing at Deal one day in August 1743. Naval gangs mustered their pressed men in the Navy Yard where they would be rowed out to warships in the Downs. A typical example occurred in 1803 when men were pressed in Dover, paraded in Deal and assigned to one of two frigates, 'Amelia' or 'Minerva', anchored in the Downs.

Once pressed, the luckless fellow remained in his fighting ship until he was paid off several years later. Even then, if it was still wartime, he might be transferred immediately to another seagoing ship or apprehended while he was ashore celebrating his freedom. Homeward bound merchantmen were fair game and pressed tenders habitually cruised the Downs ready to board them the moment they anchored. They were virtually stripped of their crews of prime seamen who were taken to a receiving ship - 'Sandwich' - stationed at the Nore.

According to the traditions and customs of the Cinque Ports, the right of impressment was vested solely in the Lord Warden but captains of naval vessels attempted to usurp this privilege. Magistrates refused to allow press gangs to operate in Deal since their activities were attended by "disturbances, riots, tumults and sometimes bloodshed". Frequently they petitioned the Lords Warden for support since boatmen went into hiding rather than risk being pressed out at sea in their boats. Economy of the port suffered as a result.

Captain Herbert of the 'Dragon' caused a furore when he had the audacity to press Deal pilots in 1670 and thereafter went in fear of his own life should he step ashore. A further hullabaloo occurred in 1702 when Admiral the Marquess of Carmarthen arrived with an armed escort and proceeded to round up local men. He was fiercely opposed by Magistrates who claimed that they had the sole right of providing seamen by this method. They petitioned the Lord Warden, Prince George of Denmark, and reminded him that the town had "encouraged and obliged about four hundred seamen of this Corporation to go on board Her Majesty's Ships of War. . . And this hath been the constant practise of furnishing the Royal Navy with Seamen from the Cinque Ports. . . and not otherwise."

Deal boatmen were recognised as providing a valuable service to the Crown as pilots and were eventually issued with tickets showing their exemption from impressment. Freedom came at a price and the town was reputed to have sold "protections" at the rate of ten shillings per head to every local sailor. Merchant seamen, though, were considered fair game. In 1793 seventy homeward bound West Indiamen entered the Downs and a general press was ordered. The result was that several hundred luckless crewmen were transferred to the Royal Navy. 'Ticketmen' escaped.

Even when the Navy press gangs were successful, they still had to fight off an angry crowd determined to release the victims. In 1655 Robert Plumleigh pressed one solitary sailor when a mob attacked and pelted his men with pebbles, driving them back to their boat. "Was there no better way to man a ship?" he asked plaintively. In

1735 a band of about thirty armed, masked men violently attacked a shore gang and released their hostages. A reward of £200 was offered for their arrest but the assailants, predictably, evaded detection.

Peter Earle in 'Sailors' (2007) asserts: "In the brutal game of manning the navy, the 'hot press' was seen as a dirty trick even by its instigators, and was only used in emergency". Press gangs ashore had three objectives: to drum up volunteers, to search for deserters and, empowered by their warrants, to compel experienced sailors into the service of the Royal Navy. The main target of a 'sweep' was inns or taverns and the subsequent affray was inevitably violent. Each man was given a shilling as press money plus three halfpence as good conduct money when marched to the assembly point.

Few landsmen, however, were conscripted and many men were released by the regulating officer as being unsuitable or unfit. Captain John Legatt complained during the reign of Charles I that the men pressed at Walmer consisted of elderly saddlers, ploughmen and maltmen. "Never was service so abused," he moaned. Daniel Lobdel, a Quaker, offered to supply legal aid to fellow Friends who might be pressed into service at the Meeting Place at Deal in 1678. (Quakers would have been of little use in wartime, anyway, because of their sworn passivism)

"There was no finer recruiting ground than the Downs", asserts J.R. Hutchinson in 'The Press Gang Afloat and Ashore' (1931) "where ships foregathered from every quarter of the navigable globe." Crews of returning merchantmen piping in from the south fell prey to press gangs afloat despite the fact that their crews fought hard to preserve their freedom. Their only hope of escape was if merchantmen entered the Downs in great numbers making it impossible for the gangs to board every vessel. Warships, themselves, however could not negotiate the beach without being reduced to matchwood nor were they able to withstand the choppy seas whipped up by a westerly wind in the Downs. Deal cutters, renowned for their seaworthiness and speed were, therefore, requisitioned for pressing in home waters. A special tender - swift and sturdy - was also stationed locally charged with the duty of being "very watchful that no vessel passed without a visit from the impress boats", according to Vice Admiral Buckle in 1778.

To replace men pressed directly from merchantmen, the Admiralty drafted 'men in lieu' or 'ticket men' to bring incoming ships safely into the Anchorage. (There were 450 of these men - mostly fishermen - in Deal, Dover and Folkestone who enjoyed exemption from the impress as a consideration for taking the luckless seamen's places). Tickets for this purpose were first issued in 1702. And after bringing a ship into port they often absconded from service in the Royal Navy. "Thirteen out of the fifteen men in lieu that I sent up in the 'Beaufort' East Indiaman have never returned," bewailed the commander of the 'Comet' bombship in the Downs. They had taken their fee and deserted.

First meetings of the Mayor and Corporation of Deal were held in a rented house owned by a widow, 'Anna Lawrence' in Lower Street (High Street). In 1702 it was decided to build a Court Hall, Gaol and Bridewell (or "a house of correction"). This purpose-built 'Guild Hall' stood between Market Street and King Street. It was a noble building surmounted by a cupola containing a "fire and market bell". Cobbles from the pavement at the rear remain to mark the site of the fish market in Market Street.

Deal's Town Hall was built in 1803. This elegant building was extended to include four police cells when the town was policed by a Town Sergeant assisted by twelve

St George's Church.

parish constables. On 1 January 1836 a Watch Committee was formed with George Hoile, a butcher, as Inspector in charge of five watchmen but later an additional Day Force was created consisting of the Town Sergeant plus two constables whose uniform resembled the London Police. About 1840 the two forces were amalgamated and a building adjoining the gaol was adapted as a Watch House. After 1888 Deal Police Force was absorbed into the Kent County Constabulary. The pavement under the Town Hall was used variously as a market place and fire station with a solitary fire engine.

There was a suggestion in the early years of the 18th century that a new chapel-of-ease should be built nearer to the foreshore to accommodate the large number of mariners who wished to attend divine service on Sundays. For centuries sailors, who might be stranded ashore for a short time only while awaiting a favourable wind to carry them on their sea voyages, were expected to walk the long distance to the parish church of St. Leonard. A proposal by the Mayor of Deal, Thomas Powell, for a new church was supported by Admiral Sir Cloudesley Shovell who was frequently stationed in the Downs. A subscription list was opened and funds were raised for building to commence on St. George's Church in 1707. Sadly, Sir Cloudesley was drowned that same winter when his fleet was shipwrecked off the Scilly Isles and with him the support of the Royal Navy for this laudable project waned.

An application was made for financial assistance to Parliament. The wording of the "Act for Completing a Chapell of Ease in the Lower Towne of Deale in the County of Kent. . ." paints a picture of the rapidly expanding community close to the shore:

"Whereas the Parish Church of the ancient Town of Deale is a full Mile from the Sea Side, where the Rendezvous of the Royal Navy in the Downes hath of Late Years so encouraged Building houses On that Shoare that a Large Spacious Brick Town, well Inhabited with all Sorts of Traders, Men and Artificers, now stands on the Beach of the Sea, and is commonly called the Towne of Lower Deale. . .”

An Act of Parliament was passed enabling a tax to be levied on coal entering the Port for a period of twenty-one years. The Corporation then mortgaged the coal dues so that construction might recommence on that "object of pity" lacking a roof.

Vignettes painted by John Lewis Roget appearing in his 'Sketches of Deal, Walmer and Sandwich' (1911) include a collier unloading sacks of coal beside a jetty on the beach at Walmer with an unsightly coal yard at the north end of Walmer Green. This tax also accounts for a slender wooden footbridge crossing the moat on the south-eastern corner of Deal Castle. Curiously, only a small portion of this fortress - the main entrance incorporating the porter's lodge - is situated in Deal. The majority of Deal Castle actually lies in Walmer where there was no liability to pay any tax on imported coal!

The Downs was practically the starting point of the overseas mails. Deal boatmen found a lucrative trade in delivering letters and parcels to ships for the Post Office. Mail bags were transported by stage coach from London every few days and put aboard vessels by regular service of the Deal boats. The same practice was applied in reverse with regard to homeward bound mails from the West Indies and Australia. Deal luggers on their westward cruises performed a useful service by intercepting ships mid-Channel and landing the mails at a convenient spot where arrangements could be made for forwarding them by road to London. At the peak of this service the Post Office paid Deal boatmen a total of £2,000 per annum but with the advent of steam all mail was dealt with at Plymouth or Southampton. Prior to the formation of the General Post Office during the Protectorate, a "foot-post" carried mail from Deal to Sandwich and then London.

During the Napoleonic Wars Deal was effectively a garrison town. Republican France declared war on Britain almost immediately after the execution of Louis XVI. Invasion was imminent and the coastline was secured. Two batteries were established on the shore north of Sandown Castle: barracks were constructed for the accommodation of troops drafted into Walmer. Shutter signal stations were built across Kent to speed communication between the Admiralty in Whitehall and Deal and the Downs. The Anchorage became highly esteemed since warships could assemble there in convoy ready to protect the Channel or retreat from enemy fire.

Lord Keith, as Commander-in-Chief of the Channel Fleet, remained in the Downs while his squadrons operated at various points along the coast from Sussex to the Firth of Forth. William Pitt, Lord Warden, who earned the title, 'The Pilot that weathered the Storm', impressed upon the Cinque Ports the importance of forming armed companies of volunteers - infantry and cavalry - to defend these vulnerable shores. Further afield, the Royal Military Canal was cut to zigzag its way across Romney Marsh between Hythe and Rye while Martello Towers were built, each one surmounted by a single deadly cannon, at short intervals along the Kent and Sussex coastline.

After a brief interlude, resulting from the Peace of Amiens in 1802, storm clouds gathered and war broke out once more between the two countries the following year.

A vast army under the command of Bonaparte assembled on the heights of Boulogne and intense preparations for our coastal defences were renewed. Pitt re-established the Cinque Ports Volunteers and, in addition to his horse and foot, a company of 'bombardiers' were mustered for exercise at Walmer Castle. Possibly it was at this time that the present guns were mounted on the castle ramparts.

Napoleon's Grand Armée - 120,000 men with guns and horses - was entrenched at Boulogne. In the Netherlands a further 34,000 Dutch and French troops were amassed. The First Consul had ordered the building of a powerful new invasion craft, consisting of sloops, barges and pinnaces, with the intention of transporting his armies across the Narrows. Precisely how his specially designed flat-bottomed boats might be navigated in poor visibility nor how they could be negotiated successfully through the conflicting tides was not considered. Arrogantly, 'Boney' declared the English Channel was merely "a ditch to be leapt by the bold". Fortunately the expected invasion never came and , in the event, Napoleon Bonaparte was subsequently defeated at sea by Nelson and on land by Wellington.

The prosperity of the port declined after the termination of the French Wars in 1815. Peace was no sooner declared than the fleets of warships stationed in the Downs were removed to Sheerness or Chatham and to be dismantled and laid up "in ordinary". According to Pritchard, "the town of Deal presented the appearance of a place deserted. . . A total suspension of trade followed. . . shops and houses were closed, and multitudes of people migrated to other places, where the prospect of trade and employment offered greater advantages than abiding in Deal." In was an inescapable fact that in times of war Deal flourished.

At the time of the French Wars the Old Barracks west of the town were demolished and North and South (or 'Cavalry') Barracks were constructed at Walmer in 1795. Originally, they were intended to accommodate 1,100 infantry and a squadron of cavalry but the premises were extended to incorporate parade grounds and a military hospital. After the Second Peace of Paris in 1815, a considerable number of troops were withdrawn and

When Dutch refugees settled in Sandwich they introduced cultivation of vegetables. The town became the first in Britain to supply markets with fresh garden produce.

The Mayor of Sandwich, John Drury, was murdered in a raid by Frenchmen in 1457. The Mayor of Sandwich still wears black robes indicating mourning. The Mayor of Deal, in sympathy, wears half mourning. The only break with tradition was when Queen Elizabeth I visited Sandwich in 1573. Good Queen Bess forbade such sombre apparel in her presence.

The loss of Calais in the reign of Mary I dealt a blow to the commerce of Deal. A considerable trade had existed with a profitable exchange of commodities that had greatly benefited the two ports.

The 'Castle Inn', also known as the 'Good Intent', was supposed to have once been the canteen to Sandown Castle. Its construction was of great antiquity and may even have dated to the completion of the castle itself.

The lantern of Deal Castle and the cupola atop St. Leonard's Church were both recognised as seamarks by Trinity House.

Walmer Green, Lifeboat House, St. Saviour's Church and makeshift boatmen's sheds and houses by Roget.

part of the Barracks was requisitioned, first by the Coast Blockade and then the Coastguard in a determined attempt to stamp out smuggling. (Blockademen and Coastguardmen were entered, in turn, on the books of H.M.S. 'Ramillies' and H.M.S. 'Talavera' stationed off Walmer). From 1839 until 1869 Walmer Barracks continued to be occupied by line regiments but after this time they were transferred to the Admiralty.

Royal Marines - "soldiers that serve at sea" - have been a strong presence in the port since their formation in the reign of Charles II. Their first permanent base here, however, was in 1861 when "coals, candles and straw" were ordered for the use of the ranks about to occupy Deal Depot. Shortly afterwards, a 'Beating Order' was issued by the Officers' Mess Committee to muster in the town. Since that time Royal Marines from Deal have distinguished themselves in countless campaigns - the Indian Mutiny, three Chinese Wars, the Crimean Wars, the Zulu Wars, the Boer War plus two World Wars. Following the detonation of an IRA time bomb which killed eleven bandsmen, the Royal Marines were removed to a more secure base at Portsmouth thus ending over three centuries of association with Deal.

Throughout the protracted wars with France and America, injured sailors were landed at Deal and Walmer and left dying in their "boat-loads" along the foreshore. After the Duke of York's disastrous invasion of Dunkirk in 1794 over one thousand soldiers are thought to have been buried in open pits in St. George's churchyard. Representatives of the Commissioners for Sick and Wounded Seamen constantly complained to the Lords of the Treasury that they were underfunded and unable to cope with the vast numbers of patients. Troops were tended in temporary tents or carted to private lodgings until funds dried up and landladies "turned the sick out of doors".

Consequently, two naval surgeons - Packe and Leith - made a contract with the

Admiralty to care for sick and wounded sailors. They converted a former French prison along Walmer Strand into a Naval Hospital and, by their laudable service, both these gentlemen secured their fortunes. Pritchard says that there was previously a large hospital leased by the Government in West Street, capable of accommodating 200 patients, and that the original French prison stood at the back of the Baptist Chapel in Nelson Street.

Eventually this Hospital was acquired by the Admiralty and replaced by a more commodious building in 1812. The Royal Naval Hospital (now luxury homes) remains along The Strand. Its pedimented facade - 365 feet long - is enlivened by a central portico and its roof is surmounted by a cupola containing a clock. The Hospital later became known as East Barracks when it housed the Depot Band of the Royal Marines in 1890. In 1930 the Depot Band was replaced by the Royal Naval School of Music and in 1950 this, too, was restyled 'The Royal Marines School of Music'.

Hasted in his 'History of Kent' (1800) pictures the port in its heyday:

"The town of Deal stands close to the sea-shore, which is a bold open beach. It is built, like most other sea-faring towns, very unequal and irregular; and consists of three principal streets parallel with the sea. . . Besides the private yards here for the building of vessels and boats, there is a King's naval officer, with storehouses and a quantity of stores, for the supply of the navy; and here are agents for the East India Company and Dutch Admiralty, constantly resident. Here is an office of customs, under a collector, comptroller, surveyor, and other inferior officers; and here are in waiting constantly a number of skilful pilots, usually called Deal pilots. . . appointed for the safe direction and

The old Customs House. Courtesy: Deal Library.

133

The Lord Warden was entitled to a salute of 19 guns from warships in the Downs.

The last time Walmer and Sandown Castles' guns were fired was at noon on 10 March 1863. The Volunteer Artillery fired a salute of 21 guns to celebrate the Prince of Wales' Wedding.

Deal was granted a new coat-of-arms in 1966. It features a shield bearing three demi-lions rampant and three demi-hulls of the Cinque Ports surmounted by a silver oar.

The silver oar is carried before the Mayor of Deal on ceremonial occasions to signify his sovereignty of the seas immediately off shore.

When the Mayor of Deal visits Royal Navy ships in home waters, he - or she - automatically assumes the rank of Admiral.

In October 1968 Deal's Middle Street was designated the first Conservation Area in Kent.

guidance of ships into port, and up the rivers Thames and Medway."

Prominent in the port were a number of maritime buildings. The Port Admiral at first occupied a grand residence at the entrance to the Navy Yard but when this became derelict a more commodious property was acquired in Queen Street. Chapman described it in detail and makes reference to the fact that it was formerly owned by a solicitor-cum-banker:

"It is a work of very substantial masonry, being built of large stones, with a domed roof and a marble floor. There is a small aperture which answers for a window that is protected with stout square bars. Entrance to this strong room was made through a massive door which was fastened by a peculiar piece of mechanism, in the shape of a very powerful old-fashioned lock. . . almost fabulous wealth was undoubtedly stored in the precincts of this historic house in by-gone days when Deal was a port of great national importance."

'Admiralty House' was a substantial building which remained the residence of the Port Admiral until 1815. In this year the office of Port Admiral at Deal terminated and the house was let. When it was finally offered for sale in 1864 an advertisement listed its features: "On the second floor four attics, on the first floor a large drawing room, five bedchambers and back stairs to the ground floor on which is a large and noble dining room, large library, breakfast room, capital hall and staircase, good kitchen, pantries, wash house, brew house with coppers, scullery and cellars." In addition, the property boasted a conservatory, kitchen gardens, stables, coach house and courtyard. In 1872 it was acquired by the eminent surgeon, Dr. Hulke, but it was later demolished to make way for the Odeon Cinema.

A strong presence from the Customs was established in the middle of the seventeenth century to deal with the landing of cargo into the port. A Customs' sloop was permanently stationed in the Downs in 1729 to escort ships up river to the Tide Surveyor at Gravesend. Its master, Philemon Phillips, estimated in 1737 that "there are upwards of 200 open boats carrying 4 to 5 hands each, employed in bringing the brandy, etc. from France, Flanders, etc. which goods are run between the North and South Forelands." The original Customs House was situated in Middle Street at the corner of Custom House Lane while a Watch House and Tide Waiter's House stood nearby at the top of King Street.

Unsurprisingly, Customs officials were unpopular in Deal. One frightful incident concerned the Collector, William Rickords, who was informed that his house was about to explode! As a result a military guard was placed along the adjacent narrow lanes of the Customs House. On 13 October 1806 'The Times' reported: "The watchman of the Customs House at Deal, on going his round about 3 o'clock on Monday morning last, discovered a large quantity of gunpowder laid under the porch of the house of the Collector of Customs and also a train of gunpowder extending nearly round the whole of the Customs House and the King's warehouse, upon which he alarmed the Collector's family; and presently perceived two men dressed in sailor's jackets who, on being called to, answered with horrid imprecations that they would blow up the Customs House and the Collector's family or hang the latter at the masthead."

A more substantial building was built by the Customs on the east side of the High Street adjacent to the 'Black Horse Inn' in 1810. This was necessary to accommodate the large staff which included a collector, a comptroller, surveyor, land waiters, riding officers, thirteen tidesmen, clerks and sitters of the boats. The new Customs House boasted a profusion of sash and dormer windows and two grand entrances - a wide one that led to the public domain and a pedimented doorway leading to the private residence of the Customs Officer. Last officer was Mr. G.W. Hider who was appointed to the charge of Customs at Deal in 1869 and he remained until its closure in 1882. He was instrumental in petitioning Trinity House for the stationing of a lightship to mark East Goodwin.

The Customs owned two quays - north and south - at opposite ends of the foreshore and their bonded vaulted warehouses (frequently burgled) existed at various points around the town. This demonstrated a concerted effort to combat smuggling in

Sketch by Henry Moses of pilots pushing their boat out alongside the timber pier.

The Esplanade and Iron Pier.

the town which was at its height during the French Wars. Regular sales of confiscated goods were held on the open beach. One typical auction in 1815 demonstrates the curious mixture of illicit cargoes: "seven scarves, 24 pieces cambric, 155 pieces of painted paper, two ivory fans, one box of pearl counters, two pairs of socks, 16lbs of candles, ten jars of succades (candied fruit) and a quantity of iron hoops". Rival Excise sales were held at the 'East India Arms' which had its own bonded warehouse.

Another maritime building was the Pilot House that stood along North Parade (or 'Pilots' Parade'). Here pilots waited their turn to be rowed across the Downs to a sailing ship signalling for their services. The Pilot House, marked by a tall flagpole, was demolished when Central Parade was extended northwards. The Cinque Ports Pilots was an unique body since for four centuries their affairs were controlled by the Court of Lodemanage presided over by the Lord Warden at Dover. In 1526 Sir Edward Guildford, Lord Warden, had established the Trinity House of the Cinque Ports Pilots under their own charter to ensure that pilots were properly qualified and their charges rigorously controlled. At that time there were fourteen licensed pilots from Dover, two from Margate and one from Deal who operated within strict territories. Sir Edward, together with four Wardens elected from these licensed 'lodesmen', formed this Court to adjudicate the laws of their Fellowhip.

In the early years the Court of Lodemanage dealt with numerous cases of negligence or misdemeanour. For instance, John Culmer, who was admitted to the Fellowship at Deal on 6 January 1629, was hired to pilot a Dutch ship, 'Crown', travelling from the Downs to London. Up river, he anchored at Limehouse where the water was too shallow and, as the tide receded, the ship went aground. He was severely disciplined. On 21 September 1743 a man-o'-war, 'Colchester', was lost during her passage form the Nore to the Downs by stranding on the sandbanks between

Longsand Head and the Kentish Knock. Forty sailors drowned. A Cinque Ports pilot from Deal was held responsible and he was tried by court martial for the loss of the ship. He was found guilty of culpable neglect and jailed for two years in the Marshalsea Prison.

After 1550 Cinque Ports Pilots were divided into two classes and entered in equal numbers in either the Upper or Lower Book. Differentiation was based upon the tonnage of ships they were allowed to escort. Rules and regulations were drawn up which ensured that pilots responded to a request from a ship's master in strict rotation. Only the pilot whose turn it was might go to the assistance of a ship in the Downs and this left him in a good position for bargaining. A scale of charges based on distance and tonnage was drawn up to ensure fair pay although there were special rates in times of war and for royal ships on state visits. East India Company ships were among the largest vessels and exceptionally high fees were earned by their pilots.

'Book Pilots' were awarded their own personal flag to identify them as they sailed through the Downs. It was obligatory that pilots should reside at their own port to remain in the Fellowship. In 1776 forty-eight pilots were listed for Deal (four were Wardens) while in 1848 sixty were recorded, all living in the North End. Although their official station was the Pilot House they also had rooms in the Customs House in the High Street. During the Napoleonic Wars Cinque Ports Pilots were employed to steer warships into the safety of the ports and harbours and, in recognition of their services, the Government issued tickets exempting them from impressment.

Pilots constantly faced danger. One of the most appalling incidents recorded

Lloyd's Signal Station and Time Ball Tower painted by Roget.

concerns the German brig, 'Guttenberg', lost on the Goodwins with twenty-five hands on 1 January 1860. Henry Pearson, a Deal pilot, was also drowned in the attempt to steer her through thick fog, tremendous wind and blinding snow. Rescue work was hampered because of the obstinacy of the Harbour Master to authorise the launch of Ramsgate lifeboat and steam tug owing to a technicality. On 22 May 1862 the pilot cutter, 'Princess', was rammed while cruising between Dover and Dungeness by a barque bound for London. Such was the force of the wind and waves that the anchor of the barque broke away and struck the cutter which lost her mast, bowsprit, sails and rigging. A Deal pilot, John Pembroke, and the mate, Joseph Pedven, tried to jump for safety but both were drowned.

A calamity involving the Dover Trinity House Pilot Cutter No. 4 was reported in 'Deal Telegram' (15 March 1879). The pilot ship left Dover Harbour for a routine night-time cruise in the Channel with a crew of eight men and twelve pilots aboard. It was run down by a Hamburg steamer just after midnight causing the death of fifteen men. All the pilots - seven from Dover, five from Deal and one from Kingsdown -lost their lives. (After 1873, Deal Pier was the point of embarkation of pilots aboard the Deal Pilot Cutter)

When the Duke of Wellington was installed as Lord Warden, he was also elected Elder Brother of the Cinque Ports Pilots. He took his role seriously and he relished the pomp and pageantry when, dressed in a blue coat with red collar, he walked ahead of the pilots, in their own smart uniform of blue coats and primrose waistcoats, in procession to St. James' Church where the Court of Lodemanage was traditionally held behind the Communion Table. The last Court was held at Dover on 21 October 1851. The Duke died shortly afterwards and thereafter the Cinque Ports Pilots came under the direct control of Trinity House in London.

Certainly, Cinque Ports Pilots were an influential body of gentlemen. They had a reputation for being difficult and refractory: they were definitely proud and haughty. They sported tall chimney pot hats when they walked to divine service on Sundays at St. Leonard's Church where they occupied their own reserved gallery built to commemorate the Great Storm of 1703. Stebbing recorded in 1937 that within memory a dozen pilots occupied this exclusive gallery (although local pilots were generally non-conformists). The churchyard has several memorials chiselled in stone: "Here Lyeth ye Body of John Blewitt Pilot he dyed November 1731 Aged 44 years". . "In Memory of John Adams pilot 1800 Aged 37 years". . . On these particular headstones carved faces beam over billowing clouds and tempestuous seas.

Lloyd's of London, the world famous corporation of underwriters, established an important station to deal with salvage services and shipping claims at Deal. Previously, shipping intelligence had been relayed to them by Messrs. George Hammond and Co., mercantile marine and consular agents, whose offices were situated opposite the Victorian pier. Business was brisk in the mid-19th century and Lloyd's realised the necessity of acquiring their own exclusive premises on the south-east coast. They found the ideal property next to the 'Port Arms' at the entrance to the Navy Yard.

'Beach House' had been the family home of the Bakers who had connections with the port since the 16th century. Sir Thomas Baker, Vice Admiral of the Red, had resided there and Captain Baker, MP for Hythe, entertained George II there in 1740. A flint-walled garden incorporated an elevated stage with a panorama of the Downs. Further, the property already possessed a tall flagpole from which the official white flag with the name LLOYD'S picked out in blue could be hoisted.

Lloyd's commenced business at 'Beach House' in December 1852. They employed their own staff who were supervised by Commander Nott, R.N. William Wells was appointed signalman at the considerable salary of 52 pounds per annum. His duties included identifying sailing ships arriving, sailing and sheltering in the Downs and reporting messages from merchant vessels when required. Firms and companies were therefore swiftly advised of the precise movements of their ships which enabled them to make appropriate preparations for docking and loading cargo.

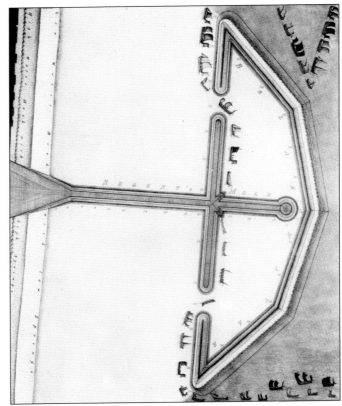

The proposed mole and breakwater by Spence in 1815. © National Maritime Museum.

When the lease expired in 1887 Lloyd's moved its signal station to an abandoned Custom's Watch House in Beach Street. The acquisition of this property was fortuitous because buildings on the east side of Beach Street were about to be removed to develop the South Esplanade. Among the ancient buildings that were demolished for improvements to the promenade were 'Royal House', owned by Richard Fox, baker and confectioner, which boasted a barometer set into the wall, and 'The Fountain Inn', where was located the Downs Pilots' bell.

Eventually, Lloyd's conceded that the old Watch House was itself ripe for demolition and they again sought alternative premises. Their third seafront office was 33 Beach Street (now 'The Fo'c'sle fishing tackle shop) opposite the iron pier where the pilots landed and were able to offer worthwhile information to the insurance company. When the number of sailing ships diminished, business dwindled and Lloyd's closed their signal station at Deal in 1903. Their affairs were handled for a modest remuneration by the Coastguard and the immense flagpole was removed to their station at the North End. This mutual agreement between Lloyd's and the Coastguard remained until 1963.

In 1855, the extent of the Port and legal Quays of Deal was defined:

Beach mission photographed by Edgar Tarry Adams.
Courtesy: National Museum of Photography, Film and Television.

"That the limits of the said Port shall commence at the Ness point corner of St. Margaret's Bay, being the eastern limit of the Port of Dover, and proceed along the coast of the County of Kent as far as a place called North Shore on the north side of the River Stour - thence along the north side of the river throughout its course over the flats and including the said river and across Brake-sand and Gull stream and north end of the Goodwin Sands to the north end of Trinity Bay, being the western boundaries of Ramsgate, including all other rivers, bays, channels, bars, strands, harbours, havens, streams, creeks and places within the said limits, and shall extend seawards to a distance of three miles. . ."

Over the centuries there were various schemes - a few perfectly feasible - to construct a harbour at Deal. The earliest known concerns "the late cut by Rogers in King Edward the Sixth tyme" which was incorporated into the plan to alleviate Sandwich Haven (circa 1548) seriously considered by the Secretary of State, William Burghley, and still held at his stately home, Hatfield House. The proposed canal would have terminated in a harbour adjacent to Sandown Castle. In 1624 Robert Jager drew up a similar plan to make a 'cut' linking Sandwich with Sandown where the harbour entrance would be guarded by a fort. Jager's map has a lengthy caption: "A true and lively description of His Majesty's Roade the Downes, and His Highenes towne and Port of Sandwich; shewing how commodious and necessary a new haven to Sandwich would be for his Majesty's Service, the good of the kingdomme and preserving many

140

hundreds of his subjects lives, ships and goods in tyme of fowle weather, staying for a wind in the Downes."

In 1735 the idea of a 'cut' was revived. The engineer, Charles Labelye, "late Teacher of the Mathematicks in the Royal Navy" was commissioned to investigate the site between Sandwich and Sandown. The coast was again surveyed and an ambitious project devised. According to Labelye the new harbour would "commodiously admit 150 sail of the largest Merchant Ships with sufficient Room in the middle for ships to pass and repass." Twin piers jutted out like callipers into the Downs and ships would pass between them along a canal to enter the oval-shaped harbour. The scheme was strongly supported by the local gentry but then the directors were accused of embezzlement. (Pritchard offers the alternative explanation that all available resources were needed for wartime engagements with France and Spain).

In 1744, a further plan was made to construct a harbour to accommodate large merchantmen and warships northwards of Sandown Castle. This, it was lauded, would be "of great use and advantage to the naval power of Great Britain, by preserving ships in distress, speedily refitting them for sea and saving the lives of His Majesty's subjects in time of war." A committee of the House of Commons reported in its favour and preparations were made to purchase the required land but when the enormous cost of the scheme was released it was vetoed. Instead, a counter proposal was made to develop Ramsgate's Royal Harbour.

In 1812 Sir John Rennie, who had designed Deal's first pier, suggested that the Small Downs, lying between the Sandhills shoreline and the bank called the 'Brake', be converted into a Harbour of Refuge encompassing over one thousand acres. His suggestion was declined once it was established that the sandbank actually appeared to move. In 1825 Thomas Telford, civil engineer, revised Rennie's proposal but applying cheaper labour and materials. This latest notion was linked with a plan to build a canal at North Deal that would run through Lydden Valley and connect with Canterbury.

Most intriguing was the plan prepared by Graeme Spence, Maritime Surveyor to the Admiralty, to construct the Regent's Mole and Break-Water at Deal in 1815. He prepared several plans of a mole stretching out from the King's Yard next to the Anchor Yard south of Deal Castle towards Deal Bank with a curved protective wall. This, he affirmed, would provide "a safe and commodious landing-place, or Harbour, for the accommodation and shelter of the Boats of Men-of-War, the Revenue, merchantmen, those belonging to Deal; and all other Boats and small craft who have Business to transact at Deal, or with Shipping in the Downs." Alas, this noble scheme did not come to fruition.

In 1838 an admirable scheme was proposed by a highly regarded civil engineer, Mr. Cundy. His idea was to construct a harbour to the north of Sandown Castle with spacious docks annexed on the site of the Sandhills. His sensible plan included a rail link via Canterbury, Chatham, Woolwich and Deptford to London. Nothing materialised. Another London engineer, Charles Capper, passed a bill through Parliament for the formation of a 'Downs Harbour and Dock Company' in 1864. The following year, Capper stood for Parliament in the General Election but was unsuccessful although he won at the by-election where he narrowly defeated Mr. Thomas Brassey, the competition revolving mainly on the harbour. Work was abandoned, despite the marginal victory and, although the scheme was revived towards the end of that century, nothing ever came of the proposed 'Deal Docks'.

Instead, it appeared to the authorities, it would be far more feasible to develop Dover Harbour. Already the advent of steam in the Victorian era meant that naval vessels need no longer halt in the Downs to take on board fresh provisions nor await a benevolent wind to carry them down Channel. Further, the lack of a suitable harbour meant that Deal could never compete as a viable commercial port despite the new fast rail link with London. During the mid-19th century Dover began to be developed on a grand scale. The Duke of Wellington, while publicly expressing sympathy with the local boatmen, was deeply involved with the expansion of Wellington Docks in Dover Harbour. Consequently Deal's prosperity as a port rapidly declined and in 1881 its status was officially demoted to that of a 'Creek'.

Promenading in Sunday best.

NAVY YARD

'The King's Store House'

DEALS' NAVY YARD , which came to prominence just as England began to emerge as the dominant sea power of Europe, was an important link in a chain of naval bases along the south coast. Its dual purpose was to repair warships and victual the fleet assembled in the Downs, that important rendezvous for men-o'-war from the 17th to the 19th centuries.

The Yard was administered by the Navy Board which, together with the Admiralty, was responsible for governing naval affairs from the reign of Henry VIII until William IV. At the height of its industry the bustling Yard employed a vast team of shipwrights, blacksmiths, carpenters, coopers, chandlers, brewers, bakers, rope and sail makers. Although the Port Admiral at Deal was nominally in charge 'The King's Store House' was administered by a civilian whose official title was 'Storekeeper'.

When Henry VIII established the Royal Navy he placed the responsibility of victualling the fleet in the Downs with Thomas Wingfield, First Captain of Deal Castle, in 1543. Later it became apparent that castle officials could no longer cope with the increasing workload, particularly during the Civil War, and so services to warships were put out to tender. In 1651 John Culmer was commissioned to take charge of a modest victualling yard although he soon complained that there was a marked lack of provision in the existing stores.

Culmer's multifarious duties were to provide food and water to ships in the Downs; to provide rope and capstans for hauling ships' boats up the beach; to provide shingle to outgoing ships requiring ballast and to sell surplus stores and redundant boats "by inch of candle". In 1657 Admiral Montagu recommended him for an increase in salary which indicates that he was certainly proficient. At one time Culmer was required to accompany Sir Richard Stayner in a house-to-house search for cargo filched from the ship, 'Princess Maria', in 1658.

In 1660, when a survey of stores was conducted on the orders of Sir William Batten, it was reported that the Naval Commissioners were responsible for "six or seven storehouses built on a waste: some call it the King's, and some the Bishop's". From this, it is conjectured, that these storehouses erected to meet the needs of the Navy were situated north of Deal Castle on land which was part of the Archbishop of Canterbury's manor.

Another important duty was to provide the fleet with water. In 1665 the Earl of Sandwich advised the Admiralty to station a pair of boats at Deal for this purpose and so Culmer obligingly equipped his own fleet of longboats and pinnaces as water boats. Culmer, too, was responsible for sweeping the roadstead for lost anchors and cables. He seems to have inherited this task from Robert Rands and George Hudson, previously engaged by the Admiralty to keep the Narrow Seas free of obstructions. Culmer's plan was to employ local boatmen in this arduous task and recompense them according to their success. Culmer died in 1671 and he lies buried in St. Martin's Church, Great Mongeham.

Samuel Pepys, the diarist, was appointed Clerk of the Acts in the Navy Office but was later promoted to Secretary to the Lord High Admiral, James, Duke of York (later James II). Pepys used his influence at court to secure for his brother-in-law, Balthazar St. Michel, the post of Muster Master at Deal. In 1668 'Balty' indeed became Muster Master for the Downs Squadron but later he seems to have combined this office with that of Admiralty Agent for the ports of Deal, Dover and Ramsgate. He continued to rent Mrs. Culmer's "ground, cellar and storehouse" and naively promised that "he will take care that she keeps the capstans in good repair". Balty lodged with his French parents at Deal. Later, Pepys arranged first for his own clerk, Tom Edwards, who was married to his servant, Jane, and then for their son, who had been named Sam in his honour, to succeed as Muster Master and Naval Agent.

During Balty's period of office a vessel known as the Deal yacht was attached to the Navy Yard. In 1674 her master was James Hudson and her crew was formed from local boatmen. In 1679 the master and mate, both described as "Downes" men, were Robert Smith and Edward Ward whilst St. Michel was styled 'Commander'. The accounts in connection with this vessel from 1674 to 1679 are signed 'B. St. Michel'.

Abraham Stock, who was Muster Master, Admiralty Agent and Store Keeper until

Launch of a lugger alongside the Navy Yard painted by Lt. Henry Wisc Harvey c.1840.

*The grandiloquent Superintendent's House
in the Navy Yard.*

1696, received a high wage. The accounts reveal that he was paid one hundred pounds annually with a generous allowance for himself and his servant's victuals. Thomas Warren, a former clerk at the Admiralty, succeeded him on 15 September 1696. Previously he had been Muster Master serving aboard H.M.S. 'William' of the Red Squadron at Spithead.

At this time the exact location of the Admiralty Depot at Deal is unknown but it seems the naval stores were scattered about the town and some were a great distance from the sea. Evidently the site of the main building proved inadequate since, according to Warren, there was "hardly room to coil a small cable for it is the worst place for a storehouse I have ever seen in my life, not only because it's so small but it's in the back part of the town which necessitates the use of carts".

Wisely, Warren suggested to the Navy Board that it would be more economical if it was situated nearer the sea. Further, a survey revealed that the stores themselves were frequently unserviceable and unsuitable for the types of warship using the Downs. This resulted in such items as grapnels, cordage and yawls being purchased from local merchants and boat builders. Prominent among these businessmen was Benjamin Hulke who was handsomely paid by the Crown for his yawls.

The proposal to build a Navy Yard on land close to the foreshore leased from the Archbishop came to fruition in October 1703. The plot defined in the lease measured four hundred and ninety feet from Deal Castle and one hundred and seventy feet from the town. It was two hundred feet on the north and south sides, one hundred and fifty feet on the east, fifty-three feet on the west and eighty feet from the high water mark. The whole area was enclosed by a wall and bordered by a six-feet wide footway on the north, south and west. There was to be a capstan ground occupying two hundred and ten feet north to south. Buildings might be erected only with permission from the Archbishop although this was never withheld.

Immediately, disaster struck! Deal and the Downs were devastated by the 'Great Storm' which swept southern England late the following month. The Yard's new storehouses, boathouses and storekeeper's abode were severely damaged. Warren requested the Navy Board to supply replacement masts, rigging, cordage, anchors and cables to patch up the surviving ships. Temporary repairs were carried out at the Navy Yard but the ships were then dispatched for major refits to the larger dockyards at Chatham, Sheerness, Woolwich and Portsmouth. Apart from the tremendous loss of life, the worst legacy was the hundreds of square miles of oak forest that was laid waste which decimated the home-grown raw material needed to provide future warships.

Work was swiftly begun on repairs. By the end of March 1704 a certificate was sent to their Lordships:

That Mr. Hall of London House, carpenter, in pursuance with his contract with the Admiralty and the Principal Commissioners of H.M. Navy of 20 April, 1703 hath (illegible) well, and in workmanlike manner framed, erected and built for H.M. Service at the South end of Deal on the ground there staked out for him:

Brick Great Storehouse	£ 419 0s 0d
One Lodging House built of brick for the Storekeeper	£ 419 16s 9d
Three Boathouses	£ 264
Sheds	£ 169 16s 9d
Fence Wall	£ 80 9d
Yard Gate ceramics instead of balls	£ 8
Five Capstans	£ 40
Iron spikes on top of fence wall	(illegible)
In all amounting to the sum of	£1749 6s 6d

This certificate was signed by Charles Finch, Matthew Spray, Thomas Warren and Benjamin Hulke.

The following additions were later considered necessary to complete the 'Queen's Buildings' at Deal:

A necessary House, there being no such conveniency provided for in the whole of the buildings. . .
An office for the Storekeeper and Clerks to write in. . .
An outhouse for washing and brewing. . .
The Water to be laid into the buildings. . . A little place for the Watchman fixed with a Bell to be struck in the night as practised in the Yards.

The cost of this supplementary work was £197 10s 0d with an extra £98 to repair the damage caused by the 'Great Storm'.

The Navy Yard had now begun its existence by the sea and it was to render valuable service to the Royal Navy for the next one hundred and sixty years. However, the Yard's early years were beset with problems since stores were imported and transported by boat because the roads were often impassable. Money was often unavailable to pay contractors' bills and the wages of seamen and labourers often fell into arrears. The political climate was precarious with Whigs and Tories constantly squabbling and government officials at that time were notorious for being inefficient or corrupt.

Warren's duties as Muster Master included checking the ships' companies in the Downs to ensure that the names and numbers borne on the ships' books corresponded with those actually on board. This was an onerous task since it was an habitual custom for Captains and Pursers to claim funds for fictitious crew members. (Even Lord Nelson was guilty of this pernicious practice) As Admiralty Agent, Warren was required to report to the Navy Board the arrival and departure of ships in the Downs (presumably by riders to and from London) provide them with pilots, act as a postman for Government despatches and also as a Judge Advocate at Courts Martial.

Another concern was for stranded seamen who required board and lodging. Superintendents were responsible for the care of sick or injured seamen landed ashore but funds for their accommodation and medication were woefully insufficient. Warren wrote a letter to the Admiralty in December, 1705, hoping to bring his plight to the attention of the Lord High Admiral, who was at that time Prince George, consort of Queen Anne:

> "This is a wild road at this season especially, and both men and boats are more exposed here than in any other part of England, and I may say that of the nine years I have lived here I never knew such storms as has been these last three winters. I thought it my duty to represent the poor seamen's case, there being no provision made for such accidents or distress."

Warren was also required to prepare estimates and settle accounts which was complicated by the fact that during the latter part of the seventeenth century there was a currency crisis arising from the debasement of the silver coinage as a result of clipping. This caused "confusion among the gentlemen and shopkeepers hereabouts." Additionally, Warren was responsible for collecting dues from shipping in the Downs for the maintenance of the Scilly and Eddystone Lighthouses. For this he was paid a handsome commission of three shillings in the pound. When he learned that other collectors were receiving four shillings, however, Warren asked the officials of Trinity House to rectify this and they responded by adjusting his payment. Warren received a separate fee for each of his numerous tasks and this ensured that he was a comparatively wealthy man.

Frequently Warren complained to the Admiralty that he was overloaded with work. Apparently he was "obliged to muster afloat two or three times a week" and he lacked both suitable craft and appropriate assistance. He was forced to hire local boats at an extravagant rate and these he dismissed as "paper-sided" since their owners were constantly claiming compensation for damage. (They were always complaining that naval ships' boats had damaged their own capstans) Further, there were no cranes at this time and therefore all the stores had to be manhandled in the Yard.

Justifiably, Warren considered his staff should be increased by one clerk and two boatmen. The clerk was required for dealing with the increasing amount of paperwork arising from the expansion of the Yard. The boatmen were needed for the salvage of anchors and cables frequently lost by warships as a result of inclement weather. A clerk, Jonathan Pordon, was eventually appointed after much haggling but recruitment of boatmen proved more difficult since they found it far more lucrative assisting merchantmen and salvaging wrecks on the Goodwins than working full time for the Admiralty.

Naturally Warren was concerned about security. He devised an alarm system for warning the town of enemy attack and organised a watch of four men from dusk to dawn. The Navy Board, however, considered the employment of watchmen at one shilling apiece unnecessary because of the close proximity of Deal Castle. Warren's response was scathing:

> "As that Garrison is at present established it is of little more benefit than barely to say we are under the protection of the Castle as being near it, for there is but four old men belong to it who don't live there but in town - two of them watch at night and generally in their cabins, for I will row every night in the week under all three Castles, and land and go round under them and never be hailed to know who or what I am. . ."

Warren was a respected figure as befitted his position as Superintendent of this important Naval Yard. He was involved in local affairs and became a close acquaintance of the Puritan Mayor of Deal, Thomas Powell. Indeed, Warren, himself, was elected Deal's Mayor in 1795. Together they signed the contract for the building of St. George's Chapel-of-Ease, a project supported by the admirals and captains of warships in the Downs. The contract for building the roof was given to the same London carpenter named Hall who had been responsible for rebuilding the Navy Yard.

Warren, himself, inhabited a substantial brick-built house in South Street. This was mentioned in a letter to the Archbishop as "a very pretty dwelling" consisting of "four small rooms on a floor". The Storekeeper's House must have been greatly extended over the years for it was described in an advertisement for its eventual sale as being "a comfortable dwelling containing twelve rooms, bath house fitted with hot and cold water, outbuildings, pleasure grounds, greenhouse, garden, stabling, etc." A public footpath ran before the house and cut slantways across the Yard in the direction of the former 'Deal Castle Inn' in Prospect Place. Another narrow footpath separated the southern limit of the Yard and the Castle moat.

At the northern entrance to the Navy Yard stood the 'Port Arms'. This was one of the hostelries that refused to billet soldiers sent to act against the smugglers in 1776. It

Prospect Place now Victoria Road.

148

seems never to have changed its name throughout its long history and its sign still proudly displays the town crest.

Prospect Place (now 'Victoria Road') marked the western extremity of the Navy Yard. Pritchard says that a rope-walk the length of Prospect Place ran from Lower Street to the Turnpike Gate which was opposite Deal Castle. A Victorian engraving by G. Hayward shows the view northwards, looking towards the belvedere surmounting Huntley's drapery and furnishing shop. On the left of the picture is a picturesque row of cottages, redolent of the sea. From the top windows of these modest dwellings there was a prospect over the roofs of the naval buildings towards the Downs. Captains, pilots and boatbuilders inhabited these homes which still retain a nautical air with their boat-shaped porches and porthole-shaped windows. Originally, the road was curved with a wide sweep at the bottom of South Street which was later widened to accommodate the busy stage coach terminus. Influential folk inhabited the grander houses of this commercial quarter. Most prominent was the residence of Comfort Kingsmill, nine times Mayor of Deal.

On the west side of Prospect Place was 'Cottage Row'. This consisted of a few small dwellings and a tiny dispensary which became the cottage hospital. From a bequest in a will land was purchased and an infirmary built for injured seamen in 1863. To celebrate Queen Victoria's Diamond Jubilee the building was adapted to a general hospital with five beds and the name was changed to 'Victoria Hospital' in 1897. Later, this noble building became the public library but it has since been converted to luxury flats.

A succession of Storekeepers followed Thomas Warren - Lancelot Burton, Jonas Benjamin and George Lawrence. Lawrence, who had previously acted as Secretary to General Byng, unjustly shot for cowardice, was appointed to this prestigious office in 1779. He was the most famous of the Storekeepers and he was responsible for the Navy Yard during its peak of expansion during the protracted French Wars. At that time it served the dual purpose of refitting and victualling the fleet although the two parts were unenclosed and undivided.

Four slipways - some double - with capstans were ordered to be assembled to enable ships' boats to be hauled up the shingle with comparative ease into the Deal Yard. There was a race against time to build these enormous slipways since the arduous task of digging away the shingle was attended by deterioration in the weather as the season advanced. Lawrence waited anxiously for timber to arrive by lighters from Woolwich and all the time he was counting the cost of the exorbitant charge for local labour.

New workshops were constructed to enable craftsmen to provide every conceivable commodity such as cables, ropes, rigging, masts, spars, pitch, planks, paint and ironmongery. Repair facilities now included saw pits, smith's shop, seasoning house and sail loft. Vast storehouses were erected to house everything from seamen's beds to signal flags although the Yard supplied mainly boats and clothing at Deal. A separate victualling house contained a wash house and cooper's shop. A bakery baked ships' biscuits while a brewhouse brewed beer. Formerly, these provisions were provided by Dover bakers and brewers but they were often stolen by privateers when ships rounded the South Foreland.

The whole area now covered five acres and was enclosed by high walls with three entrances: South Street, Prospect Place (now 'Victoria Road') and along the seafront which was also protected by a Promenade. Remarkably, gates for the Navy Yard survive and grace the entrance to Felderland Farm at Worth-next-Sandwich.

The problem of supplying the anchored fleet with fresh water remained. Originally, this was drawn from numerous wells sunk in various parts of the town. However, these were affected by the rise and fall of the tide and their water was often brackish. A concerted effort was made, therefore, to bore a deep hole to provide a better supply of water in the Navy Yard. A well was sunk to a depth of two hundred feet but the engines were unable to cope with the salt water that constantly gushed into it. The project was abandoned after the enormous sum of £8,000 had been expended on the project.

There was always a risk of fire in the Navy Yard and three fire engines were stored there for that purpose. Occasionally, townsfolk had resort to these primitive machines. In 1796, Mr King's hemp loft, which stored government property, caught alight and was totally destroyed although some new buildings nearby were saved. In 1859 plumbers restoring the ramparts of Sandown Castle accidentally melted the lead but the fire was soon under control when two Coastguards summoned the engines from the Navy Yard.

During the French Wars security was exceptionally tight. The Government ordered all beach boats to be hidden in case they could be stolen by escaping prisoners-of-war. Pilfering in the Yard increased and the guard, which had formerly consisted of the four elderly watchmen, was at last replaced by armed members of the Cumberland Militia. At first they were billeted in the crane house but a request was made for a proper guardhouse with a fireplace for winter months.

Deal Shutter Telegraph Tower.
Courtesy: Dover Museum.

Lord Nelson instructed the Navy Yard to construct craft for a midnight commando raid on Napoleon's shipping assembled off the coast of France in the summer of 1801. These were specially designed flat-bottomed boats that would slide easily into shallow harbours. Additionally, the boats were ordered to be equipped with either brass eight-inch howitzers or twenty-four pounder carronades. Mr. Lawrence assured Nelson that twelve or fourteen of these boats would be ready at the beginning of August and he immediately sent for stores and ammunition to Dover. The skilled boatmen employed in the construction of these boats petitioned the Navy Board for an increase in their pay and this was readily granted. All this activity attracted the attention of Napoleon who was assembling his Grand Armee on the cliffs at Boulogne and he despatched spies to report on the building of boats in the Navy Yard.

150

A patriotic band concert inside the navy yard.

George Lawrence died in office after nearly thirty years of loyal service. His tombstone is located in St. George's Churchyard: "George Lawrence, Esq., 31st Oct., 1897, in the 81st year of his age. Twenty-eight years Naval storekeeper at Deal". He was succeeded by Joseph Trousnell, formerly secretary to Lord Gambier on his expedition to Copenhagen.

In 1811 an Act of Parliament was passed enabling the Archbishop to grant an extended ninety-nine years' lease on the Navy Yard and the next year this was obtained by the Admiralty. The premium or fine paid was £7,959 but this included various plots of land contiguous to the Navy Yard. In 1813 another Act was passed which sanctioned the sale of the land to the Admiralty and the Archbishop, therefore, disposed of the entire property. The following year saw the Peace of France and, as a consequence, a projected further extension to the Yard was abandoned.

The Navy Yard had been the terminus in a long line of overland shutter telegraph stations that linked The Admiralty in London with the Port of Deal during the Napoleonic Wars. (Early primitive visual signalling had consisted of flags hoisted on church towers by day or fires lit in baskets hoisted at night to warn of the approach of an enemy by sea) In 1796, a shutter telegraph was installed atop Admiralty House which could communicate simple messages rapidly with the Admiralty in Westminster. This was an improvement by five hours on the slower speeds of the mail coach in the early stages of the wars. The Navy Yard purchased land on the west side of Prospect Place (now 7 - 9 Victoria Road) presumably so as not to obscure the signal being sent to the next station along the line at Betteshanger Farm. In 1815 a telegraphic chain of ships between Ostend and Deal was established, presumably using this system, when war seemed imminent after Napoleon's escape from Elba.

In 1820 a modern semaphore signalling tower was constructed just inside the northern entrance of the Navy Yard. The line from London, however, was never completed and a coastal link was formed instead which assisted the Coastal Blockade in their suppression of smugglers. In 1855 this Royal Signal Tower was equipped with a time ball which was linked by electric current directly with the Royal Observatory at Greenwich. The ball was dropped daily at 1 p.m. to enable ship's masters in the Downs to set their chronometers accurately. Coincidentally, this meant that Deal was the first town to receive Greenwich mean time. During the Great War the time ball was removed and a gun mounted on its platform atop the tower. In 1927 the time ball was superseded by radio signals broadcast at specific times for the benefit of shipping worldwide. Today, the ball is dropped hourly purely as a tourist attraction while the tower contains a museum dedicated to time and communication.

The Royal Navy Coast Blockade was formed to stamp out smuggling along the Kent and Sussex coast in 1816. Its command was entrusted to Captain William McCulloch, known as 'Flogging Joey'. He ordered fast, sleek, working galleys to assist his men in their pursuit of smugglers at sea to be constructed at the Navy Yard. These were clinker built, about twenty-eight feet long and pulling six or eight oars. Usually they were painted white in order to conceal them as they sliced through the surf.

Throughout the fourteen years of the existence of the Blockade arrangements for the supply and repair of galleys continued to be made through the Navy Yard. Boats were delivered and returned by service tender. McCulloch was keen to assure the authorities at the Navy Board: "All Bosuns' and Carpenters' stores for the service of the Blockade are drawn from Deal Navy Yard. . ." The Captain occupied a suite of rooms with his secretary in the Port Admiral's office, a grim building exposed to the elements, in the Navy Yard.

The Port Admiral, whose naval command was principally the warships in the Downs, also took responsibility for the Yard. At first he inhabited this draughty mansion at the northern entrance. In 1811 the Government purchased an alternative house in Queen Street, owned by a solicitor and banker, as the Port Admiral's residence. Stebbing dismisses this house as "a strictly utilitarian building, pine-panelled and poorly staircased, with its roof hidden behind a parapet".

Buildings in the Navy Yard. Courtesy: Deal Library.

'Admiralty House' contained one of the former banker's strong rooms where was stored considerable consignments of bullion landed at Deal. These were unloaded at the port to avoid capture by privateers and guarded by marines until they were transferred under military escort to London. In 1813 twenty-five tons of specie, gold and silver bars and gold dust were landed from H.M.S. 'Bedford'. Later that year the Navy Yard boats brought ashore two million pounds worth of money in dollars and gold from Jamaica. In July 1814 forty-eight tons of specie were landed and forwarded to the Bank of England in ten wagons under a military guard. In 1815 the office of Port Admiral at Deal ceased and the property was let.

The key to a 'Plan of His Majesty's Naval Yard, Deal' (1831) lists the important features: Admiral's office, naval officers' houses, guard house, mast house, smith's shop, saw pits, store houses, sail loft above cordage stores, officers' offices, telegraph, boathouses, slipways, cesspool, seasoning house, washing block, cooper's shop, engine house for pumping sewage with a note for the proposed victualling yards. An area marked west of the 'Road from Dover' also belonged to the Navy Yard. Probably, this is the garden that was acquired to allow the shutter telegraph to be viewed from the next station - Betteshanger Farm.

After Napoleon's defeat, the period of wars and alarms ceased for Deal and Walmer. The result was that naval presence was reduced in the Downs and fewer officers resided in the Port. After the French Wars the officer in charge of the Navy Yard was styled Captain Superintendent in line with other smaller dockyards such as Sheerness and Milford Haven. (The four main dockyards were supervised by Admiral Superintendents)

In 1830 Captain A.A. Vincent, R.N., was appointed Captain Superintendent. After two years he was promoted to Rear Admiral and he became Gentleman Usher to Queen Adelaide. He died at Walmer in 1862. Commander Edward Boys, R.N., succeeded him. He was instrumental in rejuvenating the seafront by developing the Esplanade between Broad Street and King Street in a determined attempt to "improve both the trade and the town". But when Charles Wootton was

Navy Yard gates.

The boat in which Captain Bligh was cast adrift by mutineers from 'The Bounty' was ordered to be built at Deal. At the last minute this order was rescinded and the ship's boats were made elsewhere.

In 1808 a boat from the guardship, HMS. 'Bombay', was conveying stores to the Navy Yard when it capsized drowning fourteen crew members.

During the demolition of the Navy Yard a skeleton with its skull penetrated by a canon ball was unearthed.

Apparently, the slipways for the Yard were constructed of sturdy oak timbers. They were built so high that a man could walk underneath them without removing his hat.

When supplying ships in the Downs four round trips could be made in a single day by the boatmen from the Navy Yard. Half this time was taken up in hauling up boats ready to be relaunched!

appointed clerk in charge of the Navy Yard, he closed the Naval Promenade and the northern footpath and they were not opened again to the public until Admiral Lord Paget, M.P., used his influence with the Admiralty in 1858.

A 'Journal' by Joseph Robins published in 1834 describes the Navy Yard in its years of decline:

> "The Naval and victualling establishment at this port, although, on a small scale, is of considerable importance, as being the nearest Naval station to the coast of France, and on account of the number of King's ships which, in time of war, are stationed in, and continually resorting to, the Downs. The exposed nature of the roadstead causes the frequent loss of anchors and cables; and from the facilities of this yard affords for sending off a prompt supply, renders it necessary for the ships to leave the station to repair their losses at a distant port. From thence the North Sea fleet, during the last war, chiefly obtained their supplies of stores... The acting storekeeper is Mr Pembroke."

A dramatic painting, 'Launching a Deal Lugger in a Heavy Gale' (1840) by Henry Wise Harvey shows a lugger racing down a slipway taking an anchor and cable to a warship in the Downs. Sturdy boatmen wear oilskins and sou'westers. There is a fascinating view of the gates, buildings and the watch bell of the Navy Yard. Also viewed are Walmer Road Mill northwards of Deal Castle and the Guardship moored off Walmer Castle.

Three major factors - the lack of a harbour, lasting peace with France and the advent of steam propulsion - contributed to the decline of Deal's Navy Yard. The Admiralty considered Sheerness to be far better placed to supply naval warships which now tended to anchor at the Nore. Their Lordships decided to close the Navy Yard and remove the stores to Chatham. In 1864 all the land, with the exception of the Time Ball Tower, was sold by auction to the Conservative Land Society for £13,200.

Deal's Navy Yard was demolished and laid out as a residential estate named 'Victoria Town Estate' in honour of Queen Victoria. At the period of their construction the impressive villas were considered the height of fashion and the builders were immensely proud of their achievement. Today, these desirable residences retain their florid ornamentation - portrait keystones, coloured glass and painted tiles decorated with exotic animals and birds. On the seaward side a grand esplanade was created when Pier Parade was connected with Victoria Parade in 1892. At the southern end stood the imposing Prince of Wales Terrace and the grandiloquent 'South Eastern Hotel' (later 'The Queen's Hotel') built by the South Eastern Railway Company.

THE GREAT STORM

'The late dreadful tempest'

THE GREAT STORM that swept across the country in November 1703 wreaked havoc throughout England. The full force of it was felt in the Downs where four great men-o'-war and twelve hundred sailors perished. A third of the home fleet was wiped out in a single night in an event which is regarded as the worst natural disaster in the dappled history of the Royal Navy.

During late autumn a cyclone rapidly crossed the Atlantic from the coast of North America to Britain. Duration of the storm was thirteen days overall with gales commencing on Friday 19 November and lasting for approximately three days. A period of relative calm followed, with the wind noticeably decreasing, but then it steadily increased from Thursday 25 November onwards. It reached its full strength on the night of Friday 26 November and early morning of Saturday 27 November when it battered its way through the darkness in an east-north-easterly direction across Kent.

The hurricane - "comparable to the worst in tropical climes" - was recorded by Earl Stanhope in his monumental 'History of the Reign of Queen Anne' (1780). According to this chronicler, the height of the storm was from about 11 p.m. on 26 November and continued to its full fury until about 7 a.m. the following day. All through that month the weather had been boisterous yet it gave no intimation of the impending doom. When the wind arose from the south-west it was "so high that between gusts it sounded like thunder in the distance". There was no actual thunder nor lightning - and indeed little rain - yet in some places the air was apparently full of meteoric flashes which resembled the latter. "In general, however, the darkness added to the terror," asserts Stanhope, "for it was just Full Moon."

Destruction was indiscriminate as strong winds swept Southern England - from Bristol to Norfolk - that stormy month. Trees were torn from their roots and houses were levelled with the ground. Steeples toppled and towers reeled. Lead from public buildings was torn up "like a Roll of Parchment" and blown great distances while the shredded sails of windmills were swept around so violently that "the Timbers and Wheels have heat and so set the rest on Fire." Traffic was disrupted and even stage coaches with six horses were confined to their post houses. It was estimated that eight thousand people lost their lives. Folk readily accepted that the storm was divine punishment for 'Nationall sinns'. To some, it seemed, truly the end of the world was nigh.

During the first night of the hurricane, the original Eddystone Lighthouse was swept into the sea with all its occupants. This first true offshore lighthouse had been designed by Henry Winstanley and completed in 1698. Sixty candles in the lantern room atop its sweeping stone tower warned of the danger from rocks to ships approaching Plymouth Sound. The eccentric architect was so confident of its stability that he had openly expressed his desire to be in his 'Edy-Stone Light-House' during "the greatest storm that ever blew under the face of the heavens". Ironically, he had his presumptuous wish fulfilled in a manner he had not anticipated.

In London the steeples of almost every church designed by Wren were damaged. Westminster Hall was flooded while at Whitehall the guardhouse roof collapsed. Part of the Palace of St. James was blown away and one woman was killed by flying debris. Queen Anne and Prince George were roused and escorted to safety just as a stack of chimneys crashed through the ceiling of their bedroom. They watched through the windows as acacias, limes and elms were uprooted by the savagery of the wind. Damage in the City was estimated in excess of one million pounds. (Wisely, the managers of the new playhouse at Lincoln's Inn Fields withdrew their production of Shakespeare's 'The Tempest')

London's Thames was a scene of devastation. The river became choked with wrecks and water gushed over the embankments and flooded the City. Above London Bridge five hundred wherries were lost while sixty barges sank in the region of Hammersmith Bridge. Valuable cargoes - tea, tobacco, sugar - were spoiled. Ships in the Lower Reaches were blown all the way from Execution Dock and Limehouse Hole to The Bight. There, Newcastle colliers and East Indiamen were thrown together - bow to stern - where they dashed each other to splinters.

The Great Storm of 1703 © National Maritime Museum.

In Kent alone one thousand dwellings were shattered, chimney stacks crashed in their hundreds of thousands and a great number of people were killed as they slept. At Whitstable, a hoy was sucked up by a whirlwind and thrown across the land where it struck a passer-by. At Broadstairs, blazing coals were blown from the brazier atop the tower of the North Foreland lighthouse. There was great havoc in the countryside. Rivers flooded and marshland swamped. Boats rowed through fields to rescue stranded folk. On farms, barns and stables were destroyed with injury to horses and cattle. In woods and forests, thousands of newly planted English oaks were felled. Their timber was required to build new warships and would be needed to repair those battered by the storm. Thus the Royal Navy suffered a double defeat.

Along the southern coast the damage to shipping was phenomenal. Wreckage and bodies were strewn along the shore. Havoc was caused among the great concentration of shipping in Yarmouth Roads. The worst disaster, however, occurred in the Downs. Violence began about one o'clock on the morning of 27 November when the wind - blowing from W.S.W. to S.S.W. - was whipped up to hurricane force. Over two hundred merchant vessels of all shapes and sizes - hoys, snows, brigs, brigantines - were already sheltering from the wild weather which had plagued the south coast the previous fortnight.

When the storm broke it turned the famous Anchorage into a scene of devastation. Ship after ship was ripped from its moorings and thrown upon either the Goodwins or the Brake Sand. Captains ordered hemp cables to be axed in an attempt to stop their ships capsizing and mainmasts with their torn canvases to be toppled in an endeavour to prevent them careering out of control. Distress guns boomed out from all directions and lights were kindled to call for assistance. Even the hardy Deal boatmen dared not launch into the savage seas. They were reduced to watching the sad spectacle - illuminated momentarily by sheet lightning - through telescopes from the shore.

The Grand Fleet, consisting of about eighteen men-o'-war with tenders and victuallers, under the command of Sir Cloudesley Shovell, Admiral of the White, had just returned from a fierce campaign against the French and Spanish in the Mediterranean. The return

Sir Cloudesley Shovell by Michael Dahl © National Maritime Museum.

157

voyage had been atrocious - 1,500 men had died through sickness and starvation - and three-quarters of the survivors were in poor health. Nevertheless, their captains dared not risk putting their men ashore in case they deserted. Instead, most were content to winter - undermanned - in the overcrowded Downs.

Admiral Shovell, aboard 'Triumph', decided to take advantage of a lull in the storm. Thus - on Wednesday 24 November - he decided to escort several of his stout first and second rate warships - 'Association', 'St. George', 'Russell', Dorsetshire', 'Royal Oak' and 'Revenge' - through the Gull Stream, around the North Foreland and towards the River Medway. They were joined by victualling and hospital ships whose intention was to shelter for the winter at Chatham Dockyard. Almost immediately the convoy was dispersed by the cruel wind and high waves when the Great Storm reached the North Sea.

The following day - Thursday 25 - a further number of smaller warships decided to make for the open sea since they sensed a powerful storm was brewing. Indeed, that very night a Dutch ship was blown onto the Sands with loss of all hands. It is just possible that some of the smaller merchantmen, drawing only 8 - 10 feet of water, were driven right across the sandbank at high tide and were able to make for the shelter of neighbouring harbours. The 'London Gazette' (2 December) reported that ". . . we have several of the merchant ships driven out of the Downs in the late storm safe into Ramsgate Peer."

Next day - Friday 26th - these smaller warships returned and anchored in the deeper water of the Downs, probably southwards towards Kingsdown. Martin Brayne in his modern history, 'The Greatest Storm' (2002) asserts that this disposition was crucial in determining which ships were subsequently lost on the Goodwins. "The flood tide runs up through the Downs from SSW to NNE for six hours; two hours before and four hours after high tide. There being. . . a new moon, high water in the Downs would have occurred a little before midnight. When in the early hours of the Saturday morning, the Storm was at its height it would thus have been blowing from WSW greatly increasing the velocity of the tidal stream which would set strongly towards the Goodwin Sands."

Meanwhile, the Channel fleet had joined the remaining warships and anchored in Trinity Bay under the command of the young Sir Basil Beaumont, Rear Admiral of the Blue. His flagship was 'Mary', a smaller fourth rate ship of sixty-four guns with 273 crew. Fifty years earlier she had been launched at Woolwich as the 'Speaker' but this offensive Parliamentary name was changed to 'Mary' at the Restoration. At the time of the disaster Captain Edward Hopson and his purser were on business ashore.

Thirteen warships including three third rate men-o'-war, having seventy guns and weighing 1,000 tons, now formed part of Beaumont's squadron. These two-deckers numbered 'Northumberland', (Captain Greenway with 253 crew) 'Restoration' (Captain Fleetwood Emes with 353 crew) and 'Stirling Castle' (Captain John Johnson with 277 crew plus four marine officers). They were among Samuel Pepys' 'Thirty Great Ships' rapidly constructed at Deptford as part of a massive shipbuilding programme ordered by Charles II to strengthen the Royal Navy. At the height of the storm these three sister ships lay moored in the Small Downs. All succumbed to disaster during that terrible pitch black night when the tidal current was at its strongest on that midnight high tide. . .

First to strike the Goodwin Sands was the 'Mary'. Immediately, she began to

Rear Admiral Sir Basil Beaumont by Michael Dahl © National Maritime Museum.

disintegrate. Admiral Beaumont was reported lashed to the mast and holding up valuable plate to entice boatmen to launch to his ship's aid. All was in vain. He was swept from the quarter deck while his entire crew perished. There was one exception. Thomas Atkins, coxswain of the flagship's yawl, had a miraculous escape. A freak wave washed him overboard but he desperately clung to a spar. He managed to scramble aboard the poop deck of 'Stirling Castle' - still firing her half-minute distress cannons - as she thundered past. Shortly afterwards, this great warship, too, crashed onto the Sands. Atkins, therefore, has the dubious distinction of being shipwrecked twice in a single night. He was once more cast into the sea and tossed about by tremendous waves until finally picked up, unconscious, by a Deal hooker.

In the small hours of the 27th November, the three great warships were battered by 150 m.p.h. winds, torrential rain and forty feet high waves. Vice Admiral Sir John Leake was aboard 'Prince George', a recently rebuilt second rate ninety gun three-decker, the largest and most vulnerable ship in the Downs. Captain Steven Martin and his crew of 700 sailors were "snugly" riding out the storm. But at 3 a.m. 'Restoration' parted from her moorings and drove down hard upon them. Her anchor caught fast on the hawser of 'Prince George' and for a time the two warships were locked together. Incredibly, the anchor of 'Prince George' managed to hold both ships. Finally, the cable of 'Restoration' snapped and she shifted towards her inevitable doom on the northern swatch of the Goodwins.

At the same moment 'Northumberland' broke adrift and she crashed into 'Stirling Castle', causing her to lose two anchors and break from her own moorings. 'Stirling Castle' was almost dragged onto a huge merchant ship which, by means of her own two anchors kept stable, but a large wave hit the warship and veered her away before a collision occurred. She then tripped her third anchor but was apparently left without enough cable to let out her immense sheet anchor so this lay idle on the main deck. Captain Johnson ordered her masts with their rigging to be cut to reduce wind resistance. His radical action further slowed the ship's progress towards the Goodwins.

'Northumberland' and 'Restoration' probably struck the Sands at low tide around

4.30 a.m. when they are at their most dangerous and therefore these magnificent men-o'-war would have instantly smashed to pieces with loss of all hands. 'Stirling Castle', it seems, avoided this immediate fate. She rode out the storm, caught by her single anchor on its long cable, and reached the Goodwins after the tide had turned so that she was held in deep water above the sandbank. Wind against tide, however, caused the vessel to swivel round on her cable presenting her vulnerable broadside to the angry seas.

Huge waves swamped the man-o'-war and she took on water faster than her frantic crew could pump it out. 'Stirling Castle' sank slowly, her keel touched down gently on the sandbank, with her bow facing due west. Crucially, her stern castle had remained clear of the stormy shallows long enough for seventy frozen men - including her third lieutenant, chaplain, cook, surgeon's mate and four marine officers - to be rescued by boats from Leake's fleet. (The Marine Officers were named as Capt Lt. Winwood Masham, First Lt. James Saunders, Second Lts Nicholas Shorter and Samuel Herbert from Lord Shannon's Regiment)

Josiah Burchett recorded the devastation in his 'Complete History of the Remarkable Transactions at Sea' (1720):

> It was a miserable Sight to behold many of the Ships in the Downs; for as they were almost torn in pieces by the Violence of the Wind, so it was not possible to give them any help from the shore, even when they were in the greatest Extremity, and continually firing Guns for Relief; besides the Wind was at W.S.W. and they could not possibly carry a Knot of Sail to enable them to cling to the Shore; so that many of them perished on the Goodwin Sands, and of about one hundred sixty sail, of all sorts, which were in the Downs the Day before, not more than seventy were seen the next Morning, and many of them were only floating Bottoms, for all their Masts were gone by the Board; but several of the Merchant Ships and Vessels missing were afterwards heard of either in Holland, Norway, or the Ports of this Kingdom.

Earliest eyewitness account of the calamity was written by Thomas Warren, Storekeeper of the Navy Yard at Deal. His detailed report was sent to the Navy Board "Express in the Admiralty Packet 3 oClock Afternoone". He also entered a copy in careful copperplate handwriting in the log of the Navy Yard:

Deale the 27 Novr 1703

> I am sorry I must acquaint your honrs of a miserable slaughter that has happened amongst the Shipps in the Downes, yesterday it blew very hard all day, but about midnight it came on so violently at S.W. and continued between that and the W.S.W. that about two in the morning several Gunns were soon to be fired from Shipps in Distress, but there being such a hurricane twas improbable for a man to Stand against it, much more to afford them any Boats from the shore, that out of about 100 saile of one sort or another there is not above 70 now to be seen and a great many of them Floating onely Bottoms haveing I presume cutt their Masts by the Board the Better to ride It out; of the Men of War Rear Admlc Beaumont in the Mary is missing, with the

160

Northumberland, Restoration, Sterling Castle and Mortar Bomb; the Prince George, Essex, Shrewsberry, Eagle, Constant, Chatham, Assistance, Mary Gally, and Hunter Fireship Rode it out with all their Masts, but the Nassau has cuttaaway her Main Mast, the Garland and Dunwich all their masts, and the Postillion prize her Main Mast and misen Mast, and there are five great Shipps and two smaller ones that ride to the Norward with all their Masts by the Board, two of them wee take to be Men of ware, tis a miserable spectacle to behold the Shipps in the Downes as they now Ride home almost to pieces by this Storme, and the like weather has not been known in the memory of any man born, for when the Shipps broke away, as the greatest part of them did about five in the Morning, most flashes of Gunns Being then Seen, and the wind Being then Highest at W.S.W. they could not carry a knot of Saile to hug the Shore that tis feared the Goodwin Sand took up most of those for when it was light wee could see five saile, two of those pretty bigg Shipps fast upon it, one I am afraid was a man of Warr by the Numbers of Men wee could discerne to Shelter themselves upon the Masts, who all perished as the Water flowed and the Sea broke upon her, and there is little of them now to be seen, there are likewise three small Vessells Sunk in the Roade. besides all this Damage a Float it has blown downe all the East and West fence walls of the Buildings that are erected here for Her Maty Service, & Blown off great part of the Tileing of the great Storehouse, Boat Houses and Dwelling Houses, it has Blown downe the Gibbit of the Pyrat that hung in chains att the South end of the Towne and washed the man to Sea, it has likewise blown downe all the Corne Mills here sadly, Cast downe some houses, and untiled and Damaged most of the others in Towne.

I have not any Masts or Rigging here to repaire this Damage, if it pleases God they hold the Storme out, which is something abated tho still so bad that I cannot send a boat off that I desire you will please to order a Vessel or two downe to assist those Shipps with provisions and stores to enable them to proceed where they can be better fitted and so soone as the weather will permit I will be more particular as to their wants and whether any of them wants anchors and cables I haveing but one cable in store and that for a fourth Rate which I thought fitt to let you know and am with respect

Rt. honoble
yours Thomas Warren

Miles Norcliffe, master's mate of the sixty gun 'Shrewsbury', anchored alongside Sir Basil Beaumont's flagship, 'Mary', wrote his version of the November storm in his coarse sailor's style. It was delivered to the shore when the worst of the storm had abated by a boat carrying bedraggled sailors plucked from the sea. Although not accurate concerning the number of ships nor lives lost, Northcliffe expresses the 'Horror and Consternation' of the common sailor caught up in the catastrophic events that night in the Downs:

Sir,
These lines I hope in God will find you in good Health, we are all left here in a dismal Condition, expecting every moment to be all drowned: For here is a

great Storm, and is very likely to continue; we have here the Rear Admiral of the Blew in the Ship, call'd the 'Mary', a third Rate, the very next Ship to ours, sunk, with Admiral Beaumont, and above 500 Men drowned: The Ship call'd the 'Northumberland', a third Rate, about 500 Men all sunk and drowned: The Ship call'd the 'Sterling Castle', a third Rate, all sunk and drowned abover 500 souls: and the Ship call'd the 'Restoration', a third Rate, all sunk and drowned: These Ships were all close by us which I saw; these Ship fired their Guns all Night and Day long, poor Souls, for help, but the Storm being so fierce and raging, could have none save them: The Ship call'd the 'Shrewsberry' that we are in, broke two Anchors, and did run mighty fierce backwards, within 60 or 80 Yards of the Sands, and as God Almighty would have it, we flung our sheet Anchor down, which is the biggest, and so stopt: Here we all pray'd to God to forgive us our Sins, and to save us, or else to receive us into his heavenly Kingdom. If our sheet Anchor had given way, we had been all drown'd: But I humbly thank God, it was his gracious Mercy that saved us. There's one Captain Fanel's Ship, three Hospital Ships, all split, some sunk, and most of the Men drown'd.

There are above 40 Merchant Ships cast away and sunk: To see Admiral Beaumont, that was next us, and all the rest of his Men, how they climbed up the main Mast, hundreds at a time crying out for help, and thinking to save their Lives, and in the twinkling of an Eye were drown'd: I can give you no Account, but of these four Men of War aforesaid, which I saw with my own Eyes, and those Hospital Ships, at present, by reason the Storm hath drove us far distant from one another: Captain Crow of our Ship, believes we have lost several more Ships of War, by reason we see so few; we lye here in great danger, and waiting for a North Easterly Wind to bring us to Portsmouth, and it is our Prayers to God for it; for we know not how soon this Storm may arise, and cut us all off, for it is a dismal Place to Anchor in. I have not had my Cloaths off, nor wink of Sleep these four Nights, and have got my Death with cold almost.

Yours to Command,
Miles Norcliffe

An even more dramatic account was written by John Adams, a passenger aboard a merchant ship waiting for the opportunity to sail for Portsmouth and thence to Lisbon. His own ship, recently launched, was blown out of the Downs and across the North Sea to Norway. While clinging to the shrouds, Adams watched horrified the destruction of 'Northumberland' and 'Mary' on the Goodwins, although he appears to have missed the sinking of 'Restoration':

Sir,

I cannot but write to you of the Particulars of our sad and terrible Voyage. . . There was a great Fleet with us in the Downs, and several of them were driven from their Anchors, and made the best of their way out to Sea for fear of going on shoer upon the Goodwin. The Grand Fleet was just come in from the Streights, under Sir Cloudsly Shovel; and the Great Ships being design'd for the River, lay to Leeward: Most of the Ships that went out in the Night appear'd in the Morning; and I think there was none known to be lost, but one Dutch vessel upon the Goodwin.

But the next Day, being Friday, in the Evening, it began to gather to Windward; and as it had blown very hard all Day, at Night the Wind freshen'd, and we all expected a stormy Night. We saw the Men of War struck their Top-masts, and rode with two Cables an-end: so we made all as snug as we could, and prepar'd for the worst.

In this condition we rid it out till about 12 a-clock; when, the Fury of the Wind encreasing, we began to see Destruction before us: the Objects were very dreadful on every side; and tho' it was very dark, we had Light enough to see our own Danger, and the Danger of those near us.

About One-a-clock the Ships began to drive, and we saw several come by us without a Mast standing, and in the utmost Distress.

By Two a-clock we could hear Guns firing in several Parts of this Road, as Signals of Distress, and tho' the Noise was very great with the Sea and Wind, yet we could distinguish plainly, in some short Intervals, the Cries of Poor Souls in Extremities.

By Four-a-clock we miss'd the 'Mary' and the 'Northumberland' who rid not far from us, and found they were driven from their Anchors; but what became of them, God knows: and soon after a large Man of War came driving down upon us, all her Masts gone, and in a dreadful Condition. . . I was just gowing to order the Mate to cut away, when it pleas'd God the Ship sheer'd contrary to our Expectation to Windward, and the Man of War, which we found to be the 'Sterling Castle', drove clear off us, not two Ships Lengths to Leeward...

Two Ships, a-head of us, had rid it out till now, which was towards Five in the Morning, when they both drove from their Anchors, and one of them coming foul of a small Pink, they both sunk together; the other drove by us, and having one Mast standing, I think it was her Main-Mast, she attempted to spread a little Peak of her Sail, and so stood away before it; I suppose she went to Sea.

At this time, the Raging of the Sea was so violent, and the Tempest doubled its Fury in such a Manner, that my Mate told me, we had better go to Sea, for 'twould be impossible to ride it out. . . So we slipt our Sheet Cable, and sheering the Ship towards the Shore, got her Head about, and stood away afore it; Sail we had none, nor Mast standing: Our Mate had set up a Jury Missen but no Canvass could bear the Fury of the Wind, yet he fasten'd an old Tarpaulin so as that it did the Office of a Missen and kept us from driving too fast to Leeward.

In this Condition we drove out of the Downs, and past so near the Goodwin, that we could see several Ships fast a ground, and beating to Pieces. We drove in this desperate Condition till Day-break, without any Abatement of the Storm, and our Men heartless and dispirited, tir'd with the Service of the Night, and every Minute expecting Death...

All Night it blew excessive hard, and the next Day, which was Sabbath Day, about Eleven a Clock it abated, but still blew hard: about three it blew something moderately, compar'd with the former; and we got up a Jury Main-Mast, and rigg'd it as well as we could, and with a Main Sail lower'd almost to the Deck, stood at a great rate afore it all Night and the next Day, and on Tuesday Morning we saw Land, but could not tell where it was; but being not in a Condition to keep the Sea, we run in, and made Signals of Distress; some pilots came off to us, by whom we were inform'd we had reached the Coast of Norway, and having neither Anchor nor Cable on board capable to ride the Ship, a Norwegian Pilot came on board, and brought us into a Creek where we had smooth Water, and lay by till we got Help, Cables and Anchors, by which means we are safe in Place.

Your Humble Servant,
J. Adams.

Vice Admiral Sir John Leake witnessed a melancholy sight from the deck of 'Prince George' riding in the English Channel. At first light he counted twelve warships ashore upon the Goodwins Sands, Bunt Head and Brake Sands. The Downs was littered with wreckage with a great number of merchant ships floating keel uppermost. Leake wrote a full report to Prince George, Lord High Admiral, requesting stores - anchors, cables, cordage and jury (or temporary) masts - to repair the damaged warships. His immediate reaction, however, was to order 'Anne' and all the boats from his fleet to scour the Anchorage for survivors. But even when they espied stranded sailors, they were powerless to approach the wreck before they were recalled on that short afternoon, "the sea so great".

According to Stephen Martin-Leake in his 'Life of Sir John Leake' (1920): "Having now given all possible assistance to those in distress, and taken a proper care of those that remained, his next concern was for those that had been driven out of the Downs. For this purpose, the 1st of December, he ordered the 'Assistance', 'Chatham', and 'Mary Galley', to cruise to and fro for three or four days, about the North Sand Head and on the back of the South Sand to look out for such merchant ships as might be in those parts, and in want of help, and to assist and bring them into port". Further, these ships were commanded to proceed to the North Sea and across to the coast of Holland to scout for the missing warships -'Association', 'Dorsetshire', 'Revenge' and 'Russell'- which had been driven from their anchors at the Gunfleet and had not been heard of since. The Admiralty was concerned that French privateers might set out from Dunkirk or Ostend in order to capture the crippled ships, plunder their cargoes and take their crews prisoner. After accomplishing this task Admiral Leake struck his flag and left for London leaving Captain Martin to sail with 'Prince George' to Spithead.

Captains' logs for several of Leake's ships survive and reveal their findings:

'Mary Gally' 27th Saturday
Winds WSW
Bearing the South Foreland and SSW Sandown Castle WNW
This 24 hours very hard gales and most part of the morning a violent storm at 10 last night let down our sheet anchor having brought both bowers ahead

and veered a 2r of A Cable then roade till half past 6 this morning then finding the ship to drive veered out a Cable and half one the sheet Cable a Dutch privateer being drove athwart our ships hause and carried our best bower anchor then we drove about a cables length then rid fast in the morning we saw several ships on the Godwin sands one of which was her majesty's ship with Rear Admiral Beaumont.

'Assistance'
November 27 1703
Winds SSW to WSW
This day about two in the morning we had a violent storm that held till seven the height of the wind at WSW then something abated, this night the Mary, Rear Admiral of the Blue, Northumberland, Restauration and Sterling Castle were al drove ashore on the north sand head being driven from the anchor all lost and then drowned except 70 of the Sterling Castle men, in the morning the Downes was full of Racks and sunk ships about an hundred sail of merchant ships missing of English and Flamburgher and most bound to Lisbon with the King of Spain's the Garland has lost all her masts the Nassaw her main mast the Dunwich all her mast the Litchfield her foremast and several ships all their masts at five in the morning drove with both rowers a head then let go the sheet anchor which brought us up and blessed be God no body came foul of us yesterday evening came in Litchfield and Warspight.

Contemporary accounts of the storm are, naturally, conflicting.

A correspondent of the 'Daily Courant' sent his report from his landward perspective. (The details are not consistent with Leake's version which states that 'Mary', 'Northumberland', 'Stirling Castle' and 'Restoration' were "all to pieces by 10 o'clock" in the morning):

Deal Nov 27
We had so violent a Storm at SW that the like has not been known in these parts in the memory of Man. . . it made all the houses in the town shake, uncovered several roofs, threw down chimneys, brick walls, etc. . .
P.S. at 1 in the Afternoon. It blows hard still but being cleared up to the NE we perceive 2 hulls of ships riding at anchor near the Breake which are suppos'd to be the 'Sterling Castle' and Restoration' or the 'Northumberland'; 2 other great ships were seen on the Goodwin Sands one of them being the 'Mary' who had her flag flying, but the Flood, coming on we can see no more of them".

Thomas Warren, Storekeeper, kept the Admiralty informed of developments in the Downs:

Deal the 28th November 1703

Since mine to your honour of yesterday by express the weather has been much that I have been afloat and those ships that rode to the nor-ward without masts prove to be the 'Antelope' Hospital ship, a great Hamburger and three Englishmen. That the 'Restoration', 'Sterling Castle', 'Northumberland', 'Mary' and 'Mortar Bomb' are still missing and the four former said certain to be lost upon the Goodwin Sand and if so all men lost, tho there is a hull of one of them to be seen, that I have sent boats to see what men can be saved there being a waft seen from her at daylight which are not yet come ashore. The 'Warspight' and 'Litchfield' came into the Downs the Friday afternoon before the storm and held it out, the latter with the loss of her foremast. About noon the 'Torbay' came into the Downs from the westward without a fore topmast. I find here will to be great want of cordage, jury masts, anchors and cables to service those ships that are left that I do enclose your honours account of what I have by me that you may please the better to order a fitting supply to answer...

Warren, in his letters, mentioned five ships lost on the Sands. This number is confirmed by the 'London Gazette' (27 November) "Five sail, two of which are pretty big ones, are lost upon the Goodwin Sands. No boat can yet be sent off so we know not the particulars." There has been speculation about this mysterious fifth ship. Naval historian, Sir William Laird Clowes, suggests it was the bomb vessel, 'Mortar', with her crew of sixty-five men, although Daniel Defoe in his account of the 'Great Storm' asserts she was actually lost off the coast of Holland.

In the aftermath of the storm, Warren was extremely active. He applied to the Admiralty for urgent supplies for the lame warships. He commandeered the hoy, 'Lyon', to sweep the Anchorage for lost anchors. Those from 'Northumberland', 'Garland' and 'Mortar Bomb' were soon recovered plus the great sheet anchor, complete with stock but minus its ring, from 'Restoration'. Later he arranged payment to the surviving crews and muster lists of Her Majesty's ships in the Downs. Finally, he organised a team of workmen - carpenters, bricklayers, tilers, plasters - to repair the damaged storehouse in the new Navy Yard.

Dutch bronze cannon raised from the wreck of 'Stirling Castle'.

The Royal and Merchant Navies had suffered terrible casualties. Out of the one hundred and sixty outward bound merchant ships sheltering in the Downs, not more than seventy rode out the storm and many of these were found floating keel uppermost next day. Four major warships with one thousand, one hundred and twenty six sailors perished. Across southern England the grim total was thirteen major warships lost and almost two thousand officers and men. This amounted to the greatest single loss - by storm or battle - in the entire history of the Royal Navy.

The toll might have been greater had not H.M.S. 'Prince George' with 'Essex', 'Shrewsbury', 'Eagle', 'Content', 'Chatham', 'Assistance', 'Mary' (galley) and 'Hunter' (fireship) all escaped to the open sea. 'Nassau', a third rate with eighty guns, 'Garland', 'Dunwich', 'Lichfield' and 'Postillion' all lost their masts but survived the storm. 'Association', a second rate with Sir Stafford Fairborne, Vice Admiral of the Red, aboard, was blown - severely undermanned - across the North Sea along the coasts of Holland, Norway and Sweden before limping back months later to the Nore. This was the ship in which Sir Cloudesley Shovell lost his life and his "dead Carcass spew'd upon the Shore" four years later in a shipwreck off the Scilly Isles.

"English naval supremacy was nearly broken," pronounced G. M. Treveleyan in 'England Under Queen Anne' (1930) "Never was English seamanship put to a harder test and never were ships better handled. On that awful night, and the no less awful day that followed, England was saved by the skill and courage of the crews of innumerable vessels, fighting the greatest naval battle of the war against no mortal foe."

Queen Anne, who had herself escaped with her life - declared a National Day of Mourning. Her Majesty publicly proclaimed on 12 December that the nation had experienced "a Calamity so Dreadful and Astonishing, that the like hath not been Seen or Felt, in the Memory of any Person living in this Our Kingdom." Parliament assembled to consider how to address the disaster and readily voted to grant enormous funds to build some "capital ships" to supplement the depleted Navy. A programme of repairing warships was immediately begun to quash rumours spread abroad that Britain had lost her fighting fleet.

Winter lay ahead so at least the royal dockyards would have time to build up the strength of the Navy's redoubtable 'Wooden Walls'. Ketches were dispatched to the Downs with anchors, cables and stores for the stricken ships within a week of the catastrophe. Manpower remained overstretched in all the yards - poor pay was the problem - and the Navy Board expressed concern about "the want of Carpenters, Saylemakers and Caulkers". Priority was given to the repair of the smaller and least damaged warships but it was recognised that it would be more economical to construct a fresh fleet before resuming the following summer's sea campaigns. Seven warships were completed in 1704. These numbered one magnificent first rate, 'Royal Anne', and a replacement 'Stirling Castle' and 'Northumberland'.

A greater concern was for the loss of seamen during wartime.

Rescued members of the crew of the ill-fated 'Stirling Castle' were directed to London by the Muster Master at Deal. They were transferred to 'Norfolk', a third rate of 80 guns, subsequently involved in the Siege of Gibraltar. There was still a huge shortfall in manpower at sea and the press gangs were assembled in force. Ironically, foreigners

Seaman's leather hat from 'Stirling Castle'.

The Great Storm ranks with The Great Plague and the Great Fire as the three terrible catastrophes which struck Stuart London. It was estimated that 8,000 people lost their lives in a single night across Southern Britain.

At the time of the Dutch Wars the British Fleet was divided into three squadrons - the Red, White and Blue - in that order of seniority. Each squadron was commanded by an admiral with, beneath him, a vice admiral and then a rear admiral.

The Admiral of the Red was not commonly used since, as the highest ranking officer, he was Admiral of the Fleet. At the time of the storm Sir George Rooke was Admiral of the Fleet with Sir Cloudesley Shovell, as Admiral of the White, next in seniority.

A ship's rating depended on the number of guns mounted. At the time of the storm first rates had 100+ guns; second rates 84-98 guns; third rates 64-80 guns; fifth rates 32-44 guns; sixth rates 20-30 guns.

were exempt from impressment but condemned criminals were reprieved on condition they enlisted in the Navy. Public sympathy ensured, at least, that the miserly Treasury amply compensated families whose menfolk had been lost in the Great Storm.

But there were recriminations. Daniel Defoe, author of 'Robinson Crusoe' and 'Moll Flanders', wrote his account in a booklet, 'The Storm', published in 1704. He had just been released from Newgate Prison for his "seditious" writings and was friendless and bankrupt. This was, therefore, one of his bleakest moments. (Ironically, he had forfeited his profitable building business at a time when bricks and pantiles were literally going through the roof!) The disgraced author collated material from all parts of southern England hammered by the hurricane to form the basis of his first book. Full title of this classic work of contemporary reportage: "The Storm or, a Collection of the most Remarkable Casualties and Disasters which happen'd in the Late Dreadful Tempest, both by Sea and Land".

Defoe placed an advertisement in the 'London Gazette' requesting that observers furnish him with their firsthand observations. Further, he made a "circuit. . . over most parts of Kent" to personally appraise the effects of the calamity. Nonetheless, historians in the past have tended to treat his account with caution and warned that the letters which he presented may have been embellished. Richard West, a recent biographer, praises Defoe's journalism, however, and asserts it "puts to shame all modern accounts of disaster" (1997).

Defoe also penned an epic poem, 'The Storm', in which he laid the blame for the destruction of one fifth of the Royal Navy upon the folly of the Lords of the Admiralty. They ought, he rightly suggests, to have ensured that the main fleet was safely secured in inshore harbours rather than wintering for convenience in the English Channel.

"But O ye Mighty Ships of War!
What in Winter did you there?
Wild November should our Ships Restore
To Chatham, Portsmouth and the Nore."

But his surprising censure of the Deal boatmen in prose and poetry is unjustly devastating:

"And here I cannot omit that great Notice that has been taken of the Towns-people of Deal who are blam'd, and I doubt not with too much reason for their great Barbarity in neglecting to save the Lives of abundance of poor Wretches; who having hung upon the Masts and Rigging of the Ships, or floated upon the broken Pieces of Wrecks, had gotten a Shore upon the Goodwin Sands when the Tide was out.

"It was, without doubt, a sad Spectacle to behold the poor Seamen walking too and fro upon the Sands, to view their Postures, and the Signals they made for help, which, by the Assistance of Glasses was easily seen from the Shore.

"Here they had a few Hours Reprieve, but had neither present Refreshment, nor any hopes of Life, for they were sure to be all wash'd into another World at the Reflux of the Tide. Some Boats are said to come very near them in quest of Booty, and in search of Plunder, and to carry off what they could get, but no Body concern'd themselves for the Lives of those miserable Creatures."

Defoe, however, records the endeavours of the plucky Mayor of Deal, Thomas Powell, "a slop seller by trade" (dealing in ready-made clothes for sailors) who championed public morals in Deal during the reign of Queen Anne. The author presents Mayor Powell as a local hero and his version has passed into legend. Marooned sailors, he insists, could be spotted through spyglasses from the shore clinging to the decks of submerged wrecks. Powell immediately took charge of the situation and made straight for the Customs House to request their men to launch their large, sturdy boats. He met with a curt refusal. Provoked to anger, Powell made a generous offer to the Deal boatmen of five shillings per head for all the men whose lives they could save. Then he returned to the Customs House boathouse with an army of men and commandeered the boats hove high above the tidemark.

Crewed with volunteers, these fast craft were launched to the rescue. Incredibly, it was estimated

Leather shoe from 'Stirling Castle'.

Warships of over 60 guns were classed as "ships of the line" while fourth and fifth rates were known as 'frigates'.

At the Restoration Samuel Pepys, the diarist, dined aboard the ill fated frigate, 'Mary'. Pepys, later appointed First Secretary to the Admiralty, declared her "a very brave ship".

Further local losses were 'Swan' and 'Princess', two hospital ships anchored in Westgate Bay, near 'Margett Towne', and 'Latchford', returning from London to Sandwich "with divers men and women passengers all totally lost".

In 2000 divers discovered a massive 'Prince Rupert Patent' demi-cannon complete with elm carriage and four wheels on board the sunken 'Stirling Castle'. This rare 32-pounder iron 'Rupertinoe' - named after the nephew of Charles I - is currently being restored at Ramsgate Maritime Museum.

Brass candlestick from 'Stirling Castle'.

Among the hundreds of sailors who lost their lives on Goodwin Sands were locally pressed men. 'Mary Galley' is one of those ships named as being involved in pressing men in Deal prior to the November Storm.

In 1705 members of the Cinque Ports Pilots erected their own galley at the west end of St. Leonard's Church, Deal, to commemorate the Great Storm. Timbers from ships wrecked in the hurricane reputedly were used in its construction.

Centrepiece is a curious painting of a man-o'-war under full sail showing both its bow and stern. Either side appear globes representing hemispheres while pilots of the period hold sounding lines.

that by this prompt action over two hundred sailors were rescued. "Nor was this the End of his Care," asserts Defoe, "for when the Tide came in, and 'twas too late to go off again, for all that were left were swallow'd up with the Raging of the Sea, his Care was then to relieve the poor Creatures, who he had sav'd, and who almost dead with Hunger and Cold, were naked and starving."

Powell applied to the Queen's Agent for assistance in aiding the sick and wounded but he was curtly refused. Little value was then placed upon the lives of ordinary seamen, many of whom had been pressed. Undaunted, he provided them all with billets and, moreover, out of his own pocket, supplied them with food and drink. When they had recovered he provided the impoverished sailors with money and passes to Gravesend. Those who died from trauma or hypothermia, he buried at his own expense. It was only after a great deal of persistence that he was reimbursed by the heartless government.

Defoe, while paying tribute to Powell's humanity, critised the Deal boatmen who, in actual fact, had risked their lives in attempting to rescue the shipwrecked crews. 'The Storm', rebukes these "Sons of Plunder" for their callousness in seizing cargoes while ignoring the plight of the victims of the hurricane:

"The Barbarous Shores with Men
and Boats abound,
The Men more Barbarous than the
Shores are found;
Off to the shatter'd Ships they go,
And for the Floating Purchase row.
They spare no Hazard, or no Pain,
But 'Tis to save the Goods, and not the Men. . ."

Defoe's poem, naturally, caused great offence. The author, it must be remembered, had a reputation for slander and had not long been sentenced to a spell in the stocks. The new Mayor, Thomas Horne, the Storekeeper of the Navy Yard, Thomas Warren, and several local dignitaries including Tobias Bowles, Benjamin Hulke and Thomas Powell, responded with a formal letter (21

June 1705) to the publisher, 'G. Sawbridge of Little Britain', accusing his anonymous writer of "infamous libel".

Defoe's response was to compound his condemnation in his paper, 'Review' (December 1708):

> "Let the town of Deal tell the world how in the great storm their boats went off with the utmost hazard to save the wreck and get plunder, and how they let the poor, perishing wretches that were standing on Goodwin sands stretch out their hands to see them for help in vain, deluding their dying hopes, letting them see these monsters pursue a piece of the wreck and leave the tide to flow over these miserable creatures without compassion. . . And from the shore several hundred of them were perceived walking dry on the sands in the utmost despair, running about like people out of their wits, wringing their hands, and making all the signals of distressed wretches just launching into eternity, for they were all sure to be overwhelmed by the return of the tide."

Defoe's imaginative version was not only highly offensive it conflicted with the facts reported by eye-witness observers - Leake, Warren and Burchett. During recent decades the disaster area has been carefully explored by a maritime archaeological team of amateur divers. The Thanet branch of the 'British Sub-Aqua Club' has, so far, located three of the sunken warships on Goodwin Sands. These are now all designated Wreck sites:

H.M.S. 'Restoration' has only been investigated by sonar which shows her wreckage to be both under and above the seabed.

H.M.S. 'Northumberland' which was discovered after fishermen had their nets caught and they reported it to the diving unit. Divers realised they were encountering a complete eighteenth century warship poking out of a massive sandbank. They could even lift the gunport lids and swim inside along rows of cannon. Her temporary exposure caused by a sudden movement of the sand did not protect her and she is now largely collapsed.

H.M.S. 'Stirling Castle' was also located when fishermen's nets were snagged on the Bunt Head of the North Goodwin. Subsequently her shattered hulk was investigated by a team of divers who found that she was embedded in a cliff of sand and virtually intact. 'Stirling Castle' had been built in 1679 by Jonas Shish at Deptford. Her measurements were 24 feet high, 151 long, 57 metres beam and weighing about one thousand tons. Intrepid divers swam through the gun ports of this mighty warship to explore the sandy tomb lying approximately twenty metres below the waterline.

'Stirling Castle' was listing slightly on her starboard side and her bow was facing westwards towards the shore. Her forecastle, quarterdeck and poop were missing but the remnants of her main deck were littered with cannon, cannon balls, blocks and cordage. There was no sign of her standard wooden-carved red lion figurehead nor were there any masts since these had been toppled in the attempt to prevent her from drifting towards the Sands. There was, however, a huge anchor about eighteen feet long with an enormous ring that the divers attempted to swim through. Undoubtedly, 'Stirling Castle' remains the best preserved wreck of a third rate ship-of-the-line in the world.

Subsequently the diving team raised over three hundred artefacts - pewter,

Sand glass from 'Stirling Castle'.

Centrepiece is a curious painting of a man-o'-war under full sail showing both its bow and stern. Either side appear globes representing the hemispheres while pilots of the period hold sounding lines.

In 2000 divers discovered a massive 'Prince Rupert Patent' demi-cannon complete with elm carriage and four wheels on board the sunken 'Stirling Castle'. This rare 32-pounder iron Rupertinoe - named after the nephew of Charles I - is currently being restored at Ramsgate Maritime Museum.

Marine archaeologists have found clues to suggest 'Stirling Castle' was one of the first ships discovered to have been steered by a helm.

stoneware and personal possessions of the crews - from the seabed. Scattered around the wreck were human bones clustered most thickly around a pile of onion shaped wine bottles. The divers surmised that the officers had guessed the fate of their ship and, in their abject misery, had tried to drink themselves to stupefaction. Since being exposed, the sand has once more begun to encroach and the wreck has collapsed leaving only its orlop deck intact.

The Clock House in Ramsgate Royal Harbour contains relics raised from the wrecks of 'Stirling Castle' and 'Northumberland' by the intrepid diving team from Thanet. Recovered items provided a vivid picture of the daily life of a sailor aboard a typical warship in late-Stuart times. On display are a multitude of wooden pistol stocks, hilts of hangers, clay tobacco pipes, onion wine bottles, leather book covers, pewter tankards, bone combs, iron keys, toothbrush handles, shaving kit, buttons, thimbles, an ornate ink well with a pounce pot, a candle snuffer in a case, a nest of brass weights and a rack of six brass-barrelled musketoons.

A few items of costume survive such as a seaman's single leather shoe and a leather hat. A delicate Chinese damask square woven with a design of trees and foliage would have belonged to one of the ship's officers. On a far grander scale, there is the entire pewter dinner service with the initials 'I.I'. that must have been owned by John Johnson, Captain of 'Stirling Castle'.

There is a crumbling sea chest containing a complete set of navigational instruments including a rare wooden cross-staff that was a primitive means of finding latitude. Also there is an enormous amount of surgical equipment - medicine jars, pots and bottles, optical instruments, a small wooden screw-top container for pills, a pewter porringer which doubled as a bleeding bowl and, ominously, an urethral syringe for treatment of venereal diseases. Six navigational slates, after close examination, revealed scratched references to the direction of the wind.

A great treasure is the Dutch bronze six-pounder cannon raised from 'Stirling Castle'. This is exquisitely decorated with a pair of cast-iron dolphin handles, a three-masted sailing ship on the barrel and around the breach the legend which translates: "Asseurus Koster made me in Amstredam, 1642". It was overstamped with the broad arrow of the Board of Ordnance. Perhaps the cannon was taken as a prize from a ship of the Dutch East India Company or it may have been presented as a gift during a lull in the Anglo-Dutch Wars. This magnificent specimen is, according to Martin Brayne, "a sad reminder of the guns forlornly fired to summon help as the doomed men-o'-war were driven onto the Sands".

The gilded ship's bell, marked with the Admiralty broad arrow and the date of the vessel's refit (1701), was recovered from 'Northumberland'. Another rarity rescued from the same wreck was a pair of copper kettles or furnaces, complete with brass taps, used for cooking in the ship's galley. The cook placed the company's food in mesh bags and immersed it in boiling water inside these vast kettles. Blankley's 'Naval Expositor' (1750) also informs that the same type of vessel was employed for "heating Tar at the Rope Yard". One of the kettles is exhibited at Ramsgate while the second is prominently displayed at the National Maritime Museum, Greenwich.

Yet it is the personal possessions recovered from the sunken warships that are the most poignant reminders of Britain's worst storm - a humble wooden platter scratched with the initial 'R'; a fragment of a carved draughtboard used by sailors to while away free time on a long voyage, a single drumstick that was probably part of the musical kit of a Marine drummer and a fluted brass candlestick on an octagonal base to which was still attached a skeletal hand.

BOATMEN AND THEIR CRAFT

'Riders of the Sea'

DEAL BOATMEN were world renowned for their bravery and industry. Their arduous tasks were accomplished in the most tempestuous seas and their compassion in saving lives won them high regard. Formerly, it was a splendid sight to see their noble craft with their protruding bowsprits, masts, capstans and tackle stretching in one continuous line from Kingsdown to Sandown.

Mention is made of Downs boatmen and their small craft in Tudor times but the larger class of vessels evolved over a long period of time as the port flourished. In 1616 there is a record of Deal boatmen rendering assistance to several ships stranded on the Goodwins while in 1690 a man-o'-war, 'Vanguard', mounting ninety guns, was driven onto the Sands in a gale and afterwards salved by Deal boatmen.

There were two opposing views of the Deal boatmen - saints or sinners? A Lloyd's correspondent in 1867 maintained the notion that they were a force to be reckoned with and who charged an excessive rate for their services. "Captains who hired their services found themselves the victims of seaborne extortion rackets, their cables cut, their anchors stolen and their crews overpowered." George Byng Gattie, author and patriot, defended these same boatmen from all accusations of criminal intent in his 'Memorials of the Goodwin Sands' (1890). He regarded them as "honest, well-conducted and respectable a set of men as are to be found anywhere round our coasts". And he insisted that in every known instance the boatmen put the lives of distressed seamen foremost and certainly above salvaging property.

The bravery of Deal boatmen was extolled in poetry and prose.

Charles Dickens in 'Household Words' praised the Deal boatmen:

> "They are amongst the bravest and most skilful mariners that exist. Let a gale arise and swell into a storm; let a sea run that might appal the stoutest heart that ever beat; let the light-boat, on the Goodwin Sands, throw up a rocket in the night; or let them hear through the angry roar the signal guns of a ship in distress; and these men spring into action so dauntless, so valiant and heroic, that the world cannot surpass it. . ."

Eliza Cook (1817 - 1889), a pious Victorian poet, penned a stirring poem, 'The Boatmen of the Downs':

174

"And braver deeds than ever turned
The fate of king and crowns
Are done for England's glory,
By her Boatmen of the Downs."

Deal boatmen made a precarious living from supplying anchors and chains to homeward bound ships which had slipped their cables in adverse weather and taking fresh water, provisions, men, letters and newspapers to outward bound ships in the Downs - all of which came under the curious term, 'hovelling'. The name is of doubtful origin. Elvin and Bayley both suggest it may be a corruption of the word, 'hobilers', who were light cavalry that patrolled the coast guarding against invasion during the reign of Edward III. These authors make a convincing analogy between these swift horsemen (who rode small stout horses known as "hobblers") and Deal boatmen who were "Riders of the sea".

Another task in which a hoveller (pronounced "huv'ler") would be employed was "sweeping" the seabed with grappling irons for lost anchors, cables and ordnance that were a menace to shipping. An early record mentions a government grant of £30 per annum to Robert Hudson and George Rands of Deal "on condition of their clearing the Narrow Seas for lost anchors, which cut the cables of ships, and restoring the anchors and cables of the king's ships". This was a hazardous task since boats were often overloaded with the weight of anchors but the work was lucrative. The Board of Trade offered them £2 per ton for anchors and cables thus salvaged. Those recovered were sold at auction in anchor fields situated adjacent to Deal Castle and in South Sandy Lane (Blenheim Road).

At Deal, fierce rivalry existed between the boatmen who worked on the four separate beaches - Deal North End, Deal South End, Walmer Road and Kingsdown.

'What's that on the Goodwins?' North Deal boatmen.

175

A Victorian song sheet showing a Deal lugger.

There was open hostility between the North and South Enders whose dividing line was the Royal Hotel. It must be remembered that the livelihood of one thousand men was involved in the boating trade. At the first hint of a vessel in distress they raced each other, cutting across the bows of rival boats or "taking their wind" by sailing close on the windward side, in an attempt to be the first to put a man on board. They were adept at recognising the nationality of every anchored vessel by the way she carried her masts and arranged her yards and they knew how much they could charge with impunity.

Often sets of boats could be involved since a fast rowing galley might arrive ahead of its partner, a more sturdier lugger, that would be more suitable for loading retrieved cargo. Their stations on shore were invariably identified as public houses - 'Fountain', 'India Arms', 'Harp' or 'Royal Exchange'. Indeed, the owners might be influential landlords who encouraged crews to sleep in the their taprooms and passages awaiting a call in inclement weather. Anonymous sponsors would finance a salvage operation and pay the boatmen handsome wages for the greater share of the profits - customs men, workhouse masters and devout clergymen. According to Gattie rewards for services were divided into fourteen shares: "the boat takes three and a half shares for her owners, one half share is allowed for provisions which are supplied by the owners, and one share is given to each of the men".

The amount of supplies obtained from Deal boatmen for large merchant vessels was enormous. (Buying and selling provisions at a small profit to ships was known as 'bombing') Edward Barlow in his 'Journal' mentions taking on board 'Wentworth', an East Indiaman bound for China, "fowls, hogs and sheep, geese, and turkeys, and a couple of live bulls" in 1699. He was not so lucky with his stores when he transferred to the Indiaman, 'Fleet Frigate', which he was employed to pilot to China in 1702. Customs officials got wind of the fact that the master had taken on board a quantity of French brandy which was seized before his ship set sail.

Prior to the inauguration of a national lifeboat service rescues at sea were carried out by local boats normally engaged in fishing, smuggling, salvaging or hovelling. Frequently, one hundred boats would launch to the aid of a stricken ship from the shores of Deal, Walmer and Kingsdown. First recorded instance of rescue by Deal boatmen occurred in 1563. The Earl of Warwick, Governor of Newhaven in Normandy, sailed from Portsmouth to London but was driven by contrary winds into the Small Downs. His ship, 'New Barke', was in danger but his crew were rescued by local boatmen and they were landed safely at Sandown Castle.

A later famous rescue involving local boats occurred when five luggers raced to attend the wreck of the West Indiaman, 'Belina', which struck the Goodwins on the morning of 23 November 1824. Unfortunately, only six members of the crew of this West Indiaman were saved - Captain Craig, four men and "a little black boy". The remainder were swept overboard in the height of the tempest. The bravery of the crews of the luggers, that included 'Canning', 'Sparrow' and 'Po', was celebrated by a report in the national newspapers and the publication of an engraving.

There was slim chance of remuneration for such dangerous missions but the heroes of the hour might be rewarded by the Admiralty, the Board of Trade, the Commissioners of Salvage, the Humane Benefit Society, a private owner or shipping company, a host of charities, a monarch or a head of state. Posters were printed after disasters requesting contributions from the "Affluent and Charitable" to support the

177

dependents of boatmen lost at sea. Further, boats were rarely insured since the premiums were far too high which meant that the risks the boatmen took were incalculable. Samuel Plimsoll, originator of the Plimsoll Mark, rose to the boatmen's defence and insisted they should be suitably rewarded in a public speech delivered in 1873.

The boats employed by the Deal boatmen fell into four categories.

Luggers were the most famous beach craft throughout the world. They were the largest class of boat that could be launched and beached from such a steep shingle shore with safety in a heavy sea and hauled up under the same exacting conditions with a capstan. Luggers were from forty to fifty feet long with a twelve or thirteen foot beam. In winter they were equipped with two masts - the foremast carried an enormous square dipping 'lug' sail with, possibly, a topsail, while the mizzen, positioned well aft, had a standing 'lug', but there was also a storm jib set out on a long bowsprit. Their summer rig, however, involved fitting a third mast amidships equipped with another 'lug' sail which would send them ahead, as well as to the windward, of the fastest ships that sailed beside them. Luggers were clinker-built of English elm and ballasted with bags of shingle from the beach. Crucially, they were long, lean, open boats with a shallow draught allowing them to sail over sandbanks in just a few feet of water. This meant they could reach parts of the Goodwin Sands where rival craft dared not venture.

The 'Tiger' was the largest Deal lugger. Courtesy: Deal Library.

The crew of the lugger ' Early Morn'. Courtesy: Deal Library.

Luggers were also known as 'forepeakers' because of a small cabin forward of the main mast. This cabin, (known as a 'cuddy' or 'caboose') was furnished with lockers, bunks and a stove. Here a crew of about a dozen men lived in cramped confinement in all weathers for upwards of a week. Main purpose of a lugger was to put a pilot on board ships in the Channel and therefore these sturdy craft were required to be at sea for long periods and cover great distances. At times crews would be involved in "West'ard cruises" which meant they would sail down Channel to meet homeward bound ships at The Start but they sometimes went as far as the Scilly or Channel Islands.

Each lugger had its own stage where it was hauled up the beach by old men or young boys who for a few pence were willing to turn the large wooden capstan. Night and day luggers were poised for action, straining on a slip chain at the upper part of the beach, with bows purposely pointing seawards. Deal beach is steep so that heavy luggers were able to gather enough momentum while sliding down greased skids, or 'woods', to slice through the breakers and sail straight away from the shore. Competition was fierce among the boatmen. Crews of luggers would race to a wreck in the hope of securing a salvage ahead of their rivals. They might even remain at sea for several days during a gale in the hope of being first on the scene of a shipwreck. The price of luggers was high in proportion to the precarious living their crews could earn. 'Lady Rosa', built by Henry Gardner in 1874, cost a phenomenal £400.

Names of the luggers reveal the pride and passion of their owners. Foremost was allegiance to the throne - 'British Queen', 'Victoria', 'Albert' - patriotism - 'Briton's Pride', 'Young England', 'Albion' - and hero worship - 'Brave Nelson'. There was a declaration of achievement - 'Seaman's Glory', 'Pride of the Ocean', 'Success', 'Industry', 'Endeavour', 'Guiding Star' - a sense of power - 'Tartar', 'Bouncer', 'Spartan' - and a capacity for speed - 'Wild Hare', 'Stag', 'Fly', 'Dart', 'Arrow'. There were birds and flowers - 'Petrel', 'Stork', 'Sparrow', 'Violet', 'Bluebell', 'Seaflower' - or a romantic inclination - 'Gipsy Girl', 'Garland', 'Queen of Sheba'. Often names showed a homely touch - 'Little Ann', 'Little Fred', 'Georgina', 'Florence', 'Jenny', 'Flora', and 'Lucy'. Frequent choice of children's names is explained by the fact that every eligible member of a boatman's family held shares in a lugger and so the naming of their craft was an event as significant as that of a christening.

Luggers' names were sometimes a reminder of the boatmen's hazardous calling - 'Faith', 'Hope', 'Chance', 'Speculation'. They might also be appropriate to a seaman's calling - 'Little Wanderer' (suggesting the wide scope covered by the local pilots), 'Friend of all Nations' (indicating the humanitarian aspect of the boatmen's trade) and 'Early Morn' (proclaiming the need for the hovellers to be ready at all hours to secure their work). This last name was a happy choice for a boat which won imperishable fame in the skilled hands of her intrepid crew that included Dick Roberts and Edward Hanger who were both coxswains of the Deal lifeboat.

Although there is scant information regarding the early luggers, several of the later ones achieved notoriety: 'England's Glory', described as "a stout, staunch, seatub", was associated with one of the most remarkable salvage claims in local history. This famous South End lugger, manned by a smart crew, was invariably the first boat to arrive at a salvage operation. A British brig, 'Iron Crown', sailing from Shanghai to London, laden with a valuable general cargo, ran onto the east side of the Goodwins on 7 February 1866. The North Deal lifeboat went to her assistance and prevented her from becoming a total wreck but the Walmer lifeboat, which also attended, was hampered by heavy seas that threatened to capsize her. Eventually, with the aid of two steam tugs, 'Iron Crown' was floated and towed to London. 'England's Glory' had also launched into the teeth of the "sou'westerly bluster" to assist in the salvage. Her skipper, Bill Spears, and his crew sailed across the Sands, ran off kedge anchors into deep water and helped the ship to heave herself off the Goodwins. Taking into account that the ship, her passengers and crew had all been saved, an eventual award was made amounting to a phenomenal £12,000. However, this fund had to be shared amongst over sixty local boatmen.

'Early Morn' was reputed to have been one of the swiftest luggers at North Deal. (Her only rival for speed was 'Morning Glory') Master, Edward Hanger, and his crew took part in the rescues of five vessels driven ashore between Walmer and Kingsdown in a wild, single night: 12 February 1870. More famously, they landed twenty-four passengers and crew of the screw-steamer, 'Strathclyde', which was struck twice by the Hamburg liner, 'Franconia', on 17 February 1876. Both vessels were travelling in the same direction when they collided but 'Franconia' callously steamed into harbour to ensure her own safety without stopping to render assistance to the drowning crew of 'Strathclyde'. Her captain was later tried for manslaughter in both Britain and Germany. The unsavoury episode was graphically described in an edition of 'The Illustrated Police News' (11 March 1876). Its front page was profusely illustrated with engravings of the collision, the launching and the crew of 'Early Morn'.

'Diana' was a noble lugger that won an immense number of financial awards for her salvage work in the mid-Victorian period. She was named after an earlier boat notorious for having been apprehended with a tremendous amount of contraband aboard. In February 1805 two revenue cutters, 'Tartar' and 'Lively', were patrolling the coast near Dungeness when their officers observed 'Diana' surreptitiously making for

A Deal lugger making for a ship on the Goodwins.

the shore in order to offload her illicit cargo. On board were abundant casks of brandy, rum, wine and genever in addition to tea and tobacco. Just as the Customs officers attempted to seize the prohibited goods, a gang of armed men - on foot and horse - rushed down the beach and opened fire. The officers were compelled to retreat to nearby barracks where the Lancashire Militia were quartered. Obtaining their support the Revenue Men renewed their attack and, after one smuggler was shot, the mob dispersed. A reward was offered for the capture of the rogues but it was several years before the ringleaders were identified and taken to court. Predictably the jury found them:"Not Guilty".

'Tiger', one of the more conspicuous luggers on the foreshore, was stationed near the North Deal Lifeboat House. The largest of her type, she was usually employed when the anchor and cable needed by a vessel in difficulty were beyond the capacity of ordinary first class luggers. Consequently the awards made to her crew in her heydays were exceptionally numerous. 'Tiger' was known locally as the 'Committee Boat'because she was run by a team selected from her company of one hundred and twenty shareholders. Latterly, 'Tiger' was purchased by Messrs. James Edgar and Co. to transport tinned fish from their factory at North Deal to London. The company converted her into a fishing smack and while engaged in this pursuit she was run down by a ship off Dover. In time, her stage was eroded by the sea and when she was finally removed it marked the last of the luggers to be beached at the North End. A romantic tale featuring the crew of'Tiger', who are involved in a treasure hunt on the Goodwins, appears in Herbert Russell's'The Longshoreman' (1896).

Throughout the protracted French Wars the conduct of the Deal and Walmer boatmen was exemplary. The government ordered all their boats to be hidden in case they proved useful to escaping prisoners-of-war. During the expedition to Helder local boatmen volunteered their services to embark troops free of charge from the foreshore and later they rowed across the North Sea to fetch wounded soldiers back to England. In recognition of their valuable assistance they were declared exempt from impressment. Later, a Battalion of Infantry and a Squadron of Cavalry were raised for coastal defence as 'Royal Cinque Ports Fencibles'. (Oddly, volunteers for land defence were termed 'Sea Fencibles')

At Deal thirty-five luggers, each armed with a single carronade and manned by hovellers, were reviewed by Lord Warden, William Pitt, from the ramparts of Walmer Castle, on 15 September 1803. Pitt and his colleagues then boarded one of the finest luggers commanded by Captain Thomas Canney, Warden of the Cinque Ports Pilots, and "sailed up and down and round about the little fleet . . . amidst the deafening cheers from the boats". This display of patriotism by the boatmen was remarkable since only a few years earlier Pitt had accused them of smuggling and, in an act of unprecedented vengeance, ordered the destruction of their craft. Shortly after this event Captain Canney drowned when the 'India House' yacht capsized on a pleasure trip around Ramsgate Harbour.

Life expectancy of a lugger was twenty-five years owing to the wear and tear of launching and landing on an exposed foreshore. Several of these noble luggers, though, met a premature end. 'Fawn', one of the fastest luggers on the beach, was

Keeping a lookout for ships on the Goodwins © Angus Neill.

run down by a steamer off the North Foreland in 1864; 'Topsy' was sunk by a French vessel in the English Channel in 1868. 'Pride of the Sea' was dashed to pieces on the rocks off Shanklin Bay, Isle of Wight, in 1887; 'Walmer Castle' was also lost off Ventnor, Isle of Wight, on 15 March 1892. These last two luggers were sailing far afield in search of ships requiring a pilot to guide them through the dangerous waters surrounding the Goodwins.

A tragic loss of one of the most heroic hovelling luggers, 'Reform', took place on 16 January 1871. Previously, boatmen had petitioned Deal Town Council for the demolition of the Victorian pier since it severely hampered their launches and landings but their request, unsurprisingly, was ignored. In the early hours of that fateful morning, with a south-south-westerly gale blowing, distress flares were fired from a ship in the vicinity of the South Sand Head. Immediately 'Reform' was launched from her station opposite the Time Ball Tower. Four men jumped out of the boat to lay the lower woods as the lugger slid into the water and this action saved their lives.

Once afloat the lugger needed to be pulled through the surf by means of a haul off warp. (This was a long rope fastened to an anchor a little way out to sea which was a common device employed by the boatmen at one time) The vital moment of casting off this rope was misjudged and it became entangled which resulted in the boat being turned with its head into the wind. 'Reform' was driven towards the pier, the waves threw her onto the iron piles and she was smashed to pieces. Her crew of eleven were cast into the raging sea but there were few people about on that bitterly cold day to render assistance.

Two boatmen leapt over the turnstiles and threw ropes towards them while a desperate attempt was made to launch a galley punt from the nearby 'Fountain Inn'. Three members of the Deal lifeboat manned a small boat and they managed to pick up three survivors who had clung to spars from the wreckage. Eight bodies were later recovered and at the inquest the jury recommended that a lifeboat be placed on Deal Pier and the Coastguard boat be reinstated at Sandown Castle. The funeral procession was headed by the Mayor of Deal riding in his carriage while three hundred boatmen followed the coffin on its mournful journey to St. Leonard's Church.

The vacant place on the beach left by 'Reform' was taken by 'Galatea', described as "a beautiful lugger of 20 tons burden", built by Isaac Hayward. This giant 'cat' boat was pronounced to be one of the best craft for symmetry of design ever to grace the foreshore. Sadly, the crew of 'Galatea' came to grief while attempting to put a pilot aboard a barque at the height of a storm about two miles from the shore between Dover and Folkestone on 21 October 1874. Their punt, which was being towed in tandem, capsized leaving a sole survivor to bring the lugger home and relate his tragic tale. Predictably, the barque, after observing the accident, "spread her yards and ran before the wind to the Downs without attempting to succour the drowning men." Her neighbour had been 'Renown' which occupied a prime position opposite Marine Terrace Gardens until the seafront improvements at the end of the 19th century. She was then purchased as a relic and beached in front of Walmer Place where her cabin served as a changing room for gentle bathers.

The last lugger left on Deal beach was 'Cosmopolite' presented to the Town Council as a memorial to the heroic boatmen in 1909. (She had replaced an earlier lugger of the same name lost when a Welsh schooner, 'Coal Tar', collided with her while at anchor off Dungeness on 16 October 1890) This venerable "forepeaker" was permanently exposed to the elements and her weather-worn timbers began to deteriorate but the cost of repairing her proved prohibitive during the Great War. Sadly, 'Cosmopolite' was broken up for firewood about 1925. Apparently her tarred wooden planks and seasoned varnished topsides "burned well". Afterwards, her stern outrigger, mizzen mast and long bowsprit could be seen as washing line posts in back gardens in Lower Walmer.

'Cat' boats were slightly smaller than the luggers. They were completely open which made them ideal for transporting anchors and chains across the Downs. A complete set of large anchor and cable weighed over six tons which might be transported across the surf in heavy seas in rough weather. There was a portable deckhouse placed on a platform amidships to shelter the crew. Hulls were formed of oiled timber but the single top plank was painted black.

Galley punts were sailed but could also be rowed. Apparently they were exciting to sail on account of the lightness of their construction, remarkable seaworthiness and rapidity with which their masts could be shipped. Galley punts were twenty to thirty feet long and about five or seven feet wide with a single square cut 'lug' sail amidships. They also had five rowing thwarts and were steered by oar as well as a rudder when under sail. Owing to their narrow beam, shallow draught and huge sail, they required nearly half a ton of ballast which had to be rapidly shifted to the weather side at each change of tack. Galley punts were open boats - which meant they could be extremely wet - but they were also deep and, therefore, ideal for carrying provisions and life-saving. Often their crew of three or four journeyed westwards down Channel where they were employed in the dangerous work of "hooking" incoming steamers in order to put a pilot aboard. Galley punts - a cross between a galley and a punt - were known as "knock-toes". This curious expression is explained by a puntsman in William Clark Russell's 'In The Middle Watch' (1899): ". . . our craft are so small that when we're in them we are altogether, and so knock our toes agin another."

Galleys were rowed but could also be sailed. Normally they were twenty-eight feet long with a five foot beam. Galleys (known as 'long eights') carried a single mast with a dipping lugsail but no jib. They were banked for between four, six or eight long oars known as "sweeps". Their peculiarity was that they were launched stern first and, for that reason, they had either a transom or a 'beaching' lute stern. These long, light, graceful boats had an amazing turn of speed and on calm days could outstrip every other type of craft on the beach. They were even able to cross the Goodwins at high tide while heavier craft drew too much water to achieve this daring feat.

Galleys rowing more than four oars were illegal since they could serve no other purpose than smuggling. Invariably they were painted white so that they would be concealed by the surf from pursuers. Smuggling galleys could be forty feet long and they carried an enormous press of sail. In addition, they were flat bottomed and constructed with hollow beams so that they could conceal a variety of contraband from snuff to silk. These immense craft could be pulled across to France in the short space of three hours and, if spotted on their return journey laden with contraband, they could be dragged over the Goodwins, rowed across the Downs and landed in Kent before the Revenue Cutter - in hot pursuit - could sail round the Sands.

After the Second World War only four galleys remained. The youngest was Thomas Upton's eight-oared galley, 'Seamen's Hope', built of elm by Nichols of Deal in 1907. About 1937 'Flint' Roberts presented his galley, 'Our Boys', to the Rowing Club. Two further galleys are now exhibited at Deal's Maritime Museum. 'Saxon King' (originally named 'Harold') is a four-oared galley built in 1892 by Henry Gardner. 'Undaunted' was probably built by Harry Hayward in the early years of the 20th century and was faithfully restored by Ben Bailey, son of a former cosxswain of Walmer Lifeboat. It was the last seaworthy galley to remain on Deal beach.

There were constant disputes over who had the right to a wreck which struck the Goodwin Sands. In 1602 the Lord Warden insisted that, as Admiral of the Cinque Ports, "he enjoyed all wreck of the sea" which contradicted the established tradition that the Crown was entitled to a share of the spoils from all wrecks around the coast of Britain. Richard Larn cites a letter to King Henry VIII which accuses the Lord Warden of laying an unlawful claim to wrecked goods and adds gruesome details: "When men have been found on the sea-sand their garments and their purses have been taken

Deal Pilot Boat. Courtesy: The Powell-Cotton Museum and Quex House.

from them, and their bodies left unburied, and eaten by hogs and dogs." (22 January 1533) In times of war a ship on shore with all her treasure was regarded as a "prize to the Crown". Lucrative cargoes, in reality, went to whoever arrived first on the scene of a wreck and who could artfully spirit them away.

Local boatmen were masters in this field and they gained an unenviable reputation as 'Deal Sharks'. Plunder over the centuries numbered barrels of rum, casks of wine, kegs of gunpowder, tobacco, wheat, palm oil, linseed, hides, calico, candles, tallow, soap, dye, indigo, lead, iron, zinc and plumbago from which graphite for lead pencils was obtained. More unusual "findalls" were ice, nails, wax, cement, gold dust, matches, chamber pots, lamp glasses, sewing machines, musket flints, buffalo horns, elephants' teeth, Roman antiquities and uncorked champagne. Indiamen surrendered tea, coffee, sugar, nuts, rice, rubber, cinnamon, chicory, pepper, and exotic spices. Most valued was seasoned ships' timber which was used in the construction of boatmen's homes.

Salvaging a ship brought huge rewards. Official salvors raced out from the nearest port when they noted a vessel in difficulty. If her hull was deemed to be damaged beyond repair and the ship not worth refloating they negotiated terms with her captain to make the ship secure and save her cargo. These terms often caused friction. Ship owners on both sides of the Channel protested that the Kent salvors were little more than pirates. The French constantly complained that salvors condemned ships that were still seaworthy; they forced captains to accept extortionate terms; they boarded

185

ships without consent and were far more interested in salving cargo than in rescuing either passengers or crew. In extreme cases they were even accused of deliberately scuppering a salvable ship.

Occasionally Deal boatmen were, themselves, accused of wrecking.

According to the Cinque Ports charter of 1236 a stranded ship was not considered a wreck while a man or a beast survived on board. (Otherwise, the ship was deemed a 'derelict') Larn gives the first instance of a shipwreck in the Downs as an unknown wreck off Sandwich in the reign of Edward I. Her owner, William Martyn, complained to the king that while laden with armour his ship had been cast adrift and plundered by local boatmen. Further charges concern looting of a hoy barque carrying wheat and iron lost on the Goodwins on 18 February 1542; a Portuguese vessel stripped bare in 1543 and 'Dolphin' plundered in 1585.

Elvin notes an instance of wrecking in his 'Records of Walmer' (1890). On 18 February 1807 a tremendous gale sprang up from the north-east in the early morning. In the space of a few hours several vessels came ashore between Deal Castle and the South Foreland, including a brig at Kingsdown, where all the crew perished, and a large West Indiaman at St. Margaret's Bay. Five ships were dismasted and numerous small craft found themselves in similar plight. Three warships - 'Sole Bay' frigate, 'Railleur' sloop and 'Devastation' bomb - left the Downs in great distress and rode out the gale in the open sea. Twenty-one vessels were reported lost between the Forelands. Elvin protested: ". . . to the disgrace of everyone concerned pillage is said to have prevailed to an unparalleled extent."

A more serious instance of wrecking took place aboard 'North' on Thursday 30 August 1866. The case was investigated by the Board of Trade and its findings were reported to the House of Commons. 'North' (1,238 tons) went aground on the Goodwins about two miles north-east of the South Sand lightship. She had sailed from Liverpool carrying coal for Aden and her captain had secured a return cargo of rice from Bassein in Burma. She had stopped for fresh provisions and water at St. Helena and Queenstown before proceeding up Channel for London. It was pitch black when she struck the Sands and her captain and crew promptly abandoned ship in their own boats. All were saved. The crew of the Deal lugger, 'Reform', rescued fourteen seamen including members of the steam tug, 'Wellington', which had foundered while assisting the stricken ship. In the confusion all the ship's stores, instruments, fittings, furniture, tools and personal belongings were left behind.

At daybreak the wreck was clearly visible surrounded by a swarm of thirty luggers from stations around the coast. Their crews completely stripped 'North' of everything remotely valuable - sails, rope, wire, canvas, rigging, blocks, shackles, deadeyes - so that only her masts remained. All the ship's instruments, carpenter's tools and crew's clothing vanished. Even the copper sheathing was removed from the hull as the ship lay - high and dry - on the sands. All this had long been common practice but the objection was that nothing had been surrendered to the Receiver of Wrecks. Canvas, rope and blocks from the wreck were traced to marine dealers in Deal and Dover while ships' stores were located at a firm of papermakers at River. All these firms were brought to trial at Canterbury. The case foundered, curiously, since the River firms' book-keeping proved to be sadly neglectful while all of the boatmen questioned suffered serious lapses of memory. Even the coastguards were suspected of withholding evidence and the costly case resulted in little more than minor convictions. The national press severely criticised the Deal boatmen for their greed and made them the scapegoats for the crime while ignoring the courage and compassion of the crew of the lugger, 'Reform'.

Most famous case of wrecking concerns Peter Atkins, a Deal boatman, who was sentenced to death for his dubious activities. Homeward bound, the West Indiaman, 'Endeavour', struck the Goodwins on 8 February 1805. She was carrying a cargo of rum, sugar and coffee (valued at £23,000) the property of the ship's owner, Henry Wildman, and his agent, John Kneller, who was on board. Atkins boarded the stranded vessel at daybreak and, realising the ship was doomed, volunteered his services.

Atkins hailed a number of boats to help load the cargo safely. Eight puncheons of rum were recovered and stowed aboard Atkins' own boat, 'Noble', which made for the coast. This trip was repeated three times and on the final journey Kneller climbed aboard. The boat was then loaded with four hogsheads of sugar, two tierces of coffee, a small cask of rum plus the ship's compass. About a mile from the shore, Atkins ordered Kneller into another boat from which, he said, it would be easier to embark. Meanwhile, he promised to land the remaining cargo and load it onto waiting horses.

Mr. Iggulden was appointed to act as agent for the ship's owners and all salvaged goods were ordered to be delivered into his custody. Disgracefully only a fraction of the valuable cargo was ever recovered. Wildman's son duly arrived at Deal intent upon looking after his father's affairs and, in the presence of Kneller, he questioned Atkins in the agent's office and, later, in 'The Three Kings Inn'. Atkins, at first, denied all knowledge of the missing cargo but after close questioning he protested that he had retained one small cask of rum which he had offered to sell to save the owner having to pay duty! And the coffee? Apparently it had been shared out amongst his crew.

The owners, recognising that these were blatant lies, placed the matter in the hands

An idle moment - leaning against a capstan at the north end.
Courtesy: Deal Library.

of H.M. Customs. Officers were ordered to search Atkins' house in Beach Street where they recovered two sacks of sugar. The occupant, meanwhile, had fled. A warrant was issued for his arrest but it was not for three months that he was discovered hiding in his own house. Bow Street Runners arrived from London to arrest him but they were repelled by a hostile mob. Finally, the Cavalry were called in to quell the riot and apprehend the culprit.

Atkins appeared at the Old Bailey charged with "felony and piracy on the high seas, within the jurisdiction of the Admiralty of England." He was found guilty and sentenced to death by hanging. Conveniently, Atkins' wife was housekeeper to Lady Hester Stanhope at Walmer Castle. Her Ladyship felt compelled to intervene and the sentence was commuted to transportation. Atkins was sent to Brazil where he was put in charge of the naval stores at Rio de Janeiro. Later he settled in Guernsey, then Calais, where he kept an inn, before returning to Deal in the mid-19th century. Hailed as a hero - at least in his home town - he died at the ripe old age of eighty-four.

For centuries Deal boatmen acted as unofficial pilots. The Downs was a perfect location for foreign ships to take on board a pilot who wanted to navigate either the tortuous route round the North Foreland and into the Thames Estuary or the dangerous stretch of the Goodwin Sands in this narrow portion of the English Channel. Navigators refused the services of these boatmen at their peril since they had the reputation of knowing "every spit and ridge, swatch and gulley" of the dangerous sandbanks. Further, it was said that if a pilot was wanted for any port in Europe, even up to the Baltic, one could be found in Deal. William Clark Russell interviewed a local puntsman in 'In the Middle Watch' (1885) who claimed his patch as a pilot stretched from Beachy Head to London Bridge. Commonly, pilots went far further afield and were even known to have gone in this capacity to Australia.

'Deal Luggers' painted by W.M. Williamson in 1869
© Deal Maritime and Local History Museum.

188

An early mention of a Deal pilot refers to the 'Gerald Peterson' at the end of the 16th century. The ship's master, being "vnskilful to the sandes and passadge to London hired a pilott in the Downes. . . to take chardge of the said shipp & bring her to London." At the beginning of the 17th century the Lord Warden wrote to the Mayor of Sandwich complaining that this port allowed ships from other countries to navigate the Haven without a qualified town pilot aboard. Presumably he was cautious about foreigners becoming cognisant with this area of the Kent coast.

There were dire punishments for pilots who failed to navigate correctly. Incompetent pilots in the days when aids to navigation relied more on memory rather than accurate charts might find themselves "clapped in the bilbowes". In 1585 John Vassall was piloting a ship that foundered on the Goodwins - it was disputed whether the accident was caused by the pilot or the crew - and ten years later a Downs pilot allowed a Dutch ship to be wrecked on the Sands. (The fact that this pilot had only one eye may have contributed towards the disaster) On 21 September 1743 a man-o'-war, 'Colchester', stranded on sandbanks while making for the Downs and forty sailors drowned. The Deal Pilot was tried by court martial and sentenced to two years in London's Marshalsea Prison.

Channel or North Sea Pilots were technically unqualified and therefore lacked a pilot's licence. Many had served as youths in the Royal Navy or Mercantile Service and their knowledge of the sea was unrivalled. Their practice was to acquire a testimonial after successfully piloting a ship and to offer these "testamurs" to a captain of a ship they had never before piloted once they had scrambled aboard. Masters, recognising their lack of protection, would often use local pilots as cheap labour and bargained for their services except at such times as prevailing conditions rendered their services imperative.

Deal pilots took enormous risks when searching for potential clients. Perilously a team of luggermen would cruise the Channel until they found a homeward bound vessel requiring a pilot. The subsequent attempt to board that vessel in rough weather was a dangerous mission and serious accidents occurred. Captains refused to slow down - speed was essential - so that prospective pilots were forced to climb aboard while ships were in full motion. Each boat would carry about six hands, four of whom might be transferred to ships, the other two were required to bring their lugger home. As a rule they brought a homeward bound vessel as far as Dungeness and then handed her over to an official Cinque Ports or Trinity House pilot but, under stress of weather, they might even bring a vessel into the Downs.

Pilots - official or unofficial - constantly faced danger. On New Year's Day 1861 the German brig, 'Guttenberg', smashed into the Goodwins in a snowstorm and the Deal pilot, Henry Pearson, was drowned. In May 1862 the pilot cutter, 'Princess', was struck by a barque between Dover and Dungeness while another Deal pilot, John Pembroke, was killed as he jumped overboard. A terrible accident occurred when the Dover Trinity House Pilot Cutter No. 4 was making a routine night-time cruise in the Channel in March 1879. She was run down by a Hamburg steamer just after midnight and all the pilots - seven from Dover, five from Deal and one from Kingsdown - were killed.

Deal pilots would race out in their galleys immediately upon sighting a ship's signal - burning blue lights, firing rockets or flying the ensign upside down - in order to be first to pick up the commission to guide the vessel out to sea or into safe anchorage. Captains then had a choice whether to employ a licensed or an

189

unlicensed pilot. Licences were granted to local pilots usually through a system of patronage to Freemen of Deal or Sandwich. Temporary licences were available but these were both expensive and restrictive, particularly regarding distances. One source mentions 'Three Leagues from the Land' which barely allowed a pilot to reach the back of the Goodwins.

A rare account of the life of a boatman who became an official pilot was penned by William Henry Stanton (1803 - 1878) in his posthumously published, 'Journal of a Deal Pilot' (1929). Described as "A shabby little quarto volume, painfully and clumsily written, ornamented with a few crude drawings, such as seafarers paint on their sea chests", the narrative, in fact, remains compelling. Stanton was born in Deal, educated at Walmer and sent to sea at the age of fifteen. His father had been found guilty of smuggling and imprisoned after all his possessions had been seized, leaving his family in abject poverty.

One summer evening William was strolling idly along the beach when Captain Thomas approached him and offered him a job as a hand on board his schooner, 'Nancy'. His first expedition was a cross-Channel run from Ostend to Folkestone where he helped unload the cargo, part of which was 'concealed'. Returning from a similar trip from Portsmouth the kindly yet eccentric captain became ill and William had to row ashore at Kingsdown to find discreet boatmen who would steer the schooner into Ramsgate Harbour and dispose of the illicit cargo. William's third commission was as a member of the crew of a hired smack, 'Samuel and Elizabeth', which almost sank before it reached the shore.

A company was formed by public subscription under Mr. Trownsil, Storekeeper of the Navy Yard in 1816. 'The Fishermen's Friends Society' acquired two sloops and a schooner from Sandwich for speculation in the Icelandic Cod Industry. Captain Thomas commanded one of these sloops and he offered a placement with guaranteed

South End luggers by the iron pier. Courtesy: Deal Library.

wages to William. Their ship, 'Prosperity', lived up to its name but her sister ships fared badly which curtailed further expeditions. Afterwards the company tried curing herrings for exportation but this venture also collapsed when the treasurers absconded with the profits.

After numerous trips around the coast transporting a variety of cargoes William Stanton accepted more adventurous commissions. In 1819, he joined the cargo ship, 'Lady Lushington', bound for Calcutta. There he was first shipwrecked and then chased by a tiger. Next he boarded a brigantine, 'John Cato', ostensibly sailing for Cuba, but he was alarmed when his captain became obsessed with chasing pirates. Upon his safe return Stanton decided life would be less hazardous if he invested in his own boating business.

Stanton bought a sixth share in a set of boats that included the lugger, 'Ox', a cat, 'Fox', and a galley punt. His crew ('Sea Highwaymen') were based in the snug of the 'Three Compasses' in Lower Street. Stanton was soon involved with his large company of skilled men in the dangerous round of rescue, salvage, ferrying provisions and supplying anchors to ships in trouble. His escapades are faithfully recorded in his 'Journal'. One of his first tasks was to rescue a sinking ship in which terrified female convicts were trapped. Another time he assisted in putting out a fire aboard a collier. On a third occasion he was involved in salvaging a stricken barge whose cargo included a veritable menagerie - "pigs, dogs, monkeys".

Naturally, Stanton employed his small fleet for smuggling. His 'Journal' reveals some of the tricks of this trade. Valuable cargoes of tea, silks and ribbons brought over from France were hidden among bags of ballast. Another ruse was to paint his boats white so that they were camouflaged against the surf. Often his boats made sham crossings, returning with an empty hold, so that if they were searched by the authorities it would throw them off the scent. Stanton made plenty of successful 'runs' which earned him tremendous profits. One risk was that he needed to employ a large number of people in his nocturnal activities. . . and one of them was an informer. Stanton relates an hilarious incident when 'Ox' was apprehended when beaching laden with contraband opposite the Semaphore Tower. A bitter dispute arose between the Customs Officers and the Preventive Men, both of whom claimed their "prize", valued at £10,000.

Stanton recounts the dramatic incident when he attended a German brig, 'Alexander', stranded on the Goodwins in a blizzard on 31 December 1830. He and his crew sailed their lugger, 'Ox', over the shallow waters covering the Sands during the night to reach the doomed ship. They climbed aboard 'Alexander' as she began to break up and Stanton watched, helplessly, as the owner's son drowned in the cabin. Stanton's young companion, John Wilkins, also died. He, himself, was trapped when a spar crashed onto the deck but he was mercifully released when a huge wave washed him overboard. He kept afloat by clinging to buoyant wooden railings until rescued by the crew of a lugger, 'Pink', from Ramsgate. When he presented himself at the Dover Court to claim a share of the salvage, he was curtly informed by the magistrate: "There was no precedent to award for saving life."

The inevitable result of such poor recompense was that Stanton's fleet fell into disrepair. When his boats became condemned an alternative occupation for his crew was to offer their services as official pilots. Around 1833 there was a grievance among the boatmen that they were being denied the right to become Branch Pilots. Applications depended, not upon merit or experience, but whether the boatmen were

Cigarette card showing fishing at Deal © Angus Neill.

A postal service was set up between London and the Downs by Oliver Cromwell. Horseriders brought the post over land while boatmen conveyed it to the ships, alerted by lighting bonfires on the beach.

Ships' letter bags delivered everywhere from Australia to the West Indies were landed here but this lucrative service ended when steam tugs were employed to carry mail.

A Strangers' Burial Ground where the bodies of unknown sailors were interred was situated in the vicinity of the 'Jolly Sailor' Inn and the Parish Workhouse.

Children of boatmen's families were taught to say this prayer: "God bless father and mother and send them a good hovel tonight."

First entry in St. George's Church Burial Register gives the profession of the departed as "smuggler". This indicates that the trade was then open and respectable. Vaults in the churchyard were acquired by parishioners primarily to store contraband.

Boatmen sweeping the seabed with grapnels for constricting items brought to the surface parts of a gentleman's phaeton in 1794.

Freemen of Sandwich or Dover. A petition was despatched to the Houses of Parliament and the result was that a Select Committee was appointed to question witnesses before the House of Commons. Stanton appeared in person before a distinguished panel of gentlemen where he answered their searching questions in such a brilliant manner that he won the approval of several Members of Parliament.

The Duke of Wellington, Lord Warden of the Cinque Ports, was also Elder Brother of Trinity House. He was ultimately responsible for appointing pilots. Privately, he considered that the Deal boatmen were being unfairly treated and he insisted that they should, at least, be examined. A ballot was held among the boatmen to make applications to become a fully-licensed pilot at Dover Court. Stanton was one of the men chosen. Sir Thomas Troubridge, Chairman of the Select Committee, still refused to accept Stanton's qualifications. Apparently, after all his years of service at sea in home waters, he was not yet considered competent to be a licensed pilot. His response was to petition the Duke of Wellington in person. His pluck was admired by the Iron Duke who agreed to act as his sponsor.

When Stanton finally appeared before the Court of Lodemanage, he was treated in a respectful manner. Afterwards, the Duke sent for him and invited him to dine. "I, of course accepted, and a most splendid set out it was, of every luxury you could think of." Later, an official document arrived from Dover Castle: "I do hereby certify that William Henry Stanton has been examined and found qualified to be a pilot of the

Fellowship of the Cinque Ports, and that he will be admitted therein when a vacancy shall occur"(4 November 1834). Stanton was assigned to Ramsgate.

William Stanton was forced to retire from his lucrative career of piloting after an accident when returning home from the Pilot House in 1867. Dick Roberts, Coxswain of the Deal lifeboat, who sailed the 'Early Morn' with Stanton's son,

A trio of Deal boatmen in their seal skin caps photographed by Paul Martin 1886. Courtesy: Victoria and Albert Museum.

described him as"a fine-looking but very quiet and reserved man". Stanton turned to cobbling boots and shoes to prevent him entering the Workhouse. It also gave him time to write a detailed account of his turbulent career in his 'Journal'. A modern chronicler, Bella Bathurst in'Wreckers' (2005) admits that all his life Stanton made his living, like most Deal boatmen, "through a combination of guile, courage, sharp practice and - if necessary - violence."

Deal, according to William Clark Russell, provided the best boat builders in the world. Boats built in the vicinity were the product of generations of practical experience. Apparently there were no plans but three moulds or sections were used and these were handed down from father to son. Among the famous craftsmen were Stephen Brown, John Harrison, Morris Langley, Thomas Stokes, Henry Gardener, Ratcliff and Allen, all of whom had their workshops at the North End. James Nicholas, who came from a family of boatmen, started his own building yard in 1858. He often went afloat and once assisted in the rescue of a ship, 'Atlantic', stranded on the Goodwins in 1848. Nicholas had a working knowledge, therefore, of local boats and was later able to adapt from luggers to motor boats.

Another noted firm was begun by Michael Bayly, taken over by his son, Isaac, and eventually owned by their partner, Henry Durban. Durban"like his predecessors, held a high reputation for building craft of unrivalled stability and with sailing qualities which were not excelled on any part of the coast", affirms E.C. Pain in 'Last of the Luggers' (1929). Bayly's yard was adjacent to Sandown Castle. The Kingsdown fishing lugger, 'Pilgrim', built by this firm at a cost of £400, represented the last stage in the building of local luggers. A Resident Surveyor was appointed to inspect the seaworthiness of locally-built boats.

Premier local boat builder at the beginning of the 19th century was Thomas Hayward who lived in 'Prospect House' at the end of Cottage Row (now Wellington Road). His dwelling, set in a pretty garden enclosed by undulating white palings, boasted a latticed portico and a profusion of sash windows with tall chimneys and dormers in its mansard roof. Thomas, his son, Isaac Gammon Hayward, and his grandson, another Thomas, built a great number of luggers - 'Dart', 'Renown', 'James and Thomas' and 'Foresters' Pride' - in their adjoining workshop. Their business lasted for almost a century and their advertisement cards pictured the variety of boats they constructed - luggers, yachts, doubled-bowed ships' lifeboats, ten-oared galleys (which were at that time illegal) and whalers (small open boats, pointed at both ends and steered by an oar instead of a rudder, suitable for the whaling fleet).

Thomas Hayward junior recalled: "The largest boat ever built in Deal was the 'Alexandra', for a Ramsgate owner. The shop had to be lengthened in front, and the ground dug out before laying the keel, to a depth of three or four feet, to ensure sufficient height below the flooring of the loft overhead. It was hauled up South Street by means of one of the capstans at the top. The other luggers were simply drawn up on greasy woods by means of a rope in the hands of a number of watermen and others glad to get one or two pints."

'Alexandra', named after the consort of Edward VII, cost £700 to build and she was launched on 17 February 1866. She was cutter rigged and designed to serve the dual purpose of a lugger for sturdy service in winter and a yacht for pleasure trips in the summer. 'Alexandra' was lost on the Goodwins when holed while salvaging the cargo of mahogany from the brigantine, 'Germania', on 25 March 1870. Her crew of nine scrambled into their punt in tow and rowed into Ramsgate Harbour but they were bankrupt since their lugger was uninsured. (By coincidence, another lugger destined for Ramsgate was 'Caroline', named after the luckless wife of George IV, built by Haywards in 1823)

The launching of local boats was always attended by a ceremony.

The Earl of Clanwilliam performed the naming ceremony of the splendid lugger, 'Garland', built by Hayward's and launched from a site near the Royal Signal Tower on 10 September 1867. The following year the lugger, 'Mary', described quaintly as combining all that "wisdom, strength and beauty could devise", was christened by Mrs. Henry Brassey in the presence of Mr. Henry Brassey, M.P. and Mr. Knatchbull Hugessen, M.P. Bedecked with "a profusion of flags, which gave colour to the scene, the 'Mary' glided gracefully into the water. . . amid the hearty cheers of numerous spectators assembled to witness the proceedings."

Last lugger actually designed and constructed locally appears to have been ordered for service abroad. She was built by Messrs Nicholas of North Deal for government service at Freemantle, Western Australia. The unnamed craft was of great strength and vast dimensions (length 38 ft, beam 10 ft, depth 5 ft). She had a forepeak extending to her foremast, a mainmast for use in fine weather, and a mizzen. Her keel was built of Canadian elm but additional timbers were shaped from young English elms grown in the neighbouring countryside and fixed in a green state. Finally, she was copper sheathed to the waterline. Upon completion the lugger was sailed to the India Docks in the south-west of England by James Nicholas and his two sons in July 1896. There she was put on board 'Port Hunter' to be delivered to her destination at the far side of the world.

The demise of the industry was caused by the advent of steam, the scarcity of timber and the decline of fishing. At one time there was a daily transportation of local fish by rail to London's Billingsgate Market). All the same, supplying and repairing craft for

Kentish boatmen kept several modest boatyards alive almost until the end of the 20th century. Late survivors were Able and Cory. It appears that the last timber boat, 'Golden Vanity', was built at Deal in the mid-1970s. Attendant with boat building was the sail making industry at Deal. A Mr. Finnis started his own sail making business early in the 19th century; he was succeeded by his three sons and this firm only closed in 1900. Commissions were never lacking after a storm when whole suits of sails were ordered for immediate delivery. These urgent demands, together with the equipment required by a large fleet of luggers, supported a remunerative industry.

Launching a boat directly from the shore was fraught with danger. Accidents were frequent and, sadly, sometimes involved the pupils from Elizabeth Carter House School who played among the anchors, capstans and boathouses on the foreshore. They earned the odd penny by helping boatmen haul up their luggers in rough weather and this often led to disastrous consequences. Once 'Renown' was being beached in a heavy swell which washed her broadsides back into the water. Boatmen were holding onto a rope attached to the masthead in an attempt to prevent her from rolling seawards. A few boys were asked to help but one lad neglected to let go of the rope as the boat was hit by a huge wave and he was dragged underneath her hull. Swiftly one of the boatmen pulled him from under the lurching craft by a billhook. He was lucky to escape with just a dousing and a tear in his school jacket.

In January 1863 'Albion' was returning to her stage near the Navy Yard when another accident occurred. At the critical moment when this lugger was being hauled up the shelving shingle her rope attached to the capstan snapped. She ran backwards causing the capstan to revolve at a tremendous speed. One of the spinning bars struck a labourer, Robert Vickers, a fatal blow on the back of his head. A similar accident had happened the previous winter when 'Sappho' was being hauled up the shingle opposite the 'Port Arms'. The lugger was being turned round ready for her next launch when the handful of men who were holding her back were overpowered. They jumped clear as the boat ran with gathering momentum down the slope and into the water. There was no time to "unship" the capstan bars which flew round and struck several young boys, one of whom was fatally injured. At that time the capstans were a greater distance from the sea at the South End than at the North End owing to coastal erosion.

Working boatmen were a familiar aspect of the Deal scene until the immediate postwar period. Their distinctive clothing may have been a survival of the uniform of the Navy Yard. Crews spent hours sitting in the driving spray and therefore their apparel needed to keep them warm even when soaking wet. Boatmen wore oilskins, consisting of trousers, called 'fear-noughts', which reached up to their armpits plus long coats, fastened with ropes, that covered their knees. Top clothes were heavy pilot cloth jackets, buttoned closely over their blue woollen jerseys, and painted overalls with either thick leather Wellington boots or pumps. Long woollen scarves or 'mufflers' were wound tightly round their neck but sou'westers, called 'dread-noughts', worn in foul weather might be exchanged for Elsinore woollen or sealskin caps in summer. Photographs show boatmen wearing bowlers as they turned the capstans but these hats were exchanged for derbies when the men walked to church on Sundays.

Longshoremen could be glimpsed on calm, quiet days lounging against their little tarred huts on their capstan grounds, peering through telescopes keeping "a close eye" on the Goodwins. They might be sporting nanny-goat beards or mutton chop whiskers, chewing tobacco quid or smoking short-stemmed snout warmers. At other

Winching up a boat on the beach with the lugger, 'Seamen's Hope', behind.

times, boatmen could find refuge in the various Reading Rooms, one of which was directly opposite the pier (opened by the Rector of Deal in 1858) while another was along the Strand (opened by Mrs Woollaston in 1873). Deal boatmen were treated as minor celebrities. Their gruff stern manner belied their compassion. Many of them had seen their relatives or companions drown and they, themselves, had taken part in daring rescues. George Philpott was one local hero who claimed to have personally saved one hundred lives and yet he died in poverty although he merited an obituary in the 'Daily Telegraph' in 1850.

Deal and Walmer boatmen were endowed with curious nicknames. What, one wonders, were the origins of 'Bombard' Dick, 'Cobbler' Stanton, 'Papercollar' Joe and 'Stickup' Adams? Later boatmen retained this custom. Among the more puzzling were 'Bubbles' Fouet, 'Nutty' Revell, 'Spaniard' May, 'Julia' Adams, 'Black' Harry, 'Cripple' Bill Stevens, 'Long Jabber' Marsh, 'Awful Doings' May, 'Duke' and 'Toddy' Cribbin, 'Toe' and 'Seven Belly' Budd.

In mid-Victorian times steam began to predominate the method of propulsion at sea. This was most evident locally in the majority of cross-Channel routes and regular packet services to the Continent. The presence of steamships had a marked effect on the decline of Downs Anchorage and, ultimately, the economy of the port of Deal. Formerly, sailing ships, becalmed, would linger in the vicinity but steamships could continue their journey regardless of adverse wind and inclement weather. Steam tugs began to pick up inward bound sailing ships at the end of their ocean voyages and tow them straight through the Downs, round the North Foreland and into the Thames Estuary to dock in the Pool of London. Ships had little need to moor off Deal or Ramsgate to take on board fresh water or provisions nor did they require the services of local boatmen or pilots. Further, iron chains were substituted for hempen cables so that the custom of 'sweeping' with grappling irons and salvaging lost tackle fell into disuse. Improvements to navigation resulted in the reduction of Coast Guards and Customs Officers but this resulted, naturally, in a wave of smuggling - cigars and tobacco at that time proving to be the most lucrative contraband.

Towards the end of the 19th century the construction of Dover Harbour and the building of a sea wall to protect The Marina contributed to the decline of the boating industry while abnormally high tides took their toll of the remaining capstan grounds and claimed the last of the luggers hauled ashore at the North End. The Royal Navy declined to use the Downs on a regular basis and, although coastal schooners and sailing barges continued to shelter there until World War Two, there was not enough hovelling and salvaging to support the remaining luggers at the South End after 1910. The number of beach boats dwindled and the families of boatmen were forced to rely upon the various charities in the neighbourhood for their meagre sustenance. According to Larn:". . . slowly a way of life for an entire community began to change." Distress among the boatmen, who had enjoyed prosperity during the prolonged French Wars, was already acute by the middle of Victoria's reign. Large fleets of warships no longer sheltered in the Downs and in the subsequent time of peace their services were no longer required and boatmen had recourse to the workhouses which were filled to capacity. They were forced either to seek alternative employment or emigrate in ships which departed from the Downs. One advertisement for settlers to join as civilians in the military garrison at the colony of the Cape of Good Hope appeared in 'The Times' in 1821. A group was selected from Deal and after six months the boatmen arrived in Port Elizabeth where they inhabited an area still known as the 'Deal Party'.

Thirteen Deal boatmen - Bowbyes, Bowles, Clayson, Cory, Hayward, Jarman, Neames, Newton, Norris, Roberts, Rogers, Whyman and Wilds - formed a party of

A good haul of sprats.

emigrants who boarded the aptly named, 'Mystery', bound for Canterbury, New Zealand, on 21 December 1858. These former Downs lifeboatmen and Channel pilots divided their living between Lyttleton and Timaru. There they were engaged in conveying bales of wool to coasters in summer and employed in fishing industries in winter. Letters home reveal that these immigrants were warmly welcomed and fairly treated. First rate provisions had been provided for their free voyage; boats could be easily hired for them to find well-paid work and land was sold to them cheaply to build their own homes. "There is nobody poor here," commented John Jones Bowles, a former pilot, on his Colonial life in April 1859.

Around 1880 Deal boatmen who remained turned their attention to fishing in wintertime. Luggers were constructed to surmount the difficulties of a steep beach and a heavy surf so they were not a class of boat easily adapted for this purpose. The most suitable for fishing were foresail-and-mizzen punts which proved ideal for drift netting. Mainstay was shoals of mackerel which were, at that time, regarded as a luxury and fetched high prices in the London markets. Local fish including whitebait, whiting, herring, sprats and cod were rapidly transported by rail for sale in the City. There was still the obligation to observe Fridays as fast days and therefore there was always a ready market for fresh fish (although it was often preferred smoked or salted).

There was an abundant harvest. 'Wild Girl', for instance, lost seventeen of her nets which became too heavy with her catch when fishing off the Goodwins in October 1874. It was not uncommon for luggers to lose their nets when fishing further out to sea for they were constantly cut adrift by passing vessels in the English Channel. In addition, there was great rivalry between English and French fishermen and this animosity among the boatmen, who were veterans of the French Wars, led to open warfare. On the plus side, fishing nets played a conspicuous part in concealing

Waiting for a trip to the Goodwins aboard 'Lady Irene'.
Courtesy: Tom Burnham.

198

contraband since a close examination of them was such an obnoxious task for Customs officials!

A thriving fish-preserving industry was established in Victorian times. It owed its origin to a profitable method of preserving fish in oil discovered by the French in 1840. There were two rival companies - a Scottish firm set up by James Edgar J.P. in 1877 and a French firm begun by Wenceslas Chancerelle in 1882 - that flourished at the North End. Edgar contracted thirty local luggers plus the same number at Dungeness. An average catch of sprats was thirty thousand on each tide but on 'Harvest Days' Edgar's factory caught over one hundred lasts of sprats. This firm mainly converted sprats into sardines and their 'Marie Elizabeth' brand was in great demand at home and abroad. (They were particulary popular in China and Japan) Chancerelle's 'Two Britons' factory which employed an additional forty-one boats, also possessed canneries in Brittany and Portugal. The combined firms employed around five hundred people during the height of the spratting season which contributed enormously to the town's prosperity. High tariffs of railway companies and poaching by foreign fishermen contributed to their demise. Sources, in any case, became exhausted and both factories had closed by the start of the Second World War.

Each summer, "Between the Wars", luggers were fitted out with gaff sails as pleasure boats. They were a glorious sight when launching - all sails set - directly off the open beach, overloaded with passengers packed tightly on their plank seats for a brief "trip round the Goodwins". Tripping motor boats - 'Skylark', 'Titlark' 'Moss Rose', 'Britannic', 'Lady Beatty' and 'Lady Haig' - were confined to the South End. These small craft were clinker-built and brightly varnished with either counter or elliptical sterns. They made an impressive sight with their polished brass work and short stern staff flying either the Pilot Flag or Red Ensign. Boatmen dressed smartly for the occasion in peaked cheesecutters with white tops, white shirts and navy blue guernseys. They would stand on the Promenade calling out "Lovely on the water", "Half hour trips" or "Just a-going out". Each of their boats was licensed to carry two crew and twelve passengers from Easter until September.

Boating parties were organised each autumn for visiting anglers who relished the prospect of fishing with rod and line around the sunken wrecks of the Goodwins. They were served by a fleet of motor boats which were launched stern first with a reverse gear that enabled them to pull away easily from the shore. Modern craft included 'Dido'

Hovellers who raced to salvage the American ship, 'Georgia', were disappointed to find that her only cargo was a coffin complete with corpse while other boatmen were shocked when they boarded the British barque, 'Reliance', and unpacked a canvas bag containing a human head!

In 1806 Lord Cochrane spent his prize money on commissioning a galley from Harrison's, the boat builders of Deal. The Admiralty were so impressed by the design that they ordered drawings to be made of her lines.

Deal boatmen had their own football team which played on a meadow at the North End. Freddie Upton, Coxswain of the Walmer lifeboat, played centre forward.

Deal and Walmer Angling Association - the oldest in the country - was begun in 1905. Enlisted men realised they could not fish in competition with officers and so, after the First World War, the Deal Angling Club was also formed.

199

Redsull's motor boat, 'Lady Violet', Joe Mercer's 'Sidney and Olive', painted "gashouse green", and 'Jumbo' Betts' and Freddie Upton's motorised foresail-and-mizzen punts, respectively named 'Terrier' and 'Fisherman's Pride'. A hotch potch of boats was beached along Central Parade. Prominent were the fleet of Tommy and Hannah Upton - whose tiny boathouse was replete with hanging baskets and swearing parrot - consisting of the galley punt, 'Skipjack', the elliptical-sterned 'Margaret' and the powered mizzen punts, 'Ida' and 'Minnie Ha-ha'.

Deal, Walmer and Kingsdown Rowing Club was formed in 1927 and since that time it has held a prominent place in the annals of south-east and south coast regattas. Invariably, local regattas opened with a race for foresail-and-mizzen punts followed by four-oared service galley races in which Tommy Upton's 'Seamen's Hope', Harry Upton's 'Bluebell' and 'Doctor' Bailey's 'Undaunted' fiercely competed. (A memorable occasion was when Charles Arnold's Kingsdown galley, 'Tyne', performed a spectacular feat by sailing under the pier, her mast clearing it by inches, to win the race in the early 1930s) Popular rescue races took place in the late afternoon - shops closed early so that their staff could spectate - in which most boatmen competed. When a signal gun was fired crews leapt aboard their galleys as they sped down the shingle, raising the tall mast and hoisting the huge dipping lugsail, whilst speeding through the surf. Normally the course was a two mile distance out to sea round a supposed ship on fire and then a hectic race back to the beach. Fishing boats that competed in later regattas were 'Kingfisher', 'Orange Blossom' and 'Bunch of Roses'.

At the start of the Second World War, heavier motor-boats, previously engaged in salvage work, were removed from the beach. Tank-resistant steel girders and coils of barb wire were erected along the foreshore. Later, metal pipes were laid under the promenade wall from which short tubes protruded. Vibrators, capable of creating a spark, were attached to these tubes to ignite petrol supplied from concealed storage tanks should an invasion occur. Gaps at intervals in the defences were left to enable smaller craft to launch during the fishing season.

At the evacuation of Dunkirk every available motor boat along the south-east coast was requisitioned by the Navy. Their crews, formed from mariners or landsmen, raced over to France where they repeatedly ferried allied troops from the hostile shore to their transport ships anchored in deep water while constantly under fire from enemy fighter planes. Ten fishing boats left from Deal including George Riley's 'Gipsy King', Harry Meakins' 'Lady Haig', Fred Upton's 'Rose Marie' and 'Flint' Roberts' 'Golden Spray II'. They were accompanied by lifeboats from the liner, 'Dunbar Castle', and the Belgian steamer, 'Flandres'.

'Gypsy King' worked heroically to save stranded soldiers from a sinking pontoon. 'Golden Spray', after ferrying five boatloads, returned for a sixth consignment of troops when she was swamped by the wash from three destroyers which knocked her crew overboard and disabled her. 'Lady Haig' sustained extensive damage to her hull and her engine was put out of action. Two more motor-boats were reported missing: T.H. Adams' 'Moss Rose' and H. and J. Budd's 'Britannic'. Walmer lifeboat crewed by members of the Royal Navy was also commandeered for the Dunkirk beaches but she sustained considerable damage which necessitated a refit at Lowestoft. A wartime edition of 'East Kent Mercury' paid tribute to their valiant efforts in evacuating the British Expeditionary Force.

Today, a mere dozen - mainly fibreglass - boats cluster on the beach near Deal

Castle. A larger fleet of trawlers are located at Walmer Strand where, happily, the custom continues of selling the day's catch directly from the foreshore. Oldest remaining craft is the elegant beach yacht, 'Lady Irene', built by Trott for William Meakins of the 'Port Arms' in 1907. Originally she had a lute stern, a long bowsprit, stern outrigger, gaff mainsail, standing mizzen, foresail and jib. During the autumn and winter she was used for herring and sprat fishing while in the summer she plied for "half hour trips in the Downs". In 1922 she was acquired by 'Doc' Bailey who added an engine while his son, Ben, altered the craft by adding a high counter stern for a smooth launch backwards into the waves. This rare example of a day tripper boat is now owned by artist, Tom Burnham, who has restored her to perfection.

Tommy Upton's bathing machines for hire on Central Parade.

LIFEBOATS AND LIFEBOATMEN

'Storm Warriors'

THE GOODWIN SANDS are so dangerous that eight lifeboats once served this stretch of the English Channel. During the early years of the 19th century the number of wrecks in this area rose to astronomical proportions. This resulted in four lifeboats - Ramsgate, North Deal, Walmer and Kingsdown - concentrated on just a dozen miles of the coastline with a fifth at Broadstairs, a sixth at Kingsgate and, shortly afterwards, two more at Margate and Dover - which resulted in a coverage unprecedented in the history of lifeboats.

Collisions mid-Channel also increased as the size and speed of ships increased. In the early days, hundreds of sailing ships were lost in this area through poor navigation or inclement weather. During the Victorian and Edwardian period, however, there were abundant collisions between steamships mid-Channel. Great loss of life occurred when modern steam ships accidentally rammed larger sailing ships, which sank immediately if they were fitted with iron hulls. Even today the narrow confines of the Dover Straits leave modern ships little room for error. Although the region is now almost all under continuous radar surveillance by coastguards and port control officers, major incidents still occur.

The 'Royal National Institution for the Preservation of Life from Shipwreck' was formed in 1824 with King George IV a patron and in its first year twelve stations were established around the coast of Britain. Their specially designed lifeboats were capable of working in rough water close to shore or sandbanks which offered a lower risk than the beach craft previously involved in rescues at sea. They were, however, still crewed by local boatmen whose main occupation was fishing, salvaging or putting pilots aboard ships on a normal working day. RNLI lifeboats complemented the already existing small number of lifeboats presented by private individuals or charitable associations. Besides lifeboats Manby's rocket apparatus was also supplied although this service was later transferred to the Coastguard. In 1853 the title was changed to 'The Royal National Lifeboat Institution'.

A first lifeboat to save lives from the Goodwins was presented to Broadstairs by Thomas White, a shipwright, in July 1850. This anonymous craft, launched from a horse-drawn trailer, was later named 'Mary White' after a successful mission to a brig

'Heroes of the Goodwin Sands', James Laming, Kingsdown Lifeboat Coxswain; Richard Roberts, North Deal Lifeboat Coxswain; James Mackins, Walmer Lifeboat Coxswain.

ensnared on the Sands on 6 March 1851. A second lifeboat, 'Northumberland', was privately purchased by Trinity House and stationed at Ramsgate Harbour in 1852. The Duke of Northumberland, President of the National Lifeboat Society, offered one hundred guineas as a prize for the best design and the winner, which incorporated self-righting properties, was built by James Beeching of Great Yarmouth. 'Northumberland' soon proved its worth and it was thought expedient to place a third lifeboat on a beach closer to the treacherous sandbank.

First local lifeboat was placed at Walmer in 1856. She was a self-righter (30ft x 7ft 6in) pulling ten oars and launched by carriage. And she was named after the club which presented her: 'Royal Thames Yacht Club'. She was designed by James Peake, master shipwright of the Royal Dockyard at Woolwich, and built by Forrestt, shipbuilders of Limehouse. First coxswain was William Bushell. The 'Kentish Times' reveals that her master, or coxswain, was paid a salary of £8 per year whilst her volunteer crew received 3 shillings or 5 shillings per man "depending on the weather". On her first mission she saved fifteen lives from the barque, 'Reliance', but in the next six years of service only one more person was rescued. After five years she was replaced by a second 'Royal Thames Yacht Club' (37ft x 8ft 4ins) which was longer and heavier than her namesake. She saved only five lives in 23 launches over the next ten years. All the same this was the first local lifeboat to be funded by the Royal National Lifeboat Institution.

Lifeboats were viewed with suspicion by the boatmen who regarded their installation as a threat at a time of transition to their livelihood. For centuries they had answered distress calls in their luggers and galleys and they relied upon sporadic payment for their courageous services to swell the income from salvage. Rev. Henry Teonge, chaplain aboard one of His Majesty's warships, 'Assistance', stationed in the Downs, recorded in his 'Diary' (12 June 1675) that Deal boatmen had already developed their own form of artificial respiration to resuscitate victims of drowning. Resentment towards lifeboats in general continued for a full half-century but eventually a working relationship was established between beach boats and lifeboats. Interestingly, early lifeboats copied the design and rigging of the traditional beachcraft locally since they had proved their reliability and effectiveness over decades.

It soon became evident that an additional Lifeboat Station should be established further northwards in order that further rescues might be attempted in varying conditions of wind and tide. Consequently a second lifeboat was rowed along the Thames Estuary and placed at North Deal in May 1865. She was named 'Van Kook' after Edward William Cooke, the celebrated marine artist, who was responsible for collecting most of the £450 required for her construction. 'Van Kook' (40ft x 10ft) was stationed on the beach just south of Sandown Castle and opposite the 'Good Intent Inn'.

Edward William Cooke, R.A. (1811 - 1880) painted two exquisite pictures of the Goodwin Sands calculated to promote the work of the Royal National Lifeboat Institution. The first, 'Wreck on the Goodwin Sands; Morning after a Heavy Gale, Weather Moderating' (1856) was an imaginary scene featuring both a pilot boat and the Ramsgate lifeboat, 'Northumberland', struggling to rescue a skeletal ship. (This can be identified as the East Indiaman, 'Caromondel', actually washed ashore on

The first North Deal Lifeboat, 'Van Kook'.

Yarmouth Sands). Previously Cooke had visited Trinity House Docks on the Thames to sketch a three masted light vessel undergoing repair and this appears prominently in his composite oil painting.

The artist lived and worked in London but he frequently crossed the English Channel to France and had witnessed several accidents at sea. In November 1858 the cross-Channel packet in which he was travelling ran down a French fishing lugger which carried no lights with the sad loss of two men and a boy. Cooke was greatly affected by this tragedy and he became a fervent champion of the RNLI. He kept a collecting box in his studio for patrons to make contributions for a rescue boat and he personally donated £200 towards the North Deal lifeboat.

The 'Van Kook' was a forty feet boat with a ten feet beam, built by Forrestt of Limehouse. At the time it was reported to be fast under sail, manageable under oars and having immense stability. She was also noted as the largest self-righting lifeboat in the RNLI's fleet. Cooke took time while staying at the 'Royal Exchange Hotel' to inspect this lifeboat and to approve her livery which he had chosen himself. First coxswain was Robert Wilds with Richard Roberts as Second Coxswain. Her first launch to the aid of a foreign schooner, 'George', was reported in the first edition of the 'Deal, Walmer and Sandwich Mercury' (2 June 1865).

This new lifeboat was the subject of a second painting, 'Rescue of the Crew of a Barque by the 'Van Kook' North Deal Lifeboat' (1866). In this picture the wrecked barque, viewed from its port quarter, has only her main and mizzen lower masts standing while the main yard has crashed onto her deck. Her ensign is reversed as a distress signal and the survivors are clustered in the main shrouds. The lifeboat approaches, stern to, and her crew has managed to throw a heaving line to the distressed ship. Wrecks of two boats are visible in the wild water and a Goodwins lightship is glimpsed in the far distance. The crescent-shaped lifeboat's cautious

205

'Rescue of the crew of a barque on the Goodwin by the 'Van Kook'
North Deal Lifeboat' painted by E.W. Cooke in 1866.

approach - although in a perilous situation - appears the one controlled feature in this chaotic scene.

According to the 'Lifeboat Journal' (July 1865) a lifeboat house was built at North Deal by Denne and Winn at the cost of £340. This was situated adjacent to the derelict Sandown Castle but because of sea erosion it was abandoned in 1870. A year later the old Walmer Lifeboat House was re-erected at North Deal. In 1883 the road in front of the Lifeboat House was raised and so another Lifeboat House was built on the same site by J. Wise. A famous engraving shows volunteers rushing to secure a lifebelt that would secure them a place aboard the lifeboat. Early sepia photographs show that there might be fifteen members (including the two coxswains) needed to form every lifeboat crew.

North Deal Lifeboat Station, which was once sandwiched between two public houses - 'North Star' and 'Lifeboat Inn' - remains along The Marina. This prim, symmetrical, blue and white painted building has lost its wide recessed doors, service boards, giant lantern and bell turret but it retains the distinctive oriel window from which lifeboatmen used to keep a watch over the Downs. Terracotta roundels depict an early lifeboat surrounded by oak leaves and a crown above the date: 1883. Now, it is the headquarters of the Deal Sea Angling Club.

On 7 February 1865 the two lifeboats - 'Royal Thames Yacht Club' and 'Van Kook' - combined in their endeavours to reach the fully-rigged sailing ship, 'Iron Crown', driven by a south-south-westerly gale onto the Goodwins. One of the Deal luggers, 'England's Glory', also came to its aid and six of her crew scrambled aboard the disabled vessel. The 'Royal Thames Yacht Club' was prevented by the heavy seas from coming alongside 'Iron Crown' but 'Van Kook' proved more tenacious and, under the direction of Coxswains Wilds and Roberts, succeeded in putting a further six men aboard. These skilful boatmen contrived to hurl a kedge anchor from high up on the foreyard and when the drift of the ship was checked all other anchors were simultaneously released. As she lifted high on the rising ride, cables were attached to three steam tugs who towed 'Iron Crown' triumphantly into the deep water of the Downs.

The following year it was felt necessary to station a third lifeboat southwards under the cliffs at Kingsdown. It was considered to be the ideal position since, despite obvious difficulties in launching from the exposed foreland, this lifeboat, once afloat, and with a southerly wind and a lee tide, would be in a far more favourable position for reaching ships grounded on the southern point of the Goodwins.

First lifeboat at Kingsdown was 'Onzio' (33ft x 8ft) renamed 'Sabrina', built by Forrestt. Donated by William Ferguson at a cost of £300, she arrived by train and was drawn to the village by six horses and forty boatmen. At 33ft in length, with a beam of 8' 1" and weighing a mere 2 tons, she was one of the smallest craft built for the RNLI. She was soon replaced by a slighter larger vessel, the gift of the same gentleman, a self-righter also named 'Sabrina' (36ft x 9ft). Her coxswain was Jarvist Arnold and she remained on station until 1882 when she was transferred to Newquay, Cornwall. Initially, Kingsdown lifeboat was beached directly on the shingle but soon she received her own boathouse. This was sited one hundred yards from the sea to allow the lifeboat a good run down the beach. The silhouette of this distinctive building under the White Cliffs remains today although it has now been converted into a holiday home. High tides now lap close to its door which means that storm shutters are essential to prevent shingle washing into the panelled sitting room, even in summer...

Thus, by 1866, the Goodwin Sands were strongly guarded by a fleet of sturdy lifeboats capable of launching in the fiercest storms that frequently lash this corner of the Kent coast.

In 1870 five sailing ships were driven ashore between Walmer Castle and Kingsdown Cliffs. A south-westerly gale blew for three days and reached hurricane force on the night of 12 February. One fully rigged ship, 'Glendura', of Liverpool, from Java and bound for Rotterdam with a cargo of rum, spices and sugar was caught in this storm accompanied by sleet and snow. Fortunately a Deal pilot, Simon Pritchard, was on board and he had the presence of mind to steer the ship towards the shore in the direction of Kingsdown Lifeboat Station.

The vessel beached - stem on - minus both anchors but with her foretopsail set, just two hundred and fifty yards from land. Yet that stretch was a turmoil of wild surf with a vicious undertow sweeping back from the shore. A cork fender on the end of a line was thrown from 'Glendura' and this was caught by a lifeboatmen. Coxswain Arnold launched 'Sabrina' and his crew pulled her through the breakers towards the sinking ship. The lifeboat was constantly filled with water so that her crew were drenched and numb with cold. Despite these difficulties, 'Sabrina' made a total of five round trips with the same coxswain but a constant change of crew. Twenty-nine survivors were brought ashore, including the captain, his wife and son. Afterwards Coxswain Arnold found that his oilskins were so stiff with ice that when he managed to pull them off they stood up on their own accord!

Jarvist Arnold, master of the 'Earl of Zetland' lugger, was also a Channel pilot. He was a tough, humorous, experienced mariner. He was coxswain at Kingsdown for twenty years from 1866 to 1886. Sadly, when he retired the RNLI neglected to recognise his life-saving efforts with a medal. Throughout his service he was assisted by James Laming who succeeded him as coxswain from 1886 to 1907. One of their shared missions was to the barque, 'India', from which they brought ashore sixteen men after they had been afloat for twelve hours in appalling weather. These stalwart lifeboatmen crossed and recrossed the Goodwins four times which testifies to their tremendous skill and stamina.

All three lifeboats were launched from an open, exposed shore. They

Kingsdown Lifeboat Coxswain, Jarvist Arnold.

were nearly all fitted out with two masts with lug sails so they could reach far out beyond the Goodwin Sands and into the English Channel. But they also carried either ten or twelve oars because lifeboatmen preferred to row to their destination which, although difficult, was far safer. The Coxswain was paid £1 per launch by the RNLI but the stations relied upon volunteers who were paid a pittance to man their lifeboats. Only the first thirteen to answer the summons and don cork lifejackets and sealskin caps would secure a place. Launching also required men to hold the lower woods or greased skids in position to enable lifeboats to run down the beach at great speed and get afloat.

Essential equipment carried included a lantern, a compass, lifebuoys and lifelines festooned round the sides to enable survivors still in the water to climb up into the boat. Further lifelines were attached to corks so that they could float or be thrown from the lifeboat when alongside a wreck. Additionally, there was a pair of grappling irons - one at the head and one at the stern - to throw into the rigging of wrecked ships plus a sharp hatchet. The canteen was sparse and consisted simply of a jar of water, a little rum and a few biscuits. Further rations were obtained from passing vessels although sometimes this was refused, even from crews of the ships they were involved in rescuing.

In 1871 a third lifeboat, 'Centurion' (36ft x 9ft 4ins) was presented to Walmer by

George Aston, a London businessman. A dramatic depiction of this lifeboat on her first mission to rescue the crew of the schooner, 'Hero', stranded on the Goodwins on 16 October 1872, was painted by Charles Robert Ricketts (1838 - 1883), a former naval officer. Described as "a remarkably good boat", on one occasion 'Centurion' proved her excellent qualities by righting herself when capsized under canvas. She remained for thirteen years, making 38 launches and saving 72 lives. In 1880, 'Centurion' rescued no fewer than 26 people from 'Colombo' of Greenock. The Lifeboat House was specially built to house 'Centurion' and its "chapel-like" appearance perfectly complements adjacent St. Saviour's Church.

Walmer and Kingsdown lifeboats worked in tandem to assist one of the first steamships to be stranded on the Goodwin Sands. In the early hours of the morning of 17 December 1872 Coxswain Arnold in 'Sabrina' and Coxswain Bushell in 'Centurion' launched in a south-easterly gale to search for the reported wreck. After sailing through the surf in the darkness they located a large screw steamship homeward bound from the Mediterranean to Newcastle, laden with grain, but now held fast on the South Calliper. By the time they reached her the tide had fallen which allowed the lifeboats to put aboard half their crew to assist in lightening the steamship's load. There would then be a slim possibility that she would relocate on the next tide...

Meanwhile, the steamer's crew worked feverishly to pump out water and jettison her cargo but at dawn it became obvious that S.S. 'Sorrento' was doomed. Her back was broken. The tide rose swiftly, the gale intensified and huge waves swamped the decks. Both crew and lifeboatmen took refuge in the bridge. Patiently, they awaited the

The launch of the North Deal lifeboat, 'Mary Somerville',
attracted large crowds.

chance to abandon ship and jump into one of the lifeboats. Just then a huge breaker forced down upon them and snatched away the ship's boats. The mooring cable which held the Walmer lifeboat alongside was torn in half sending her spinning wildly among the wreckage. 'Centurion' was swept over half a mile to leeward before she could be checked by her anchor but with a depleted crew battling with the furious wind and tide there was slim chance of her returning to S.S. 'Sorrento'.

Coxswain Arnold now faced one of the most difficult challenges in his career. He had the unenviable task of attempting a second assault on the sinking steamship which held, not only thirty-two crew members, but fourteen lifeboatmen, including three of his own sons. The cluster of men stranded on the tiny bridge watched helplessly as the two lifeboats drifted beyond their reach. They repeatedly attempted to pass a sturdy rope down to the Kingsdown lifeboat and when eventually a line came within the grasp of the bowman's boathook, 'Sabrina' was able to draw alongside so that all the crew were safely boarded. As the captain stepped into the lifeboat, the steamship's masts and funnel collapsed and she snapped in two. Coxswain Arnold then sailed 'Sabrina' - wind and seas dead aft - straight across the broken waters of the sandbank and, 'Centurion' trailing behind, the two lifeboats made for Broadstairs.

Seamanship demonstrated by captains of ships passing through the English Channel in the nineteenth century was of a poor standard. Coxswain Wilds, who won the RNLI silver medal in 1877 and a second clasp to the silver in 1882, was involved in the rescue of the crew of a large Canadian vessel that drove onto the outer edge of the Goodwins in 1880. Later, it was revealed the captain did not employ a pilot, lacked the appropriate charts, failed to take soundings and had no knowledge of local waters.

Throughout the 1870s and 1880s 'Van Kook' constantly attended similar incidents. One such routine rescue resulted in serious damage to the lifeboat despite the coxswain's undoubted skill. The Downs was crowded with shipping when a sudden storm arose. There was the usual flurry of activity as luggers and cats raced to the assistance of vessels in difficulty. Second coxswain, Richard Roberts, was among the boatmen who were swept up in the maelstrom and he was forced to sail his cat, 'Early Morn', into Margate Harbour. He returned to Deal by train to be immediately told of a series of warning guns from the Gull lightship and flares in the direction of the Brake Sands.

Coxwains Wilds and Roberts launched 'Van Kook' - "under close-reefed mizzen and double reefed storm foresail" - but before they reached the ship which had grounded on the Brake, it had broken up and vanished without trace. Whilst they searched in vain they noticed another flare and changed tack. Almost immediately they were confronted by another ship close by, her decks awash and heeling so that her yardarms dipped into the water. It was a French brig, 'D'Artagnan', whose terrified crew hesitated to jump into the refuge of the lifeboat. Coxswain Wilds veered down on his cable anchor so that he was nearly touching the ship's stern while Second Coxswain Roberts climbed aboard, seized the men and lifted them one at a time into the lifeboat.

The Frenchmen's prevarication caused considerable damage to the lifeboat. Huge waves had lifted 'Van Kook' and thrown her against the brig's transom. All the crew had been rescued but both port and starboard bows of the lifeboat were stove in.

Undeterred, Coxswain Wilds turned the battered lifeboat in the direction of the wreck that had originally burnt the flare. It was a Swedish barque, 'Hedvig Sophia', now fast breaking up. 'Van Kook' dropped anchor to windward and steered tentatively among the raffle of wreckage in an effort to rescue the crew. This time it was the captain's wife who refused to trust herself to the swaying lifeboat. At dawn, 'Van Kook' limped home with her motley crew - five Frenchmen and twelve Swedes - to safety. The RNLI awarded both the Coxswain and Second Coxswain of North Deal silver medals for gallantry.

Two years later Coxswain Wilds rescued another petrified foreign crew. On 28 December 1879, in the early hours, guns firing from the South Sand Lightship warned of vessels on the Goodwin Sands. 'Van Kook' was launched and headed for the south-east spit of the sandbank where a barque was fighting for her life in the vicious gale. As the North Deal lifeboat neared the barque all her mast crashed into the frenzied foam. In the distance another vessel disappeared before the lifeboatmen's eyes - lost with all hands.

Coxswain Wilds dropped anchor to windward and slowly drew closer to the stricken vessel which was identified as the German ship, 'Leda', bound for Hamburg. Just as a line was thrown to the sinking ship, a massive wave lifted the lifeboat almost as high as the wreck's foreyard. As she came down her port bilge caught the bulwarks and she almost capsized. Swiftly, two lines were rigged across and the German crew were encouraged to transfer from ship to lifeboat. First man across was a veteran since he had been rescued twice before by the North Deal Lifeboat!

In 1881 'Van Kook' was renamed 'Mary Somerville' and this first North Deal lifeboat saved 281 lives in 23 years of service. Confusingly, this last name was retained by a further two boats: ON 178 built by Forrestt and ON 227, a self-righter (42ft x 11ft) pulling twelve oars built by Woolfe. This latter lifeboat came on station in 1888 and remained in service for the next 17 years. Rescues by these noble craft included 'Ganges' (an iron ship from London bound from Middlesborough for Calcutta which stranded on the Goodwins in 1881) and 'Frederick Carl' (a small Dutch schooner from Oude-Pekela loaded with oats which struck the North Sand Head in 1885). During this last disaster, Coxswain Wilds was seriously injured and he was replaced by Second Coxswain Richard Roberts.

Robert Wilds was Coxswain of the North Deal lifeboat from 1865 until 1885. He was the first local boatman to receive the coveted RNLI silver medal awarded for the rescue of two sailing ships driven ashore. Further, he had been responsible for rowing Sir George Airy, Astronomer Royal, around the Downs in his galley searching for a suitable site for Deal's time ball which was eventually located atop the former Semaphore Station. Richard Roberts, who replaced him, had already been awarded the silver medal but then won a second and third clasp during his twenty-two years as Coxswain. During his forty-two years service at the North Deal Station he rescued four hundred and forty-one lives and died at the ripe old age of ninety-five. Second Coxswain was now Edward Hanger and the regular crew comprised famous local boatmen - Adams, Bailey, Baker, Betts, Brown, Budd, Erridge, Marsh, May, Mockett, Pain, Redsull, Riley and Stanton.

211

North Deal lifeboat, 'Charles Dibdin', and crew.

At Walmer 'Centurion' remained until 1884. She was replaced by 'Civil Service No. 4' ON 34 (40ft x 10ft) a self-righter built by Forrestt which served until 1895. This boat made nine launches and brought back a total of six survivors in eleven years. (A temporary lifeboat replaced her when she was sent away for repairs in 1891-2 and 1895-7) She was followed in 1897 by a second 'Civil Service No. 4' ON 394 of similar dimensions but built by Hansen of Cowes. This boat rescued one hundred and fifty-five lives in fifteen years. Her most notable rescue was when she brought thirty-five people ashore from the wreck of S.S. 'Carlotta' on 9 October 1900. Coxswain was John Thomas Mackins and the Second Coxswain was Henry Parker.

Coxswain Mackins was at the helm of Walmer lifeboat for twenty-three years from 1881 until 1904. He gained the RNLI vellum for his rescue, in conjunction with Kingsdown lifeboat, of the crew of the steamer, 'Mersey', Christmas, 1901. He was succeeded by Harry Wolstenholme Parker who had previously been afloat in the lugger, 'Pride of the Sea', as a Channel pilot. Parker held the position of coxswain for fourteen years but was then forced to retire through ill health. Among notable missions in which he was involved are the four-masted Norwegian ship, 'Mersey'; the Italian steamer, 'Carlotta'; the Belgian steamer, 'Cap Lopez'; the fully rigged ship, 'Hazelbank', wrecked on the Goodwins on her maiden voyage; the German steamer, 'Asia'; the barque, 'John Lockett' and the wreck of S.S. 'Sorrento'. Second Coxswain was Thomas Heard.

Kingsdown Station was served by 'Charles Hargrave' (36ft x 9ft) a self-righter built by Forrest, between 1882 and 1890 and a larger lifeboat of the same name, ON 306 (40ft x 10) another self-righter built by Woolfe in 1890. Her Coxswain, James Richard Laming, was once described by Treanor as "a man of undoubted courage and pure words". Laming was born in Kingsdown and had served as a Channel pilot. Once, he had a narrow escape from drowning whilst aboard the barque, 'Childwall', of Liverpool on route from Iquique to Antwerp, which collided with a steamer, 'Noorland', off Flushing, on 2 January 1892. 'Childwall' was almost sliced in two and, as she began to sink, Laming with eight members of the crew climbed into the rigging where they remained until they were rescued by the Harwich steamer, 'Ipswich'. Laming was connected with the Kingsdown lifeboat for forty-one years and was Coxswain for twenty-seven years when he was credited with saving 118 lives.

On 12 December 1889 the sailing barge, 'Mandalay', of Glasgow, sailing from Middlesborough to the River Plate, miscalculated her position and strayed into one of the swatchways of the Goodwins where she foundered. Gunfire from the Goodwins lightships thundered out their summons while their rockets soared into the frosty sky. Coastguard maroons echoed their call on shore and in the early hours of the morning the North Deal lifeboat, 'Mary Somerville' launched. 'Mandalay', weighed down by her heavy cargo of railway sleepers, was sinking deeper into the Sands so that at low tide she stood unsupported on the northern swatch. The lifeboatmen, under the direction of Second Coxswain Hanger, assisted the ship's crew in a vain attempt to release her before she inevitably broke her back. They were busily engaged in jettisoning her cumbersome cargo as the long stretch of hard sand was rapidly covered by the encroaching surf whipped up by an unrelenting wintry gale.

The tug, 'Bantam Cock', arrived to offer aid and she was soon joined by the lugger, 'Champion'. Several galley punts also drew alongside but all these vessels were forced to return to shore as the south-west wind strengthened to storm force. At midnight heavy seas were breaking over the deck of 'Mandalay' so that salvage work was abandoned and the hatches battened down. 'Mary Somervile' continued to ride the heavy swell while a new tug, 'Cambria', arrived and cautiously crept along the narrow swatchway. Lifeboatmen had the dangerous task of passing the tug's steel hawser aboard the stranded ship to enable her to be towed to safety. At one point the taut towing hawser became entangled underneath the lifeboat and lifted her high into the air. She came crashing down onto the ship's bulwarks. Chaos reigned. Meanwhile, the crew of 'Mandalay' had secured another towing rope from a second tug, 'Iona', Paradoxically, the huge wave that nearly destroyed 'Mary Somerville' had released the ship from the sandbank and she was slowly slewing round. Eventually, 'Mandalay' was towed off into deep water - to a chorus of tug's whistles and jubilant cheers - and into the shelter of the Downs.

Richard Roberts became Coxswain of the North Deal lifeboat upon Robert Wilds retirement in 1885. He was in the lifeboat service for forty-two years, serving as coxswain for twenty-two years, and was concerned with the rescue of 441 lives. During that time he earned three silver medals from the RNLI. He was described as "short of stature, keen-eyed, well-knit, sturdy and agile". He was the first local lifeboatman to be awarded three silver medals by the RNLI. Coxswains Roberts and Hanger both retired in 1907.

Meticulous records of each launch were entered into the 'Returns for Services'. Coxswain Roberts laboriously wrote his accounts in careful copperplate immediately upon returning ashore and several entries reveal his frustration at an abortive mission:

5 Nov 1886

About 5 A.M. I was called by Coastguard as the Gull Light & East Good Wind were a fireing of Rockets & Guns I Immediately summoned a Crew and Proceeded to the Goodwin Sand and waited till daylight and as we Could not see anything Ashore we returned.

8 Dec 1886

I received a Telegram from Harbour Master Ramsgate saying could see People running about on the Lee Part of NSH of Goodwin I come to the Conclusion that I was justified in going owing to the low tide I took a Crew to assist us affloat and we proceeded and went Along the Sand until our Boat took the Ground and when we had knocked clear of the Sand our Boat was amongst a quantity of Nets and Barrels and unfortunately there was no one to be seen and we left and made fast to Margate jetty for two hours.

9 Nov 1888

Whilst Proceeding to London with the Late Mary Somerville when close to the Tongue Light vessel about 6.30 A.M. we observed signals flying we hailed her the answer was I have a Shipwreck Crew on Board Will you take them We put the Boat along side and took them in our Boat Proceeded and Landed them at Gravesend at 1 P.M.

Shortly before Richard Roberts left the service, the second 'Mary Somerville' was replaced by 'Charles Dibdin' ON 552 (43ft x 12 ft) a self-righter built by Thames

Kingsdown lifeboat, 'Sabrina'. Courtesy: R.N.L.I.

Ironworks in 1905. This was an extremely heavy boat (weighing 10 tons 6 cwt) and it had to be dragged a considerable distance across the shingle prior to launching at low tide. She was one of four Deal lifeboats named after the founder of the Civil Service Lifeboat Fund who had proved to be an indefatigable Secretary of the RNLI. (This historic craft was recently traced to the Helford River in Cornwall where she was being converted into a cabin cruiser by a private owner) Her Coxswain was William Adams and during her long service (1907 - 31) 'Charles Dibdin' saved 443 lives.

Naturally, the presence of four lifeboats in such a confined area led to confusion and rivalry. When a lightship summoned help or a boatman raised the alarm, several lifeboats might launch to assist the same wreck. This caused unwelcome competition which stretched valuable resources. Instructions issued to the local coxswains towards the end of the 19th century were vague:

> "In really bad weather, the action of several lifeboats will not be scrutinised too closely, but, as a general rule, the windward boat is to be launched. The lee boats are not to launch unless the coxswain considers it absolutely necessary. In fine weather, the windward boat of the group is to be the only one launched. If the wind is offshore the boat in the most advantageous position with regard to wind and tide, and distance from the casualty, is the only one to be launched."

Walmer had a new lifeboat, 'Civil Service No. 4' ON 34 (40ft x 10ft) a self-righter built by Forrestt on service from 1884 - 5. She, in turn, was followed by a second 'Civil Service No. 4' ON 394 which was of similar dimensions but built by Hansen of Cowes. This boat saved 155 lives before the station was temporarily closed in 1912. At the turn of the century, Walmer lifeboat saved thirty-five people from the steamer, 'Carlotta'. Again, in 1900, 'Civil Service No. 4' rescued the entire crew of the South Sand Head lightship.

Incredibly, Walmer Lifeboat crew became involved in a heated dispute and went on strike! On New Year's Eve 1906 a public enquiry headed by Lord George Hamilton, captain of Deal Castle, and attended by dignitaries from both the Lifeboat Institution and Trinity House, was held at the Town Hall. It centred upon a difference of opinion between the central and local committees of the RNLI regarding the launching of the lifeboat the previous Spring. Friction between the two authorities had resulted in the refusal of the crew to man the Walmer lifeboat. (While their claim was in dispute, the crew nobly continued to attend shipwrecks in their own beach boats)

Coxswain Harry Parker of 'Civil Service No. 4', explained the circumstances when a vessel, 'Mersey', had collided during the night and all four Goodwin lightships had fired distress rockets to summon aid. Exercising his discretion, Coxswain Parker had ordered Walmer lifeboat to be launched in thick fog and this craft was not only the first afloat but the first to reach the Goodwins. Indeed, Walmer lifeboat had rescued several members of the ship's crew before the rival Kingsdown lifeboat had even arrived. Local secretary, Rev. T.S. Treanor, recommended that the crew should be paid but this claim was rejected by the London Central Committee who insisted that Walmer lifeboat should never have launched in the first place. Walmer lifeboatmen won their case and their fee was paid. Clearly, it was not only the "weather rule" that was the cause of the problem but that there were now too many lifeboats along this stretch of the coast. The decision was made that one of the three Downs lifeboats must be withdrawn.

On 21 December 1907 the Belgian steamer, 'Cap Lopez', stranded on the South Goodwins. Both the Walmer lifeboat, 'Civil Service No. 4', and the Kingsdown lifeboat, 'Charles Hargrave', attended. The sea was rough. Walmer lifeboat was lifted so high it crashed onto the ship's deck and was seriously damaged. New Coxswain, James Pay, managed to steer the Kingsdown lifeboat alongside the wreck and the captain, his crew of thirteen men plus a dog were rescued. In addition to rescuing the survivors Coxswain Pay had to tow the Walmer lifeboat ashore.

On 9 April 1909 'Charles Dibdin' joined 'Francis Forbes Barton' of Broadstairs and 'Charles and Susanna Stephens' of Ramsgate in assisting with the rescue of the crew of 'Mahratta' of Liverpool which had gone aground on the Goodwins. All three lifeboats stood by the vessel until the subsequent high tide - twelve hours later - hoping in vain that she would refloat without assistance.

When it became apparent that the ship was doomed, 'Charles Dibdin' ferried fourteen people ashore while tugs remained to try and release the ship from the sandbank. When the two Thanet lifeboats returned to harbour, 'Charles Dibdin' kept vigil for a second night. Next day it was obvious that she would break up and so all the passengers were taken off, followed by the captain and his officers. 'Charles Dibdin' had saved two dozen people after an exceptionally long service of over fifty hours.

North Deal reserve lifeboat,
Francis Forbes Barton © Angus Neill.

In 1912 a meeting was convened to review the performance of all three Downs lifeboats. From the time of their installation they had saved a combined total of 760 lives - North Deal (428) Walmer (171) and Kingsdown (161). It was proposed that Walmer Lifeboat Station should be closed but this did not meet with general approval and was rejected in a free vote. Nevertheless, the RNLI made the decision that year to close Walmer Station.

During the First World War there was great difficulty in

manning all three lifeboats. Younger boatmen of fighting age enlisted in the Naval Reserve to serve in trawlers, drifters or minesweepers. Nonetheless, the Deal lifeboatmen saved a total of three hundred lives, including fifty British naval officers and men. The RNLI decided that, after the Germans made merchant vessels a target of their submarines in the English Channel, a second lifeboat should be placed at North Deal. Consequently, 'Charles Dibdin' at North Deal and 'Charles Hargrave' at Kingsdown were joined by 'Francis Forbes Barton' from Broadstairs in 1915.

'Francis Forbes Barton' (40ft x 10ft) was a self-righter built by Rutherford. She arrived on station 1 March 1915 and remained until 1921 when she was transferred to Ramsgate. Coxswain was William 'Cobbler' Stanton with second coxswain Thomas Adams junior and later Robert Holbourn. Stanton, a true 'storm warrior', had already served under three previous coxswains and he and Holbourn both received silver medals for their rescue of the crew of the American freighter, S.S. 'Siberia' which struck the Goodwins on 20 November 1916.

Censorship of all radio and newspapers means that there is scant record of wrecks and rescues during most of the First World War.

The Downs was a designated protected anchorage and formed the base where a fleet of patrol boats and minesweepers operated against the enemy. A submerged German submarine fired a torpedo near the South Sand Head which struck the torpedo gunboat, H.M.S. 'Niger', acting as a guardship, at midday on 11 November 1914. The warship had become a familiar sight stationed locally since the beginning of hostilities. North Deal and Kingsdown lifeboats launched simultaneously despite being hampered by

Walmer Lifeboat Civil Service No. 4 photographed by Edgar Tarry Adams. Courtesy: National Museum of Photography, Film and Television.

wrecks along the coast but it was the galley punt, 'Hope', that reached the imperilled vessel first. All ninety-five members of the crew were hauled aboard. Meanwhile, H.M.S. 'Niger' stood almost vertical with her bows touching the seabed in fifty feet of water with her forepart belching thick black smoke. She sank in full view of observers just one and a half miles away onshore.

North Deal lifeboat was launched again in a furious gale on the night of 8 December 1914 in response to rockets fired by the South Goodwin lightship. Luckily, it was a full moon which offered some relief from the impenetrable darkness. (Shipping was prohibited to display its navigational lights in wartime). The lifeboatmen made towards the South Sand Head but were surprised to find that the lightship herself had parted from her cable and risked being blown onto the Goodwins. They watched horrified as the lightship sheered the sandbank and drifted out into the open sea. The English Channel had been sown with mines and the coxswain was forbidden to enter the danger zone. (Later the lightship was towed back to her station unscathed)

North Deal lifeboat, Kingsdown lifeboat and Ramsgate lifeboat all launched during the violent storm on Sunday 19 and Monday 20 November 1916. In the space of twenty-four hours this gallant fleet saved eighty-two lives from steamers that went aground on the southern part of the Goodwins. At dusk a south-south-west wind reached hurricane proportions and a mountainous sea was pounding over the Sands. Signals of distress were sent up from the Italian freighter, S.S. 'Val Salice', laden with over 4,000 tons of coke and coal, on her voyage from Sunderland to Savona.

At Kingsdown, Coxswain Pay, with a depleted wartime crew, prepared to launch 'Charles Hargrave' since she seemed in the most favourable position to reach the south-west sandbank but she was immediately thrown back on shore. Once the tide had risen sufficiently Coxswain Bill Adams felt confident in launching 'Charles Dibdin' from North Deal and her crew, which had raced back and forth between the two lifeboat stations, now headed - braving rain squalls and intense darkness - for the Goodwins.

Around midnight 'Charles Dibdin' located the wrecked Italian steamer. The guardship in the Downs obligingly turned on a searchlight to guide the rescuers since there was an enforced blackout. The lifeboat struggled to combat the formidable breakers that lifted her almost to the level of the steamer's masthead. Coxswain Adams dropped his anchor although he realised there was little hope of the lifeboat remaining close to the ship for any length of time. The Italians, donning lifejackets, were induced to trust themselves to the rope ladders hanging down the sides of their ship and, directed by the shielded beam of the searchlight, they scrambled aboard. Miraculously, the entire crew of thirty were taken safely aboard 'Charles Dibdin' as she surged momentarily alongside the steamship. The last man to leave the sinking ship was her master, Captain Bolognini.

All three lifeboats were involved once more in an incident which occurred only four hours later when distress signals were sighted from an American steamer, 'Siberia', that lay - hard and fast - on the Sands just southwards of 'Val Salice'. Initially, North Deal reserve boat, 'Francis Forbes Barton', alone launched, under the direction of Coxswain Stanton, towed by a tug from Dover. But the weather had deteriorated and conditions were now so perilous that the lifeboat could not get alongside the stricken steamer which was breaking up fast. Further, the lifeboat was constantly filled with water, risking capsizing, and finally Stanton had to admit defeat. Even the Ramsgate lifeboat which took up the struggle was forced to return to harbour.

Later the next day a renewed effort was made to reach 'Siberia' by the Kingsdown lifeboat, 'Charles Hargrave'. Her coxswain, James Pay, was then sixty years old and his crew comprised veteran boatmen since the younger men from the village were away fighting in the Great War. A tow from a naval vessel brought the lifeboatmen alongside

218

'Siberia' which by then was completely awash. Huge waves lifted the lifeboat to the level of her damaged bridge where she was in danger of being smashed against the splintered metal. Despite the herculean task fifty-two men were rescued from the steamer and returned safely ashore. The President of America presented a gold medal to the Coxswain and monetary awards to the crew to show his country's gratitude. The RNLI also awarded James Pay, who had been coxswain since 1907, the silver medal for gallantry.

Another arduous mission was that towards the American Government steamship, 'Piave', of 5,000 tons, on her maiden voyage, laden with food, from New York to Rotterdam. The New Jersey steamship, with her crew of ninety-six men, grounded on the Goodwins on 29 January 1919. North Deal lifeboat, 'Charles Dibdin', alerted by gunfire from the Gull lightship, launched and stood by the vessel for two whole days while the crew jettisoned her cargo. Several salvage tugs arrived on the scene but they were unsuccessful in dislodging the stranded cargo ship.

On the third day the weather turned into a blinding snowstorm. S.S. 'Piave' broke her back and tilted over onto her port side. This created an alarming situation whereby the crew were stranded on the starboard side in pitch darkness with an angry sea rolling over them. The crew abandoned ship. Men either jumped into the lifeboat or boarded the ship's own boat, precariously lowered. A further catastrophe occurred when this boat became entangled and was strung by the bows so that the occupants were catapulted into the sea. There was then the added danger of them being crushed between the ship and the lifeboat.

Lines were thrown and - aided by pocket torches - twenty-nine men were pulled to safety aboard the North Deal lifeboat. The tug, 'Champion', with the Ramsgate lifeboat arrived and located the remainder of the crew. Just as the overloaded 'Charles Dibdin' cleared the wreck, she was caught in a whirlpool and spun round alarmingly before she could be extricated by Coxswain Adams. Eventually the exhausted lifeboatmen with the terrified survivors returned to shore after their arduous experience. The lifeboat crew had been afloat for a total of fifty hours and each man received a gold medal from the President of America in gratitude. (Coxwain Adams was presented with a gold watch)

A further notable rescue by Coxswain Adams and the North Deal lifeboat occurred when the Estonian three-masted schooner, 'Toogo', struck the northern part of the Sands in a furious gale on 1 November 1919. 'Charles Dibdin' launched with two extra hands in response to rockets and gunfire from the vigilant lightships. Even with an additional two men aboard, it took the lifeboat three hours to reach the Goodwins. They found that 'Toogo' was held broadsides on the sandbank with her crew stranded in the rigging. But before the rescuers could reach her, the schooner sank beneath the waves. The lifeboat cruised among the wreckage, her crew aware of pitiful cries for help yet powerless to help. Only at daybreak were two survivors located clinging to an upturned boat. Another man was picked up by a passing steamer. The rest of the ship's crew, including the captain's wife, had drowned. On their return the lifeboat was swamped by mountainous seas; one wave knocked down and injured both the Coxswain and Second Coxswain. For this rescue Coxswain Adams received his third silver medal from the RNLI.

Meanwhile, more vessels were reported in trouble and the reserve lifeboat prepared to launch. Coxswain Adams had been seriously injured in the previous rescue and so Second Coxswain William Stanton took over the helm. He organised a fresh crew for 'Charles Dibdin' to return to the Goodwins. By now the gale had developed into a hurricane and the sea became so rough that it took almost six hours for the lifeboat to reach the Sands. The fatigued lifeboatmen managed to reach the ketch, 'Corinthian', from Antwerp, and rescue three men desperately clinging to the rigging. Upon his return Stanton went straight home to bed. He was suffering from throat cancer. He received a bronze award for his bravery but it was his last mission. His place was taken by William Hoile with Thomas Cribben as Second Coxswain.

Senior Coxswain of North Deal throughout the Great War was William 'Bonnie' Adams. Master of the fast second class lugger, 'Albert Victor', he was described as a "sturdy figure" with a "ruddy countenance" and "placid features". Adams spent fifty-two years of his eventful life in the service of the RNLI and he was Coxswain of the North Deal lifeboat from 1907 until 1921. His famous rescues numbered S.S. 'Val Salice', 'Toogo', and 'Piave' but he was best remembered for assisting the armed Admiralty steam trawler, 'De La Pole', which was breaking up on the Goodwins in a gale on 4 February 1916. Officially, he was credited with saving 321 lives and he was awarded a trio of silver medals for gallantry from the RNLI.

There was a marked reduction in shipwrecks along this part of the coast "between the wars". Briefly, 'Barbara Fleming' ON 480, built by Thames Ironworks in 1902, served Kingsdown Station (from 1926 - 7). By then it had become increasingly difficult to find a crew owing to the decline of the seafaring population of the village and it was often necessary to send for volunteers from Deal or Walmer when it was expedient to launch from that southerly point under the cliffs. Eventually, there was only the Coxswain (James Pay) and Second Coxswain (William George Sutton) left and so the RNLI made the decision to transfer the Kingsdown lifeboat, 'Barbara Fleming', to Walmer and the North Deal reserve lifeboat, 'Francis Forbes Barton', to Ramsgate. Kingsdown Station, which had saved 241 lives in sixty-one years with a total of five rowing and pulling lifeboats, was closed in 1927. North Deal Station, which had saved 859 lives in 419 launches over a period of seventy years, was closed in 1932. Her last lifeboat, 'Charles Dibdin' - still dependent on oars and sails - had served for 27 years and saved 395 lives.

Walmer Station was therefore reopened in 1926. Henry Pearson was appointed Coxswain with Joseph Mercer as Second Coxswain. 'Barbara Fleming', which served from 1927 until 1933 at Walmer, was credited with saving only three lives for this period yet she took part in the longest stand-by of a vessel held fast on the Goodwin Sands. This involved the American ship, 'Hybert', of Wilmington. Walmer lifeboat spent around sixty hours beginning 6 November 1931 while a number of salvage tugs attempted to refloat the ship. Eventually, seventeen tugs released 'Hybert' from the grip of the sandbank after she had jettisoned most of her cargo of cotton bales. The strain on the ship as she was pulled free by the tugs was terrific and, according to one lifeboatman, "her rivets were going off like pistol shots".

The RNLI was developing a fast new motor lifeboat that could be launched down the shingle and there were plans to introduce this innovative craft to serve the Goodwin Sands. Accordingly, in 1933, the revolutionary life-saving craft, 'Charles Dibdin Civil Service No 2' ON 762 (41ft x 12ft) propelled by two 35 mph. twin-screwed engines which gave a speed of over 7 knots, arrived at Walmer. She had been built by Groves and Guttridge of East Cowes at a cost of £6000. Apart from being able to launch directly from the beach, she was fitted with relieving scuppers which, even when completely flooded, she could be freed from water in seconds while her 130 separate air cases rendered her unsinkable. Her equipment included a searchlight, radio telephone, loud hailer and a line throwing gun. And in addition to carrying her crew of ten men she could hold a maximum of a further seventy-six people. The new lifeboat was certainly elegant. Her keel was made of teak, her stem and stern posts were of English oak while her timbers were of Canadian rock elm and she was planked with a double skin of Honduras mahogany.

The lifeboat station was specially reconstructed to include a mechanic's workshop. First Coxswain was Henry Pearson who later piloted many of the cross-Channel swimmers. When he died of exposure in 1937 he had spent over fifty years in the service of the lifeboat. This first local motor lifeboat gave outstanding service and eventually rescued a total of 387 lives. Indeed, she became the most famous lifeboat in the country.

At the commencement of World War Two, the Downs was a Contraband Control Base crowded with shipping. 'Charles Dibdin Civil Service No. 2' was at the forefront of activity and frequently launched to assist vessels which had been in collision or had been mined. She operated with great difficulty from a narrow gap in the barbed wire opposite the lifeboat house. Her wartime Coxswain was Joe Mercer and her mechanic was Percy Cavell. The first true call came during the 'Phoney War' when she landed a crew of forty-four from 'Kabinda' wrecked on the Sands near Trinity Bay.

During the Second World War, 'Charles Dibdin' was launched sixty-seven times. In the severe winter of 1940 she was launched 26 times and saved 45 lives in just four months. All these early efforts were carried out despite the danger of magnetic or acoustic mines in the Downs. Indeed, on one occasion, while searching for a stricken steamer in Pegwell Bay, the lifeboat was caught in the beam of a searchlight and machine gunned by an enemy aircraft. Luckily, nobody was hit. After the fall

Lifeboat Doctor, James Hall O.B.E, with Coxswain, Freddy Upton.

221

of France, it became impossible, not only to man the lifeboat, but to safely enter the Downs Anchorage. For a time the station was closed. The lifeboat did, however, assemble a Royal Navy crew to take part in the evacuation of Dunkirk.

After Walmer lifeboat returned from an urgent refit a retained crew was selected from the men still available. Brothers Joe and Dick Mercer were First Coxswains; Freddie Upton, Bill Willis, 'Jumbo' Betts, 'Fido' Bailey and George and William Riley took turns as Second Coxswains. Percy Cavell and John 'Lardy' Dadd served as mechanics. Harry Axon and Len Mercer were employed to operate the electric winch and hauling tackle, both skilled jobs on which the lives of the crew might depend. Soon, however, the regular crew was reduced to nine experienced but elderly boatmen. Throughout hostilities, 'Charles Dibdin Civil Service No. 2' did yeoman service and when she was retired after 26 years she had been launched 241 times and saved 412 lives. She had earned the reputation of being the busiest lifeboat in the world.

Joe Mercer was Coxswain of Walmer lifeboat from 1935 until 1945. Curiously, many of his notable rescues were in local boats rather than the official lifeboat. As a youth, Joe and his companions went to the rescue of a blazing German steamer, 'Patrio', in their galley pount, 'Welcome'. Their boat struck on timbers and sank instantly, throwing all its occupants into the cold, black water. Thus, at eighteen, Joe was an experienced boatman and welcomed into the lifeboat service, working his way up from acting boatman to Coxswain of Walmer lifeboat. He was awarded the Bronze Medal for gallantry for the wartime mission to the Admiralty anti-submarine boat No. 25 which hit the Sands at top speed on 18 January 1944.

During the Second World War Dr James Hall O.B.E. (1899 - 1973) assumed the role of lifeboat doctor for shipping in the Downs. In his autobiography, 'Sea Surgeon' (1960) he describes how he began casually to operate a casualty service afloat, being transported by a rota of dedicated boatmen in their own boats and later in Walmer

Walmer Lifeboat, Civil Service No. 4.

lifeboat. When the majority of his patients were evacuated from the area Dr Hall became the official visiting surgeon attached to Walmer lifeboat.

Dr Hall's visits were usually attempted in nightmarish conditions - stormy weather, thick fog, snow storms and dark nights during the regulation blackout. In those perilous times no radio contact was permitted between the Coastguard, the lifeboat and the motor boats that ferried Dr. Hall across the Downs. The only signalling was by flag in good visibility or, alternatively, with an Aldis-type lamp flashing Morse code. (The international flag, 'W', or the Morse code - one short, two longs - signalled 'I require medical assistance') Additionally, there was the precarious task of boarding a large vessel from the confines of the lifeboat in rough seas often strewn with floating mines. Finally, captains and crews of Allied ships requiring his attention were sometimes unable to communicate in English.

When the Royal Navy gained control of the English Channel in October 1944 a medical service afloat was resumed. 'Charles Dibdin Civil Service No. 2' (under the direction of Coxswains Joe Mercer and Freddie Upton) was constantly employed in incidents mid-Channel. Dr Hall was often called upon to accompany the crew and his patients included an injured medic, an insane fireman, a rescued airman and several wartime stowaways. Consulting his diary, Dr. Hall recalled with humour that the most frequent illnesses he had to treat in our sea port were related to injuries, insanity, appendicitis and venereal diseases. Dr. Hall made an estimated total of forty lifeboat trips and three hundred in motor boats to render aid to seamen of all nationalities in the Dover Roadstead.

Freddie Upton, who was Coxswain from 1945 to 1962, is perhaps the most famous

Lifeboat roundel.

Communication between the three local lifeboat stations in any emergency was at first by messenger on horseback.

A painting by Charles Ricketts', "A Deal Lugger and the 'Sabrina', Walmer lifeboat, assisting the 'Honi Sverne' wrecked on the Goodwin Sands, October 11th 1870", was shown at the Royal Academy of Arts in 1871.

Coxswain Adams and the crew of the North Deal lifeboat took part in the Lord Mayor's show in London in 1919. They were heartily cheered as they rode along in a smaller borrowed lifeboat mounted on a trailer.

Bill 'Bonnie' Adams was the first lifeboatman to feature on a "live" radio broadcast. He proudly wore his medals which rattled when they struck the table and the listening public assumed he was counting his loose change!

Highlight of the Deal regatta, which was on a grander scale to the Walmer regatta, was the annual race between the Deal, Walmer and Kingsdown lifeboats.

name in the history of Walmer lifeboat. This sturdy boatman came from a generation of boatmen on both his paternal and maternal sides. As a youth Fred used his own sailing boat with which he frequently ferried pilots. In the First World War he served in the minesweepers and in the Second World War he helped service shipping in the Downs. He was master of the 'Rose Marie' motor boat involved mainly in sprat fishing beached on the foreshore at Deal. He gained two RNLI silver medals for his epic rescues and also the Maud Smith Award for the bravest lifesaving act in 1948. His name is inevitably coupled with his engineer, Percy Cavell, who was awarded a bronze medal.

In the immediate postwar period Walmer was the busiest lifeboat station in the British Isles. During this traumatic time there was an astonishing series of wrecks of American liberty ships caused by the stubborn refusal of the United States authorities to employ pilots to navigate the Dover Straits. First disaster was 'Abraham Baldwin', laden with tanks, aground in Trinity Bay in 1944. A number of British and American airmen were picked up in dinghies and the entire crew of thirty-one were rescued by Coxswain Upton and 'Charles Dibdin Civil Service No. 2'.

One of the most difficult rescues was to 'Luray Victory', a 9,000-ton vessel, of Los Angeles, travelling from Norfolk, Virginia, to Bremerhaven, laden with grain, which struck the southern edge of the Goodwin Sands on 30 January 1946. Walmer lifeboat sped through heavy surf at dead of night but found her fast aground surrounded by such mountainous seas that it was impossible to ride alongside. It stood by all that night and most of the following day but the weather deteriorated so that efforts to tow her off at high tide proved impossible. The lifeboat crew returned to shore for fresh provisions and clothing but when they next appeared they were dismayed to find that conditions had actually worsened.

Volunteers rush to crew the North Deal lifeboat.

The wind had turned to southerly and was blowing a gale while the ebb tide was rushing past the sides of the steamer as she began to disintegrate. The ship creaked, decks bulged, derricks toppled and masts tumbled while down below water gushed through the wide rents in the hull. A furious surf and racing tide still prevented the lifeboat from fastening a tow rope while the sands beyond the stern were starting to dry. Speed was essential to ensure that the rescuers themselves did not become trapped. Coxswain Upton reversed the lifeboat so that she approached the steamer bows on and pulled the crew - one by one - to safety by means of rope ladders suspended from her sides. In this manner a record number of forty-nine men were saved at one time.

On Christmas Eve another liberty ship, 'North Eastern Victory', of New Orleans, smashed into the South Goodwins in thick fog. When Walmer lifeboat reached her she had already broken her back and the engine room was completely flooded. The crew of thirty-six were quickly taken off but the captain stubbornly insisted that he and six officers should remain on board the two halves of the broken ship despite fuel oil pouring out of her bunkers. The lifeboat returned to shore but as the weather deteriorated the decision was made to stand by throughout the night. At dawn the remainder of the crew were removed because the liberty ship was breaking up. Afterwards the lifeboat crew returned to their own Christmas celebrations.

On 8 March 1947 Walmer lifeboat attended the Greek steamer, 'Ira', an ex-Liberty ship laden with 8,000 tons of coal for Antwerp. She had grounded in an awkward position between the two halves of 'Luray Victory' and close to 'North Eastern Victory' on the southern part of the Goodwins. When the lifeboat arrived the demoralised crew were in a fearful state and many of the survivors needed treatment for their injuries sustained in their attempt to escape. "I have never seen such a panic in all my life," reported Coxswain Upton. "Ship's lifeboats were being lowered at random, men were jumping into them and just drifting away on the tide. They leaped into the lifeboat yelling at us to get away from the ship. We almost had to fight them to keep alongside. My bowman who had got aboard 'Ira' said that men and baggage were

Walmer lifeboat, 'Charles Dibdin Civil Service No 2', manned by a crew from the Royal Navy, took part in the evacuation of Dunkirk. Years later an unexploded shell was found embedded in her hull.

Walmer was one of only three beach-launching lifeboat stations. The two others were at Aldeburgh and Dungeness.

A flag flying from the masthead of the lifeboat was a sure signal that a rescued crew was on board.

Traditionally, the three maroons fired were interpreted as: one, "stand by"; two "launch" and three, "doctor required". After the second maroon crew members might rush from seafront pubs, flag down passing motorists and expect to be driven at speed to Walmer Lifeboat House along the Strand.

Shopkeepers along the Strand used to open their back and front doors whenever the maroons sounded to allow the crew to take a short cut to the lifeboat station.

The last Walmer Lifeboat 'Hampshire Rose'.

jammed in the gangways and those who fell were trampled on without mercy. He got them off, however, and then we had to chase around to pick up those adrift in the ship's boats."

Another ship requiring the services of Walmer Lifeboat that year was 'Helena Modjeska' which also grounded on the Goodwin Sands. Walmer lifeboat raced to the rescue - the sea oily calm - of this massive ship with a general cargo destined for Northern Europe. This was one of the rare occasions when a wreck survived long enough for all her freight to be recovered. The main reason was that she went adrift on the inside of the Sands at Trinity Bay whereas a ship of similar dimensions would rapidly disappear on the seaward side of the Goodwins. Her crew of thirty-nine were rescued plus two German prisoners-of-war who had stowed away.

Perhaps the most challenging service for Coxswain Upton and the crew of Walmer lifeboat occurred on 2 January 1948. At sea the weather was appalling but in a brief lull the Coastguard spotted a ship aground on the Sands. 'Sylvia Onorato', a 2,300-ton Italian vessel of Naples, laden with plumbago, bound from the Adriatic for Rotterdam was held fast on the Goodwins. The lifeboat launched but as she neared her target her crew found conditions far more perilous than imagined. At one time the lifeboat was lifted so high by the waves that the crew were looking down on the bridge of the stranded vessel. Walmer lifeboat itself risked becoming another victim of the Sands.

Meanwhile, tugs had arrived although the ship was in such a precarious situation that it was impossible to secure hawsers. The captain resolutely refused to abandon ship even though the gale was clearly increasing and the fate of his ship was sealed. Walmer lifeboat returned to station to refuel but when she stood by the next day the captain remained adamant. When the lifeboat launched a third time the captain was persuaded to leave his ship after he received a radio message from Lloyd's agents informing him of an imminent Force 9 SSW gale. He ordered his men into the lifeboat.

The rescued crew comprised twenty-eight men, two German stowaways and one Alsatian dog. Coxswain Upton was awarded the RNLI silver medal and his mechanic, Percy Cavell, the bronze medal.

On 13 January 1952 the French freighter, 'Agen', 4,000 tons, of Rochelle, bound from Dakar to Hamburg, carrying a mixed cargo, struck the southern tip of the Goodwins. The fury of the seas ensured that she broke her back almost immediately. By the time Walmer lifeboat reached her she had snapped in two and her crew were huddled in the bows. The jagged metal of her broken hull made it dangerous to reach 'Agen' in the darkness. Walmer lifeboat actually made thirteen attempts! Gingerly, Coxswain Upton managed to steer the lifeboat between the two halves of the ship and reach the forward part of the wreck. The crew of thirty-five plus two passengers slid down a rope into the lifeboat but inevitably the captain refused to comply. Coxswain Upton could not risk the lives of the survivors because of the captain's obstinacy and so he made for the shore. Later, he returned to the stricken ship and persuaded the captain to enter the lifeboat since the weather had worsened. Coxswain Upton was awarded another silver medal and Percy Cavell another bronze medal from the RNLI.

In 1959 'Charles Dibdin, Civil Service No. 32' ON 948 (42ft x 12ft 3ins), a Beach-type motor lifeboat costing £30,000 built by William Osborne of Littlehampton, came on station at Walmer and served until 1975. Her speed was just over eight knots and she carried sufficient fuel to 'steam' at her maximum speed for 220 miles with refuelling. Even in rough weather she could accommodate seventy people some of whom were sheltered in the cabin forward of the engine room. During the first ten years this lifeboat saved eighty-nine lives and five of her crew were awarded badges for meritorious service. (Altogether she was launched 162 times and saved a total of 412 lives)

On the night of 12 November 1961 the East Goodwin lightship broke adrift in a storm and was driven southwards along the outer edge of the Goodwin Sands. Coxswain Upton and his crew reached the lightship in an hour just as an emergency anchor checked the drifting vessel. Walmer lifeboat kept up a seventeen hour vigil - steaming forever around the lightship - until the arrival of the Trinity House vessel, 'Vesta'. Even then the lifeboat could not return to shore since the storm had caused

Tally of the last Walmer lifeboat, 'Hampshire Rose', included the rescue of a cat and a dog.

Kingsdown Lifeboat Station formed the background for scenes in the film, 'Isadora Duncan' (Universal 1968). The eccentric dancer was played by Vanessa Redgrave.

Queen Elizabeth, the Queen Mother, visited Walmer Lifeboat and presented a centenary vellum to the station in 1956.

Children's entertainer, Mr. Pastry, once advertised Walker's crisps for a television commercial by sitting in a deckchair on the beach. He escaped by a hair's breadth as Walmer lifeboat raced down the slipway.

On 1 September 1974, BBC's 'Songs of Praise' was broadcast from Walmer Lifeboat Station. A poignant moment was when a helicopter flew over the Goodwin Sands to the accompaniment of 'Eternal Father, Strong to Save'.

In preparation for the General Election, Prime Minister Margaret Thatcher visited Walmer Lifeboat Station on 24 May 1983.

tremendous erosion of the coastline and so she had to seek temporary shelter in Dover Harbour.

Both Freddie Upton and Percy Cavell (who had served under four coxswains) retired in 1962. There followed a succession of three fine coxswains at Walmer. Ben Bailey, a prominent boatman, served from 1962 until 1966. Harry Brown then took over until 1973 when Norman Griffiths deputised for a few months only. Afterwards Bruce Brown, the former mechanic, became Coxswain and he served until 1982. He was the nephew of Harry Brown and he was the fourth generation of boatmen in his family. At one time Bruce had to rescue his Second Coxswain, Cyril Williams, who had become trapped aboard a sinking cabin cruiser, 'Shark'. When Bruce Brown relinquished his role in 1982, he became the Station's mechanic, and Cyril Williams was made Coxswain.

Last lifeboat at Walmer, which stood proudly on her turntable opposite Walmer Green, was named 'Hampshire Rose'. She was a Rother class wooden boat (37ft x 11ft) adapted for beach launching with twelve watertight compartments built by Osborne's. She was equipped with modern safety devices and navigational aids including radio telephone and echo sounders. She had two diesel engines, a speed of 8 knots and she carried a crew of seven. A gift of the people of Hampshire (and Sussex) whose county emblem is a rose, she was launched by Lady Rose, wife of Sir Alec Rose, round-the-world lone yachtsman, on 6 September 1975 to commemorate the 150th anniversary of the RNLI.

The character of the Lifeboat Service in Kent has changed owing to the increased navigational aids for ships and the service now operates mainly to assist pleasure craft rather than commerce. Generally, calls are to attend cabin cruisers, yachts, speedboats and catamarans that have become dismasted, broken down or gone adrift, plus sea anglers with engine trouble or explorers trapped by the incoming tide under the White Cliffs. Trials had already been made of an inshore lifeboat of the 'Gemini' type at Walmer in the summer of 1964. The result was the installation of an Atlantic 21 fast inflatable rigid rescue dinghy, named 'James Burgess'. Manned by junior members of the lifeboat crew she was intended for summer operational duties only.

Today Walmer Lifeboat is manned by volunteers who are all alerted by telephone or on bleepers by the Coastguard. The exception is a full-time motor mechanic who ensures that the engines, radio and electronic equipment are working and that the boat is ready for service at any time of day or night. Coxswain Denis Brophy served from 1988 - 1990. "I used to help with the fishing boats on the front and lots of the boatmen were involved with the lifeboat so I went along and became a shore helper," he reveals. He started as an emergency mechanic, became second coxswain but then was voted Coxswain. Later, he was promoted to Operational Manager, the modern term for Honorary Secretary.

Present Walmer lifeboat is the offshore rigid inflatable Atlantic 85, 'Donald McLauchlan', which came into service in December 2006. Launched by tractor-trailer, she carries a crew of five including her helmsman. She is supported by the smaller D-Class lifeboat, 'Duggie Rodbard', which deals specifically with inshore rescues. This was the first time in the history of the RNLI that two lifeboats arrived and were named on station consecutively.

ELIZABETH CARTER

'A Woman of Wit and Wisdom'

ELIZABETH CARTER (1717 - 1806) was a celebrated author, poet, essayist, linguist and translator who became the most prominent member of the 'Bluestockings', an exclusive literary society in Georgian London. Her scholarship won her world renown and even elicited praise from Dr. Samuel Johnson, who admired both her studiousness and domesticity. She won from him this accolade: "My old friend, Mrs. Carter, could make a pudding as well as translate Epictetus and work a handkerchief as well as compose a poem."

Elizabeth's father, the intolerant Nicolas Carter, M.A., D.D., was born in the village of Dinton, in the Vale of Aylesbury, in 1688. He was descended from a long line of farmers and graziers who hailed from Bedfordshire and Buckinghamshire. They took pride in the fact that they could trace their ancestry back to the Norman Conquest. The Carters had fought for Parliament in the Civil War and one even preached before the House of Commons. Nicolas graduated from Emmanuel College, Cambridge, in 1710 and six years later he was appointed to the parish of Tilmanstone-with-Sutton. Later, he became Rector of Ham and Woodchurch. He was a learned cleric, restless and volatile. . . and a fervent anti-Jacobite. He was one of the six appointed preachers at Canterbury Cathedral and several of his sermons were published anonymously. In 1718 he was installed as the incumbent of St. George-the-Martyr at Deal where he remained for a remarkable spell of fifty-six years. Sadly, these years of service were marked by violent clashes of opinion between church and council.

Nicolas Carter's first wife was Margaret Swayne, an heiress from Bere in Dorset. She bore him two sons and three daughters - John, Elizabeth, Margaret, Nicolas and James. Nicolas' portrait, apparently, showed a strong likeness between the cleric and all his children. The eldest son, John, a Cambridge graduate, joined the army and first served in the 'Regiment of Foot' commanded by Lieutenant Wolfe. John's portrait by Highmore painted in 1756 depicts a sensitive young officer wearing a red uniform with dark blue facings and large silver braid. Later, Captain Carter settled in Deal where he was highly regarded as "a magistrate, a gentleman and a scholar" but, like his father, he was known all his life for his short temper and uncertain health. The two youngest brothers, Nicolas and James, became lieutenants in the Royal Navy and both died on foreign service. Margaret married Dr. Thomas Pennington, Rector of

Mrs Elizabeth Carter by Joseph Highmore c.1738. © Deal Town Council.

Tunstal, and their son, Montagu, also entered the church. He was Elizabeth Carter's favourite nephew.

Rev. Montagu Pennington became Curate of Old St. Mary's Church at Walmer for twenty years before he was appointed Curate of Sutton, Vicar of Northbourne and finally Perpetual Curate of St. George's at Deal. He must have been a persuasive preacher. In 1832 a tremor struck the church - a huge crack appeared in the roof and the organ dropped three inches - but the preacher was able to pacify the congregation until they were escorted to safety. On Sunday 4 December 1842 he preached before the young Queen Victoria and Prince Albert at Walmer Castle. Rev. Montagu Pennington composed a 'Memoir' of his aunt - possibly under her guidance - published posthumously. This was a strange commission since Elizabeth professed to scorn the injudicious publication of her confidential letters.

In the absence of a Vicarage Nicolas Carter lived in a property (since demolished) in Park Street. It was such a cramped house with a warren of little rooms that Elizabeth referred to it as the 'Vinegar Bottle'. There was a garden in which she could play push pin, ball and battledore with her brothers and sisters. For Elizabeth, however, there was little time for sport. When her mother lost her substantial fortune in the collapse of the financial scheme known as the 'South Sea Bubble', she never recovered from the shock and died prematurely. Elizabeth, who was then barely ten years old, was expected to take over the running of their home.

Dr. Carter admitted that after his wife's death he was "pressed by want of money" and he struggled to cope with his young family on his modest stipend of £100 per annum. His finances were only resolved when he took a new wife, the kindly Mary Bean, who hailed from Deal. She bore him a son, Henry, called 'Harry', and a daughter, Mary, nicknamed 'Polly'. Elizabeth will have developed her skill as a cook in these years although she could make disastrous mistakes. She once prepared a ginger pudding which she "overcharged with pepper and brandy that it put the whole family in a flame". Neighbours, though, requested her recipes for Christening cakes and "plum puddings". And she was expected to make shirts for her brothers and trim bonnets for her sisters which, incidentally, she continued to do when she became famous and had moved to London.

Unusually, Rev. Nicolas Carter took a keen interest in all his children's education - boys and girls - and taught them Latin, Hebrew and Greek. Pennington insists his aunt had been a slow learner but Nicolas Carter regarded his daughter, Elizabeth, as a prodigy. His patron, Sir George Oxenden M.P., Lord of the Manor of Dene on Barham Downs, near Canterbury, was greatly impressed by a letter Elizabeth had written at the age of twelve. Dr. Carter was so proud of his daughter's achievements that he sent her to study French from a Huguenot refugee minister in Canterbury. Later, Elizabeth became friendly with Dr. Lynch, Dean of Canterbury, and his daughters and she frequently stayed at the Deanery.

There she was woken each morning by the rooks lodged in the elms outside her windows and she laughed one night when the watchman fled from the imagined apparition of a white horse "perched on the steeple like a weathercock". One evening the chimney caught fire and Mrs. Lynch and her maids fought to extinguish it with long brooms. At Canterbury Elizabeth attended a ball on Twelfth Night at which officers from Flanders were present to set young hearts aflutter although her greatest delight was to attend divine service and listen to the Cathedral choir.

Elizabeth became involved with more influential families in Kent. The closest friendship was with Mr. and Mrs John Underdown who lived at Shepherdswell. Indeed, Elizabeth once described Hannah Underdown as "my chief friend in this place". The two families - Carters and Underdowns - frequently exchanged visits and spent weekends together. At one time Dr. Carter hosted a dinner party for Mr. Underdown at 'The Three Kings' at Deal. The two families' relationships were sealed when Elizabeth's elder brother, John, married their much loved daughter, Frances, in 1755. Inexplicably, Elizabeth did not attend their wedding. Sadly, Frances died three years later and although John grieved greatly he married twice more.

Elizabeth found she had a thirst for education and taught herself nine languages including French, Italian, Spanish, Portuguese and Arabic. (Her preferred tongue was German) She shared her knowledge with her half brother and tutored Henry in the classics in preparation for his entrance into Cambridge University. Her command of languages meant that she had direct access to the sources of knowledge and debate while her ability to read Hebrew and Greek allowed her to discourse with leading theologians. Sir George Oxenden, who was a friend of the Prime Minister, Robert Walpole, offered to find Elizabeth a position at court as a governess where her fluent German would have found favour with the Hanoverian King, George II. Characteristically, Elizabeth declined.

There is a glimpse of life in the Carter household in a letter Elizabeth wrote to a friend in 1746:

"As you desire a full and true account of my whole life and conversation, it is necessary in the first place you should be made acquainted with the singular contrivance by which I am called in the morning. There is a bell placed at the head of my bed, and to this is fastened a packthread and a piece of lead, which, when I am not lulled by soft zephyrs through the broken pane, is conveyed through a crevasse of my window into a garden below, pertaining to the Sexton, who gets up between four and five, and pulls the said packthread with as much heart and good will as if he was ringing my knell...

"When I have made myself fit to appear among human creatures we go to breakfast, and are, as you imagined, extremely chatty; and this, and tea in the afternoon, are the most sociable and delightful parts of the day. Our family is now reduced to my eldest sister, and a little boy, who is very diverting at other times; but over our tea every body is so eager to talk, that all his share in the conversation is only to stare and eat prodigiously. We have a great variety of topics, in which every body bears a part, till we get insensibly upon books; and whenever we go beyond Latin and French, my sister and the rest walk off, and leave my father and me to finish the discourse, and the tea-kettle by ourselves. . .

"I fancy I have a privilege for talking a vast deal over the tea-table, as I am tolerably silent the rest of the day. After breakfast every one follows their several employments. My first care is to water the pinks and the roses, which are stuck in about twenty parts of the room; and when this task is finished, I sit down to a spinnet, which, in its best state, might have cost about fifteen shillings, with as much importance as if I knew how to play. After deafening myself for about half an hour with all manner of noises, I proceed to some other amusement, that employs me about the same time, for longer I seldom apply to any thing; and this between reading, writing, twirling the globes, and running up and down stairs an hundred times to see where every body is, and how they do, which furnishes me with little intervals of talk, I seldom want either business or entertainment."

The curious 'Larum' which Elizabeth rigged up with the assistance of an obliging Sexton prevented her from oversleeping so that she could enjoy early morning walks in the neighbouring countryside or across clifftops. She seems to have made only one excursion to the Isle of Thanet in order to observe some scientific experiments made by a clever tavern keeper in July 1750. Elizabeth joined a party of friends who were rowed across to Ramsgate in an open boat which was at one time swept dangerously out to sea. Wisely, her friends decided to hire a fleet of coaches and chaises to return home although Elizabeth chose to walk conducted by a couple of guides. Her ruddy complexion, caused by her constant rambling over the countryside, might result, she once joked, in her being "clapped in the stocks for a vagrant".

Elizabeth was encouraged by her father to visit London. At first she lodged with his friend, Edward Cave, whose printing works occupied a large vaulted room above the medieval Gatehouse of the Priory of the Order of St. John at Clerkenwell. Cave was a man who took risks and had already published several of Dr. Carter's controversial tracts and sermons written in "a plain but nervous style." He was also the founder of the prestigious monthly 'Gentleman's Magazine' which openly encouraged women writers. Elizabeth, at the age of sixteen, contributed a riddle on 'Fire' under the pen-name 'Eliza' (4 November 1734). A certain Mr Johnson, seizing upon the opportunity for self-publicity, responded to her in print. These two correspondents struck up a lasting friendship and when Dr. Johnson - who achieved renown as a lexicographer - launched his own journal, 'The Rambler', in 1750, he invited Elizabeth to contribute articles.

Elizabeth Carter was not a prolific author. Cave published a slim volume of her verse, 'Poems Upon Particular Occasions', anonymously in 1738 (revised in 1762 and again, with additional poems, in 1776). She wrote a poem on the death of Queen Caroline, consort of George II, which was presented to the king by Sir Robert Walpole. She translated from the French a critique on Pope's 'Essay on Man' and translated a review of Sir Isaac Newton's philosophy, 'Explain'd for the Ladies'. Privately, she compiled a 'Dictionary of Arabick'.

Initially, Elizabeth published anonymously or under pseudonyms in an endeavour to safeguard her modesty and guarantee an unbiased critical response. Yet her youth, talent and sex tempted Cave to promote her as a sensation. He advanced her position further as a rising star by publishing a series of poems and epigrams that claimed she was the rightful heir to Alexander Pope, then regarded as England's leading poet and satirist. Pope was "an infamous scourge of women writers" and the obvious talents of the young Elizabeth Carter challenged his reputation.

Privately, Elizabeth confessed she was a slow study and could only concentrate for short intervals. Habitually, she would sit up late at night writing, kept awake by "chewing" green tea and sipping coffee or taking pinches of snuff perfumed with lily-of-the-valley as stimulants. Her father firmly disapproved of this last habit to which she became addicted. Often, though, she ended up propped up in an elbow chair with a damp towel wrapped around her head, nursing headaches, all night.

All his life Dr. Carter retained a high respect for his daughter and he corresponded frequently with her while she was away from home. His letters are an endearing jumble of fatherly advice, family gossip, political opinion and domestic details:

"Betty Belcey sends her duty and is sorry she can procure no lavender. It has all been bespoken beforehand, and sent on board ships."

"Such an army of sprats have been taken, they are sold today for 2d a gallon; a thing never known before. Harry had two feasts of them - He is not quite well!"

Elizabeth Carter's emblem, an owl, features on her bookplate.

"Before you come down, when it suits you, you must buy sugar of all sorts, according to your judgement, except that of the very coarsest kind. . . Powder blew and stone blew. Starch according to your will, and whole rice. Flower of Mustard, Sallad Oyl, Nutmegs, Cloves. Anchovies, Icing-glass. Peper. Morells. Best Almonds. Raisons. Coffee. Add anything else, of whatever kind you think is wanting. Your brother will receive money from me, and you may have from him what you want."

An earlier commission had requested: "needles and a yard and 3/4 of black binding for Polly's bonnet" with a brisk reminder that "Jack wants a dozen shirts. Peggy is to make three and send three to you to make."

Elizabeth enjoyed the stimulus of living in London and frequently attended concerts, plays and exhibitions although she rigorously avoided "Routs, Drums, Hurricanes, Balls, Assemblies,

Ridottos, Masquerades, Auctions, Plays, Operas, Puppet-shows and Bear gardens." She was thrilled by Charles Macklin's portrayal of Shylock in 'The Merchant of Venice' at Drury Lane theatre but was dismissive of the "rarities" at the Royal Society Museum which, she teased, included: "Pontius Pilate's Wife's Maid's Grandmother's Hat". One public entertainment she firmly declined was an invitation to watch the execution of five malefactors at Tyburn on 24 November 1740.

She far preferred the simple pleasures of exploring the wintry "Landskip" of Hyde Park or Kensington Gardens although a great high point was when she gained entrance to Pope's private riverside garden at Twickenham. While strolling in the Mall she observed an eclipse of the sun (July 1748) which, for some, heralded the Day of Judgement. Often she was invited to dinner parties where her sparkling conversation enthralled the guests who might number Dr. Johnson, Dr. Burney, Samuel Rogers and Sir Joshua Reynolds. All the same she never kept "bad hours" for, as she said, "except upon public occasions ten o'clock was my unvariable hour".

One valued new London acquaintance was Catherine Talbot, ward of Dr. Secker, Dean of St. Paul's and Bishop of Oxford. She became a lifelong friend and, when apart, they frequently corresponded. In 1757 Miss Talbot secured for Elizabeth private apartments above a cabinet maker's at the sign of the elephant opposite the south door of the Cathedral. Catherine Talbot would then be a near neighbour since she often stayed with her guardian at the Deanery. Later, when Dr. Secker became Archbishop of Canterbury, he removed to Lambeth Palace where Elizabeth was a welcome guest. She occupied a room in the tower where she could view the Thames by moonlight.

Whilst in London, Elizabeth, at the instance of Dr. Secker, began to translate the works of the Greek scholar, Epictetus. She began her translation in 1749 and completed it with an introduction and annotations almost ten years later. 'The Life and Works of Epictetus' in one volume large quarto was published by subscription (price one guinea) by Samuel Richardson, the novelist, in April 1758. The Prince of Wales was numbered among the subscribers. It sold out almost immediately and so, at the suggestion of her father, she printed "a 1/4 of a thousand more". Royalties of the first edition amounted to a phenomenal £1,000 which guaranteed her financial security for the rest of her life.

Epictetus, a first century B.C. Greek philosopher, was the great champion of Stoicism. He was born a slave in Hierapolis but he eventually gained his freedom although he was later exiled by Domitian. The Stoic sect had been founded by Zeno, a fourth century B.C. Greek philosopher, and their members fervently studied logic, physics and ethics. They condemned the passions and conceived the highest state mankind might achieve is virtue. Stoics believed that since the world is the creation of divine wisdom and is governed by divine law it is the duty of man to accept his fate. The sect fell out of favour with the expansion of the Roman Empire and the rise of Christianity.

Elizabeth was, herself, "a paragon of Virtue" simply because she was a devout Christian. She firmly believed that Christianity alone offered true solace from life's problems and that Stoicism was "a mere moral system". It did not offer the spiritual reward of everlasting life nor the intimate relationship with the Christian God. Nevertheless, she and her friends recognised that this pagan philosophy wisely counselled its disciples with emotional self-restraint and physical self-discipline.

Elizabeth Carter's immaculate translation - published for the first time under her own name - brought her worldwide fame. Instantly, she became a topic of conversation amongst lettered aristocracy, scholarly lecturers and educated clergy. The 'Critical Review' commented: ". . . it is not a little extraordinary to find a woman mistress of the Greek language, sounding the depth of antient philosophy, and capable of giving a faithful and elegant translation of one of the most difficult authors of antiquity." (August 1758) According to Pennington, it made "a great noise all over Europe" and challenged the minds of thinkers as diverse as Jeremy Bentham, Immanuel Kant and Frederick the Great. Empress Catherine of Russia expressed her admiration for the author while Queen Charlotte commanded that Elizabeth Carter be presented to her at Lady Cremorne's House in Chelsea. (Indeed, this translation of 'Epictetus' remained the standard version until the beginning of the twentieth century)

And because of her renowned scholarship, Elizabeth Carter was invited to join that exclusive Georgian society known as the 'Blew Stockings'. The term "blue stocking" was first applied by Admiral Boscawen to members of the literary circle held at Montagu House, the London home of Elizabeth Montagu, a wealthy patroness of writers and artists. Mrs Montagu, one of the leading hostesses of the day, was "brilliant in diamonds, solid in judgement, critical in talk". At her gatherings there was no ceremony, no cards and no supper. . . instead educated people of both sexes indulged in intellectual conversation and cultural debate. According to Pennington: "Even dress was so little regarded, that a foreign gentleman who was to go there with an acquaintance, was told in jest, that it was so little necessary, that he might appear there, if he pleased, in blue stockings." Another source states that one of their members Benjamin Stillingfleet, an eminent botanist, was the first to wear blue rather than the fashionable black stockings at their meetings. (Wearing informal blue worsted stockings instead of black silk stockings would indicate that members of this elite circle scorned fashion for learning)

Elizabeth Carter lent the Bluestocking Circle the aura of solid learning and religious piety although she could be uncomfortable in large gatherings since she suffered from short sight and social awkwardness. The female members of the groups formed a close bond. They numbered Catherine Talbot, Hannah More, Charlotte Lennox, Hester Mulso (later, Mrs Chapone) who was once dubbed 'the little spitfire' and Mrs. Jersey, a kindly but nervous woman who was exceedingly deaf and hosted her parties with a variety of hearing trumpets jangling from her waist. Presiding over this 'Army of Blues' was Mrs. Elizabeth Montagu who had been instantly struck by the composure and dignity of this classically educated woman from Deal. Apparently, she had known Eliza from childhood having been brought up in her family home, 'Horton', near Hythe.

Mrs. Elizabeth Carter was lionised by London Society who hailed her as the most learned woman in England. (Mrs. was a courtesy title since she never married although there was a host of suitors) She rarely dined alone unless prevented by illness from leaving her apartments because a succession of carriages and chairs were sent for her to sup. She ate frugally, preferring vegetables and pastries to meat, and drank modestly. She was required to assist Mrs. Montagu, 'Queen of the Blues', with her breakfast parties held at Adam's famous Chinese Room in Hill Street and the 'Bas Blue' assemblies at her home in Portman Square which boasted a curious 'feather room' adorned with the plumage of exotic birds. All the same, she sought to avoid her stifling friendship and was relieved to find that:"My London life has not that hurry and bustle it might have if I was of more importance."

Letter writing remained Elizabeth Carter's passion and her correspondence was voluminous. Postage was expensive and paid by the recipient but her letters were treasured by her family who copied them out and circulated them among their friends to be poured over at their "Tea tables". (Frequently, she wrote to her father in Latin purely as an intellectual exercise) Nevertheless, Elizabeth could be careless with her handwriting, scratching the paper with her pen once the ink ran dry, so that she often apologised for her indecipherable "Scrawl". Indeed, her manuscripts were so full of "blots and interlineations" that she was once upbraided by her publisher, Cave. She became extremely short-sighted and could not read without the aid of a 'Glass'. Her letters are full of interjections - "My paper runs low", "The bell rings for church, so I must quit you."'Supper's upon Table' - which give immediacy to the reader. She became so absorbed in her letter writing that it often took her into the late hours - "Dear, how the watchman made me jump!", "My candle is out, so Goodnight"."I am writing by owl light, and shall put out your eyes and my own, but as this is one of the most summer-like evenings we have had, I was willing to enjoy as much as possible the sitting without candles." (9 July 1768)

Modern writers dispute Montagu Pennington's guarded portrayal of his aunt in the 'Memoirs' as an amateur who strayed into a literary world and they regard Mrs. Carter as a professional letter writer of enduring merit. Subject matter ranges from the trivial, such as her fondness for dancing or flirting with young officers, to issues of national importance where, for instance, she expresses approval for Prime Minister William Pitt's abolition of the slave trade. Elizabeth Carter's letters "are central to her role as a Bluestocking," adduced Judith Hawley in her study, 'Bluestocking Feminism' (1999) "In her letters she is witty, ironic, flirtatious, and light-hearted, as well as weighty and learned..."

Over the years Elizabeth Carter built up a pattern of travel sharing her time between the city and the coast. In summer, autumn and early winter she was usually in Deal but then she returned for the London Season in the spring. By 1762 she could afford to rent her own comfortable apartments on the first floor of 20, Clarges Street, near Piccadilly. By coincidence, the house was built in 1717 - the year of her birth - on the site of Clarges House, a property owned by the family of Ann Clarges, wife of General Monk, Duke of Albemarle. There she would have been on nodding acquaintance terms with Admiral Lord St. Vincent, Edmund Kean, Charles James Fox and Lady Emma Hamilton. Later, she moved next door to No 21 where she eventually died.

Her father's lowly position as Perpetual Curate did not allow for the family to own either a carriage or a horse. Her normal mode of transport was, therefore, the stage-coach which she abhorred. She spurned the fast mail coach in favour of the lumbering night coach, principally used by country folk travelling intermediate or short distances upon the road. She claimed familiarity of the neighbourhood between Deal and Canterbury and could recommend the safe routes to her friend, Miss Talbot. "In the first place, I will infallibly, if I live and prosper, meet you on Tuesday, May the 8th, at the King's Head (the posthouse) in Canterbury. The road from thence to Dover I never travelled, but my brother assures me 'tis a very good one. The inn to which all strangers go there is the Ship. From Dover to Deal is eight miles, a good road, excepting the hill, which may be walked up, and there is a beautiful romantic prospect from the top of it. From Deal to Canterbury is sixteen miles, a most excellent road." (30 April 1750)

Longer journeys were slow, tortuous and fraught with danger. In winter there was the further risk of being stranded in a snowstorm. Generally, she found herself "jolted black and blue" squashed inside the coach between idle gossips and local pilots returning from the packet boats. Her pattern of travel to London was to set out from Deal by bright moonlight at 8 p.m. in order to reach Clarges Street by 11 a.m. the following day. The first part of the road was free from robbers and daylight protected the travellers as they "rattled about the coach" through North Kent. Everyone held their breath as they passed through the notorious 'Hanging Wood', haunt of highwaymen, and they did not stop for breakfast until they had reached the safety of Dartford. On the return journey her father often sent his chaise to meet her at Rochester but she was extremely grateful when her brother-in-law, Dr. Pennington, placed his carriage at her disposal for the full extent of the journey.

Elizabeth Carter was now a wealthy woman. Royalties from 'Epictetus', bolstered by an inheritance from her uncle which, ironically, she invested in a stock of annuities in the South Sea Company, brought her financial independence. (Later still she received a sizeable legacy from Mrs. Montagu which gave her a "plentiful Fortune") It enabled her to lease from Dr. Thomas Secker, Archbishop of Canterbury, four adjoining tenements a stone's throw from the beach in 1762. The buildings were on the southern extremity of the town and commanded views of both the country and the sea. Formerly, the house was bounded on the east by boats' stores connected with a landing stage while to the north was the 'South Foreland Inn'. Eventually, Elizabeth was able to buy the freehold and have them converted into a single dwelling where she and her father, following the death of his second wife, set up home together.

While her new premises were being refurbished Elizabeth took the opportunity to tour the Continent with her distinguished friends. The large party roamed the countryside in a variety of equipages and while jolting around in one of the grander coaches Elizabeth continued to write letters - she improvised with a thimble as an inkwell - describing her adventures. During the course of their travels, the friends were introduced to minor royalty, all of whom failed to impress Madame Carter and, although she evidently put her faith in the restorative properties of the polluted spa waters, she dismissed the "trifling fopperies of Popery" displayed in all the Catholic churches. (For instance, at the convent in Lisle she was shown the actual kitchen, complete with iron stove and brass kettle, belonging to the Virgin Mary) Poor health ruined her enjoyment of the holiday and she was glad to return to the comfort of her new seaside home.

Today this charming pink-painted confection at the top of South Street with its ornate plaque and distinctive front door lit by bottlenose glass has been greatly altered over the centuries. The solid Georgian house has a series of beautifully proportioned rooms with low beams, fine panelling and marble fireplaces. There is a welcoming hall with a wide staircase opening onto a sunny landing. Originally, this stairway linked the two separate properties occupied by father and daughter. Elizabeth's quarters were part of the grand projection which formerly had a profusion of windows that faced seawards. None of these were sash windows since Mrs. Carter spurned their addition as "modern foppery".

According to her nephew, Montagu Pennington, father and daughter: "Each had their separate library and apartment, and they met but seldom, except at meals." Mrs. Carter's library, as might be expected, was extensive and there is a reference to it in Ireland's 'History of Kent' Volume 1 (1828): "The library of the late Mrs. Carter completely fills a large apartment, and is composed of the best editions of approved classical and scientific productions." Precious books were sent by friends in London via the reliable twice-weekly hoy around the coast to Sandwich and from thence "paquets" were conveyed to Deal by cart. Elizabeth was most content when spending her time "quietly and decently in the sober conversation of books". For her bookplates Elizabeth adopted an owl - the emblem of Minerva - perched on a tree by moonlight and encircled by a ribbon bearing the motto: 'Ask it of God'.

Mrs Elizabeth Carter by Catherine Read. Courtesy: Dr. Johnson's House.

Elizabeth's apartments stood "quite open on three sides, with a very wide space in front, where there is not anything to shelter it." From the top windows of her "airy abode" there were uninterrupted views easterly of the sea. A variety of sounds - from the "howling North east wind" to the "Thunder of Cannon" - drew observers. Here events were keenly noted - two ships driven ashore on the Sandhills in boisterous weather. . . a privateer bringing into the Downs a prize of a French East Indiaman. . . maimed and wounded sailors being landed on the foreshore and a burial at sea." The solemn of intervals of the minute guns, the languid dashing of the oars, the melancholy murmur of the surge on shore, the pausing beat of the drum, and the mournful strains of the dead march, formed one of the most pathetic concerts I have ever heard."(20 June 1780) Occasionally, events of national importance were observed - the ascent of M. Blanchard by balloon over the English Channel in 1785 and the embarkation of troops to Holland during the French Wars in 1799.

Elizabeth took immense pleasure in converting the"strange wild stony spot"in front of her house into a garden. She gave periodic reports of its progress to friends."It is smaller than you can imagine, but it will be full of roses and honeysuckles, and I am pleased and thankful for it. . ." (25 May 1763) "As I was watering my myrtles and geraniums the other day, in a little court before my house. . ." (26 Aug 1765) At night the perfume was exquisite and she was delighted to be serenaded by nightingales. She was apprehensive, however, each time her elderly father mounted a precarious ladder to prune his vines.

In this sunny courtyard Elizabeth planted an acorn which became a flourishing oak that she claimed was the most easterly in England. Miss Cornelia Knight, companion to Princess Charlotte, felt compelled to celebrate this tree in verse:

> "But every Muse will guard from fortunes stroke
> Minerva's Olive and Eliza's Oak".

Over the years ivy clinging to the trunk sapped its life so that only its trunk remained. Nevertheless, it bore a plaque until recently proclaiming its noble origins.

From living in such close proximity to the sea, Elizabeth Carter could not fail to observe the clandestine activities of the smugglers. She recognised that almost everyone in the town was engaged in this activity to"the utter destruction of all honest industry"and that their attachment to the illicit trade was so strong"that most of them had rather suffer want and hunger than apply themselves to anything else." Smuggling, she deemed,"a plain, practical sin".

Parson Carter's daughter was an outspoken critic of these illegal practices although she blamed the nobility for encouraging the "nocturnal trade" by purchasing "run goods". She deplored the fact that the main customers were gentlefolk foolishly influenced by fashion, "which makes us break the law and smuggle for the sake of getting French finery." She scolded her friend, Miss Sutton, that "if ever I see a prohibited gown, or a smuggled pair of ruffles, in your possession, you must expect no quarter." It disgusted her to see the carriages of people of the first rank of the land leave Deal laden with every kind of contraband. "I hear nothing here but tea and brandy, and prohibited clothing," she complained, "which is bought up with a scandalous degree of eagerness by people of fashion and people of fortune, who either come or send commissions from all quarters." (1772)

The military were frequently drafted in in a concerted effort to stamp out smuggling."I hear we are to have the Essex Militia quartered at Dover and Deal,"she reported."There have been sad disorders here lately with the smugglers; they have killed one poor custom house officer, and dangerously wounded another. The villains who did the mischief are fled to France, where they may be very useful to give our enemies all the intelligence of our coast in their power. Surely if people did but consider what a set of wicked wretches they encourage by the dirty practice of dealing in smuggled goods, they would make more conscience of it than they do." (1779)

She revealed that the Preventive Men temporarily gained the upper hand when they made a surprise search for hides. "We have had lately sad devastations amongst our smugglers, and the amount of the seizures is very great; but so are their gains: they reckon if they save but one boat out of three that they are quits, so judge what their profits are. . . Their trade is no doubt very justifiable but it must very much raise one's indignation to see the rich and the great avail themselves with impunity of the frauds (by buying these goods, little of which) can be consumed in this town." (1783)

Her complaints against the smugglers generally met with deaf ears. Once when she was travelling by stagecoach she dared to air opinions publicly and was upbraided by a Walmer resident who bluntly told her to mind her own business!

Press Gangs were another serious threat to this seaport during times of war. When the Marquess of Carmarthen turned up with an armed escort to press boatmen there was an almighty "hullabaloo". Mrs. Carter commented on the affray to Mrs. Montague in 1776: ". . . we have press warrants come down here backed by a precept from the Lord Warden; but our Magistrates refuse to back them; and will suffer none to be taken on shore but such as they themselves find to be proper persons. As their protection does not extend to the sea all our fishermen keep snug on the land to the great dismay of all people who set their minds on whitings and sprats, of which there is none to be got."

Deal provided her with constant stimulus and her letters mention interesting occurrences in this historic port. The Coronation of George III was lavishly celebrated by the townsfolk. "We had great illuminations, and firing of canon here. There happened to be nineteen men of war in the Downs besides sloops: and 21 guns from each made a noble peal of thunder." (September 1761) A far more alarming noise came from the thunderstorm which hit East Kent on 20 July 1788. "My house did not suffer from it, but the lower part of the town was presently two feet deep in water, and in some places much more; quite at the north end they could only move in boats and a very great deal of damage it has done to many families, whose ground floors were filled, and their furniture floating about." (20 July 1788) Newspapers gave sensational reports of imminent invasion during the French Wars but Mrs. Carter was able to gain first-hand knowledge of the true situation from Mrs. Lutwidge, wife of the Port Admiral. "We have had the Images of war brought very near to us, by the Sight of a French Frigate in the Downs, captured this week in Dunkirk Road. It was boarded in the night by one of our Gun Vessels; & the French officers fought with such desperate Valour that none above the rank of a midshipman was left alive." (12 July 1800)

On a lighter note, there are numerous references to seabathing which at that period was hailed by quack doctors as curing a multitude of illnesses. The cure was recommended to be taken in the cold winter months in the early morning and from a bathing machine which offered privacy.

"Lady Charlotte Finch had brought Miss Finch to bathe in the sea for the recovery of her health. . . her disorder seems to be merely nervous. . . the air of the place has done her good." (August 1770)

"Lord and Lady Ancram and their family are come to Deal, so our sea bathing season begins very early; indeed ours is such a fine open coast I wonder more people do not come to us, the water is so fine." (June 1771)
"Our little Prince Octavius (George II's eighth child who died the following year aged four) is very well in health and the eruption is much mended since his bathing in the sea." (1782)

Another sickly son of George III and Queen Charlotte was sent to the seaside to recover his strength after being innoculated against smallpox. Apparently, he soon endeared himself to "an old bluestocking lady" by graciously waving to her. Alas, the royal infant did not benefit from his spell of seabathing and, being the thirteenth child, he was sadly the first of the royal offspring to die.

Royalty - both the brother and wife of George IV - visited Mrs. Carter at her residence. The Duke of Cumberland was Colonel of the 15th Regiment of Light Dragoons and he inspected them when they were stationed at Walmer Barracks. He made time to call upon Mrs. Carter and his arrival caused much excitement among the neighbours. The Duke of Cumberland was the fifth son of George III and he later became King of Hanover. A short time before this visit Caroline, Princess of Wales, who was staying for some months in the Isle of Thanet, sent a message that she would come to Deal and drink tea with Elizabeth Carter. Her Royal Highness accompanied by two ladies-in-waiting arrived to take a dish or tea - and a homemade apple pie - with Mrs. Carter just before six o'clock and stayed for two hours.

Elizabeth Carter confessed she was no horsewoman (she was once badly thrown from her mount) and so she kept herself healthy by vigorous walking. Regularly, she rose between four and five o'clock so that she could walk out in the company of her dog, Rover. She was always content to exchange the "noise & dust & smoke" of London for the "flowry fields of Kent" where she could wander among "Eglantines and Honey Suckles". Habitually, she strolled out to visit friends in the surrounding villages of Sholden, Eastry, Northbourne, Woodnesborough and Wingham. She thought nothing of walking the sixteen miles to Canterbury. Once, she scorned to travel by the "drawling" stagecoach which plied between Deal and Canterbury and strode briskly ahead!

Her correspondence mentions "moonlit walks in the snow" and ventures into the countryside to go "a nutting". At the seaside she collected seashells on the foreshore or seaweed from under the White Cliffs. In winter she indulged in invigorating walks after first securing her cap and bonnet with large pins to prevent them from being "blown to the Goodwin Sands". Often she strolled in the direction of Kingsdown where she sat alone on the steep cliffs to relish the seascape by moonlight. She would often sit alone by the seashore writing extempore poetry or contemplating the panorama over the Channel.

Astronomy fascinated her. She enjoyed stargazing from the beach on mild autumn evenings and relished tracking the stars, planets, auroras and comets. "I walked last night at some unseasonable hour, and seeing the stars glitter, I could not help getting up to take a view of the sky, and I think I never saw a finer glow of constellations in my life," she wrote. "Orion and Sirius quite dazzled me." She had been introduced to Edmund Halley, Astronomer Royal, at Greenwich, and employed Thomas Wright, an astronomer, to help her identify all the features of the night sky. "Does not Venus make a fine appearance?" she asked. "You cannot think how I long for a telescope." Her other interests were mathematics, religion, ancient history and geography.

Elizabeth was musical. Among the instruments she played was a German flute. In Deal she owned a spinnet (rarely tuned) but in London she played a harpsichord which doubled as a writing table. Her favourite composer was Handel and she would spend hours copying out his music by hand. When young she was extremely fond of dancing quadrilles and subscribed to both the Deal and Sandwich Assembly Rooms. Another passion was amateur theatricals. She once wrote her own play for her family to perform, borrowing properties and costumes from her wide circle of friends. Her voice when performing or reading aloud was reportedly quiet yet full of inflection. She could knit and crochet and might be found engaged in "working (embroidering) a pair of ruffles (lace frills) and a handkerchief". She was not accomplished at drawing but preferred to play a sociable game of cards, particularly "sixpenny whist with her country neighbours". Naturally, she declined to gamble at the gaming tables although in old age she was not averse to the occasional quiet rubber.

Despite her shyness and modesty Elizabeth Carter was a decided presence in the London Salons and when she made her entrance the room fell silent. Elizabeth Sheridan, sister of the playwright, caught sight of her at an assembly in 1785: "After tea our circle was increased by the arrival of Mrs. Carter - on her being announced you may suppose my whole attention was turned to the door. She seems about sixty and is rather fat; she is in no way striking in her appearance, and was dressed in a scarlet gown and petticoat, with a plain undress cap and perfectly flat head - A small work-bag was hanging at her arm, out of which she drew some knotting as soon as she was seated; but with no fuss or airs. She entered into the conversation with that ease which persons have when both their thoughts and words are at command, and with no toss of the head, no sneer, no emphatic look, in short, no affected consequence of any kind."

Contemporary descriptions of her appearance reveal that Elizabeth Carter, in middle age, had a fair complexion, curled hair and hazel eyes. She spurned make-up and applied only Hungary or lavender water as cosmetics. She had an expressive face that animated her lively conversation but her shyness was aggravated by short-sightedness and to correct her vision she employed a glass. In later years, she tended towards corpulency and deafness. Although Elizabeth considered, herself, that she dressed "awkwardly" she was regarded as a woman of fashion in Deal. She paid particular attention to sleeves and altered their length to suit the current trend. Her one idiosyncrasy was to wear a single rose or sprig of jasmine which set her out as a "true Country Girl". Surprisingly for such a modest person, red was her favourite colour and she caused comment at wearing scarlet in public when in her seventies.

Elizabeth Carter sat for her portrait on numerous occasions. One portrait (circa 1738) shows her as a young woman in graceful pose standing in a garden holding an open book. She is wearing a borrowed cream duchesse silk satin gown with lace decorating the wide neckline of her bodice and a double tier of lace flounces (or "engagements") under her ample cuffs. Her modest hairstyle is enlivened with fresh flowers and strings of pearls. Two allegorical figures - Fame and Learning - hover overhead holding a laurel wreath. The National Portrait Gallery's catalogue for the exhibition, 'Brilliant Women' (2008) proposes that this portrait provides "a visual analogue of the literary celebration of her visit to Pope's garden" and was "designed to advance Carter's professional identity". The portrait proclaims metaphorically that Mrs. Carter has stolen Pope's laurel crown for literature.

The oil painting is by Joseph Highmore whose daughter, Susannah, was a close friend of the sitter. She lived in London's Lincoln's Inn Fields, where she moved in literary circles, but frequently visited Hythe. Highmore also painted a pair of portraits of her brother, John, and his wife, Frances, née Underdown. In 1762 Susanna married the Rev. John Duncombe, Master of the Hospital of St. John and one of the Six Preachers at Canterbury Cathedral. Highmore retired and went to live with the couple in Canterbury until his demise in 1780. His portrait of Elizabeth Carter was presented by her nephew, Montagu, when Perpetual Curate of St. George's Church, to the Corporation of Deal in 1815. It hangs prominently in the Town Hall.

A far more striking portrait was painted by John Fayram (circa 1741). It portrays Elizabeth Carter in playful guise as Minerva, Roman goddess of wisdom. She is dressed in full armour with plumed helmet and round shield but instead of a sword she wields a copy of Plato. (Amusingly, an owl is concealed in her headress) This portrait with its extraordinary composition blatantly presents Mrs. Carter as the foremost intellectual of the day and prepared for war against her contemporary critics. The portrait remained

Carter House by Pat Moody © Deal Maritime and Local History Museum.

in the Pennington family for decades, was returned to Carter House late last century but is now in private ownership.

A third portrait by Katherine Read, a leading portrait painter, was commissioned by Mrs. Montagu around 1765. This oil painting shows a gentle, assured, middle-aged Mrs. Carter in scholarly pose holding a quill and leaning on a volume of 'Epictetus'. She is wearing a long yellow scarf wound over her hair with a green shawl draped over her shoulders. Her averted gaze and matronly attire indicate a return to feminine modesty. It now hangs prominently in Dr. Johnson's House in Gough Square.

A fourth oval pastel by Thomas Lawrence dates from 1788/9. This homely portrait shows a profile of Mrs. Carter in ripe old age. She is dressed in a dark brown silk dress, a black silk shawl, white neck

Mrs Elizabeth Carter by Thomas Lawrence © National Portrait Gallery.

frill with pink bow and a white lace cap tied with a broad red ribbon. An eye-glass hangs from a black ribbon round her neck. A cameo copy carved in ivory by the Belgian sculptor, Karl Hendrik Geerts of Louvain, rests on mauve velvet in a carved oak frame in the Mayor's Parlour at Deal Town Hall. It conceals a collection of six autographed letters from Mrs Carter to Miss Highmore donated by her niece, Hannah Carter Smith, in 1854. In 1800 Lawrence attempted another painting of Mrs Carter wearing a bonnet but it was never finished.

Dr. Johnson's House preserves several items of furniture which reputedly belonged to Elizabeth Carter. There is a grand mahogany bureau with a flap which unusually lifts down to reveal a writing slope; a three-tiered whatnot and a ladder-back armchair which Dr. Johnson supposedly acquired from his friend on permanent loan.

Dr. Nicolas Carter, who had always tended to be a hypochondriac, became increasingly deaf in old age. Indisputably, he was a man of great faith but he was also undoubtedly obstinate and bigoted. Even in his advanced years he had made regular trips to London hoping to find a possible third bride. He died after a prolonged illness in October 1774 fighting his ecclesiastic superiors to the bitter end. He was buried in Ham Churchyard where since 1734 he had held the rectory with those of Tilmanstone, Woodnesborough and Sutton. Dr. George Redsull Carter, who had presented the magnificent organ to St. George's Church, also commissioned the stained-glass east window depicting Faith, Hope and Charity as a tribute to his ancestor's memory in 1867.

Naturally, Elizabeth Carter valued education highly. A Charity School was founded by Rev. William Backhouse, Rector of St. Leonard's Church, at Upper Deal in 1786.

Thirty-five village children were taught reading and writing plus the catechism. Mrs. Carter volunteered to subscribe fifteen shillings annually to sponsor one child's education. During the ministry of Rev. Robert Brandon, who succeeded Dr. Carter as Perpetual Curate of St. George's Church, Deal Charity School was also opened in 1792. It appears this school, which was funded by private subscription, began in a modest way. It first occupied a house leased from the Hulke family in Lower Street. Later it was enlarged and moved to the south end of Middle Street in the vicinity of 'Carter House'.

Deal Charity School catered for twenty-five boys and twenty-five girls from the age of six onwards. Eminent townsfolk were invited to support the children's education and Mrs. Carter sponsored a boy with the surname 'Carter'. It also appears she taught voluntarily at this school and took pleasure in organising nature walks in the country. This new Charity School existed from 1802 to 1813 when it transferred to St. George's Hall and because of its location was renamed Deal Central School. A considerable number of boys left to attend Deal Nautical College, which was administered by nine Naval Officers and had a fine record of achievement. In the first seventeen years of its existence over two hundred and fifty boys left to embark upon a seafaring career.

During her advanced years Elizabeth Carter found the cold weather in Deal a trial and so she usually chose to pass the winter months in London. "If I had no other motive to bring me to London than to avoid the hollow blasts of the wind," she once wrote, "I would sit through the wintry months listening to the tempests, and looking at the dashing ocean with great tranquility, but Dr. Johnson says "London is the land of ideas" and I say that it is the land of friendship." She was also suffering from a painful illness, then commonly known as 'St. Anthony's Fire'.

'St. Anthony's Fire' was the popular name for ergotism which was a poison produced from a fungus that grew on rye. Apparently, it was first noticed in the Middle Ages when it was responsible for causing the deaths of thousands of people. There were two forms of the disease: one that results in convulsions and the other that causes gangrene. (St. Anthony's Fire refers to the latter form of the disease) The patron saint of victims of ergotism was St. Anthony because it was primarily the Order of Saint Anthony that treated these patients. In the 17th century it was discovered that bread containing ergot was the likely cause of these mass poisonings but with the improvement in farming methods the epidemics decreased. Undoubtedly, the disease caused considerable pain. One of the popular treatments was to apply a poultice made from the plant, 'Shepherd's Purse', which was thought to relieve the inflammation.

On 16 December - which coincided with her birthday - Elizabeth Carter received her final sacrament. She dined with her nephew and insisted he read out the whole of her will so that she could give last minute directions to her executors. Then, despite a severe attack of her illness, she demonstrated remarkable stoicism by her determination to see her old friends in London. She travelled there in time for the winter season and arrived on Christmas Eve, 1805. The journey would have been made in great discomfort and she probably guessed she was dying. Elizabeth was nursed by her devoted companion, Lady Cremorne, but after a brief, but protracted final bout of sickness, she died "without a struggle" on 19 February 1806.

Elizabeth Carter was interred in the grounds of Grosvenor Chapel, an appendage to the Church of St. George, Hanover Square. It was a private funeral attended, as was the custom, only by her close male relatives, and she was quietly buried, in accordance with her express desire, "with as little expense as possible". All traces of her tomb have long since vanished but a marble mural monument to her memory remains on the east wall of the chancel in St. George's Church at Deal. "In deep learning, genius and extensive knowledge she was equalled by few, in piety and the practice of every Christian duty excelled by none".

Pennington's 'Memoir' portrays a quaint, harmless, revered aunt who, by chance, became one of the leading intellectuals of the Georgian age. Despite this muted version of his relative's fame, the true character of Elizabeth Carter - opinionated, determined, ambitious - shines through. She was, after all, the favourite daughter of a notorious cleric skilled in self-promotion, and her "launch into society" was no mere accident but achieved through immense application and hard work. Mrs. Carter was "deliberate, determined, focused", according to Norma Clark in 'Dr. Johnson's Women' (2000) and she had clearly "resolved from an early age on literary scholarship and celebrity".

THE OLD PLAYHOUSE

'an excellent set of actors'

A PROSPEROUS THEATRE patronised by the officers of the Royal Navy when stationed in the Downs graced the port in Georgian times. Distinguished patrons who flocked there to be entertained by a company of skilled actors, singers, dancers and acrobats included the royal brothers, Frederick, Duke of York, and William, Duke of Clarence (later King William IV).

Strolling players were an inexorable part of any nautical town where they were guaranteed a new audience almost nightly from the constant arrival of ships whose crews were eager for diversions. Indeed, John Bernard, a theatrical manager who operated a maritime circuit extending practically the entire length of the east coast, observed: "Sailors in general, I believe, are very fond of playhouses: this may be partly because they find their ships workhouses, and partly because the former are the readiest places of amusement they can visit when they are ashore."

At Deal, however, the frenzied attempts by touring companies to attract customers by either literally drumming up trade or parading in costume drew scorn from the highly literate Elizabeth Carter: "Everybody else in the family and indeed the town too, is gone to see a show to which people are called by beat of drum...'tis not a raree-show, but a play. Do you not often lament, dear Miss Talbot, that this sort of entertainment which might be rendered so useful to the interest of virtue, is so very ill-regulated that it is hardy proper?" (29 October 1747) "I am credibly informed we have an excellent set of actors coming to Deal, who want very few qualifications but washing their faces and learning to read." (30 November 1751)

At first these versatile troupes set up their stages in inns, barns or even the open air until eventually a permanent venue was secured especially equipped for dramatic performances at Deal. The date of the original Playhouse remains a mystery but there is a suggestion that it may have been converted from a derelict malthouse. Certainly, it was the scene of lively entertainment, providing amusement for the local inhabitants and visitors alike. A succession of insignificant companies - Perry's, Dymer's, Burton's, Diddiar's, Copeland's, Glassington's, Hillyard's - played limited seasons with varying success at this seaside venue which had the reputation for being exceedingly tough. Actor and writer, William Oxberry bluntly declared Deal to be "the worst theatrical town in England... avoid it."

Deal's Playhouse is clearly marked on Dodd's map of 1810. It stood prominently on the west side of Lower Street (now High Street). Photographs which survive present the theatre in its later stages when it had been miserably converted into a furniture-cum-antique warehouse. A plain, three-storeyed building is shown with bric-a-brac - copper warming pans and iron hip baths - piled high on a cobbled forecourt and faded playbills still peeling on the walls. The building seems to be divided into two: one part having three windows and the signs 'The Old Playhouse' and 'Furniture and Bedding' painted on it while the second has four sash windows above an arcade entered by three sliding doors. Above appears the legend: 'Henry Dunn Senr., Broker, Paper-Hanger, Upholsterer, Dealer in Antique Furniture'. The addition of a date, 'Est. 1798', probably refers to the foundation of the family business since Deal's Theatre was then in its heyday and had for some time been presided over by the vivacious Mrs. Baker - first woman theatre manager in England.

Mrs. Sarah Baker (c1736 - 1816) dubbed 'Governess-General and Sole Autocratix of the Kentish Drama', was perhaps the most colourful character to have inhabited Deal. Sarah, who was born in a tent, travelled around the country with her mother, Ann Wakelin, an acrobatic dancer from Sadler's Wells. They exhibited various sideshows and provided all manner of entertainments ranging from clowning to rope-dancing at fairs and festivals. Sarah was an accomplished dancer and puppeteer in her youth and for a time she operated her own Punch and Judy show. Eventually, Sarah Wakelin married a member of her mother's nomadic troupe, an acrobat named Baker. Alas, he died within a few years and Sarah found herself a widow with three small children to support. When old Mrs. Wakelin retired, her stage properties passed to Sarah who continued to tour although she became adept at adapting her entertainment to meet public demand. She introduced Shakespeare, standard classics and popular plays of the day interspersed with comic songs, jigs and gymnastics. Her ambition was to establish theatres throughout the southeast where she might present the legitimate drama with professional actors.

Mrs Baker achieved her aspiration and she dominated the theatrical scene in Kent and Sussex for almost half a century. She presented spectacular entertainments at every military or naval town, astutely timing the arrival of her company to coincide with major events such as Tunbridge Wells Spa Season or Canterbury Races. Her reputation was so great that she could command the services of famous actors. Several times she engaged the Regency clown, Joseph Grimaldi, to play at Rochester, Maidstone and Canterbury where he appeared in pantomime to great acclaim and packed houses. He recalls his eccentric manageress with affection in his 'Memoirs' (1838) which he related to Charles Dickens.

Sarah built no fewer than ten theatres entirely at her own expense although she only rented suitable premises at Deal. Her own theatres were constructed to an identical plan - a plain, rectangular auditorium with folding doors screening the central entrance with its solitary paybox - and this ploy ensured that her scenery fitted all venues. Invariably, there was a dwelling-house attached. Her portable wooden stage was ideal for presentation of interludes, operettas and bowdlerised hit plays direct from London such as 'She Stoops to Conquer', 'The Beaux Strategem', 'School For

Scandal' and 'The Beggar's Opera'. (At Deal, unsurprisingly, the pantomimes, 'Harlequin Invasion' and 'Robin Hood', proved far more popular than Shakespeare's 'As You Like It' and 'Twelfth Night')

Sarah Baker's theatrical company was at Folkestone in April 1771 and, presumably, it was at that time she first ventured into Deal. A notice in the 'Kentish Express' (19 November 1772) announced that a Sadler's Wells Company under her own management would soon appear at Canterbury in a programme of rope dancing, musical interludes, tumbling and burlettas and further promised that the clothes, scenery and machinery would be "entirely new". When Sarah Baker finally established her own grand theatre in this Cathedral City she made only intermittent forays into Deal and the surrounding district.

Sarah found she had a formidable rival in the person of Charles Mate, a sea captain whose wife owned a prosperous tavern in Dover. Mate had control of the Dover circuit and he presented plays at every coastal venue between Rye and Margate. (Margate's present 'Theatre Royal', which dates from 1787, evolved out of a makeshift theatre in a barn behind the 'Fountain Inn' in King Street) A true eccentric, Mate, after forsaking his naval career for one on the stage, addressed his players in nautical terms directing them to "go on the larboard tack" or "pass to port" whenever he wanted them to cross the stage! The two managers - Baker and Mate - fought zealously for control of the Kentish circuits, both attracting capacity audiences.

Mrs. Baker's was a salaried company and consequently she charged high prices (3/- 2/- and 1/- in Deal in 1780). Charles Mate, to attract better custom, always strived to undercut her. Sarah, however, managed to keep in profit despite the fact that she had enormous expenses which included the fees of her carpenter, doorkeeper, lamp trimmer, scene shifters, members of the band, cast refreshments and playbill printing. Furthermore, she had the expense of transporting her scenery, wardrobe, properties and stage, either by handcart or foyboat. Nonetheless, she was generous to her loyal band of theatregoers and frequently let children in to watch her shows for just a few pence. Sometimes she even acted as an unofficial pawnbroker by allowing patrons entrance in exchange for trifles - knives, badges or scissors - which had to be redeemed the following day for the full price of a pit seat. At one time she gave a 'benefit night' for the pupils of Deal's Charity School. Sarah Baker disdained banks and kept her substantial takings in several large punch bowls that stood on the top shelf of her bureau which travelled with her to every new venue.

Sarah's attempts to build a theatre at a cost of £500 on a site adjacent to the parish church of St. John that would rival Mate's 'Theatre Royal' at Margate was thwarted when the latter artfully secured a royal charter which granted him the sole right to present plays in that popular resort. Sarah, conceding defeat, divided her wooden theatre into four sections and packed it aboard a sailing vessel where it was conveyed round the coast to Faversham. Undaunted, she gained control of the Canterbury circuit comprising Rochester, Sittingbourne, Maidstone, Tunbridge Wells, Faversham, Folkestone, Dover, Sandwich and Deal in 1785. Sarah, although illiterate, became a phenomenally wealthy woman who met with instant success wherever she presented her programme of plays which rarely fell below three pieces. That she had been able to accrue such a fortune she ascribed to the fact that she had always been her own ticket taker. Nightly, Mrs. Baker might be seen at the entrance of her own theatre collecting the money for Boxes, Pit and Gallery (there were reduced prices for late admission) whilst bestowing honours on all and sundry. As each patron approached, he or she was greeted with 'Your Grace', 'Your Highness' or some similar ennoblement. Once they had paid, Sarah hustled them in through the door with the admonishment, "Pass on, Tom Fool!" These alternating hot and cold receptions were the cause of merriment to the crowd swarming round the doors. During the performances Sarah would steal into the auditorium and watch the action from a gap in the pit entrance which offered her an uninterrupted view of the stage.

Widow Baker's own company was very much a family affair. Her two daughters performed regularly - Ann played tragic roles while Sally appeared in comedy - while her son, Henry, though certainly not a matinee idol, was a proficient actor. Her sister, Mary Wakelin, was an occasional performer and her cousin, Ireland, was the band leader. (There were only three musicians) Prominent among the players were a very rough actor called Rugg, a youth named Smith, a comic wag known as Frisby, a mysterious Twiddy, the Marriotts and the Glassingtons (who were brother and sister). These actors all received decent salaries and were not subject to profit share, with its fluctuating payments, cautiously adopted by Charles Mate.

Luckily, there is a glimpse backstage of the workings of this seaside Georgian Playhouse. Thomas Dibdin (1771 - 1841), son of

The Old Deal Playhouse.

Charles Dibdin who composed a host of popular patriotic ballads, recorded his experiences in 'Reminiscences' (2 Volumes, published 1827). While acting with the Dover Players, Thomas was offered an engagement to play at Deal by Jem Gardner, manager of Mrs. Baker's company, in 1789. The new contract offered was to be paid on a salary and was therefore regarded by this ambitious young actor as a definite step forward in his career. His first meeting with the enigmatic Mrs. Baker was one of sheer delight. Arrived in high spirits at Deal, Dibdin was introduced to his benefactress who was, in her own words, whiling away the time and keeping her company together until her new "great grand theatre" (a phrase to which she was evidently partial) was built at Canterbury.

On making a low bow in Sarah's 'salon of residence', Thomas was greeted by two ladies who rose and - both being excellent dancers - made an elegant curtsy. The first was Mrs. Baker's sister, Ann Wakelin, whose talents seemed inexhaustible: "principal comic dancer, occasional actress, wardrobe keeper and professed cook". Indeed her services were regarded as indispensable so that apart from receiving free board and lodging, she was paid a guinea and a half each week in addition to being granted a benefit night in every town in which the company played. The second lady was, of course, Mrs. Baker herself. Immediately, Sarah struck the newcomer as being warm-hearted, genteel and delightfully eccentric. Quite unlearned, totally illiterate, she could with difficulty barely sign her name. Dibdin was amazed how that, being left a widow so early in life and without any tangible means of support, his commandress had created such a talented and prosperous company entirely through her own determination and industry.

Her generosity, too, was soon in evidence. "On my first announcing my name in her presence," Dibdin recalls, "Mrs. Baker asked, without waiting a reply, whether I was not very young on the stage, whether I had got a lodging, and whether, after my journey, I did not want some money; adding, with her usual rapidity of utterances, 'I am sure you do, and I won't have my young men in debt in the town: here is a week's salary in advance: show the people a little of this and they will be sure to be civil in the hopes of seeing the rest of it'." So saying she pressed a scattering of coins into the surprised novice's hands adding, "Pooh! Nonsense! The silver is all good: I took it all at the doors myself last night. Miss Wakelin shall inquire about a lodging for you, and you will find Jem Gardner at the theatre: we don't live there ourselves, because it is not mine, I only rent it: but at Rochester, and Maidstone, and Tunbridge Wells and my new 'great grand theatre' at Canterbury, I have dwelling-houses of my own."

Dibdin went in search of lodgings and by pure chance alighted upon Sarah Baker's own apartments: "I was now asked to tea, and introduced to an interesting looking consumptive gentleman named Campden who had, at Miss Wakelin's request, procured me a lodging, and being Mrs. Baker's artist for scenery (and no humble one for such an establishment) I found a very great acquisition in his society: he was, like myself, averse from the pot-companion system, which in that day too much obtained among the heroes of the stage. . . With Campden I therefore passed many a rational evening (on non-play nights) of reading and sketching designs for scenes."

Thomas Dibdin's own lodgings appear to have been in the manner of modern 'theatrical digs': "The apartments he engaged for me were in Middle Street facing an opening toward the sea through which, while lying in bed, I had a good view of the numerous Indiamen which entered, anchored in, and set sail from the Downs. My landlady was a very pretty and intelligent young woman, with a still prettier infant, which she seemed as affectionately devoted to as her husband - a Jersey man, of the most ferocious and diabolical disposition I ever witnessed: his wife's father and sister lived in the house; and upon the slightest pretence (for provocation he never received) he would beat the grey-headed man, both the sisters, and even the infant with savage cruelty; and when ordered off to sea towards evening (for he was in the service of the government, in some way connected with carrying out anchors and stores, in bad

*Final days of the old Playhouse photographed by Edgar Tarry Adams.
Courtesy: National Museum of Photography, Film and Television.*

weather, from the Royal Yard to the King's ships in the Downs) he would take, not the key of, but the street-door itself way with him. . . My amiable landlord, Mr. Norman, afterwards received his dessert, for he was hanged, under an alias, as one of the principals in the mutiny at the Nore."

At the theatre the young actor was introduced to no less a personage than Governor Trott - "a whimsical character, and amateur actor well-known to all who have been at Deal, particularly to naval officers". This slim youth was a fine singer and also proprietor of the local bathing-rooms where he amused patrons with his comical anecdotes and "good natured oddities of his own eccentricity". When Dibdin first saw Sam Trott he was in a more sombre mood, however, playing the role of second executioner!

Thomas Dibdin.

Apart from appearing in the current repertoire of plays Dibdin was expected to lend a hand backstage. "Besides my performing a new character in play or farce almost every night, I improved rapidly, under friend Campden, in the art of scene-painting, thankfully giving him my labour in return for his instructions.

My principal attempts were in the scenery of 'Richard Coeur-de-Lion' and the 'Destruction of the Bastille' - both which pieces were produced and acted with more propriety and expensive decoration than could have been expected in a small theatre."

Mrs. Baker "went every morning to market and kept the box-book, on which always lay a massive silver ink-stand which, with a superb pair of silver trumpets, several cups, tankards, and candlesticks of the same pure metal, it was the lady's honest pride to say she had paid for with her own hard earnings - she next manufactured the daily play-bill by the help of scissors, needle, thread, and a collection of old bills, cutting a play from one, an interlude from another, a farce from a third, and sewed them neatly together; and thus precluded the necessity of pen and ink, except where the name of a former actor was to make way for a successor, and then a blank was left for the first performer who happened to call in, and who could write, to fill up."

Dibdin's 'Reminiscences' are brimful of amusing anecdotes:

"When Mrs. Baker first engaged a living company, she not only used to beat the drum behind the scenes, in Richard, and other martial plays, but was occasionally her own prompter, or rather that of her actors. As has before been hinted, her practice in reading had not been very extensive; and one evening, when her manager, Mr. Gardner, who was playing Gradus, in the farce of 'Who's the Dupe?', and imposing an old Doiley, by affecting to speak Greek, his memory unfortunately failed him and he cast an anxious eye towards the promptress for assistance; Mrs. Baker having never met with so many syllables combined in one word, or so many such words on one page as the fictitious Greek afforded, was rather puzzled, and hesitated a moment; with Gardner's distress increasing by the delay, he rather angrily, in a loud whisper, exclaimed, 'Give me the word, Madam'. The Lady replied, 'It's a hard word, Jem!' - 'Then give me the next' - 'That's harder' - 'The next?' - 'Harder still'. Gardener became furious; and the manageress, no less so, threw the book on the stage, and left it, saying 'There, now, you have 'em all, you may take your choice."

Dibdin vividly portrays every member of that illustrious company: "Her eldest daughter, Miss Baker, was the Lady Macbeth, Euphrasia, Priscilla Tomboy, and Spoiled Child of the corps; Miss Sally Baker (since married to Mr. Dowton) was the Miss Alton, Leonora in the Padlock, Polly in the Beggar's Opera, etc. Mr. Gardner, the stage manager, played all the heroes, Falstaff, and the violincello, set accompaniments for the orchestra, taught the singers, and sometimes copied the parts: he was a gentlemanly man of some education, without the slightest objection to a second bottle at seasonable hours, or a third at any time, and sometimes - but we will wind things up by saying that his conduct to those under his direction procured him the honourable appellation of 'The Actor's Friend'."

Alas, Thomas Dibdin's account of the Deal thespians ends here for, as he records: "After a brief, though successful sojourn at Deal, we removed one fine afternoon to Sandwich, only five miles distant, where there was a pretty sort of amateur theatre at the 'New Inn'." The career of this handsome, talented actor flourished and he became an actor, writer and manager at several leading theatres in London. Mrs. Baker, herself, continued to bring her company to Deal for a regular three month season each year until her "great grand theatre" at Canterbury was finally opened around 1789. After that time she abandoned the smaller venues and concentrated mainly on larger venues which brought her greater income although she continued to present occasional plays at Deal. She died in 1816, only a few months after she had retired, and handed over the business to her son-in-law, by now a celebrated character actor, William Dowton. At that time he had numerous professional engagements so he immediately passed on the care of the circuit to his son, also called William, although the success of this travelling theatre rapidly declined. The cessation of the Napoleonic Wars meant that the military and naval presence in the seaports was vastly reduced while the advent of the railways meant that audiences could travel into London to seek alternative entertainment. Mrs. Baker, throughout her lifetime, had ruled over a prosperous empire and in her will she disposed of her ten profitable provincial theatres.

The withdrawal from Deal by Sarah Baker left this lucrative venue open for her rival, Charles Mate, who in the spring of 1788 announced in the 'Kentish Gazette' "that a large and commodious THEATRE, is now fitting up with the greatest Care and Attention opening on Easter Monday for a stay of two months." This seems to indicate that the Playhouse provided just a basic venue for travelling companies to 'fit up' their

Perry's Company which played Deal in 1751 claimed historical accuracy for its production of 'Cato' that featured "new Roman dresses".

Madame Tussaud's presented her famous waxworks at the Assembly Rooms, Deal, in 1818. Ninety figures were displayed including Nelson, Wellington, Shakespeare and Sleeping Beauty.

The Victorian midget, Tom Thumb, and his family appeared at the New Assembly Rooms at Deal on 14 August 1865. Billed as "the four smallest beings in the world", this diminutive family made a special tableau dressed in their wedding costumes.

Lord George Sanger's Circus paraded along the Promenade to advertise their arrival in Deal in 1898. When the elephants were taken for a bathe in the sea the boatmen objected to their presence and forced them to "skedaddle".

own portable stage with wax lights and heavy drapes. From that time onwards scarcely a programme appears without his name prominent on the playbills and he was successful in attracting top names to appear at the Deal Playhouse.

In 1794 Deal Playhouse welcomed George III's son, Frederick, Duke of York. The 'Kentish Gazette' (3 March) reported the Duke's arrival in Deal en route for Ostend and his taking up residence at 'The Three King's Hotel' (now 'The Royal'). Graciously, His Royal Highness appeared on the balcony "at the back of the hotel next the sea" where a large crowd gathered to greet him. It was stated that the Duke would visit the Playhouse that same evening and in deference to the royal taste the bill was hastily changed from 'King Lear' (mad monarchs were a touchy subject in Georgian times!) to 'Wild Oats', plus a farce, 'Sprigs of Lavender'. Hopefully, this frivolous entertainment took Prince Frederick's mind off his current disastrous campaign on the Continent.

Presumably, Thomas Dibdin, despite his fame, continued to tour the provinces because a playbill for Saturday 16 December 1797 advertises a benefit night for his wife, Ann, a singer and actor, at Deal's New Theatre. Once again there was a diversity of presentation. Shakespeare's 'As You Like It' (which to add to its popularity was subtitled, 'Love In A Forest') was sandwiched between the adventure, 'Robinson Crusoe', and a farce, 'The Irish Widow'. In the Shakespeare's romance Jem Gardner was tempted back to play the comic, Touchstone, while Dibdin awarded himself the walk-on part as the elderly servant, Adam. Mrs. Dibdin strutted the stage in the breeches role, Rosalind, and her rendering of the Bard was enlivened with the 'Cuckoo Song'.

A pantomime, 'Lord Mayor's Day, or Harlequin in London', included fantastic scenery which Dibdin painted specially for the occasion. A grand parade through the audience featured the Lord Mayor riding in his state coach attended by his mace bearer, liveried footmen and a man in a full suit of armour. These dramatic performances were interspersed with songs, including 'Landlords of Deal' or 'A Song About Signs'. Every member of the audience was provided with a songsheet to encourage them to join in the chorus.

There was a dramatic curiosity when Messrs Fitzmaurice and O'Rourke presented a 'Gallimaufry' at the Deal Theatre on 30 and 31 August 1805. This strange entertainment consisted of a mixture of recitations, songs and music. Fresh from their season at the Theatre Royal, Margate, Mr. O'Rourke sang comic songs, providing his own accompaniment on the pianoforte, and Mr Fitzmaurice played the bagpipes. The flyers made the tantalising offer that: "Any Lady or Gentleman may have a Private Performance at their own House by giving a few Hours Notice".

One playbill (Wednesday 11 November 1807) advertises a German historical play, 'Pizzaro',

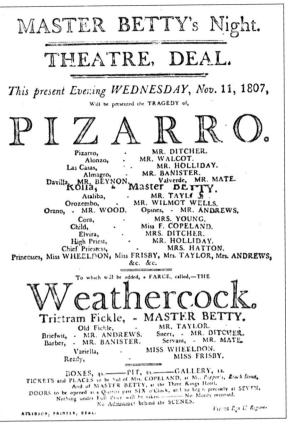

Poster advertising the appearance of Master Betty at Deal's Playhouse in 1807.

concerning the Spanish Conqueror of Peru, adapted by Sheridan and premiered earlier that year at Drury Lane. Acting the heroic epic role of Rolla was the child prodigy, 'Master Betty' (1791 - 1874) whose popularity rivalled even Kemble when he appeared nightly at West End venues at the turn of that century. Preposterously, he was compared with the celebrated Roman actor, Quintus Roscious Gallus. At Deal's Playhouse, this 'Young Roscius' made one of his last appearances as a child where he matched his performance in tragedy with an appearance in farce. He played Tristram Fickle in Allingham's broad comedy, 'The Weathercock', in which Mr. Mate also deigned to appear as 'Servant'.

Master Betty, whose meteoric flight to fame began when he was only twelve years old, amassed a fortune by such appearances in the provinces where audiences were astounded by his mastery of Shakespeare. (His favoured role was Hamlet) Inevitably, the teenage actor was snapped up by Mrs. Baker while at Canterbury and he made a return visit to Deal under her management in 1813. Playbills generally announced certain strictures that would be applied to his prestigious performances: "Nothing under Full Price will be taken. No money returned. No admittance behind the scenes." An even more remarkable performer was Clara Fisher, who specialised in male leading roles from Shakespeare. She appeared at Deal Playhouse, when only eight years old, where she alternated Richard III with Shylock, in 1819.

Another playbill for Charles Mate's company advertises Mrs. Taylor's Benefit Night (29 June 1811) on which occasion the regular company appeared in support - Mr. Holliday, Mr. Banister, Mr. and Mrs. Wells and, naturally, Charles Mate, this time in the all important role of 'Postboy'. The programme was a mixed variety of drama and song, the accent being firmly on comedy. Topping the bill was the riotous romp, 'The Clandestine Marriage', written in collaboration by David Garrick and George Colman the elder, based on Hogarth's series of engravings, 'Marriage la Mode', and produced for the first time in 1766. For good measure there was a performance of a new two-act comedy, 'The Budget of Blunders - or Madness Rules the Hour', which had enjoyed a run of 45 successive nights at Covent Garden "with the most distinguished applause", and, during the course of the evening, cheerful interludes were provided by the singing of comic songs and ditties all arranged by "particular desire" to maintain the happy tempo.

Dorothy Jordan (1761 - 1816) former mistress of the Duke of Clarence who abandoned her when he became King William IV, played at Deal in February 1815. Left in great financial difficulties, Miss Jordan found that she could still earn a decent living by returning to her former profession as a comedy actor. She was engaged for two nights to play the heroine in 'The Soldiers Daughter' which drew packed houses. Audiences were keen to get a late glimpse of the most celebrated comedienne of her day. Soon afterwards she appeared for ten nights at Margate's 'Theatre Royal' (she had first appeared there in August 1797 when she played Peggy in 'The Country Girl') before finally retiring from her career on the stage which had spanned forty years.

A stray playbill (undated) gives further insights into the fare offered at Deal. It advertises a double bill: a comedy, 'The Jew or the Benevolent Israelite', and an historical drama, 'The Voyages of Captain Cook'. This latter piece featured such sensational scenes as 'Capt. Cook is Stabbed in the back' and 'The English Fight for the Body'. Tickets could be obtained in advance from Mr. F. Savill, 100 Beach Street (for whose 'benefit' the performance was staged) or at the theatre where "the Box plans will lie for inspection every morning from Ten till Two." The same bill gives advance notice of two spring pantomimes: 'Whittington and his Cat', on Easter Monday, and 'Cinderella and her little glass slipper' on Tuesday.

Incongruously, 'Cinderella' was played out before a panorama - purportedly painted expressly for the new pantomime - "Portraying the progress of a steam vessel on her voyage to India commencing at Gravesend and proceeding in its passage by the Nore Light-Vessel, Nore and Entrance to the Medway, Reculver, Margate and North Foreland, Ramsgate Harbour with the Royal Sovereign Yacht sailing from it with His Majesty on board on his way to Calais, Deal, Dover and Shakespeare's Cliff in the distance. . ." The panorama ended with the sunrise at Calcutta which, presumably, formed the backdrop for the walk down.

An anonymous patron left a revealing account of a performance at the Deal Playhouse in 1815. (The evening included a cameo appearance of Governor Trott who was, by then, past his prime) "After tea we all assembled and went to the Play. Deal

Theatre is very small and built in a square manner. Jane Shore was acted very well. Mr. Montgomery and Miss Fitzhenry were the best two actors. Jane Shore was rather overdone. The bill said 'The Lawyer' was to be acted, but 'Gloucester' came forward to say they could get no book and would substitute 'The Purse'. or 'Benevolent Tar', which was acted very well. A pantomime came next but I, being close, saw all the tricks. They had about 6 Scenes to it all. We then went home and very soberly to bed."

"I forgot to mention that one of the Band sang 'Oh Nancy' very well and also that Mr. Trott the Bather thought he could sing so well that he could please the people, but, however, he was hissed pretty well."

Sadly, the Old Playhouse had fallen into decline during the early years of the nineteenth century. After the Battle of Waterloo the threat of a French invasion was stalled which meant that a large number of soldiers and sailors, who were regular patrons, left this garrison town. Rate books confirm that the premises had been acquired in 1804/5 by Charles Crickett, a carpenter and alderman, who owned pockets of land in Lower Deal. Twenty years later the building ceased to be hired out to theatrical companies and provided temporary accommodation for a school.

Eventually, the site was acquired by the Dunn family as their secondhand furniture store. After the death of Henry Dunn, the building was purchased for £1,450 by Sydney Pittock whose own store was adjacent. In 1911 the Playhouse was demolished to make way for the spacious furnishing department of Messrs John Pittock and Son who later sold them to Messrs. Brown and Phillips. Customers for a long time recalled the former theatre with its cobbled forecourt, long passageway leading down to the central Box Office and remnants of the Gallery and Side Boxes.

PLAYS, SONGS AND BALLADS

'a monstrous place for wickedness'

A SURPRISING NUMBER of plays, songs and ballads have been set in and around Deal.

'The Fair Quaker of Deal, or The Humours of the Navy' is a comedy written by Charles Shadwell. Little is known of the author except that he was the son of Thomas Shadwell, the successful Irish dramatist who succeeded Dryden as Poet Laureate.'Fair Quaker' was first performed at London's prestigious Drury Lane Theatre in 1710 and repeated there in repertory over successive seasons.

Shadwell's play is regarded as the most faithful contemporary literary representation of naval life in the eighteenth century. (This is despite the fact that all of the action takes place on land and none of the characters are shown on active service at sea).

The slender plot revolves around match-making and matrimony. Dorcas Zeal is a virtuous Quaker who is wooed by Worthy, "a Captain of the Navy and a Gentleman of Honour". There are several other suitors for both the hero and the heroine who try to deceive the couple through false letters and feeble disguises. Everything is resolved rather too simply and the action would not hold the attention of modern audiences who require more realistic situations. There is a little local colour - Dorcas lives in the North End, there is an assignation at Deal Castle and the Goodwin Sands has a passing mention - but most of the play takes place in the fictitious 'Mariners Inn'.

There is a topical reference to the Dutch in the Medway but Deal is presented in an unflattering light. Rovewell, "a Gentlemen of Fortune", exclaims: "This is a monstrous Place for Wickedness! Fornication flourishes more here than in any Sea-Port of Europe."

Flip, the illiterate drunken Commodore, lodges at 'The Three Mariners' where "The Husband keeps a Bom-boat, the wife a Brandy-shop, and the two Daughters are let out to all Comers and Goers."

Chief delight is the character, Mizen, an effeminate fop who languishes in an exquisitely furnished cabin, holds a visiting day aboard his ship and has wild plans to reform the Navy:

> "I am now compiling a Book, wherein I mend the Language wonderfully; I leave out your Larboard and Starboard, Hawsers and Swabbs; I have no such

thing as hawl Cat hawl, nor Belay, silly Words, only fit for Dutchmen to pronounce. I put fine Sentences into the Mouths of our Sailors, deriv'd from the Manliness of the Italian, and the Softness of the French. And by the time I am made an Admiral, I doubt not of bringing every Sailor in the Navy to be more polite than most of our Country Gentlemen; and the next Generation of them may pass very well for people of the first Quality. I'll get an Order for removing them from Wapping into the Pall Mall: and instead of frequenting Punch, Musick and Baudy-Houses; the Chocolate-Houses, Eating-Houses, and fine Taverns shall be oblig'd to receive them."

Mizen's vision is of a "polite" Navy peopled by "proper, handsome, well-drest Fellows" sporting "glittering, shining coats, powder'd Wigs, Snuff-Boxes, and fashionable airs" so that, when they appear abroad, they will be regarded as the "Wonder of the World".

Bernard Capp in 'Cromwell's Navy' (1989) makes an incisive comment on the relationship between the officers and their men evident in this play. 'The Fair Quaker of Deal', he says, "... shows well the startling familiarity which could exist between naval officers and their men." Commodore Flip makes a point of getting drunk with each mess every week, confident that in return the seamen will serve him all the more readily. "My joculousness with 'em makes 'em fight for me", he explains. Shadwell does not sentimentalise the relationship, and depicts the commodore as a man of rough and capricious ways. But Flip has spent his whole life at sea, serving in every post from cook's boy upwards, and has remained close to the ordinary seaman, familiar with their ways, their jokes, and their needs. "I love a sailor," he says simply.

'Black-Ey'd Susan' by Douglas William Jerrold (1803 - 1857) an actor, journalist and manager of Sheerness Theatre, was first produced at London's Royal Surrey Theatre on 8 June 1826. Described as "a nautical and domestic drama", this two act play closely follows the story-line of John Gay's earlier ballad of the same name and it is enlivened by a selection from

Miss Pope as 'Dorcas Zeal' from a playscript of 'The Fair Quaker' (1777).

261

'Dibdin's Naval Airs'. 'Susan' was Jerrold's greatest success: it was one of the first plays to run for one hundred consecutive performances in England.

The story, which is set entirely in and around Deal, has two plots running simultaneously although both are contrived. Sweet William, a jovial sailor, has gone to sea and left his young wife, Susan, in impoverished circumstances, lodging with the ailing Dame Hatley. Wicked Tom Hatchet, a smuggler, plans to marry Susan. First, he intends sending his accomplice, Raker, to convince her scheming uncle, Doggrass, to turn her out of her cottage because of arrears in rent. Hatchet will then appear at the eleventh hour in the guise of an heroic saviour to pay off Susan's debts and take her for himself.

Susan does have a couple of loyal friends - Gnatbrain and his sweetheart, Dolly Mayflower - who are more than a match for Doggrass and his assistant, Jacob Twigg, the Bailiff. A comic scene takes place at Dame Hatley's cottage. While the Bailiff attempts to seize Susan's modest furniture, her neighbours are passing it out of the bedroom window!

When Hatchet arrives he hands over thirteen pounds to pay off Susan's debts but his scheme to marry her is thwarted by the timely arrival of William, accompanied by his shipmates, Seaweed and Blue Peter, in the Downs. Susan is soon reconciled with her husband. Their reunion is a comic one for Raker, a sailor, is in the midst of relating the details of William's demise when - lo and behold - he flings open the door and

Susan boards a ship in the Downs.

rushes into his wife's arms! Doggrass attempts to convince William that he has cared for Susan and that he is pleased to see him safe and sound. . . but the shrewd sailor is not convinced. He dismisses his uncle with the phrase, "Go tell it to the marines."

The plot takes a further turn, however, when William's Captain, intoxicated one night, is attracted to Susan and attempts to seduce her. William rushes on with cutlass drawn and strikes his superior. Immediately, he is arrested and taken on board ship.

At his Court Martial the Admiral, although sympathetic, insists that justice must be done and he sentences the luckless hero to be hanged from the fore-yard-arm. He is escorted below deck to await his fate. Susan is brought to his condemned cell where she bids her husband a tearful farewell.

After their leave-taking William is taken to the place of execution when

Sailor William wields his cutlass on this 'penny plain' Victorian illustration.

- in the very nick of time - a repentant Captain Crosstree appears to confess his fault. He had secretly secured a discharge for William who is reunited with his wife.

The success of Jerrold's play owes a great deal to its inclusion of the famous ballad, 'Sweet William's Farewell to Black Ey'd Susan'. This song was composed by John Gay to include in his own play, 'Polly', intended as the sequel to his highly popular, 'The Beggar's Opera'. This was suppressed by the Lord Chamberlain in 1728 before it could be performed because one of its characters was a thinly-veiled satire on the statesman, Sir Robert Walpole. The delightful ballad was therefore independently published:

> All in the Downs the fleet was moor'd,
> The streamers waving in the wind.
> When black-ey'd Susan came on board,
> Oh! where shall I my true love find?
> Tell me, jovial sailors, tell me true,
> Does my sweet William sail among your crew?
>
> William, who high upon the yard,
> Rock'd with the billows to and fro;
> Soon as her well-known voice he heard,
> He sigh'd and cast his eyes below.
> The cord slides swiftly through his glowing hands,
> And quick as lightning on the deck he stands.

So the sweet lark, high-pos'd in air,
Shuts close his pinions to his breast
(If, chance, his mate's shrill call he hear)
And drops at once into her nest.
The noblest captain in the British fleet,
Might envy William's lip those kisses sweet.

O, Susan, Susan, lovely dear,
My vows shall ever true remain;
Let me kiss off that falling tear,
We only part to meet again.
Change, as ye list, ye winds; my mind shall be
The faithful compass that still points to thee.

Believe not what the landsmen say,
Who tempt with doubts thy constant mind.
They tell thee, sailors, when away,
In every port a mistress find.
Yes, yes, believe them when they tell thee so,
For thou art present whereso'er I go.

If to fair India's coast we sail,
Thy eyes are seen in di'monds bright;
Thy breath is Afric's spicy gale,
Thy skin is ivory so white.
Thus every beauteous object that I view,
Wakes in my soul some charm of lovely Sue.

Though battle call me from thy arms,
Let not my pretty Susan mourn:
Though cannons roar, yet free from harms,
William shall to his dear return.
Love turns aside the balls that round me fly,
Lest precious tears should drop from Susan's eye.

The boatswain gave the dreadful word,
The sails their swelling bosom spread;
No longer must she stay on board;
They kiss'd; she sighed; he hung his head;
Her less'ning boat unwilling rows to land;
Adieu! she cries, and waves her lily hand.

A local legend provided Jerrold with a stage sequel. This was the fictional tale of Ambrose Gwinett who supposedly met the man for whose murder he was hanged after escaping the gallows and travelling abroad. The convoluted story was the notion of an Irish dramatist, Isaac Bickerstaff, yet it is often presented as gospel truth by reputable researchers. 'Ambrose Gwinett, or A Sea Side Story', was first performed at the Coburg Theatre on 6 October 1828 but since then it was frequently revived, especially in Victorian times. Two early playscripts survive: Dick's Standard Plays, which includes the original cast list, and Cumberland's Minor Theatres Edition embellished with engravings of scenes, descriptions of costumes and directions for staging.

One long forgotten play set entirely in and around Deal was 'Deal Boatman' which is a remote dramatisation of Dickens' 'David Copperfield'. The script was printed by Samuel French in an acting edition (No. 888) price 6d. 'Deal Boatman' was written by F.C. Burnand who also penned such uninspiring titles as 'Easy Shaving', 'Turkish Bath', 'Alonzo the Brave' and 'Ixion, or The Man at the Wheel'. 'Deal Boatman' is a play in two acts, the first part of which takes place inside the seaside cottage of Jacob Vance, the boatman of the title, on the evening of the marriage of his ward, Mary, to his nephew, Matthew. Described as "a serio-

BLACK EYD SUSAN.

Susan gathers flowers in this 'tuppence coloured' Victorian illustration.

comic drama", it follows the hackneyed storyline of the seduction of a young maiden by a villain although she is rescued from this fate worse than death by a dashing hero. The melodrama, which has little merit, was first produced at the 'Theatre Royal', Drury Lane on 21 September, 1863. It had a short run at Margate's 'Theatre Royal' in 1869 when Nat Gosling played the title role under the direction of the celebrated manageress, Mrs. Sarah Thorne.

Two eighteenth century ballads speak of further sorrowful lovers. 'Peggy of Deal' was prevented from marrying a 'Banished Sailor' by her father who mercilessly confined her to her bedchamber. The narrative verse continues - jumping inexplicably from first to third person after the third stanza - to relate a midnight parting between the lovers at the bedroom window. Afterwards, Peggy ("tall", "handsome", "her eyes as black as sloes") dies "raving distracted" and in agony. This mournful single sheet ballad, illustrated by a lively woodcut of a sailor dancing the hornpipe, was printed by John Pitts, "Wholesale Toy & Marble Warehouse", of Seven Dials, London, about 1802. It also appears in 'Batchelar's Pleasing Songster', a chap-book printed in London in 1825, and a two volume collection of songs, 'Kentish Garland', published in Hereford in 1881.

Near the fam'd town of Deal, close by the sea-side,
I courted young Peggy to be my sweet bride,
But her father was hasty, and would not comply,
And it's all for my Peggy I languish and die.

She's tall and she's handsome, her eyes black as sloes,
The delight of my fancy, wherever she goes;
And could I persuade her old dad to comply,
How happy I'd live, and contended I'd die!

As my love and I were walking the meadows so green,
Her surly old father he stept in between,
Saying, "Ere that my daughter a sailor should have,
I sooner would follow her down to the grave!"

Then straight to her chamber he this damsel confin'd,
Which caused her vexation and a sad troubled mind,
Which caused her vexation and a sad aching heart,
To think her sailor so soon she must part.

One night to her window went this sailor so brave,
Saying, "My dear Peggy, your pardon I crave;
Here is a letter I wrote with my hand,
It is for to let you know I am at your command."

"O then" said sweet Peggy, "see how I am confin'd,
I am loaded with sorrow, no comfort can find;
My hard-hearted father will not pity me,
And he from confinement will not set me free!"

"O Peggy, my darling, our ship's ready for sea;
May vengeance befall them that keep you from me!"
This fair maid wrung her hands, beat her bosom and cried,
And raving distracted, in agony died."

'Ben Hawser' similarly met with harsh treatment from his fiance's harsh parents (which seems to be quite the rule in nautical ballads). After being parted from 'fair Kate of Deal' for several years at sea, Ben is killed on his homeward voyage and his corpse floats to her feet as she strolls forlornly on Deal beach. This sorrowful ballad, which originally appeared as a pamphlet, is contained in a collection entitled, 'Excellent New Songs', printed by A. Bell of Penrith in 1805.

Ben Hawser lov'd fair Kate of Deal,
And woo'd her for his blooming bride;
But ah! her Friends, with hearts like steel,
This much-wish'd happiness denied.
For they were proud, and Ben was poor,
Though none like him was e'er so true;
But all in vain, they clos'd the door,
Nor let him take a last adieu!

Ben droop'd and pin'd with sad despair,
For much he wish'd his Kate to see;
But to the Beach he did repair,
And brav'd once more the stormy Sea;
And as the Vessel, from the Flood,
The lest'ning Shore still kept in view,
Upon the deck he ling'ring stood,
And sigh'd and said, "Sweet Girl, adieu!"

Ben plough'd the Deep for many a year,
And oft in Battles hot was he;
In danger still devoid of fear,
And to his Messmates kind and free.
Returning home, the Foe drew nigh,
A fatal ball unerring flew;
Ben fell, and heaving forth a sigh,
"Tis past," he cried, "Sweet Girl, adieu!"

The Morning smil'd, the day was fair,
When Kate, who still did faithful prove,
Breath'd on the Beach the vernal air,
Deep musing on her long-lost Love.
When floating on the Wave she spied
A Corse - it was her lover true!
Soon as she saw, she shriek'd and cried,
"I come, - no more we'll bid adieu!"

MARY BAX

'Murder Most Foul'

A WAYSIDE STONE marking the location of a brutal murder stands atop a grassy knoll alongside the Ancient Highway connecting Deal with Sandwich. The winding track is a distinctive feature of the sandhills which stretch five miles along the coast north of Sandown to Pepperness.

This track, which is part of an old Roman Road, was once described as "so brode as 2 or 3 cartes maie meete". Boulders were placed at intervals to mark the precise route which was "not very deepe or fowle (savinge two or three places) which have needed of amendment." It became a bustling highway during the construction of the three castles commissioned by Henry VIII in 1540. Caen stones were landed at the quay in Sandwich and brought by carts across the Sandhills to the building sites along the foreshore. Artillery and furniture were conveyed to the completed castles; beer and provisions were carried for the Navy.

Eminent persons have travelled along the same pathway which is also referred to as the 'Downs Road'. In 1518 the Papal Legate, Cardinal Campeggio, sent to adjudicate on the legality of Henry VIII's marriage to Catherine of Aragon, landed at Deal and was escorted by bishops and gentlemen to his lodgings in Sandwich. In 1573 Elizabeth I was conveyed in style on a litter from Sandown Castle to Sandown Gate at Sandwich during her royal progress through Kent. (The gilded heraldic beasts which ornamented it are now on display in the Guildhall) Good Queen Bess invariably toured the country in summer to avoid contamination by the plague in London. Normally her retinue consisted of about five hundred courtiers, officers and servants with a seemingly endless procession of thousands of horses and hundreds of baggage carts. Consequently an alternative title is the 'Queen's Road'.

Charles II, supposedly the year before his Restoration, visited Sandwich where he drank a glass of sack at the 'Bell Tavern' before being escorted, presumably along the Ancient Highway, to Deal by the Mayor and Corporation. At the time of the Napoleonic Wars frequent movement of troops was observed between Walmer Barracks and the two batteries in the Sandhills while in Victoria's reign drovers herded their cattle along the Ancient Highway from Deal to Sandwich Market.

Two streams - south and north - crossed the Sandhills. The latter, through which the sea once flowed, was known as the 'Guestling'. Here, felons were once drowned and their bodies were then carried by the tide into the Downs. A gibbet is marked on several early maps on the shoreline between Deal and Sandwich.

Victims of battles fought in the Downs during the Dutch Wars were buried in open pits. During the Restoration non-conformists defied the law and worshipped secretly at dead of night in the Sandhills.

Two naval officers from a frigate, 'Gloucester', fought a duel in the Sandhills on 13 September 1713. The result was fatal. Lieutenant Wye shot Captain Carlton through the head on the first round. He then made a quick escape whilst the seconds were administering to the dying man. The lieutenant was later arrested in Middle Street. At his subsequent court martial he was convicted of manslaughter and sentenced to be branded upon one hand. Duels were also fought between Lieutenant Morgan and the captain of the 'Maidstone' at Deal in 1761 and two officers of the Royal Flintshire Regiment in a meadow near Sandown Castle in May 1798.

Pritchard in his 'History of Deal' lists the numerous plants and herbs found growing in the Sandhills. A number of them provided food for families or fodder for cattle. Others provided simple remedies for ailments. Rushes were used for making rush lights or woven for matting; reeds were used as thatch for cottages or turned into ropes; cotton grass provided wicks for candles while sea holly was crystalised and eaten as a confection. Most interesting was woad. Blue dye extracted from its leaves was daubed on the skin by the Ancient Britons who repelled Caesar.

The Sandhills was regarded as a place of assembly for amusement. When the Ancient Highway became flooded people often skated over the frozen surface in the vicinity of 'The Chequers' while a line of bathing machines lined the beach between the old windmill and Sandown Castle. To celebrate Queen Victoria's Golden Jubilee in 1863 a procession headed by the Town Band led to the Sandhills where entertainment for the children included races, swings, conjuring tricks and donkey rides. A field at Sandown marked the starting point of the mile-long course of the Deal and Walmer Races which attracted great interest in Edwardian times. When the Prince of Wales (later George V) visited Deal to inspect the Royal Marines in 1909 he played a round of golf at the Cinque Ports Golf Club which thereafter applied the prefix, 'Royal'.

Throughout history access along the 'Ancient Highway' has been in dispute. In 1275 there was an argument between Simon of Ercheslowe (Archers Low) and Roger de Shalford, the warrener of Lydd Court. Simon had blocked ditches in the marshes and caused the road to be flooded so that it became impassable. The warrener seized Simon's cattle grazing in nearby fields as a penalty. In retaliation Simon rallied his friends from Sandwich who rescued the cattle and beat the warrener.

The Year Book of Sandwich, which recorded the town's affairs between 1551 and 1568, states that there was another dispute between the Mayor of Sandwich and Thomas Rolfe, tenant of Lydd Court. In March 1563 Rolfe ordered his bailiff assisted by labourers to plough up the highway and sow it with corn. This "malycyous and develyshe" act was referred to the Star Chamber where the Archbishop of Canterbury and Sir Richard Sackville gave their judgement "that the way now used over Lydcourt ground, and wherein the riding and carriage of beach stone was, shall be laid out and left unsown sixteen feet broad, for all the queen's liege people freely to pass". There

269

was a stern warning that travellers should not trespass from this ample cart track onto the corn growing on fields either side of the highway. At the hearing it was described as "leadynge from Sandwiche towne out of Sandedowne-gate unto the Downs-gate, and so from thence over Lydde Court, and from thence over the late Maison Dieu ground to the Downes and so to Deale. . ."

It must be remembered that for centuries this was the main road for horse traffic from Deal to Sandwich. The alternative route was a long and circuitous one. It left Deal by a narrow track, Five Bells Lane (now Queen street) and soon veered round to the right along Middle Deal Road to Upper Deal. A number of historic properties are still located along this former main road including 'Sherrard', 'Rosway' and 'Berkeley House'. By St. Leonard's Church the road turned sharp right and continued in a southerly direction as far as Foulmead near Sholden. Then it deviated along Finglesham and Ham and did not return to its present route until reaching the lane opposite 'Upton House' in Worth. In 1800 a direct toll road was laid from Upper Deal, via Sholden to the west of Cottington, Foulmead and Worth, to Sandwich.

Fussel compares these two routes in 'A Journey Round the Coast of Kent' (1818):

> "The coast between Sandwich and Deal almost entirely consists of an accumulation of sand which forms irregular eminences very arid and dreary in appearance, and interspersed with bog and marshy ground very deceitful to the foot of the passenger; so that travelling by way of the sandhills, as the inhabitants of the neighbourhood denominate them, is both disagreeable and dangerous and the other road more inland is usually preferred, although it considerably lengthens the journey."

Certainly, the Sandhills always had a poor reputation for safety.

Mary Bax's desolate memorial is set into a low, grassy bank slightly northwards of the 'Chequers Inn'. (It must be remembered that the true course of the Ancient Highway actually runs through the golf course) The inscription reads:

On this spot
August the 25th 1782
Mary Bax, Spinster,
aged 23 years
was murdered by
Martin Lash, foreigner,
who was executed for the
same.

Mary Bax, a young woman from Deal set out to walk alone at about ten o'clock in the forenoon along the winding road in the direction of Sandwich. Halfway she was approached by a rough sailor who demanded the parcel she was carrying. When Mary refused to surrender it, the stranger snatched it from her and removed her shoes on which presumably were valuable buckles. Mary resisted and the sailor struck her violently before slitting her throat. To conceal his crime he threw her body into a dyke

The 'Mary Bax' stone on the Ancient Highway.

and tried to submerge it in the murky water among the reeds and bullrushes.

A young lad named Rogers, the son of "a looker on the Marshes", witnessed the perpetration of this vile deed. He was sheltering from a sudden shower under a haystack at a nearby farm. Fearing a similar fate he lay concealed until the stranger had walked a fair distance in the direction of Sandwich. Then he sped back to Deal where he met a labourer named Tomlinson, also "a looker", who escorted the boy to the Magistrate.

The alarm was raised and the townsfolk were stirred into pursuit but the murderer cunningly doubled back to Folkestone. There, Martin Laas, a Norwegian, who had deserted his ship in the Downs, was apprehended as he lay fast asleep in long grass at the foot of a tombstone in the parish church. Beside him lay incriminating evidence - the stolen parcel. Since the crime had taken place on the Sandhills which lay beyond the jurisdiction of both Deal and Sandwich, Laas was taken to be tried at the County Court at Maidstone where he was eventually convicted and hanged for murder most foul.

Sole eye witness at the subsequent trial was Rogers, the looker's son. 'Looker' is a Kentish colloquialism for a sheep minder. A looker's cottage was once a feature of the barren landscape of the sandhills. It figures prominently as a seamark on charts of the Downs by Captain Hurd R.N. (1808) and J.W. Norrie (1830). It was destroyed by vandals who set it alight in the middle of the nineteenth century. A sepia photograph of this building exists and shows it to have been a large, rambling dwelling with a thatched roof. It was situated east of No. 2 Battery and north of the isolated 'Chequers Inn' adjacent to the Ancient Highway.

The looker's cottage was excavated by the Deal and Walmer Local History Society. Its foundations dated back to circa 1650. Possibly, it was built as an inn although it ended its days as a farmhouse. Confusion arises because the building is marked on early maps as 'Half-Way House', a name that was later transferred to the Chequers which also bears indications that it was built in the 17th century. Pottery has been unearthed which confirms that the site was occupied around 1250 - 1350 A.D. At that period the land was owned by a monastery and it is thought that in medieval times the area was rented by a sheep farmer or a family drawing their living from the sea.

Mary's murder appears to have taken place on Monday 23 August 1783. (The modern inscription on the memorial stone perpetuates the wrong year) According to the records of St. Peter's Church, Sandwich, Mary's body was buried in the churchyard on 28 August 1783. There are, however, further discrepancies with the dates in contemporary accounts.

This brutal crime naturally caused a sensation in the town and the inside story was given by Mrs. Elizabeth Carter (whose brother, John, was a local magistrate) in a letter to her London friend, Mrs Vesey:

July 30 1784

"We have been in great agitation in this place on account of a murder committed on Monday last, at a place about two or three miles from this place. The utmost activity and diligence has been exerted to find the murderer, and I am glad to say they have succeeded. He was for some hours last night under examination by my brother, who sent him to jail. The subject of this dreadful affair was a poor young woman, who was walking to Sandwich with a bundle. The wretch threw her into a ditch in order to rob her, and there she was smothered. A boy about thirteen years old saw the whole transaction, and gave a very clear account of it: but was so sadly ignorant on other respects, that my brother could not administer an oath to him. However, there will be sufficient evidence, from a handkerchief that was found on the prisoner, which the poor mother of the girl swore to be her's. He was exhorted to confess; but answered he would confess only to God. He attempted to prove an alibi: but was seen by so many people near the time at this place, that there seems no doubt of his person, which is marked very strongly by a wound on his cheek, which he received in the engagement with the Ville de Paris. He is a Dane, but was in our fleet."

A report of the murder appeared in the Annual Register (1784):

Martin Laas, a sailor, was in April convicted of murdering a young woman at Worde, near Sandwich. Throughout the whole of his trial he treated the witnesses very insultingly, and gave three loud cheers before he was removed from the dock. Upon this, the Judge gave strict orders for him to be chained to the floor of his dungeon, where he afterwards confessed his crime. He said that on August 25th, as he was sitting on a roadside bank near the halfway house, between Deal and Sandwich, Mary Bax passed by, upon which he followed her and inquired the way to Sheerness. She told him he was a great way from the place; whereupon he said he had no money, and must have some. She had none, she said, for him. He then pushed her into a ditch, and jumped after her, into the mud and water, which reached to the middle of him. Taking the bundle she was carrying, and removing her shoes from her feet, he made off across the marshes, towards Dover. The shoes he immediately threw away, and hid the bundle near where he was taken.

The prisoner, giving this account, did not seem to feel the least concern for the crime, or its consequences, but appeared, on the contrary, very cheerful, saying he had been fated to commit it, and to suffer for it, as he had been told, years before, by an old Spaniard.

He was a native of Bergen, in Norway, twenty-seven years of age, and had served under Lord Romney, in H.M.S. Fame, for upwards of two years. He was, however, extremely penitent when brought to the place of execution, acknowledging the justice of his sentence, and prayed with great fervency.

The tragic story of Mary Bax is also rehearsed by R.M. Ballantyne in his novel, 'The Lifeboat' (1870). Here, the hero of the tale, which has a distinct local setting, is Mary's cousin, John. In chapter eight the murder is described in detail by David Winter on his way for a pint at 'The Checkers of Hope Inn': "It stands in the midst of the solitary waste; a sort of half-way house between the towns of Sandwich and Deal; far removed from either, however, quite beyond earshot of human dwelling. . . an irregular old building. . . the scene of many a savage revelry and many a deed of darkness. . . a celebrated resort of smugglers in days gone by." (Chapter VIII)

John Winter, brother of the youth, aged seventeen, had been an admirer of the beautiful Miss Bax and it was through his endeavours that the villain described as 'a Lascar' (a sailor from India or South-East Asia) was apprehended. Martin Laas, we learn, was hanged close to the scene of his dreadful crime. Afterwards John Winter left the country and he did not return for thirty years by which time the incident had long been forgotten. His little brother, the author tragically relates, was later drowned at sea.

Records of the Kent Lent Assizes at Maidstone for 1784 exist. They reveal that on Friday 19 March, Martin Laas, aged 27, was found guilty of the wilful murder of Mary Bax. He was sentenced to be hanged the following Monday and afterwards his body was to be "dissected and anatomized". (It must have been little comfort to him that he was found not guilty of stealing goods from her to the value of 1s/8d) The accused was denied both the benefit of a lawyer to represent him or an interpreter to explain the situation and therefore, by modern standards, this could not be regarded as a fair trial.

Looker's Cottage on the Sandhills. Courtesy: Deal Library.

J.M.W. TURNER

'the painter of light'

J.M.W. TURNER (1775 - 1851) Britain's finest marine artist, whose career culminated in such masterpieces as 'Rain, Steam and Speed' and 'The Fighting Temeraire', completed numerous paintings of Kent. At one time this artistic visionary and impressionist secretly set up home with a buxom widow at Margate. From there he departed on sketching tours around the south-east coast and he often ventured into Deal to paint its spectacular seascapes.

Joseph Mallord William Turner (his family called him 'William') was born above a humble barber's shop in Covent Garden when this crowded district was still fashionable. Although he lacked the advantage of being born into an artistic family, his own talent was evident from early childhood. His father encouraged him in his pursuits and he proudly pinned up samples of his son's sketches in his hairdressing shop where they attracted the notice of gentry.

Young Turner's footsteps led him daily to the nearby banks of the River Thames where he studied, first-hand, ships from all parts of the world as they sailed along the bustling waterway. He learned to sketch their masts, sails and cordage and became fascinated with the fast-flowing water of London's tidal river. The metropolis was then known as the 'Great Smoke' and his juvenile experience of rigged ships viewed through mist remained with him to colour all his mature work.

At the age of ten Turner went to lodge with his maternal uncle at New Brentford. His visit introduced him to the countryside for, at that time, the town was pleasantly ringed by "gardeners' gardens with fruit trees all in full bloom". This became a favourite haunt to which he returned frequently in later life. And it was here, apparently, that Turner first expressed a serious interest in painting.

At eleven or twelve years of age, he was packed off to Margate to lodge with relatives, possibly because his mother's mental health was deteriorating. There, Turner attended a non-conformist school attached to the Methodist Chapel in Love Lane which was presided over by a fervent preacher, Thomas Coleman. A handful of early sketches, which the boy made whilst still at school of this popular Thanet resort, survive. One view of the Old Town reveals a complicated perspective of a sloping street with its jumble of house fronts and quaint rooftops while a harbour scene presents his earliest depiction of seagoing vessels.

J.M.W. Turner © National Portrait Gallery.

A client at the barber shop, Rev. Robert Nixon, a clergyman from Foots Cray, North Kent, recognised the boy's talent and brought his sketches to the attention of an influential friend who just happened to be a member of the Royal Academy of Arts. The promising young artist was soon invited to study at the prestigious Academy at Somerset House in the Strand where he proved a dutiful and dedicated student. He was encouraged to take a series of journeys, sketching from nature, so that by the age of thirteen he was producing "astonishing precocious drawings".

While studying under a variety of innovative tutors, Turner continued to travel around the countryside armed with his sketchbook. In 1791 he visited the West Country and the following year he strayed into Wales. The selection of subjects in his second surviving sketchbook, produced when he was sixteen, reveals that the more natural and dramatic scenery was beginning to stir his imagination. The year 1793 brought him again into Kent and an uncompleted work, 'Storm off Dover' (now in the British Museum) shows the pier in the foreground, a flag at half-mast and a vessel with lowered sails on the horizon.

Another clergyman, Rev. James Douglas, chaplain to the Prince Regent, was also a client of the barber's shop in Covent Garden. This benevolent artist and antiquary noticed the youth drawing in the back parlour and admired his creativity. Immediately, he took Turner under his patronage and invited him down to Rochester to experiment in painting in oils directly from nature. There Turner depicted fishermen drawing their boats ashore in a gale with the castle in the background. Apart from a self-portrait, this scene (now lost) would appear to have been Turner's earliest known oil painting.

Turner's father's hairdressing and wigmaking business faltered when the Tory government of William Pitt the younger introduced a tax on hair powder in 1795. Instantly, this curtailed the trend for powdered wigs and ruined his profitable trade. Turner decided to employ his father as his assistant, stretching and priming his large canvasses, in his newly acquired London studio. While his father thrived, his mother, shamefully, was left - forgotten and unvisited - a raving lunatic in Bedlam.

Towards the end of the eighteenth century there was a vogue for topographical views, particularly those with a romantic aspect focusing upon wild and rugged scenery. When still a student Turner was commissioned to sketch town views that would be turned into cheap engravings by skilled craftsmen for publication in magazines. This was a lucrative project - and Turner was highly mercenary - and an excellent way of bringing his name and style to the attention of the general public. The middle classes, who could not afford the high prices of the original paintings, astutely realised the intrinsic value and superlative quality of these faithful reproductions, "after Turner". The scheme proved to be an exhausting task but it demonstrates admirably Turner's industry in relentless travelling - often rising early to catch the sunrise - across rugged terrain in all weathers to research material. The first engravings were so successful that similar projects followed - the Isle of Wight and South Wales (1795) the Lake District and Scotland (1797) and North Wales (in both 1798 and 1799).

Turner's travelling, although necessary to his work, might be deemed obsessive. His journeys were always carefully planned and involved various modes of transport - hired horses, stagecoaches, rowing boats... but mostly he walked. According to James Hamilton in 'Turner, A Life' (1997) the artist's purpose was "to experience, practise, look, sketch, remember - and earn". He rarely painted in the open air, especially larger canvasses, but made rapid sketches and copious notes which could be consulted back in the studio. His habit was to research in the summer and paint in the winter. All the same, his life was spent in "perpetual motion".

At the age of twenty-one Turner went once more to Margate to sketch and paint. This was the time of the threatened invasion by Napoleon and so the militia was doubled in strength. There Turner fell in love with the sister of a former schoolfriend but their affair was unrequited and blighted by separation when the artist left for a sketching tour. It seems he never got over it. Robert C. Leslie, the son of Turner's friend and fellow artist, wrote later that when he was living in Deal about 1869: "... my next-door neighbour was an old lady of the name of Cato, her maiden name was White; and she told me that she knew Turner as a young man, also the young lady he was in love with. She spoke of him as being very delicate, and said that he often came to Margate for his health. She seemed to know little of Turner as the artist."

In 1805, Turner ventured once more into Kent to sketch the 'Victory' as she entered the River Medway bearing aboard Nelson's body. Immediately, he set to work on a large oil painting of 'The Battle of Trafalgar' which he proudly exhibited three years later at his own gallery. It is one of the complexities of Turner's career that throughout his life he manipulated two artistic styles with equal versatility - oil and watercolour. Masterly views of Kent in the former medium painted during the early part of the 19th century include 'Sheerness and the Isle of Sheppey' (1807) a dramatic image of storm clouds parting to reveal sunshine, and 'Margate' (1808) a tranquil scene with the harbour and far distant cliffs shrouded in morning mist. For the artist the money rolled in even though he asked excessive prices for his canvasses. When customers cavilled he demanded more. Rarely did he give any of his own work away although there is an accredited story that he once presented a boatman with a sea-picce to settle his account for rowing him around Margate Harbour.

276

Topographical views, however, were still Turner's main source of income. Over the years he built up a team of talented and experienced craftsmen - Horsburgh, Radclyffe and Lupton - to translate his watercolours into fine engravings. Their difficulties, as might be imagined, were immense: By reducing large paintings in size how could the intricate detail be maintained? In the atmospheric landscapes how might a scene be evoked by line drawing alone? And how could the artist's vivid oranges, pastel pinks and yellow hues be transposed to monochrome? Incredibly, over eight hundred different engravings were made from Turner's works which at that time expressed "the collective identity of Britain". Invariably, Turner supervised the production of these superb engravings and they nearly all bear traces of the artist's own hand. His criticism, however, was not always welcome and his relationship with his engravers proved to be every bit as stormy as certain of his sea-pieces.

After a less successful attempt at being his own editor and publisher of a large series of views divided into five categories - History, Mountains, Pastoral, Epic Pastoral and Marine - Turner accepted a commission from W.B. Cooke to produce forty paintings to be turned into engravings for a new project entitled, 'Picturesque Views of the Southern Coast of England'. To gather material for this ambitious venture the artist set out resolutely on a sketching tour of the coastline, journeying from Whitstable to Minehead, in 1811. The watercolours he produced were again turned into engravings under Turner's watchful eye and, as a result, they preserve remarkably the light and atmosphere of his original conception. Published singly between 1814 and 1826, and collectively in volume form in 1826, the scenes for 'Southern Coast' include Ramsgate, Margate, Hythe, Whitstable Oyster Beds, Dover from Shakespeare Cliffs, Smugglers at Folkestone and a dramatic 'Deal in a Storm'.

Deal is fortunate in possessing its own original Turner which is displayed in the Mayor's Parlour of the Town Hall. 'Deal in a Storm' (6"x 8") was painted for the series, 'Picturesque Views of the Southern Coast of England', circa 1824. In this subtle watercolour the town extends from left to right along a sloping beach. Heavy waves fill the foreground and the spars of a vessel wrecked on the Goodwin Sands floats in the distance. Boatmen are shown hastily preparing boats to be launched on a life-saving mission while other people watch wreckage being washed ashore by the angry waves. Two flags on a mast in the centre stand out against a louring sky and a streak of ribbon lightning zigzags from the right. (This is the only instance of a Turner painting depicting a full flash of lightning)

Surprisingly, Turner has gained his stormy effect through the pale greys of the gathering clouds contrasting with the bright yellow shingle and pastel pinks and creams of the ramshackle dwellings on the foreshore. The detail is meticulously painted so that it bears examination under a magnifying glass: the sails on the hovelling luggers, the design on the flags, the crumbling buildings with their smoking chimneys and Flemish gables and, in the far distance, the tiny silhouette of Sandown Castle. This modest watercolour was engraved by W. Radclyffe and became the third subject to be published in the 'Southern Coast' series in 1826.

Turner's expensive leather bound sketchbook with its strong brass clasp is preserved in the Tate Gallery (where it is known as the 'Holland' sketchbook). It reveals that the

'Deal in a Storm' by J.M.W. Turner c.1824. Courtesy: Deal Town Council.

artist relentlessly traipsed the foreshore between Deal and Walmer making notes and drawings of all the familiar landmarks: Walmer Castle against a background of Kingsdown Cliffs. . . Royal Naval Hospital. . . Walmer Road windmill. . . Deal Castle with the governor's lodgings. . . Customs House boathouse. . . a hovelling lugger drawn up on the shingle adjacent to the Royal Signalling Station which - uniquely - shows the twin arms of Popham's semaphore relaying a message to shipping in the Downs. Towards the North End the artist sketched the boats belonging to the Customs House and the numerous houses and inns (labelled 'Royal Exchange Inn' or 'Hoop and Griffin') lining the seashore.

Later, either in an inn or back at his studio, these sketches were "worked up" into an imaginary scene that captured perfectly the atmosphere of this bustling port. Indeed, Leith Ritchie, a journalist who wrote the travelogue that accompanied Turner's engravings observed that when he was in Turner's presence he was "frequently surprised to find what a forcible idea he conveyed of a place with scarcely a single correct detail." (This novel method would explain the fact that no one has yet been able to identify the precise location which Turner painted of Deal beach)

Whilst in the neighbourhood Turner took the opportunity to accompany an expedition to the Goodwin Sands where he drew working luggers and a sunken wreck. He also watched a cricket match, organised by Captain Kennet Martin, Harbour Master of Ramsgate, which he recorded for posterity. His rapid sketch shows a rather static scene composed of watercolour, chalk and gouache with a flat ground and a passing steamship on the horizon. The original artwork is preserved at the Yale Center for British Art in Connecticut.

Deal appears a second time as the last of the plates in Turner's series of watercolours, 'Harbours of England'. Little more than spirited sea-pieces, the

278

'Off Deal' by J.M.W. Turner c.1828.

subsequent engravings by Thomas Lupton covered twelve of the least important ports at that time. (Deal, in any case, never possessed a harbour) It was merely a mixture of an abandoned 'Ports of England' project, begun in the early years of the nineteenth century, with additional plates. The turbulent scene, 'Off Deal' (9 x 6) originally painted between 1826 and 1828, is held by the Walker Art Gallery, Liverpool. Here Turner demonstrates his fondness for detail by depicting a cluster of ships battling against the waves with a hovelling lugger manfully striving to reach them through the spray and spume. Prominent on the shoreline are five signal flags hoisted on tall masts which was then an effective means of communication between shipping companies on shore and their ships at sea.

It is often assumed Turner was rowed out around the Downs by local boatmen to make sketches for this evocative painting. However, Turner's biographer, James Hamilton points out that, after leaving Margate, "the steam packet service ran on round the North Foreland to Ramsgate, and then on down past Deal, St. Margaret's-at-Cliffe, and round to Dover. This coastal journey, by now so easy to take, was one which Turner made at will." Turner, the artist, would have been tempted by the opportunity to sketch the inspiring coastline from the deck of this convenient packet service around East Kent.

"The key to these series of landscapes is memory," Hamilton remarks. "None of the watercolours was painted on the spot, but this was almost always Turner's practice as a watercolourist. They were made instead at his painting table at Queen Anne Street, under the London north light that filtered through the panes, some from pencil studies drawn as much as twenty years earlier. Reminded by his sketchbook studies, Turner would add topographical details from memory, exaggerating or diminishing as he chose. . . and effects of weather for mood."

When 'Harbours of England' was published posthumously in 1856, the set of engravings was accompanied by an illustrative text by Turner's ardent admirer, John Ruskin. The Victorian critic noted Turner's fascination with this "neat, courageous, benevolent, merry, methodical" town. He described the crowded seascape, contrasting the "disorder and distress among the boats on the left with the boat going out to help them" with the "precision of the little town stretching in sunshine along the beach".

Turner, himself, is supposed to have penned this colourful description of the port:

> "It was very strange to me, knowing that whatever was brave and strong in the English sailor was concentrated in our Deal Boatmen, to walk along that trim strip of conventional beach, which the sea itself seems to wash in a methodical manner, one shingle-step at a time; and by its thin toy-like boats each with its head to sea at regular intervals, looking like things that one would give a clever boy to play with in a pond when first he got past petticoats, and the row of lath-cots, all tidiness and telegraph, looking as if the whole business of the human race was to know what o'clock it was, and when it would be high water - only some slight weakness in favour of grog being indicated here and there by a hospitable-looking open door, a gay bow window and a sign intimating that it is a sailor's duty to be not only accurate but 'jolly'."

While sketching on the Kentish coast Turner chose Margate as his headquarters because it was within easy reach of London by stagecoach, corn boat and, eventually, steam railway. In the 1830s the journey from London to Margate became far speedier with the introduction of packet steamers, 'The Magnet' and 'King William', that departed regularly from London Bridge to Margate Jetty.

One ballad, 'The Margate Voyage' (1841) captures the thrill of the departure from Blackfriars or Greenwich in the steamboat, 'Adelaide':

> "Off we went with our tall chimney smoking,
> Five hundred, all squeezing and choking,
> Some their heads o'er the vessel's side poking. . ."

Apparently, Turner spent most of these voyages leaning over the stern mesmerised by the swirling foam or setting sun. (There is an amusing glimpse of the artist eating shrimps out of an immense red silk handkerchief laid across his knees as he rocked back and forth on the Margate paddle steamer) Having in mind to paint the splendid sunsets for which the resort was famous - he was, after all, known as "the painter of light" - Turner stepped onto Rennie's spanking new stone pier and immediately sought lodgings with a westerly view in the hilly area known as Cold Harbour.

By chance, Turner knocked on the door of a certain Sophia Caroline Booth who, having moved from her native town of Dover in 1827, had opened a boarding house with the approval of her husband, a retired sea captain. Her terrace property was just east of the little harbour underneath the clifftop fort and its front top windows were ideal for an artist to paint from since they offered an oblique view of the sea. Apparently, when requested to tender the usual references, Turner proffered a handful of banknotes and sovereigns and testily replied: "My good woman, I will buy your house outright!" The final difficulty, the disclosure of his name, Turner solved by telling the landlady that if she were 'Mrs. Booth' then he might as well be 'Mr. Booth'.

A fictional tale - Mr. Booth was very much alive at the time - but Turner did remain the sole lodger and soon indulged in an unconventional alliance with his landlady, a plump yet attractive woman. Sophia was not well educated and had an earthy country accent but she was fairly wealthy and was respected by the townsfolk. At first Turner was an intermittent visitor but gradually he became the sole - and cosseted - guest. It was only when the real Mr. Booth expired that he, in truth, took upon himself the pseudonym, 'Booth'. Everybody in the locality came to know him as such, the house for instance being rated in that name. Alas, the ratebooks do not specify which house. Probably, it was the modest dwelling squeezed in between the Customs House and the 'Foy Boat Inn', since demolished, a favourite haunt of seafarers. (Turner probably resorted here to sample his favourite tipple - half a bottle of brown sherry!)

Sophia Booth had been baptised at Dover on 3 February 1799. In 1818 she had married Henry Pound, a Margate mariner, by whom she had a son, Daniel John. When Pound died by drowning in 1821, she was snapped up by John Booth, a prosperous, Kentish gentleman. Their only son, John Pound Booth, died prematurely at the age of seven in 1832. This tragedy must have hastened her second husband's death for he

The cricket match on Goodwin Sands played in 1824, painted by Turner.
Courtesy: Vale Center for British Art, Paul Mellon Collection, USA.

died aged seventy-one the following year and was buried next to his son in St. John's Churchyard, Margate. He left his widow a substantial inheritance which she wisely invested in property throughout East Kent. It seems Sophia preferred the company of older men for the eccentric artist from London was twenty-five years her senior. Exactly when Turner and Mrs. Booth began cohabiting is not known but it probably began during the early 1830s. Turner wrote poetry to his tall, lusty mistress and took a fatherly interest in her son, Daniel, by her first marriage and encouraged him to train as an engraver.

Turner, in middle age, had changed from the dapper youth, distinguished by his elegant clothes and immaculate hairstyle, into a grotesque figure. He was fairly short - about five feet four inches in height - according to information supplied by his tailor. He had a large head with a ruddy complexion and his low forehead sloped back under a shock of brown hair, roughly parted in the middle. He had a great beak of a nose and penetrating blue-grey eyes under beetling eyebrows. His sturdy figure was supported by bandy legs and he had large, ungainly feet. His contemporaries described him variously as looking like "a long-stage coachman", "the captain of a river steamboat" or even "an English farmer". He painted under the shade of a giant umbrella whose handle concealed a dagger and doubled as a makeshift fishing rod.

Fish, for Turner, was a passion. It was said "he painted fish, wrote fish, thought fish and dreamt fish." Indeed, fish appear profusely in his sketchbooks. (And after drawing them, the fish he caught could be cooked and eaten!) Fishing boats, too, appear in abundance - moored in the harbour, drawn up on the beach or afloat at sea. Painting and fishing was the obvious combination for such a solitary man. Apparently, Turner would sit patiently for hours at a stretch, "perhaps without a single nibble". And the coastal towns of Margate, Ramsgate and Deal provided him with ample opportunities for this dual pastime - fishing and painting his catch.

In April 1827, the year in which he became Mrs. Booth's lodger, Turner had written to a friend, James Holworthy, the watercolour artist: "What may become of me, I know not what, particularly if a lady keep my bed warm, and last winter was quite enough to make singles think of doubles. Poor daddy never felt the cold so much." By the autumn of 1833, Turner had most certainly turned "singles" into "doubles" for he was living openly with his landlady.

From Margate Turner roamed the Kentish coastline. He toured from the Medway round to Folkestone and sketched Whitstable, Ramsgate, Deal and Dover. He travelled in stagecoaches or on borrowed horses. He walked the beaches and headlands in fair weather and foul. He hired boats to row him a little way offshore to sketch the harbours, cliffs and headlands. He thought nothing of walking thirty miles a day carrying his painting paraphernalia wrapped in a cloth and tied to the end of his furled umbrella. A vast number of Turner's late watercolours are indifferently titled but they have the feel of being painted around the familiar coast of Kent. 'Sunset', for instance, may have been painted at Pegwell Bay while 'Shipping' features Deal luggers and so appears to show a scene mid-Channel. But it was the Thanet skies which had the greatest appeal to him and he repeatedly returned to Margate to sketch from the upstairs front windows of Sophia Booth's guest house.

Turner was determined to preserve his anonymity while at Margate.

Presumably, gossip became rife and his cover was blown because he persuaded Sophia to move to Deal in 1836. The advent of the railways brought day trippers from London and there was therefore a strong chance that he would eventually be recognised. At Deal, being totally unknown, he could successfully pose as her husband. At that time she was approaching thirty and "if a little full-blown" was, apparently, "still comely enough to appeal to susceptible males". Modern writers have depicted her as tall, massive and "Junoesque". She was certainly generous because it is well attested that her partner had the furtiveness of a bankrupt and contributed "not a farthing" towards his considerable upkeep. Further, she proved to be a loyal companion to her cantankerous, arrogant, avaricious partner because she accompanied him to London without a murmur when Turner's health began to fail and he decided to look for a second home in London.

After living in several houses across the capital, the couple finally settled on a small cottage in Chelsea overlooking the River Thames in 1846. Widow Booth paid cash for a twenty-one year lease on the riverfront property in an area which then had the reputation of being a resort quaintly known as 'World's End'. There they lived in peaceful seclusion although they were only a stone's throw from Cremorne Pier and Pleasure Gardens. Their new home, now part of Cheyne Walk, was adjacent to a boatbuilder's yard and a couple of shops selling beer, wine and ginger ale. There the residents, watching with amusement Turner lurching home a trifle drunk, irreverently christened him 'Puggy Booth'. (More respectful residents thought the artist resembled a retired sea captain and referred to him as the 'Old Admiral')

Turner continued painting and far from showing signs of fatigue, "there is a sense of an artist moving across the paper with untrammelled freedom and panache," according to Anthony Bailey in 'JMW Turner, Standing in the Sun' (1998). The artist continued to depict stormy seascapes off the coast of south-east Kent. By now his scenes were highly impressionistic and few topographical details are evident. A view of 'Margate Harbour' (1840) may have been painted from the artist's former lodgings but identification of the scene rests entirely upon its traditional title; 'Off Ramsgate'

Turner's watercolour, 'Deal in a Storm', was acquired by Deal Borough Council in 1950. The generous donor was reputed to have paid the princely sum of £90.

Turner wrote a long poem to accompany the excellent engravings of his watercolours included in the 'Southern Coast' series. It was never published and is now lost which is a pity because his poem would possibly have mentioned Deal.

According to his mistress, Sophia Booth, Turner owned a house at St. Margaret's-at-Cliffe. The house has never been positively identified although one suggestion is 'South Sands House' (formerly 'The Hermitage') which has a sea view.

Sophia Booth lies buried with her second husband and their only son in the south portion of St. John's Churchyard, Margate.

*Turner's sketchbook shows a Deal lugger and the Royal Signal Tower.
Courtesy: The Tate.*

(1840) is identified by the hulk of a ship presumably stuck on Goodwin Sands while
'Folkestone' (1845), a painting with a markedly green tinge, reputedly the artist's least
favourite colour, has the tall, bleak sail of a lugger as the only discernable object. Turner
continued to be engaged by the sea's destructive force and a great number of his
marine paintings featured storms and squalls, wrecks and rescues.

Surprisingly, two further paintings of Deal by Turner recently came to light. At first
they were viewed with suspicion which is demonstrated by the remarkably low price
of £800 realised at auction by Sotheby's in 1960. They were both painted between 1835
and 1840 and presented with true generosity to Mrs. Booth. Presumably they hung in
her parlour at Deal.

The first oil painting, 'Off Deal' (9" x 12"), completed by the elderly artist, was
acquired by the National Museum, Stockholm. It is a haunting evocation of a wintry
shoreline crowded with boats and boatmen pitted against the elements. Discernible
are the orange masts of luggers and the crews of galleys battling to reach the shore. A
cluster of sailing boats in the distance indicate violent struggles with wind and weather
further out in the Downs.

The second oil painting, 'Sailing Boat off Deal' (9"x 12"), a technically looser painting
of slightly higher quality, is exhibited at the National Museum of Wales, Cardiff. In
this scene the horizon is obscured by mist and spray while the parchment-coloured
sails of a hovelling lugger are just visible through the haze. The whole dramatic effect
is achieved by pastel shades of yellow, pink and blue with occasional bold strokes of
fiery red. A stretch of pale blue above blotchy grey clouds gives promise of better
weather ahead.

Sophia Booth had insisted that she retained her seaside homes. She returned to
Margate with Turner in 1847 and to Deal in 1849. There was an epidemic of cholera

between 1847 - 9 which killed 53,000 people in Britain and Wales (14,000 in London). Chelsea, then a poor area of London with bad drains and prone to flooding, was listed as having the highest rate of mortality north of the river. Symptoms of this dreadful disease were vomiting, diarrhoea, severe cramps of the stomach and limbs. . . and frequently death. Inevitably, Turner caught the dreaded disease. Sophia proved a sympathetic nurse and she brought him to Deal to convalesce. Her trusted physician, Dr. David Price, was brought over from Margate to attend the temperamental patient.

Dr. Price was a much respected practitioner. He was a consulting surgeon at the Royal Sea Bathing Hospital, a Justice of the Peace and a Town Councillor. He must surely have recognised his patient but he played the game by prescribing remedies for "Mr. Smith or Thomson or whatever name he called himself." The good doctor's opinion was that Turner's bout of cholera should have killed him "had he not had the most extraordinary constitution." Presumably, his habit of consuming alcohol in vast amounts rendered him immune. Sophia attended constantly. . . "most unwearied, being up day @ night, indeed he wanted for nothing." Incredibly, Turner, refreshed by the bracing sea air, made a full recovery: he returned to Chelsea and he began painting once more.

Typically, Dr. Price was not paid by Turner for his services although he had made ten return journeys from Margate to Deal between August and September in 1851. Later, he claimed in a sworn affidavit that he had not received any remuneration since 1850. "And I say that I so attended the said Testator at his request at Margate and at Deal during a severe attack of Cholera and a serious illness consequent upon it where he resided in a house of the defendant Sophia Caroline Booth. . . and that I was on various occasions summoned to Deal by messages through the Electric Telegraph."

Time and tide, however, could not prevent the onslaught of further incapacities. William Turner was now a chronically sick man, and although he continued through sheer determination to paint, he was susceptible to infection and cold. In his final days he had become an invalid and he was reduced to sitting in his wheeled chair studying the changing lights of the river from his bedroom window at Chelsea. This "prophet and poet in colour" breathed his last on 19 December 1851. It was a red, misty morning but the wintry sun fell full on the face of this dying man - the son of a common barber and a mental lunatic - regarded as one of the founders of English watercolour landscape painting. He was buried in St. Paul's Cathedral next to Sir Joshua Reynolds, a former President of the Royal Academy, having bequeathed, in a confused will, his entire paintings to the nation.

SAINT ANDREW'S CHURCH

'the boatmen's church'

SAINT ANDREW'S CHURCH , built of Caen stone with a handsome tower and spire, was immediately recognised as a decided "ornament to the town". Opened in 1852, this was the third of Deal's maritime churches built to serve the seafaring population of our ancient port.

When the church was dedicated in the mid-19th century, however, the port was in decline. Steamships had already begun to replace sailing ships in the Channel and these vessels, being largely independent of the wind, had no need to pause in the Downs to take on provisions. Dover Harbour, under the direction of the Duke of Wellington as Lord Warden of the Cinque Ports, was extended during this period and local trade, accordingly, diminished. Deal boats had not been built with fishing in mind and they were quite unsuited to this purpose. Hardy boatmen faced poverty, starvation, homelessness. . . and they began to contemplate emigration.

An idea for a new church to minister to the impoverished boatmen was suggested by Rev. Archibald Hamilton Duthie when he became Rector of St. Leonard's Church in 1846. He canvassed fervently for support in the town and he called a public meeting to promote this new 'Chapel of Ease'. A subscription list was opened headed by Queen Adelaide who donated £50. The Dowager Queen always held Deal in affection since she constantly recalled the warm welcome the townsfolk had given her when she had landed in 1818 prior to her marriage to the Duke of Clarence (later William IV, the 'Sailor King'). Several houses in the Conservation Area are named after this kindly consort and, indeed, the 'Three King's Hotel' was renamed the 'Royal Hotel' in her honour.

Many illustrious personages gave generously to the scheme and there were donations, too, from both the directors of the South Eastern Railway Company and the Gas Company whose offices lay in the North End. Churchgoers were issued with collecting books and sent to knock on doors seeking small donations. These miniature books survive and record all the willing contributions which were often akin to the biblical 'widow's mite': 'Bill' and 'Puss' gave 6d each, 'two Neighbours' £5, 'a friend in Jamaica' £5, 'two ladies' 1s 3d, 'A Bachelor' 1d, 'A Well Wisher' 1s, 'A Churchman' 1s and 'A Servant' 1d.

St. Andrew's Church.

The architect chosen was Ambrose Poynter of Westminster while the builders were Collyer and Son of Dover. Originally, the intention was to build the new church in a more central position in the town. The site preferred was described as "garden ground situated in Lower Street" but the architect advised the land was unsuitable and compensation had to be paid to the owner since the contract had already been signed. An alternative site for the proposed church was located - the defunct parish workhouse in West Street - and this was eventually purchased for a miserly £900.

Deal's Workhouse had been built in 1796 following an Act of Parliament which provided for the relief of the poor in every parish. Described as "a large and commodious Poor House", it was capable of accommodating between two and three hundred paupers. Plans exist showing this formidable building which was entered through a magnificent portico. On the ground floor were the Master's Room, a committee room, a dining room, a spinning room, a wash house and exercise yards. Twin staircases - one for men, the other for women - at the front of the building led to dormitories on the top two floors. In addition, there were "cells for correction and insane", hospital wards for both sexes, a school room and - ominously - a 'dead house'.

This massive 'Poor House' had been necessary for the bustling port to provide, not only for the elderly and infirm, but also any inhabitant stricken with disease or plague, soldiers dismissed from armed services in times of peace and widows with large families whose menfolk had been drowned. In 1835 a new poor law system came into force and removed the direct responsibility from local bodies to a central institution and the destitute people of Deal were transferred to Eastry Union. This was felt to be a great trial to the aged and infirm by "severing the ties that existed between them and their families and friends, without any hope of seeing them again, unless without a permissive order and trudging a distance of full twelve miles to Eastry, there and back." Union Road and 'Beggars' Alley' (or 'Paupers' Alley') a straggling path bounded by high brick walls, are reminders of Deal's Workhouse.

Eventual cost of the church was approximately £4,500. One further scheme was put forward for collecting money to support the church once it was opened was the antiquated custom of pew rents. Handwritten lists are extant naming the townsfolk who desired to rent seats in the new church. These lists are fascinating since they record the names of many of the earliest worshippers together with their addresses and occupations. It was intended that there should be 483 reserved "sittings" plus a large number which would be free of charge. Originally, the long pews extended almost to the walls of the church (these were shortened later for processions) but all bench ends retain their former numbering - with brass rails for umbrellas - and some bear the inscription: 'Free'.

On 28 May 1849, the foundation stone was laid by Mrs. Archibald Duthie and a sermon was preached by "Mr. Penny, ye new Rector of Great Mongeham". The Corporation of Deal and the Fellowship of Pilots were invited to attend the ceremony. A workman was paid eighteen shillings for "hoisting flags" for the festivities. (Surprisingly, the foundation stone cannot now be located) On the same day the Archbishop of Canterbury preached a sermon at St. Leonard's after which a further collection was made for funds and endowments. Building commenced in earnest and devotional services were held in the builders' huts as the work progressed.

The consecration ceremony for the completed church was performed by the Archbishop of Canterbury, John Bird Sumner, on 31 October 1850. Saint Andrew was deemed to be a suitable patron for a boatman's church since this apostle was, according to scripture, a fisherman from Bethsaida. The Rev. Martin Edgar Benson, former Curate of St. Leonard's, was instituted and inducted as Vicar. At the time of consecration the church was regarded as a 'Chapel-of-Ease' attached to St. Leonard's and the area around the church was declared to be an "ecclesiastical district". 'The Dover Telegraph and Cinque Ports General Advertiser' reported the occasion and commented on the architecture: "The general aspect of the church, as an ecclesiastical structure, is handsome. At the western extremity is a tower from the centre of which rises a tall and elegant spire. Upon the whole, the church must be considered as an ornament to the town..."

The area in the immediate vicinity of the church was once devoted to market gardening. Much of this land was owned by two brothers, Peter and Duke Hayman, whose names are commemorated in the later developed streets, Peter Street and Duke Street. Garden Alley, part of which remains northwards of the church, connected Western Road with the High Street. By the early 19th century this land was developed for housing to accommodate the Deal Pilots. These early navigators were responsible for piloting ships entering the Downs where they were immediately confronted with the treacherous Goodwin Sands. Duke Street, Peter Street, Robert Street, Nelson Street and Middle Street all contain houses favoured by these intrepid pilots.

In addition, boatbuilders' yards and numerous hostelries abounded in the district. 'The Deal Hoy', opposite the church, takes its name from the type of boat commonly employed for conveying goods from the shore to shipping in the Downs. This was a flourishing trade among the North End boatmen in the 18th and early 19th centuries. Grander villas fashionable in the late Victorian period were erected in streets which took the names of saints - St. George's Road, St. Patrick's Road, St. David's Road and St. Andrew's Road. A special entrance to the churchyard was created for inhabitants of these dwellings to attend the new church.

The 'Register of Marriage' is complete from 1852. First entry, dated 31 May, records the marriage of Frederick William Woodward Goodborn, a painter from North Sandy Lane (Golf Road) and Sarah Eliza Steel, daughter of Edward Steel, a plasterer who lived in Duke Street. This ceremony was solemnised by Rev. M.E. Benson, Perpetual Curate. Signatures of all parties are carefully inscribed in copperplate handwriting but the subsequent entry reveals the next couple to have been illiterate: "William Ladd X his mark; Susannah Goodchild X her mark".

The first leather bound 'Register of Baptisms' (1852 - 1861) carries the royal coat-of-arms embossed in gold. It is a fascinating document for it reveals the diverse professions of the parents who took their infants to be baptised there in the mid-Victorian era. Trades include coachbuilder, sadler, victualler, confectioner, maltman, chimney sweeper, basket maker, whitesmith, miller, pastry cook, bookbinder, brushmaker, gasman, waterman, sawyer, hawker, servant and groom. The arrival of the Minster-Deal branch of the South Eastern Railway in 1847 evidently provided employment for a great number of townsfolk: engine cleaner, railway blacksmith, platemaker, switchman, carman, stoker, porter, guard and gatekeeper.

The majority of occupations, naturally, relied upon the sea: sail maker, rope maker, fisherman, sailor, steward, mariner, boat builder, shipping agent, Coastguard, master of the pilot cutter and Chief Engineer of H.M.S. 'Princess Royal'. Yet this is primarily a spiritual document and it is encouraging to find that many of the familiar names of local boatmen - Atkins, Norris, Roberts, Erridge, Stanton, Pritchard - appear with regularity. (Alas, there appears an uncomfortable number of 'single' women - perhaps not so surprising in a maritime town - who brought their offspring to be baptised at their parish church)

St. Andrew's Church was well patronised. In 1865, owing to the increasing congregation, the Rev. Martin Benson resolved to enlarge his church. The north aisle was extended to create ninety extra seats and the chancel was enlarged. (A decorative iron cross on the church marks the original boundary of the nave) Major alterations were also carried out under the direction of the new incumbent, Rev. Charles Shirley Woolmar, who was appointed in 1866. (Formerly, he had been Chaplain of Maidstone Gaol) The cramped vestry was demolished in order to extend the south aisle, the organ was removed from the north aisle into the new aisle and the entire north chancel aisle was converted into free seating. Dormer windows were inserted into the roof to give more light and increase ventilation while two windows, 'The Good Shepherd' and 'The Raising of Lazarus', originally placed at the east end of the north and south aisles respectively, were removed to the south aisle. As these were of different sizes; they could not be paired but they were matched with two new windows. Further, a spacious vestry was built on the north side of the church which was used for Sunday School, Bible classes and choir practice.

Although St. Andrew's has been altered and extended over many periods, the interior, which is light and spacious, presents a certain harmony. It is particularly

Interior of St. Andrew's Church.

pleasing at festival times - Christmas, Easter and Harvest Thanksgiving - when its lavish decorations attract a host of visitors. Constructed in the Early English style, the church contains several features that complement the local boatmen. The chancel arch is unique in that it takes the form of a clinker-built boat while a large stone lantern on the eastern exterior is shaped like a beacon to guide shipping safely into harbour.

A board displayed inside the church lists the incumbents. First named, Rev. Martin Benson, served as Vicar but in 1867, during the incumbency of Rev. Charles Shirley Woolmer, a tithe was purchased at Sibertswold (or Shepherdswell) and presented to the benefice. Thereafter, St. Andrew's assumed the title 'Rectory'. At the same time the parish of St. Andrew came into existence and the complicated boundaries were defined in the 'London Gazette'.

St. Andrew's possesses a large number of colourful late Victorian stained-glass windows by the celebrated artist, Alexander Gibbs. These depict events from the life of Christ and the ministry of his apostles (several scenes are duplicated). An exceedingly fine window in the north aisle is a copy of the famous pre-Raphaelite painting, 'The Light of the World', by William Holman Hunt. Nearby is a representation of Saint Nicholas, patron of sailors, above a window showing Jesus walking on the water. The tall-masted sailing ship and shoal of fish in a rough sea are further reminders that this is primarily a boatmen's church.

Many of the windows commemorate past members of the congregation.

A double light in the south aisle recalls an influential benefactor and freemason, William Matson Cavell (1804 - 1879) who was an Alderman, Magistrate and four times Mayor of Deal. There is a suggestion that the face of Moses standing beside the Burning Bush is a portrait of this worthy gentleman. A window near the vestry featuring healing miracles of Christ remembers Dr. Frederick Hulke (1833 - 81), a respected magistrate and skilful physician who attended the Duke of Wellington at Walmer Castle. The funeral of this highly respected professional man was a magnificent affair attended by Deal Corporation, Royal Marines, The Coastguard, Members of Parliament and Brethren of the Freemasons Society.

The original east window, which was dedicated to Elizabeth, Countess of Clanwilliam, was destroyed by enemy action in World War Two and it was subsequently replaced by an Ascension window. The pretty west window which was carried off by the same bomb has been less happily filled in with knapped flint.

The Victorian font is constructed of Caen stone and stands on a Portland stone base. Octagonal in shape, it has a carved oak cover and a basin lined with lead. The brass lectern with its eagle head and jewelled collar dates from late Victorian times.

The ornate oak choir stalls have faces hidden among the carved poppy heads. The rood cross which carries the figure of the crucified Christ was carved in Byzantine style. Its design incorporates the symbols of Alpha and Omega, the Blessed Sacrament and the Holy Trinity. The artist included a 'chi ro' on the reverse so that the choir could share in the symbolism.

The Sanctuary was formerly far more colourful than at present. A dove radiating light was painted at the apex of the east window while on either side angels appeared kneeling in adoration. On the south wall of the choir was depicted an angel holding a scroll and on the opposite side appeared St. Andrew with a cross. Although all these decorations have vanished, the set of murals composed of painted tiles remain, dating from around 1882. They were produced by the renowned Gibbs' firm which is more usually associated with stained glass in 'high Gothic' style. Subjects represented there are Melchizedek, King of Salem, offering bread and wine; the Israelites gathering manna in the wilderness; Christ feeding five thousand and the wedding at Cana.

St. Andrew's possess both sedilia (stone seats for clergy) and piscina (a basin for cleansing sacred vessels) in the sanctuary. It is unusual to find either in a post-Reformation church. A true English (or 'Sarum') altar was added in 1934. This has two candlesticks placed on the table with four more carried by the riddel posts painted green and gold with the thistle and cross of St. Andrew. The elaborate oak pulpit carries painted panels of the three evangelists and four doctors of the early church with a statue of St. Andrew in the centre.

Originally, there were no chapels. In 1891 the north aisle was altered to accommodate a memorial chapel which later became the Lady Chapel. The Blessed Sacrament is reserved in the aumbry in the north wall where it is protected by an ornate pewter door.

Prior to 1948 the organ was positioned against the east wall of the south aisle and the remaining space was utilised as a Memorial Chapel to the Fallen of the First World War. Once the organ pipes were removed to the gallery the South Chapel was created and dedicated to All Souls. The first organ was built by James Eagles and placed on the north side of the chancel in 1857.

This organ was entirely rebuilt at a cost of £500 by the celebrated firm of F.H. Browne and Sons. Their workshop had been established in 1871 at the disused Baptist Chapel in Nelson Street. Browne's organs are to be found in several local churches -

New St. Mary's, St. Saviour's, St. George's, Victoria Baptist Church, the former Congregational Church and Wesleyan Chapel - while others appear nationwide or have been exported abroad. Truly, the organ at St. Andrew's was a splendid example of their craft - a three-manual pipe organ which was once hand pumped by the indefatigable Mr Tookey.

Queen Victoria's coat-of-arms with the motto, 'Dieu et mon droit' is displayed in the centre of the gallery over the west door. At first this neat gallery was reached via a short flight of wooden stairs in the tower. Children were provided with special seats for them to view the service when not attending Sunday School. Apparently, these children did a great deal of marching to and from their classes and during the collection. Their robust activity was admired by visiting inspectors.

The stately tower with its stone spire surmounted by a copper cockerel weather vane is a landmark in the North End. This tower houses a single bell, 27" in diameter, weighing 4 cwts and tuned to the note F#. It was cast in 1850 by the Whitechapel Bell Foundry whose more famous bells include Big Ben and Bow Bells.

First sexton charged with tolling the bell prior to services was a certain Mr. Lowndes employed at ten pounds per annum in 1857. A curious survival is the system whereby a tiny spring bell was set up in the porch and connected by a wire to the vestry. This enabled the Priest to signal to the sexton to cease tolling when a service was about to commence.

A fascinating legend concerns the eight medieval gargoyles (or "grotesques") that adorn the tower. In the late 1840s the boatmen of Reculver learned that a church was about to be built for the seafaring populace of Deal and they obtained a series of gruesome stone carvings from a ruined church which they brought around the coast

St. Andrew's Church.

in rowing boats. The identity of the church remains a mystery and, indeed, there may be no truth in the story at all!

St. Andrew's Church is surrounded by one acre of land. Formerly, this was landscaped (at a cost of £13) and a 'carriageway' ran from the roadside to the door. The original entrance was through a lantern-lit gateway in West Street but later an opening was made in the boundary walls to allow access through St. Andrew's Road. At one time the churchyard must have presented a colourful sight with flower beds, shrubs and a drive lined with sycamore trees. The churchyard was encompassed by red brick walls and spear-headed railings. A wayside calvary with a willow figure of the crucified Christ still stands at the eastern approach.

St. Andrew's lantern.

In 1865 a house was purchased for a Rectory. 'Clarendon House' stood at the corner of Lower Street (now the High Street) and Union Road (which once led to the Workhouse). Described in 1936 as "a good Queen Anne building", this was a magnificent, red brick, double-fronted house with shuttered windows and an imposing porch approached by a short drive. Although the house was a three-storey affair, the front and the back were on separate levels so that one zig-zagged one's way to the top. The roof was surmounted by a belvedere which gave spectacular views over the Downs.

The Rectory was a spacious building. At the front there were a large dining room and a drawing room separated by a wide hall and open stairway which led to bedrooms and a study on the top two floors. At the rear were a large, old-fashioned kitchen, scullery, pantry and wine cellars. There was a circular terrace, a conservatory and french windows set into the drawing room bay with steps leading down onto the croquet lawn.

The garden was extensive. It was bounded on the west by a high wall where a stone informed that it was erected by "My Hayman in 1797" although, in fact, the foundations were of an earlier date. Trees abounded - an avenue of sycamores, horse chestnuts, ash, crab apples and, in the front garden, a mulberry. In addition there were stables and a well which

Fashion icon, Hardy Amies, designed the set of vestments for the Priest to wear during High Mass. He presented them to the church in memory of his mother.

The original rectory was the brewer's residence for the Hayman brothers at the foot of Farrier Street.

At one time St. Andrew's sported a football team.

reputedly supplied pure water to shipping in the Downs. This lovely garden was the scene of countless fetes and bazaars in summer.

Eventually, the upkeep of such a grand house proved too expensive and it was abandoned in favour of a Victorian terrace property, 'Brooke House', in Cowper Road. Sadly, although 'Clarendon House' was a listed building, it fell into disrepair and it was demolished in 1964. Meanwhile, the present Rectory was built. As this occupies a corner of the churchyard, an order needed to be signed by the Queen in Council before building could commence. St. Andrew's Rectory is the first to be built on consecrated ground since medieval times.

Education has always been a concern of St. Andrew's. In 1792 Deal's first Charity School had been instituted by St. George's Church to provide free education for fifty pupils. This school was transferred to the present St. George's Hall in 1814 where "a hundred poor boys and a hundred poor girls are taught reading, writing and arithmetic". St. Andrew's decided to combine with St. Leonard's to open a similar establishment in London Road. Donations from private individuals were supplemented by grants from the Diocesan Board and the National Society.

Deal Parochial School was opened on 18 August 1853. It cost £2,300 and the architect was again Mr. Poynter of Westminster. The school combined two long halls (one for boys, the other for girls) with an infants' room adjoining. Each classroom had galleries, high windows and access to the playground. Houses were provided for the master and mistress, Mr. and Mrs. C.J. Hopping, and for the infants' teacher, Miss S.A. Cooper. 'The Illustrated London News' published an engraving of the school together with a report of the opening ceremony: "The Schools will accommodate about 300 children: and it is hoped that those for whose benefit they were intended will avail themselves of the privilege of the instruction hereby so generously afforded." A modern Parochial School patronised by all three churches now occupies a site on the former Royal Marines sports ground while the original Victorian building has been demolished.

St. Andrew's also ran an infant school for the children of labourers and boatmen in Duke Street. The property purchased has had a chequered history. It was built in 1806 as a Wesleyan chapel and a Sunday School was established at the rear. A grander Wesleyan (Methodist) School was opened in 1860 and a Wesleyan Chapel moved to an adjoining site in Union Road in 1867. The vacant hall was acquired by the Roman Catholic Church for occasional celebration of Mass. There are several indications that this building - now private houses - was once a chapel. The southern end retains its curved apse while a decorative lantern appears over the doorway.

This infant school was well-attended and averaged 135 pupils. Although education was by that time made compulsory, a weekly payment of 'school pence' was required from each pupil. Headmistress was Miss Elizabeth Grace and she adopted the 'Monitorial System' whereby a succession of young pupil/teachers taught the infants under her direction. The classrooms were warm but gloomy and the desks were arranged in formal rows. Yet the pupils seemed happy and well-cared for so much so that a proposal was soon made to adapt the adjacent Parish Room into an extension of the thriving school. This room, like St. Andrew's Hall, has been converted into a private residence but its fascia still bears the faint inscription: 'British School'.

St. Andrew's Church football team in 1902. Courtesy: K.J. Hilton.

During the Second World War St. Andrew's Hall welcomed evacuees from London and North Kent. It provided them with both accommodation and education. Later, the children of Deal were themselves evacuated to Wales where they were administered to by Rev. N.C. Bowman, Curate of St. Andrew's Church. After the war the Hall was sold to the Deal Branch of the Old Age Pensioners' Association. By that time there was little to indicate that it had been a flourishing education establishment. The warren of little rooms did, however, retain their decorative cast-iron fireplaces, original gas brackets and stout wooden pegs for children's outdoor clothes.

In a further endeavour to evangelise the boatmen St. Andrew's Church acquired a Mission Chapel at the North End of Deal. This was a compact, corrugated iron construction dating from around 1883 which stood in Sandown Road. Hemmed in by iron railings, it was approached by a flight of stone steps leading to a tiny wooden porch. It had plain arched windows and a steep, sloping roof surmounted by a miniature steeple that housed a tinpot bell.

Although the Mission stood in the centre of the boat building and fish curing industries, it has to be admitted that the mariners for whom it was intended showed little concern for evangelism. Nevertheless, it was a happy place of worship with a lively congregation ministered to by the Curate. The Mission continued until the outbreak of the Second World War when it was damaged by a bomb. A private house now occupies the site.

During the traumatic years of the First World War the Anglican churches in the district made a concerted effort to cope with major crises locally. They saw the war years as a spiritual challenge offering a real opportunity for missionary work in the district. Lack of attendance at services, admittedly, was a matter of grave concern for the clergy and "the habit of motoring, the wireless, the servant problem, the custom of weekends in country houses and the playing of games on Sundays" were some of the excuses offered for diminishing congregations.

Similar problems were encountered during the Second World War. Minute Books record the difficulties faced by the Deal churches. Petrol rationing prevented pastoral visits, clergymen declined to serve as Air Raid Wardens and - ominously - arrangements were made for "the burial of the enemy dead". Decisions regarding action to be taken following an air raid during a service were left to the discretion of the celebrant, "black-outs" threatened to disrupt wintertime assemblies while the ceasing of church bells was thought to have "a depressing psychological effect on the community".

For a time St. George's Church was left without an Incumbent but St. Andrew's carried on stoically. Devastation occurred when a direct hit by a shell on an air raid shelter in Robert Street killed members of the family from 'Faber Villa'. This same blast carried off both the east and west windows of St. Andrew's. The church was temporarily closed but an altar was set up in the parish room and regular services continued. The Sunday School also functioned and one of the teachers offered the cellars of her house in Ivy Place for shelter in the event of future bombardment. The flat roof of the Rectory in the High Street was deemed an ideal place for Fire Watching. And from September 1940 until August 1942, the Rector, Rev. W.G. Illingworth, was appointed to serve a church near Bedford. In the face of all these tribulations the local clergy seized the opportunity for home mission - among the distressed and bereaved, American soldiers stationed in the vicinity and the "return of men and women from the Forces after the Conclusion of War".

Processing at St. Andrew's Church.

After the surrender of the garrison at Calais and, concomitantly the cessation of shelling from long range guns, an open air service of thanksgiving was organised in Alfred Square by the new Rector, Rev. V.D.W. Hyde, for people living in the blighted North End on Sunday 8 October 1944. The church choir was accompanied in their rousing singing by the Salvation Army band. The Mayor and Mayoress (Alderman and Mrs. E.J. Dobson) attended.

The first official duty by Dr. Geoffrey Fisher, Archbishop of Canterbury, after his visit to the Pope in Rome was to perform the Institution and Induction of Canon Lyonel Lancaster on 6 December 1960. (The Primate's address to a full congregation at St. Andrew's attracted a great deal of attention from the national press) The Rev. John King came to St. Andrew's from St. Laurence in Thanet where he was also Chaplain to R.A.F. Manston. Present Rector is the Reverend Christopher Lindlaw who was previously Curate of St. James the Less in Lancing, Sussex. Father Christopher was once a freelance wine maker who operated his own company specialising in English sparkling wines. "My task", he declares, "is to foster and develop in the parish the Catholic Faith as the Church of England has received it."

REV. THOMAS STANLEY TREANOR

'Sky Pilot'

REV. THOMAS STANLEY TREANOR (1837 - 1910) was appointed Chaplain to the Missions to Seamen for Deal and The Downs in July, 1878. A scholar and an author, Treanor could read Greek and converse in many languages and his passion for souls, coupled with masterly seamanship, earned him the affectionate title 'Sky Pilot'.

The days of Deal's prominence as "the greatest seaport in the world" were truly over but the Downs remained an important anchorage for shipping to and from the port of London. On a single night in his first year of office Treanor counted five hundred ships with an estimated five thousand sailors sheltering off Deal and in a later year he counted twenty steamers passing through the Channel in addition to three hundred smaller vessels. Naturally, the Missions to Seamen regarded the Downs as one of its "twelve great roadstead stations".

The mission in the Downs served five main groups: merchant seamen of many nations, foreign seamen passing through the port; the Royal Navy represented by five local coastguard stations; nine lightships in the English Channel and, closer to home, the Deal boatmen. (The coastguard stations were visited in turn by the scripture reader, Mr. J.W. Lowe, since this was regarded as shore work)

Treanor listed the great variety of ships passing through the Downs in an article he wrote for the journal, 'The Sunday At Home': "From London alone we find ships bound to India, Australia, America and the Cape; to Nova Scotia with half a cargo on board, or round to Cardiff in ballast. Besides these vessels there are to be found in the long heaving line of shipping in the Downs stately clippers from Dundee and the North of England, outward bound to Calcutta or Kurrachee, or Chittagong, or Yokohama; German barques, Norwegian timber ships, Italian, Greek, French and Spanish merchantmen, besides numbers of our own colliers. Barges, too, in number are found here; French chasse-marées, pilot-boats, English tug boats and sometimes men-of-war, and torpedo vessels or cruising gun boats swell the total; while far away on the horizon gleam the dull red hulls of the nearer lightships round the Goodwin Sands, the more distant ones being out of sight." (25 August 1888)

Originally founded by Lord Shaftesbury, The Downs Mission Station was opened in 1859. Later, funds for Boatmen's Rooms were raised from a bazaar in Deal Castle organised by Lady Granville and Lady Sydney. Rear Admiral Sir John Hill, last Captain of Sandown Castle, gave permission for stones from the demolished fortress to be used in the foundations. The Lord Warden, Lord Palmerston, generously presented a library, two telescopes and a clock. This imposing Gothic building facing the sea near the former North Deal Lifeboat House was opened in 1884. The symmetrical red brick building on stone foundations has stout chimneys poking through its tiled roof with a decorative finial on its apex. It was primarily for boatmen's recreation and the reception of shipwrecked mariners but there was also a spacious office for Treanor. Here the Vicar of the Downs held Sunday services exclusively for the families of boatmen living at the North End.

Lord Shaftesbury had previously opened a smaller Reading Room at the top of Five Step Alley opposite the iron pier in 1861. Lord Palmerston, Warden of the Cinque Ports, donated a barometer and telescopes. The Rooms remained a hive of activity until after the Second World War with its cluttered interior - Hurricane lamps, fishing tackle, nautical paintings, glass floats, fishermen's chest, model boats and stuffed fish - as a reminder of marine life. The Old Boatmen's Rooms is now a private house.

Thomas Stanley Treanor was born on 2 December 1837, puzzlingly, according to his birth certificate, at the "Forge" in the hamlet of Farlow, near Stottesdon, Shropshire. Presumably, his father, Rev. John Treanor, was Curate in charge of the Chapel of St. Giles which was demolished in 1857. The Norman font, where Thomas would have been baptised, is preserved in the replacement Victorian edifice. According to his obituary in the 'Deal, Walmer and Sandwich Mercury' (19 Nov 1910) which gives several inaccurate biographical details, Rev. John Treanor, who hailed from Scotland, was later Rector of Galway. He was a cousin of Lord Traynor who held considerable estates in western Ireland.

Treanor served for a short time as a midshipman in the Royal Navy before entering upon his own clerical career. In 1855 Thomas entered Trinity College, Dublin, where he won the Ecclesiastical History Prize and a championship cup for athletics. (This combination of successes in religion and sport stood him in good stead for his later career as Chaplain to Seamen at Deal) He graduated with a B.A. (1862) and later gained an M.A. (1877) He was ordained Deacon (1862) then Priest (1863) and finally Curate (1864) at Tuam, a market town in County Galway. There his wife, Charlotte Elizabeth, died at their home 'The Grove'. Naturally, this was a time of great unhappiness for Treanor which is why he may have been tempted to find solace abroad.

In 1865 he became Chaplain at Arcachon, a fishing port in south-west France. He returned to Ireland when he was appointed Rector of Shrule, a parish in County Longford, in 1870. Two years later he was made Rector of Achill Island (also known as 'Eagle Island') a tiny fishing village at Mayo on the west coast of Ireland. There, he married for a second time. His new wife, Anita, née Silletoe, who bore him five daughters and a son who was named after his father.

After the disestablishment of the Irish Church, Treanor accepted an invitation to become Chaplain to the Missions to Seamen for Deal and The Downs. Now his parish was the open sea. The Mission's responsibility extended to lightships and coastguard

Treanor reads to boatmen in the Downs.

stations and, most importantly, the welfare of the Deal, Walmer and Kingsdown boatmen. At the turn of the century there was estimated to be around one thousand boatmen and fishermen in the vicinity. In one year Treanor expected to visit four hundred boatmen's homes plus eight hundred and ninety ships, spending an average two hundred and fifty days afloat annually. At first he hired local boats but eventually the Mission acquired its own galley punt at a cost of fifty pounds. Bishop Parry of Dover dedicated 'The Countess Sydney', which was later joined by a second galley, 'Evangeline'. The two worked in tandem until 1906 when they were replaced by 'Quiver IX'. The crew of the Mission boats comprised George Norris (coxswain) and Stephen Wilds (bowman). The chaplain steered.

Treanor was the ideal man for the job. He had a working knowledge of the sea from his youthful days in the Navy and he maintained his robust physical fitness since he continued training in athletics. In latter years he became a member of the Alpine Touring Club and he could boast that he had scaled the highest mountains in Switzerland. All these attributes earned him the respect of the hardy local boatmen. Indeed, his bluff, hearty manner and his personal pluck tempered with a hint of wry humour were just the right qualities to appeal to sailors.

This stalwart crew assembled for prayer before every launch and, after commending themselves and their work to the Almighty, donned oilskins, sou'westers and cork lifejackets. The boat lay in front of the Mission Rooms, near the capstan by which she was heaved along the shingle, a distance of fifty or sixty yards, ready for launching. "Twenty willing pair of hands stand by to rush the good boat into the water," wrote Treanor, "the long expected 'smooth' comes, and she is quickly afloat. . ."

'Countess Sydney', a twenty-two feet long galley punt, her familiar 'Blue Angel' flag streaming in the breeze, would then sail to the nearest Merchant Navy ship in the Downs. There, the crew, destined for a long voyage and caught in a moment of 'loneliness and leisure', would welcome Treanor. The chaplain, with amazing agility, would climb a rope thrown over the ship's side - a most dangerous operation - while the crew hauled up his collapsible harmonium. Treanor was an accomplished organist and he had an excellent singing voice which could carry across the still waters to the decks of neighbouring ships. The captain would then summon his crew - everyone from the cook to the cabin boy - and passengers of all nationalities for a simple service in the fo'c's'le.

Treanor - "close clipped beard, full moustache, watcher's eyes" - was a staunch Irish Protestant. Habitually he wore "high sea boots, thick Cardigan vest and pilot jacket". His photographs show a rugged, muscular figure, scarred by sea and storm. The chaplain's deep, powerful voice carried easily across the open decks as he preached for upwards of an hour. He carried Bibles in twenty languages and the prayer book in ten plus one hundred hymn books. Treanor was a linguist but his main accomplishment was to read Greek. In addition he carried a formidable array of temperance cards, medals and tracts - 'Atonement for Sin', 'Judgement to Come', 'Resurrection of the Dead' - "words to make the heart quake and the very ears of impenitent sinners to tingle". On a lighter note there was an assortment of gifts for the crew: newspapers, magazines, scrap books, needle cases, mufflers, mittens and helmets knitted by the Deal ladies.

Most distressing for Treanor was to learn via the London newspapers the fate of ships on whose decks he had recently held divine service - "all hands lost" - wrecked at sea. This happened frequently. One chilling occasion, he recalled, was when he visited the lightship placed temporarily near the wreck of the ill-fated S.S. 'Scholten', that had foundered five miles off Dover. "Entombed in her hull, probably one hundred bodies lay, and no preacher or moralist could have pointed a more solemn lesson than did that grim and lonely wave-washed mast."

Numerous visits were made to the four Goodwin Sands lightships.

Their isolated crews were delighted to receive gifts of fresh bread, fruit, flowers, vegetables, newspapers, letters from home and an exchange of library books. Grateful lightshipmen never forgot to pass enamel mugs of tea in a bucket over the swaying taffrail and down to the frozen members of crew patiently waiting in the mission boat below. The North, South and West (Gull) Lightships were easily accessible but the East Goodwin Lightship, ten miles from land and a mile and three-quarters from the outer edge of the Goodwin Sands, was difficult and dangerous to reach. The Mission boat often returned in dense fog across the dreaded sandbank.

Lightships further afield were sometimes included in parish visits. The Tongue, off Margate, and the Varne, off Folkestone, lay about ten miles from the nearest land and a strong off shore breeze made it sometimes difficult for the mission boat to return to base. It could be a twelve hour journey. The Edinburgh lightship, twenty-five miles off Ramsgate, might only be reached on spring tides with favourable winds and fair weather. Most isolated were the Galloper and Long Sand Lightships, both fifty miles from Deal and thirty miles from land, anchored on the confines of the North Sea. Habitually, Treanor visited them on the same day by employing a crew of five, leaving at seven in the morning, in a magnificent twenty-ton lugger, 'Guiding Star'.

Visits to remote lightships were arranged to take place prior to Christmas so that the missioners could bring maximum cheer. Ladies made plum puddings and mince pies while the men provided rounds of beef and plucked turkeys. Holly, ivy and laurel were gathered by their children. Christmas cards, letters and gifts in profusion would be sent from friends ashore. The service in a cabin would feature familiar carols and centre around readings from the Nativity.

Treanor's sheer determination is demonstrated by his efforts to reach the Varne Lightship, twenty miles off Folkestone, in the summer of 1891. The crew of the mission boat with the coxswain of the Deal lifeboat set off loaded with provisions in the large and powerful galley punt, 'Success'. Ten miles from the intended destination the sea became heavy, gigantic waves almost deluging the boat, spray stinging the men's faces, nearly blinding them, so that they were forced back to the shelter of Dover Harbour.

A second attempt a fortnight later began with a favourable light wind and ended in thick fog when the crew could barely see the length of their boat. "All kinds of ghostly shapes and spectral ships, all manner of imaginary noises and sounds came at us out of that wreathing, vaporous fog." Although they came within five hundred yards of the lightship the men were once more forced to return.

On their third attempt a suitable tide carried the galley straight to the lightship and the sailors enjoyed the missionary's three hourlong visit. There were welcome gifts of fruit, flowers, vegetables, newspapers and the inevitable woollen wear from the ladies. And it was a glorious evening when the boatmen took their leave but the wind had dropped and the crew would have to struggle to return home. "Our splendid boat, though built for speed and strength under sail, was too weighty and too big for rowing" - but row they did, the whole twenty miles, dressed in cumbersome sea boots, oilskins and sou'westers.

Treanor penned his own account of his valiant attempt to reach the North Sand Head and East Goodwin Lightships. The North Sand Head Lightship lay about a mile from the northernmost point of the Goodwin Sands, about seven miles from the nearest land and ten miles from Deal. On such occasions a larger, more powerful boat was required and this was obtained from Richard Roberts whose galley punt measured thirty feet long by seven feet beam. Roberts, the celebrated coxswain of Deal lifeboat, would then act as fourth man. Even so, it was a matter of considerable risk to venture so far from land in an open boat and attempt to sail round the Goodwin Sands. Their journey might take twelve hours during which time any change in the weather might occur.

"We sweep outwards and onwards before a strong flood tide and a good breeze that swells our great sail into curves of canvas, under the pressure of which the sharp boat curtsies to the wind and hisses through the parting waves. Sheet, halyard, bowline and backstay were all tight as fiddlestrings, and humming to the increasing wind, the noble boat leans over till the bubbling water boils up in an arch over her lee gunwale, without, however, a drop getting aboard, and then, as she "spings her luff", comes upright again in her onward flight."

Doubling the southern extreme of the Brake Sand, the party came into the deep water of the stream of the Gull Lightship, for which Treanor had some London newspapers to throw aboard. "If we have time enough to haul down sail and unship our mast, we go leeward of her, and keeping a little ahead of her, pull with all our might at our oars, the chaplain steering as well as pulling, until we almost touch her - not her cutwater, or she would drive us clean under - and get our boarding hook, with towline attached, into her chain or rigging. This done the chaplain resigns the helm of the mission boat and jumps aboard the moving vessel. Books are left, a precious text is repeated and pressed, a hymn perhaps is sung, and a short prayer is said on deck, and five minutes afterwards the mission boat is half a mile wide, riding alone on the waste of waters."

On this occasion, although surrounded by ships of various nations, they visited no passing vessel but stood on for the still distant lightships. Next they plunged into the expanse of sea round the attractive North-West Goodwin Buoy. Then they skirted the North-West edge of the Goodwins, giving the tossing breakers on it a wide berth, and, slacking their sheet, they ran between the little shallow patch called by the boatmen, 'Sawney's Knoll', and the Goodwins themselves. . .

"While we are still far off," Treanor records, "the lightship crew recognise the mission boat and flag on the cock-staff in our bows. We on our part look carefully to see on which side of the lightship her boat lays outside by its davits, or whether it is inboard altogether. This is of vital importance to the safety of our mast. Getting out our fenders, we steer for the side we have decided on, tide, wind and sea having also to be considered, and shooting round her stern, we run up along, let us say, her starboard side, for the lightships's head is lying W or WNW. Quickly we haul down sail and clamber on board, leaving the boat with one man in it, to steer off from the vessel and ride by a long scope of hawser."

"I am never tired of looking with admiration at the beautiful Deal boats which float the water with the native grace that comes of symmetry and power, and the lightshipmen join in singing their praises", Treanor enthused. "It is a real pleasure to see the lightshipmen again, and they are as obviously glad to see us as old friends." There was the usual exchange of gifts newspapers, books and flowers - followed by an inspection tour of the lightship, Treanor being fascinated to discover on this occasion that a telephone wire had been laid connecting the vessel to the mainland, of immense importance in alerting the coastguards and directing life-saving craft to the exact location of ships in distress in this treacherous part of the English Channel. After a long survey of the ship, all hands gathered for a brief service in front of the Trinity flag spread across a deal table.

During service a clap of thunder and a roar of wind brought the missionaries onto deck where they discovered that there had been a short thunder squall with hail in which, while it lasted, the wind blew a gale. No time to waste! Collecting their belongings and transporting them hastily to the boat, the Deal party moved off to catch the first of the ebb tide which would carry them to the East Goodwin Lightship.

This second lightship was six or seven miles distant SSE and to reach her their course lay outside the Goodwins along the outer edge of which, keeping at a safe distance, the boatmen made one or two tacks. The great quicksand with its buoys and swatches, its stump of masts and ribs of forgotten ships, held their interest -

Christening a new mission boat.

particularly to the coxswain of the lifeboat - but the ebb tide would not permit them to linger. They reached the East Goodwin Lightship in about one hour and a quarter from the first vessel.

The East Goodwin Lightship lay about one and three quarter miles from the farthest point of the Goodwin Sands, in about thirty fathoms of water. So valuable a marker, she was frequently struck by mid-Channel shipping. Vessels, taking the lightship as their point of departure from that treacherous area of quicksand, came too close or, not making sufficient allowance for the strong current, often drove right into her. Treanor wondered that she had not, in fact, been sunk, a collision having occurred just prior to his visit and he pondered upon the considerable risk a lightshipman daily faced.

Service over, the missionaries prepared for the homeward journey:". . . as the evening was falling in, and as we shoved off in our boat, and we were steering straight for the Goodwins, the great green light of the ship, which revolves every fifteen seconds, began north of the South-East buoy, through which we passed safely."

Returning home, Treanor's crew invariably hitched a lift by hooking onto a passing steamer at full speed in the manner of the audacious Deal boatmen. Their mission boat might be towed at a speed of twelve knots before casting off and beating to windward towards the shore. Treanor, himself, once described this difficult and dangerous undertaking in 'The Cry From The Sea': "We had rowed sixteen or seventeen miles since morning, and some of us thought that we had had enough of it. We all without exception looked round, hoping for something to turn up, when between us and the land, about a mile astern of us, we saw a tug-boat."Down sails and row!"

"This we did with all our might to get within hailing distance of her, and then I stood up and waved my cap. The master of the tug-boat kindly sheered out to us, and without stopping his vessel took our boarding hook and tow-line aboard him, whilst I was steering so as to avoid the swirl of the propeller, deep in the water though it was, and to get our boat end on for the first giant pull the steamer would give us.

"Nothing I know gives one such an idea of force as this first jerk. Then, bows up in the air, we rushed after the tug through a foaming cauldron of waters, which raced past and alongside us, and now and then sent a cataract of spray - salt sea-spray - sometimes fine as dust and then rattling like hailstones on our oilskins."

And so in this daring manner the tired, intrepid boatmen, flew homewards covering the remaining six miles in less than half an hour.

Treanor wrote a trio of books recording his missionary work and chronicling the dramatic exploits of the renowned Deal boatmen: 'Heroes of the Goodwin Sands' (1892) 'The Log of a Sky Pilot' (1894) and 'The Cry From the Sea - And the Answer From the Shore' (1899) published by The Religious Tract Society. In his first and most famous book, 'Heroes of the Goodwin Sands', he relates graphically the incidents surrounding the daring sea rescues of 'The Frederick Carl', a Danish schooner which struck the outer part of the North Sand Head in October, 1885, during which life-saving mission the brave crew member, George Marsh, was drowned; 'The Golden Island', a three-masted schooner lodged on the Goodwins during a gale at midnight in May, 1887, all saved, and 'The Indian Chief', which was attended by the Ramsgate lifeboat, 'Bradford', assisted by the steam tug, 'Aid' in January, 1881. He also pays tribute to Jarvist Arnold, Coxswain of the Kingsdown Lifeboat, and her indomitable crew who saved forty-seven lives from S.S. 'Sorrento', the first steamer to be lost on the Sands - shortly before Christmas 1872. All these books attracted a wide circulation.

Treanor was Honorary Secretary of Goodwin Sands and Downs Branch of the Royal National Lifeboat Institution and was therefore responsible for the Kingsdown, Walmer and Deal Lifeboat Stations. He rarely accompanied the lifeboat crew but remained ashore ready to offer spiritual comfort to returning rescuers and survivors. Further, he was a noted journalist and his articles appeared regularly in national magazines. His lively contributions detailed his experiences at sea and featured the work of the local boatmen.

One article gave a superb picture of the famous Deal luggers:

"In those days all Deal and Walmer beach was full of those wonderful sea boats hauled up on the shingle, while their mizzen booms almost ran into the house on the opposite side of the roadway. The Deal luggers are about 40ft long and 13ft beam, more, or less. The small luggers are called 'cats'. There is a forecastle, or 'forepeak', in the luggers where you can comfortably sleep - that is, if you are able to sleep in such surroundings, and if the anguish of the sea sickness is absent. There is a movable 'caboose' in the 'cats' right amidships, in which three or four men packed close side by side can lie. These large boats are lugger rigged, carrying the foremast well forward, and sometimes, but very rarely, like the French 'chasse-marées', a mainmast also, with a maintopsail as well, of course, as the mizzen behind. The mainmast is now hardly ever used, being inconvenient for getting alongside shipping, and therefore only survive the foremast and mizzen, the mainmast being developed out of existence. The luggers are splendid sea boats, and it is a fine sight to see one of them crowded with men and close reefed, crusing in the Downs, 'hovelling', or 'on the look-out' for a job in the gale. While ships are parting from their anchors and flying signals of distress, the luggers supplying their wants or putting pilots on board wheel and sweep round them like sea birds on the wind. . ." ('Leisure Hour' 1892)

Treanor was well known to visitors since he organised an annual summer concert at the Pier Pavilion in aid of funds for the Mission to Seamen. There, supported by the sturdy coxswains of the Downs lifeboats, he spoke in stirring language of the dangers that beset mariners, the perils of the lifeboatmen and the aims of the society worldwide. He was frequently invited to speak from the pulpits of the local churches whose congregations fervently supported him in his missionary work. On a secular note, Treanor was a dedicated Unionist and a member of the Primrose League.

Treanor lived at 'The Laurels', a grand house adjacent to the War Memorial Hospital. Funds for the purchase, apparently, came from the sale of twelve private capstan grounds. This was an imposing Victorian property with a conservatory and a croquet lawn. On a triangle of land at the junction of London Road and St. Leonard's Road there is a tall brick ball-capped edifice which puzzles passers-by. It is said to be a replica of the watch tower that once rose above the house and

The chaplain boarding a moving steamship.

gave Treanor an unrivalled view over his maritime parish.

This twice-widowed cleric needed a sizeable establishment to accommodate his large family. Indeed, his children were so numerous that his memory failed him when he filled in their dates and places of birth for the 1881 census. He notes his eldest daughter, Charlott (sic) was born in Arcachon in 1865 which was the year that his first wife, Charlotte, had died, presumably in childbirth, in Ireland. His memory of the dates for his five other daughters by his second marriage - Louie, Mabel, Sarah, Violet and Florence - are hopelessly vague since the dates given are approximate and do not tally with their birth certificates! His son, Thomas Stanley, who was born in 1877 at Westport, Co Mayo, appears later to have served with the Army in South Africa. Treanor retained two Irish servants - Ellen and Marshole - and employed a governess, Johanna, to look after his offspring.

Treanor married for a third time. His new bride was a society woman, Louise Ann Atkinson, whose family had lately returned from India. She resided at Hyde Park Mansions, London, and, by all accounts, they had a splendid wedding held at Marylebone Church on 28 August 1890. When Treanor wrote an account of his conversion in 'The Log of a Sky Pilot' he mentions that his young wife adopted the Christian faith at a later stage.

Treanor arranged for twelve almshouses and a large beach plot and capstan grounds to be made available for retired boatmen. He died on Friday 11 November 1910 and his funeral service at St. Leonard's Church was attended by the Mayor and Corporation, a large number of clergy, representatives of both the Lifeboat Institution and Missions to Seamen, coxswains of the three lifeboats, local boatmen and residents "of all classes". Principal mourners were his four sons-in-law. There was no address but tributes had already been paid to him by all the local clergy from their pulpits on the previous Sunday. Typical was that read by the Rev. C. Pendock Banks, Rector of St. Andrew's: "We all recognise his manliness and courage, his sincerity and straightforwardness, his vigorous intellect, his sturdiness of religious conviction, his consistency in practising what he preached. . ."

Treanor lies buried in an untended grave beneath a spreading yew in Deal Cemetery. A stone cross bears a text from the epistles ("But if we walk in the light. . . we share a

Treanor's watchtower.

The redundant Mission was converted into a character seaside home. One occupant was Arnold Cawthrow (1913 - 1993) Big Chief editor of the popular 'I Spy' books.

People can still remember the public barometer displayed in a niche on the north side of the Boatmen's Rooms at the top of Exchange Street.

On the day 'Countess Sydney' was launched it was found that the mission boat leaked badly. She had to return hastily to shore to avoid drowning her crew which included the Bishop of Dover.

common life."1 John 1 v 7) and the information that he was "Chaplain for 32 years to the Missions to Seamen". A new mission motorboat was named in his honour, 'Stanley Treanor'. His successor was the Rev. P.L. Negus. The Downs Mission Station was the last station actively involved in work afloat at sea. The Missions to Seamen Boat Station closed in September 1927 and the boat was transferred to Ramsgate. Before his death Treanor had reported only 1,840 ships at anchor in a single year yet by the time of the mission's closure in 1931 the work was practically limited to seasonal visits to the Goodwin Lightships.

Presents of flowers, fruit and vegetables to the lightshipmen.

CELEBRITY CORNER

'distant summers and sweet idleness'

ARTISTS, authors and actors have found Deal conducive to their creative talents. They have been joined by a variety of poets, painters and performers.

Poet Laureate, Robert Seymour Bridges, was born at 'Roselands', Upper Walmer, in 1844. The grand house, long since vanished, was set among pleasant walks and gardens. Bridges recalled his boyhood delight at spying tall ships rounding the South Foreland. His family, who had been "substantial yeomen" since the early sixteenth century, were acquainted with the Duke of Wellington. The Poet remembered how every Sunday the Duke would pause by their pew in church and graciously bow to his mother, Harriet. He was awestruck when he noticed the flag flying at half mast over Walmer Castle, signifying the death of the Duke in 1852:

"I had seen his castle-flag to fall half-mast
One morn as I sat looking on the sea,
When thus all England's grief came first to me,
Who hold my childhood favour'd that I knew
So well the face that won at Waterloo."

Elegy: The Summer-House on the Mound (1899)

Charles Dickens was a guest speaker at a dinner to celebrate the opening of the Deal - Minster Railway on 30 June 1847. The author, summoned by electric telegraph, hastened over from Broadstairs to deliver an incoherent speech in which he, at least, praised the gallantry of the local boatmen. (He refers indirectly to Deal boatmen in his appreciation of "the seaside town without a cliff" in 'Household Words' 28 June 1856) Dickens stayed at 'The Swan Inn' (formerly 'The Five Bells') on what was at that time the main road between Dover and Sandwich. This was an important posting house with stabling for fifteen horses and tethering for a further one hundred. A toll gate stood directly outside the inn at the entrance to Queen Street (Five Bells Lane). Dickens is thought to have written several chapters of 'David Copperfield' (1850) while staying there.

When Dickens wrote his convoluted novel, 'Bleak House' (1853) he included several scenes set in Deal. Esther Summerson, recovering from smallpox, visits her friend,

Richard Carstone, stationed at Walmer Barracks, with her maid, Charley. By chance Esther encounters her former lover, Allan Woodcourt, a naval officer, recently returned to England after surviving "shipwreck and peril".

There is an evocative description of the Downs in the early morning viewed from the window of a seaside hotel (presumably 'The Royal'):

> "Our little room was like a ship's cabin, and that delighted Charley very much. Then the fog began to rise like a curtain; and numbers of ships, that we had no idea were near, appeared. I don't know how many sail the waiter told us were then lying in the Downs. Some of these vessels were of grand size: one was a large Indiaman just come home: and when the sun shone through the clouds, making silvery pools in the dark sea, the way in which these ships brightened, and shadowed, and changed, amid a bustle of boats pulling off from the shore to them and from them to the shore, and general life and motion in themselves and everything around them, was most beautiful." (Chapter 45)

Thomas Hughes conceived the idea of writing 'Tom Brown's Schooldays', while lodging at 'Leicester House', a prim, detached dwelling in Victoria Road in 1856. His story about life at Rugby during the headship of the famous Dr. Arnold has become a children's classic. Hughes was holidaying with his son in this "ridiculously small house" when he had the idea for his story. ". . . we turn out to the beach every morning at 7 to bathe," he wrote to Lord Goderich, "a source of danger just now as it is very rough with a great undertow, delicious swimming."

'Tom Brown's Schooldays' was published anonymously but the book was greeted with such acclaim by press and public that the publishers "soon revealed the secret", and to Hughes surprise, he instantly "became famous". The writing was vigorous, convincing and moving and this modest author was hailed for creating a new literary genre. According to his biographers, Mack and Armytage, "His was literally the first work of fiction to present a real world of boys in the setting of a real English public school." Sadly, his eldest son, Maurice, for whom Hughes wrote the book, died before reaching maturity.

William Makepeace Thackeray may have visited Deal to gain local colour for his unfinished novel, 'Denis Duval', which centres upon smuggling on the south coast. Chapter eight was the last instalment Thackeray

Looking southwards along the Esplanade.

wrote before he died and this was published in the June issue of 'Cornhill Magazine' for 1864. This final chapter is set almost entirely in Deal and concerns the young hero's enlistment in the Royal Navy. Denis' mother, who owns a prosperous fishing fleet, awaits her son at the 'Blue Anchor Inn', which was actually situated in West Street. She kits him out in the correct uniform, hastily made by a local tailor, and then takes immense pleasure in strolling with him, thus attired, along 'The Mall'. The next day Denis with his neatly packed sea chest is put on board 'Serapis' under the watchful eye of Captain Pearson who will steer him through his examinations so that he will eventually become rated as a midshipman. The proud mother, certain that her son is in safe hands, departs, holding back the tears, in "her little chaise. . . without looking back".

William Clark Russell, regarded as one of the greatest nautical writers of the Victorian age, lived in Deal. This handsome, dapper, keen-eyed, moustached American had been born in New York. His father was a composer and his mother was related to William Wordsworth (after whom her son was named). Russell joined the Merchant Navy and made voyages to India and Australia before fighting in the Second Chinese War. He abandoned his career at sea to concentrate on writing and he became a prolific author completing over sixty titles including 'Life of Nelson', 'Wreck of the Grosvenor', 'A Voyage at Anchor', 'In the Middle Watch' and 'The Ship, Her Story'. As a writer of sea stories he ranked with John Masefield, Richard Dana, Alan Villers, Herman Melville, Basil Lubbock and Robert Ballantyne - all of whom had connections with Deal.

Russell's novels mirrored the hardships faced daily by merchant seamen and his writings alerted the reading public to their injustices which led to social reforms. He was a champion of the Deal boatmen and offered strong support when their precarious livelihood was threatened with extinction. His book, 'Betwixt the Forelands' (1889) is a tribute to the port he greatly loved: ". . . a salter, a tarrier, a woodener, more box-ended hull of a place, I defy the imagination to figure". 'What Cheer?' (1907) which echoes the cry of the landsman as the hovellers return to shore, is a novel centred wholly around the Deal boatmen.

Indeed, Russell was held in such high esteem by the local boatmen that he was presented with a splendid mallet by boatbuilder, Thomas Hayward, which he had used for launching a craft he built in 1890. Russell lived at 3, Sandown Terrace (now 'Marine Terrace') a substantial building constructed in 1844 on land developed by William Betts, a railway contractor, between Sandown Castle and the Coastguard Station. The author relished the seaview from his study: "You might fish with a rod out of the windows," he declared.

Dornford Yates, one of the instigators of the 'Clubland Heroes', whose market was dominated by John Buchan and 'Sapper', was born at 'Wellesley House' (a former home of the Duke of Wellington) at Upper Walmer in 1885. His real name was Cecil William Mercer (which he hated!) He attended St. Clare, a nearby preparatory school for boys, once the beautiful home of Lord Conyers. Described as "a great, rambling, creeper-clad house with some thirty acres of gardens and playing fields", St. Clare was built by Andrew Gram, a Norwegian merchant, in 1806. The school was founded in 1891 by Alexander Murray and he enlisted his three daughters to assist with teaching. Youngest daughter was Charlotte Murray, poet and novelist, who was also a strict Protestant.

According to Yates her "penetrating clear blue eyes enormously magnified behind her glasses" watched disapprovingly his every move.

Yates wrote over three dozen romances and thrillers which retained their popularity throughout the 20th century. It seems strange that no seafaring character appears in any of his novels since he came from a distinguished nautical family. His great-grandfather, Lieutenant Josiah Dornford, commanded the brig, 'Thresher', in the attack on the Boulogne flotilla and served at sea during the Walcheren expedition before he transferred to the Coastguard. His grandfather, Captain Samuel Mercer, R.N., was Superintendent of the Packet Service at Dover before he retired to 'Swiss Cottage', Great Mongeham. Swindling solicitors, however, abound. His great uncle, George Mercer, a local dignitary, was a partner in a firm of solicitors. He was guilty of embezzlement and committed suicide to avoid prosecution. Yates' father took over the firm for a while but he was haunted by the memory of the fraud and soon moved his family to Harrow.

Another pupil of St. Clare's was Richard Aldington, poet, critic and essayist, who wrote 'Death of a Hero', one of the finest novels of the First World War. As a boy he remembers "skirting the castle grounds on dismal crocodile walks" but his childhood ramblings may have inspired him to write his 'Life of Wellington'. He lived first above his father's office at 5, Cannon Street, Dover, a street "full of umbrellas and horses"; then moved with his family to Warwick Court, Waterworks Road (now St. Richard's Road), Deal. Later still he inhabited an unidentified house in St. Margaret's-at-Cliffe. He recalls in his autobiography, 'Life for Life's Sake', that he slept there in a room with the "flash of the Foreland lighthouse winking through a gap in the curtain."

Deal was Joseph Conrad's favourite seaside town, according to his son, John. This master mariner began to write novels after he retired from service in the Merchant Navy in 1894. Prosperity came late to this Polish born English author but when his literary talent was firmly established he rented a handsome Georgian country house, 'Oswald's', in Bishopsbourne, near Canterbury. He once brought his crippled wife, Jessie, for a brief autumn holiday to Deal in 1920. They stayed at the 'South Eastern' which later became 'The Queen's Hotel'.

Conrad relished the view over the Downs from his hotel window and he took pleasure in naming the sails of the tall ships as they were being rigged. He encountered an old shipmate, George 'Frenchie' Baker, in whose company he rounded the Cape of Good Hope in a sailing ship, 'Riversdale', bound for Madras. The two friends reminisced one day as they rowed along the coast in a hired fishing boat. "Loyalty to memories of the past and to the men he had worked with at sea and on shore was a deep, abiding trait in his nature," assured his friend, Edward Garnett, an influential publisher's reader who had encouraged Conrad in his literary aspirations. (Alas, there is a only passing reference to Deal in Conrad's controversial novel, 'Heart of Darkness', based on his experiences in the Congo)

Playwright and novelist, J.B. Priestley, spent one summer with his family in a rented house, 'Wardley', along The Marina. He found it convenient for visiting his sister who owned a cosy tea shop (now 'The Golden Hind Bookshop') opposite 'The Royal Hotel'. Priestley was delighted by the furnished seaside property and wrote in 1928: "One of my ambitions has been realised at last. For the past two months we have been living at the very edge of the sea. . ."

Priestley completed his frothy novel, 'The Good Companions' (1929) which he called his "daydream", while at Deal. This tale, later dramatised, is often held to have catapulted him to instant fame and fortune. It was published in a time of economic gloom, rising unemployment and political unrest. The novel caught the imagination of the reading public and became one of the outstanding best sellers of the interwar period.

The story follows the adventures of a pierrot troupe travelling around the English coast in the 1920s. Priestley's description of the quaint seaside town of Sandybay sounds familiar: ". . . it was a clean, friendly little town, open to salt winds that as yet only had a healthy chill on them. In the mornings, when the October sun struggled through, there was a fine sparkle on the sea, the air was crisp and sweet as an apple, and it was delightful to swing along the promenade. In the centre, the old part, Sandybay was still a fishing village, a fascinating higgledy-piggledy of boats, nets, capstans, blue jerseys, mahogany faces and queer inns. . ."

> "Sandybay was a growing but 'select' resort; and here you found the Beach Hotel. . . a Circulating Library. . . and the Pier. This Pier went forward for about twenty-five yards, then swelled out in a rather dropsical fashion to support a Pavilion, which looked like an overgrown and neglected greenhouse. . . and ended in a subdued riot of little kiosks and automatic machines, the whole dominated by Refreshment Rooms, where the very red-faced men who took out monthly angling tickets could obtain a little Scotch or Draught Bass."

J.B. Priestley also wrote a series of essays with a local flavour published in a strangely titled book, 'The Balconinny' (1929) which was the name given by his daughter, Barbara, to the cramped balcony facing the sea. The panoramic view it afforded over the Downs delighted the author: "But that very morning, in came a Dutch mine-layer or mine-sweeper. . . and this is to say nothing of the regular traffic of this magic street; the great P & O and Union Castle liners, the tankers and grain ships and tramps and tiny coasting steamers, the brigs and luggers and little racing yachts. . ."

Lieutenant Evelyn Waugh of the Royal Marines was stationed at Kingsdown. In January 1940 he was transferred from Chatham and arrived at 'Kingsdown House', then "a derelict Victorian villa surrounded by little asbestos huts used in the summer as a holiday camp. One bath for sixty men, one washbasin, the WCs all frozen up and those inside the house without seats. Carpetless, noisy, cold. . ." He and a fellow officer took refuge in the Deal and Walmer Union Club (later known as 'S.P.Q.R'.) adjacent to Deal Castle. Waugh deemed it a "club for retired buffers" with some "old bores to talk to" but, at least, its facilities included a bath. Later, when permission was granted for officers to live out, he rented rooms for himself and his wife, Laura, at 'The Swan Hotel'.

Waugh remained unimpressed by the way the army camp was organised and its emphasis on lectures, strategies, field exercises and firearms practices. Nevertheless, the experience gave him ideal material for his superb war novels. He recorded in his diary the grim view from the frosted windows of his snowbound hut: "The prospect is extraordinary with white foreground and dingy sea background full of a hundred or more neutral ships awaiting contraband control. One, an Italian, was wrecked last night." (Thursday 18 January 1940)

Further southwards along the cliffs towards St. Margaret's Bay, Private Peter Ustinov was more philosophical about his military service. Playwright, actor, raconteur. . . Ustinov recalled his wartime experiences in his memoirs, 'Dear Me'. Early in January 1942, this raw recruit reported for duty, still wearing his civilian clothes, at an infantry regiment stationed on the clifftop. "In time of war", St. Margaret's "was melancholy indeed. The bungalows on the beach were deserted, and had been used as part of a street-fighting course by the military. Complicated barbed-wire constructions to a height of over ten feet added to its desolate hostility. Up on the cliffs was the village itself, and countless holiday homes, now largely taken over by the army. Dominant among these was the Granville Hotel, a white building with slatted verandahs, redolent of distant summers and sweet idleness."

His potential for leadership was soon recognised. He was temporarily promoted to officer status and put in charge of a pillbox on the Western Heights. The beach below was a tragic and sinister place where the debris washed up by each tide numbered a burned aviator's cap, crumpled pieces of metal from crashed aeroplanes and charred wood from sunken ships. He endured with fortitude: "The quizzical whistle of shells and bombs, earth-shaking explosions, the barking of incomprehensible orders. . ."Ustinov, even under duress, demonstrated his sense of humour and eye for the ridiculous. At his interview before the selection board he had expressed his desire to join the tank corps. The reason he gave was that he preferred "to go into battle sitting down".

Sir Noel Coward by Ida Kar
© National Portrait Gallery.

Immediately after the war Noel Coward leased a seaside property, 'White Cliffs', at St. Margaret's Bay. The house, with its russet roofs and myriad shutters, can be readily identified, perched precariously under the crumbling chalk face at the north end of the beach. At the time of his occupation, however, the foreshore was still cluttered with wartime debris and barbed wire. Selfishly, Coward bought four neighbouring houses at a time of acute housing shortage simply to ensure his own privacy and questions were asked in Parliament regarding the extent of his refurbishments during that age of austerity. 'The Master' enjoyed entertaining in his novel home and house guests included Gertrude Lawrence, Ivor Novello and Ian Fleming.

Coward's valet, Cole Lesley, set an idyllic scene: "Noel adored the sea, and. . . the house was almost in it; depending on the weather the waves either lapped against or lashed the end wall of the house, and this was to become the wall of his bedroom, against which was the head of the bed. The drama of this situation of course appealed strongly to him, the drama intensified by the White Cliffs of Dover rising steeply on his right, only a yard or two from where he lay. To his left he could look at, or step out on to, a little low-walled lawn beyond which stretched the changing colours of the sky and the English Channel; the never-ending traffic on the latter further enhancing the visual pleasure."

A few light-hearted references to Deal appear in his diary published posthumously:

Monday 19 November 1945
Went for a walk to the lighthouse. A grey pearly light over everything; very lovely. Went shopping with Cole in Deal and bought fourteen old and scarifying paintings with good frames and canvases. Worked on the synopsis (for a new operetta set on a mythical South Sea Island) from 5 p.m. till 10 p.m. and finished it. Dinner in bed. There is a sea mist and the Goodwins fog-horn is going.

Monday 1 July 1946

I woke early and wrote the first scene of the last act because, atom bomb or no atom bomb, I intend to get the operette finished.
In the evening Cole, Joyce, Graham and I went to Deal and saw the film of 'Bitter Sweet' (M.G.M'.s Technicolour version of Coward's play in 1940) Having only seen it once we had forgotten the full horror of it. . . After this vulgar orgy of tenth rate endeavour, we sat on the front and watched the hardy English children and a few adults advancing, mauve with cold, into the cheerless waves.

In 1952 the lease on this "extravagant" property was taken over by Ian Fleming. It became his weekend hideaway for the crucial decade in which he conceived the James Bond books. First novel to feature the super spy with a licence to kill (007) was 'Casino Royale', published that same year. Much of Fleming's inspiration came from his own experiences as a Naval Intelligence Officer during World War Two, a traveller and a journalist. The author, who was born at Pett's Bottom, near Canterbury, already knew the area intimately and so it is not surprising to learn that several of his superspy's escapades took place locally. James Bond's thrilling encounter with Auric Goldfinger on the golf course was played out at Royal St. George's (thinly disguised as 'Royal St. Mark's') Sandwich while Sir Hugo Drax's atomic rocket research station was - incredibly - based at Kingsdown Cliffs. Two famous car chases occurred between Bond and those arch villains across East Kent - one in the Aston Martin CB III in 'Goldfinger' and the other in a 4-litre supercharged Bentley in 'Moonraker'.

315

At one point Bond strolls with a plucky, auburn-haired heroine, Gala Brand, across the clifftops:

"It was a wonderful afternoon of blue and green and gold. . . To their left the carpet of green turf, bright with small wildflowers, sloped gradually down to the long pebble beaches of Deal and Walmer, which curved towards Sandwich and the Bay. . . It was low tide and the Goodwins were golden and tender in the sparkling blue of the Straits with only the smattering of masts and spars that stretched along the length to tell the true story. The white lettering on the South Goodwin lightship was easy to read and even the name of her sister ship to the north showed white against the red of her hull. Between the sands of the coast, along the twelve-fathom channel of the Inner Leads, there were half a dozen ships beating up through the Downs, the thud of their engines coming clearly off the quiet sea, and between the evil sands and the sharp outline of the French coast there were ships of all registries going about their business - liners, merchantmen, ungainly Dutch schuyts, and even a slim corvette, hastening down south, perhaps to Portsmouth. As far as the eye could reach the Eastern Approaches of England were dotted with traffic plying towards near or distant horizons, towards a home port, or towards the other side of the world. It was a panorama full of colour and excitement and romance and the two people on the edge of the cliff were silent as they stood for a time and watched it all."
(Chapter 16)

Ian Fleming by Mark Gerson
© National Portrait Gallery.

Fortunately, little damage occurs - apart from the Goodwins Lightships breaking their moorings - when Drax's atomic bomb explodes in the English Channel.

Romantic novelist, Victoria Holt (who also wrote under the name 'Jean Plaidy') roamed the historic streets of Deal searching for inspiration for plots in the 1970s. Miss Holt stayed with friends at the 'Scarborough Cat' on the seafront before purchasing 'The King's Lodging' in Sandwich. A pivotal scene in her adventure, 'The Shivering Sands' (1969) focuses upon the Goodwins and there are delightful vignettes of the Edwardian town.

L.S. Lowry's 'Deal Beach' (1947).
Courtesy: Felix Rosentiel's Widow & Son Ltd (on behalf of the estate of L. S. Lowry).

A variety of artists have had a brush with the town.

John Hassall, pioneer of commercial art, was born along The Beach at Walmer in 1868. His father was Lieutenant Christopher Clark Hassall, R.N. John was actually the second son although, since his elder brother, Ralph, died in infancy, he actually became the eldest in a large family. Young John was sent away to be educated in Worthing but during that time his father had an accident on board ship and was partially paralysed. The next time John returned home he was shocked to find that his father had become a bitter invalid. When Lieutenant Hassall died John's mother, Louisa, married a military man, William Wright (later General Sir William Purvis Wright, K.C.B.) The family moved from Walmer to grand homes in Tunbridge Wells and London. The stepfather cared for John and encouraged his talents as an artist. Eventually, John began to specialise in children's book illustrations, theatre programmes, posters for London Underground and advertisements for products as diverse as Veritas Mantles and Colman's Mustard. John Hassall is most famous for his Edwardian holiday poster featuring a jolly boatman skipping along the sands with the caption: 'Skegness is SO bracing'.

Laurence Stephen Lowry ventured into Kent. He made a number of drawings in chalk and crayon on different coloured papers of Canterbury and Westgate-on-Sea during 1912. At the same time, while experimenting with his artistic style, he sketched Deal. Although Deal became one of his favourite venues, Lowry did not turn his sketch into an actual painting until thirty-five years later. 'Deal Beach' or, simply 'The Beach', depicts the North End of Deal with 'The Royal Hotel' prominent on the far left, a cluster of houses on the foreshore and neatly spaced boats pulled up on the shingle. Their tall, slender masts echo the familiar primitive 'matchstick' children playing at the water's edge.

Edward Ardizzone (1900 - 1976) war artist and book illustrator, was introduced to the area when his brother, Philip, rented a house at Kingsdown sometime in the 1930s. When he visited one summer he was enchanted to hear the bands on the decks of liners passing close inshore from his balcony on warm, summer evenings and he was fascinated by the beams of the lightships flashing round the walls of his bedroom late at night. There he felt, "as much afloat as ashore". It gave him the idea for a series of popular children's books featuring Little Tim whose delightful

An Edward Ardizzone illustration for his Little Tim series.
Courtesy: Frances Lincoln Publishers.

illustrations often include local landmarks. In 1976 Ardizzone bought his own holiday home in Deal in order to escape the bustle of London.

Norman Long, a popular performer between the wars, was the first entertainer to be made a star by radio. He was born in 1893 above his father's shoe shop in Deal High Street. Pain's Directories for the late Victorian period advertise: "LONG and Son, boot and shoe manufacturers and portmanteau warehouse, 10, 12, 13 High St." Norman started life as an insurance agent but found a talent to amuse soldiers in his regiment during the First World War. He composed his own comic songs which were first heard via the "cat's whisker" on 28 November 1922.

This cheeky, chubby comedian was initially billed as 'A Song, a Smile and a Piano' but this was changed to 'A Song, a Joke and a Piano' since a smile was difficult to appreciate on radio. (This did not deter him from mystifying his listeners with card tricks!) Norman was proud to have been the first entertainer to broadcast from both the studios at Marconi House and Savoy Hill. Yet another achievement was when he took part in the first Royal Command

Wills cigarette card of the radio celebrity Norman Long.

Performance on radio in 1927. After the war Norman Long's popularity waned and he retired from show business to run a hotel in Salcombe.

Actress, Dorothy Summers, ran a seafront café called 'Mrs. Mopps'. She was famous as the office charlady in the wartime radio comedy show, 'It's That Man Again', shortened to 'ITMA'. ('That Man' referred to Hitler!) This surreal programme starred Tommy Handley as the mayor of a disreputable seaside resort improbably called 'Foaming-at-the-Mouth'. Each episode featured a bizarre group of characters who would enter a studio door one at a time to converse with him. They would each utter their own catchphrase, speak a few lines and abruptly exit. Miss Summers, who played the charlady, Mrs. Mopp, would call out in her strident voice above the clatter of her bucket: "Can I do you now, sir?" British families would gather round their wireless sets to listen every week in the blackout. The show ran from 1939 until 1949 when Handley died after which time Dorothy retired to her café at 81, Beach Street (later known as 'The Lobster Pot').

Wartime humorist, Nathaniel Gubbins, retired to Deal in 1947 where he lived first along The Beach and later atop Dover Road. Discovered by Lord Beaverbrook, his weekly column, 'Sitting on the Fence' in the 'Sunday Express' helped to keep up morale during World War Two. Gubbins' characters - The Man in the Pub, Sally the Cat, The Awful Child, The Worm's Wife - captured the imagination of the nation during those bleak times. He was admired by Coward, who invited him to lunch at The Savoy, and Churchill, who sent a car to fetch him to dine at Chartwell. It was rumoured that

Queen Elizabeth read his satirical pieces to King George VI over breakfast every Sunday morning. Nathaniel Gubbins lies buried in Walmer Churchyard.

Big Chief I-Spy, Arnold Cawthrow, lived for a time in the converted Boatmens' Rooms at the top of Exchange Street. The forty slim volumes, published originally by the defunct 'News Chronicle', were popular with children in the 1950s and 60s. Their titles, which ranged from 'I-Spy at the Seaside' to 'I-Spy at the Zoo', required young observers, or 'Redskins', to spot objects on a theme in return for fake feathers to add to their Red Indian headdress. Cawthrow, described by his assistant, 'Hawkeye', as "a frightfully camp antiques trader", was actually the second Big Chief. He ran his company from the 'Wigwam on the Green' (a seedy office above a hardware store on Paddington Green). When Cawthrow's tribe came completely under the influence of television, he hung up his tomahawk and retired gracefully to his unique home overlooking the seafront.

On a classical note, Dame Ninette de Valois, director of Sadler's Wells, which became the Royal Ballet at Covent Garden, spent her childhood at Walmer. Her real name was 'Edris Stannus' but she adopted her grand stage name because of a tenuous link with the French royal family. She was born at 'Baltiboys', a late Georgian country house, near Blessington, Co. Wicklow, Ireland, in 1898. Her father was a lieutenant-colonel who achieved a D.S.O. and her mother was a glassmaker who contributed tableware for Queen Mary's doll's house. While still young, Ninette moved with her family to lodge with her grandmother who owned a large Victorian house along The Beach at Walmer.

The Esplanade by the Victorian Pier.

Once a week Dame Ninette was driven with her governess in a hired brougham to 'The Oaks School for Girls' which later became 'Tormore School for Boys' at Upper Deal. There she was taught gymnastics by a Royal Marines sergeant-major who treated all his pupils as soldiers. More happily, Ninette relished her classical ballet lessons at this same school conducted by an accomplished teacher who travelled especially from London. At home, on winter's evenings, she would push back the heavily fringed antimacassared chairs in the drawing room to leave a small clear space on the thick Oriental carpet where by the light of the fire she would dance to her heart's content. Her grandmother, dressed in her stiff black moire gown, accompanied her on the upright piano, following the music with the aid of her gold-rimmed pince-nez. "I would experience a strange sense of happy achievement," Dame Ninette recalled in later years. "I would go contentedly to bed, wrapped in my new-found secret happiness."

The composer, John Ireland, rented a flat in 'Comarques', a fine Georgian town house in the High Street, for a short period before the Second World War. Habitually he made the tortuous steam train journey down at weekends from Charing Cross. His landlady remembered that this shy, introspective, lonely man spent hours locked away in his study writing music "without a sound coming from the piano, other than an occasional chord". There he wrote a short piece for string orchestra, 'Concertino Pastorale', although his most acclaimed work was 'Sea Fever' which incorporates words by poet, John Masefield. His friend and neighbour, Herbert Brown, a local solicitor, attempted a biography but found Ireland reluctant to release personal details and so he abandoned this project. A shell fired from across the Channel partly destroyed 'Comarques' but, by then, the composer had moved to the Channel Islands. When he did return for a brief period

G.P.R. James, a popular historical novelist, lived at 'The Shrubbery', a mock Tudor mansion, at Upper Walmer. A former occupant was Princess Amelia, daughter of George III.

Captain Marryat stayed regularly at the 'Star and Garter', a former hotel on the seafront. His novel, 'Poor Jack', recalls the deeds of the Deal pilots.

Henry Russell, father of the author, William Clark Russell, composed 'A Life on the Ocean Wave', adopted as the regimental march of the Royal Marines.

A pupil of St. Clare's Preparatory School was the popular comedian, Jimmy Edwards, distinguished by his handlebar moustache.

Captain Hornblower, C.S. Forester's fictitious hero, was, according to the books, born at Worth, near Deal.

John Willis, owner of 'Cutty Sark', lived for a time at Marine Terrace, Sandown.

W. G. Grace once played cricket on the lawn of 'Rosway', a Queen Anne manor in Middle Deal.

Mrs Pewtner Butt, owner of 'Sholden Hall', wrote ghost stories. She encountered the ghost of an admiral who had been resident in the 18th century.

immediately after the war, he commented wistfully:"It is a strange experience to see Deal again - and the sea."

Joseph Lister, pioneer of antiseptic surgery, spent a peaceful retirement at 'The Coach House' along The Beach at Walmer. He opened the door to modern surgery by recognising that germs spread disease and infect wounds which was an advance on the theory of Louis Pasteur. Baron Lister had heard of Walmer's "bracing air and quiet attraction" from a friend and made what was intended as a brief visit in the summer of 1908. He decided to make Walmer his home and settled in this grand house with its enviable view of "the wide stretch of sea separated from the house by a narrow lawn". Until he became an invalid Baron Lister was able to enjoy country drives and visits from younger members of his large family. On fine mornings he sat in a chair to watch the sun rising over the sea and he relished the seclusion of this "sleepy old Cinque Port". The people of Deal and Walmer, in their turn, expressed honour at having this modest yet diligent medical man amongst them in his evening light.

Charles Hawtrey.
Courtesy: Peter Rogers Productions.

Edward Banks, J.P., "a great cricketer and gardener", resided at 'Sholden Hall', formerly 'Sholden Lodge', which stands opposite St. Nicholas' Church. This splendid Georgian mansion (circa 1805) is approached by a tree-lined sweep from the London Road. It retains its pillared portico and grand belvedere, reached via a winding stairway, with a view over the Downs. Opposite the grand bay on the north side is an ivy clad stone arch that once led into the extensive kitchen garden.

Banks was born in Swansea in 1820 and while still an infant he was brought with his younger brother, William, to live at 'Oxney Manor' between Deal and Dover. The boys soon developed a love of cricket and eventually played for the county. In 1845 Edward turned out for Kent against all England and the following summer he played against Surrey in the first ever match at The Oval. (He made 37 runs which was the second highest score for his team in that match) The famous cricketer, Fuller Pilch, proclaimed Edward Banks "the greatest fielder of the day".

When Edward married, he moved with his wife, Nancy, to Sholden. He suffered from poor health so it is not surprising he took up the gentle pursuit of floriculture as a profession. He erected a number of greenhouses in the grounds - only one remains with its wide slate shelves - and started propagating fuchsias. This exotic plant in which he specialised had been introduced commercially into Britain at the end of the

18th century. He produced a host of new cultivars annually - one was named 'Beauty of Sholden' - which he sold to the London nurseries where he was hailed as 'King of Fuchsias'. His 'Forget-me-not' is now the emblem of the British Fuchsia Society. Edward Banks was a generous benefactor and he donated land on which Sholden Primary School was built in 1877.

The all-round sportsman, Gilbert Compton Elliot, lived at 'Hull Place', Sholden. Cricketer, boxer, golfer. . . Gilbert is credited with introducing ju-jitsu from Japan. Early in the nineteenth century, he began to convert this hidden ancient manor house into a comfortable family home. The plain brick frontage was remodelled in the Georgian style, reputedly by Sir Edwin Lutyens, while

Sir Norman Wisdom by Godfrey Argent
© National Portrait Gallery.

the celebrated gardens were redesigned, reputedly by Gertrude Jekyll. During the planting of the rose garden foundations of a Roman villa were discovered, complete with traces of painted frescoes on the walls. Inside the house the Tudor dining room was retained, including a stone fireplace and wooden panelling, behind which was found a smugglers' "hidey hole".

Gibert welcomed royalty to his modernised residence. The Prince of Wales stayed at 'Hull Place' on several occasions when visiting Royal St. George's Golf Club in the 1920s. Prince Albert (later King George VI) was another house guest while the Duke of Kent and his bride, Princess Marina, spent the first night of their honeymoon there on 28 November, 1934.

Gibert's daughter, Cynthia, served as a driver with the British Women's Mobile Canteen attached to the French Army during the Second World War. She was captured by the Germans, but, being a non-combatant, she was soon repatriated. In 1944, Cynthia shocked society by marrying a man twice her age, Leslie Hore-Belisha. He was the Minister for Transport who introduced the Belisha Beacon at pedestrian crossings. Ten years later Hore-Belisha was created Lord Devonport but, as there were no children by the marriage, the title became extinct.

Members of the millionaire Astor family owned a holiday retreat, 'Rest Harrow' (named after a plant which grows wild in the Sandhills) at nearby Sandwich Bay. Waldorf and his American wife, Nancy, relished this sprawling Arts and Crafts house at right angles to the sea along Princes Drive. The Astors habitually motored down from their luxurious mansion, 'Cliveden', overlooking the River Thames, for golfing weekends. Occasional house guests included T.E. Lawrence, the author, archaeologist, soldier and explorer, and Joachim von Ribbentrop, the German Foreign Minister who was lodging in a bungalow at Minnis Bay.

Nancy Astor became the first female Member of Parliament and she made her maiden speech to a packed house on 24 February 1920. She became a far more influential politician than her husband and concerned herself with the introduction of women police, widows' pensions, juvenile courts, female unemployment, child abuse, education and housing. Her brother-in-law, Colonel John Jacob Astor V, First Baron Astor of Hever Castle was for a quarter of a century M.P. for Dover. He proved to be a more conventional Tory politician who enjoyed socialising with his constituents. "We put in a good week at Deal last week," he wrote to Waldorf, "golf every morning and 2 or 3 meetings and concerts every afternoon and evening." (29 January 1921). The legacy of this wartime Member of Parliament is the 'Astor Theatre' (previously known as both 'Stanhope Hall' and 'Winter Gardens Theatre'). He presented this building upon his retirement to the inhabitants of Deal and Walmer in recognition of their courage and fortitude during the Second World War.

Two comedians spent time in Deal.

Charles Hawtrey, star of television's popular 'The Army Game' sitcom and cinema's interminable 'Carry On' series, bought a house upon a whim in the Conservation Area in 1970. This capacious Georgian terrace house was once described as "a warren of tight passages, stairs that need careful mounting and odd little cupboards and nooks" ('The Times' 23 September 2000). Sadly, Hawtrey, because of his aggressive alcoholism and dubious lifestyle, brought disrepute upon the town. Roger Lewis in his scurrilous biography, 'Charles Hawtrey', describes the fallen star as "sweet as strychnine". This seems apt. His erratic behaviour culminated in a fire which totally destroyed the interior of his historic property and for that reason Charles Hawtrey is probably the least deserving personality to have a blue plaque erected to his memory. Kenneth Williams, in typical vitriolic style, mentions a fleeting visit to his friend (Sunday 10 May 1970) in his posthumously published 'Diaries' (1993).

Sir Norman Wisdom, by complete contrast, is a celebrity who retains both the nation's and the town's affections. To escape his disfunctional family, Norman and his brother, while still schoolboys, took shelter with their guardians in Walmer. Norman attended Canada Road Junior School and became an enthusiastic member of Walmer Sea Scouts. Later, he worked as an unofficial station porter and as an errand boy for both the 'Home and Colonial' and 'Lipton's' grocery stores in the High Street. Once, this loveable latchkey kid stayed up all night to watch a film crew on location at Walmer attempting to capture the lifeboat battling against a storm at sea. This novel experience inspired him to seek an alternative career as an entertainer on stage, film, radio and television.

Perhaps the pop world has been the least represented in postwar Deal.

The original 'Rolling Stones' - Mick Jagger, Bill Whyman, Keith Richards, Charlie Watts, but not Brian Jones who was ill - performed (fee £55) at the Strand Palace Theatre, Walmer, on 5 September 1963. This was at the start of their cult career and only a short time before their big break on national television. Bill Whyman, in his autobiography, 'Stone Alone' (1997) describes the venue as a "dump" and the audience as "thugs"! Later, the distinctive angular building was converted into car showrooms.

Cross-dressing pop star, Boy George (born 'George Alan O'Dowd') founder of the cult group, 'Culture Club', spent reluctant boyhood holidays at Deal. His Irish father, Jerry, was a keen angler and would pack the family in the back of his broken-down van for occasional days away from London. "I hated fishing," confesses George in his autobiography, 'Take It Like A Man' (1995). "It always seemed like a good idea when we started out, but I'd get bored quickly and moan about going home. I would sit in Dad's van slouched in the front seat with my legs on the dashboard and arms folded, sulking." Misery, indeed.

The great number of celebrities who have graced Deal and Walmer with their presence for holidays, retreats and retirement gives the lie to the old adage - "As dull as Deal in times of peace".

BIBLIOGRAPHY

Stuart Admiral *Sir Cloudesley Shovell*
Nicholas Ardizzone *Edward Ardizzone*
Tony Arnold *The Coldest Place in England*
Tony Arnold and Alan Percy Walker *Deal's Lanes and Alleys*
Tony Arnold and Alan Percy Walker *Sketches of Deal*
Anthony Bailey *Standing in the Sun*
Jocelyn Baines *Joseph Conrad*
Margaret Baker *The Folklore of the Sea*
Frank Barlow *The Goodwins*
Bella Bathhurst *The Wreckers*
John Beattie *Lifeboats to the Rescue*
Lilian Boys Behrens *Under Thirty-seven Kings*
Helen C. Bentwich *History of Sandwich*
Howard Biggs *The Sound of Maroons*
John Blake *Sea Charts of the British Isles*
David W. Bone *Merchantmen-at-Arms*
J.P. Bowen *British Lighthouses*
Martin Brayne *The Greatest Storm*
Stephen Brindle *Brunel, The Man Who Built The World*
Alan Brooke and David Brandon *Bound for Botany Bay, British Convict Voyages to Australia*
David Blayney Brown *Turner and Kent*
Josiah Burchett *Complete History of the Remarkable Transactions at Sea*
Wes Butters *Charles Hawtrey, That Funny Fella with the Glasses*
Janet Cameron *Haunted Kent*
Bernard Capp *Cromwell's Navy*
D.P. Capper *Moat Defensive*
Elizabeth Carter *Letters Volumes 1 - 4*
David Chamberlain *Lost and Found*
David Chamberlain *Saga of the Goodwins*
David Chamberlain *Tales from Around the Goodwins*
David Chamberlain *The Goodwin Sands Man-Of-War*
Henry Stephen Chapman *Deal Past and Present*
Mark Chetwynd-Stapylton *Discovering Wayside Graves and Memorial Stones*
Kate Chisholm *Fanny Burney*
E.W. Clark *Reminiscences of Old Deal*
Norma Clarke *Dr. Johnson's Women*
Barbara Collins *A Short History of the Civic Church of St. George-the-Martyr*
Barbara Collins *Discovering Deal*
David G. Collyer *Deal and District at War 1939-45*
David G. Collyer *East Kent at War*
David Cordingly *Cochrane the Dauntless*
Vaughan Cornish *The Churchyard Yew and Immortality*
Patricia Cornwall *Portrait of a Killer*
David Cuppleditch *The John Hassall Lifestyle*
Marquess Curzon of Kedleston *Walmer Castle and its Lords Warden*
William Dampier *A New Voyage Around the World*
Michael Davie (Ed) *The Diaries of Evelyn Waugh*
Daniel Defoe *A Tour thro' the Whole Island of Great Britain*
Thomas Dibdin *Reminiscences Vol 1*
Charles Dickens *Memoirs of Joseph Grimaldi*
Peter Earle *Sailors*
Elizabeth Eger and Lucy Peltz *Brilliant Women, 18th Century Bluestockings*
Martin Easdown *Piers of Kent*
Adam Edwards *A Short History of the Wellington Boot*

C.R.S. Elvin *Walmer and Walmer Castle*
Stewart P. Evans and Keith Skinner *Jack the Ripper: Letters from Hell*
Bernard Falk *Turner the Painter, His Hidden Life*
Flora Fraser *Princesses - The Daughters of George III*
Robert Fulton *Torpedo War and Submarine Explosions*
George Fox *Journal*
Edward Garnett (Ed) *Letters of Joseph Conrad*
George Byng Gattie *Memorials of the Goodwin Sands*
Alice C.C. Gaussen *A Woman of Wit and Wisdom*
Boy George *Take It Like A Man*
D.E.W. Gibb *Lloyd's of London*
Sir Rickman John *Godlee Bt Lord Lister*
Rev. John Gilmore *Storm Warriors*
George Goldsmith-Carter *Looming Lights*
George Goldsmith-Carter *Sailing Ships and Sailing Craft*
G.A. Gollock *At the Sign of the Angel*
Ivan Green *The Book of Deal and Walmer*
John W. Graham *William Penn*
William Hague *William Wilberforce*
Dr. James Hall, O.B.E. *Sea Surgeon*
James Hamilton *Turner, A Life*
James Hamilton *Turner's Britain*
Peter C. Hammond *The Parson and the Victorian Parish*
Gwen Hampshire (Ed) *Elizabeth Carter, 1717 - 1806, An Edition of Some Unpublished Letters*
G.G. Harris *The Trinity House of Deptford 1514 - 1660*
Claire Harman *Fanny Burney*
Selina Hastings *Evelyn Waugh*
Judith Hawley (Ed) *Bluestocking Feminism Vol 2*
Caroline Hillier *The Bulwark Shore*
John Hilton *Joseph Hatch, the Ulcombe Bell Founder*
S.N. Holbourn *A Boatman's Tale*
Gregory Holyoake *St. Andrew's Church*
Mary Hopkirk *Queen Adelaide*
J.H. and E.C. Hubback *Jane Austen's Sailor Brothers*
F.J. Hunt *Deal, Walmer and Kingsdown Amateur Rowing Club*
J.R. Hutchinson *The Press Gang Afloat and Ashore*
John Ingamells *Mid-Georgian Portraits 1760 - 1790*
Roy Ingleton *Policing Kent*
Anthony Lane *Calamity Corner*
Anthony Lane *Guiding Lights*
Anthony Lane *Shipwrecks of Kent*
Richard and Bridget Larn *Shipwrecks of the Goodwin Sands*
Erik Larson *Thunderstruck*
Cole Lesley *The Life of Noel Coward*
Roger Lewis *Charles Hawtrey: The Man who was Private Widdle*
John Longmire *John Ireland, Portrait of a Friend*
Basil Lubbock (Ed) *Barlow's Journal*
Basil Lubbock *The Log of the Cutty Sark*
Andrew Lycett *Ian Fleming*
Kendall McDonald *Dive Kent*
Edward Mack and W.H.G. Armytage *Thomas Hughes*
Alan Major *The Kentish Lights*
Howard Mallinson *Send it by Telegraph*
G.E. Manwaring (Ed) *The Diary of Henry Teonge*
Colin Martin and Geoffrey Parker *The Spanish Armada*
Stephen Martin-Leake *Life of Sir John Leake Vol 1*

Robert B. Matkin *Maritime Thanet*
Jeffrey Meyers *Joseph Conrad*
Elizabeth Melling (Ed) *The Poor*
Geoffrey Moorhouse *Great Harry's Navy*
Malcolm Morley *Margate and its Theatres*
John Munday *E.W. Cooke, A Man of His Time.*
Sylia Harcstark Myers *The Bluestocking Circle*
Gertrude Nunns *A History of Deal*
Patrick O'Brian *Men-Of-War*
E.C. Pain *Deal and the Downs in the War of Liberation 1939 - 1945*
E.C. Pain *History of Deal 1914 - 1953*
E.C. Pain *Last of Our Luggers*
W.D. Parish and W.F. Shaw *A Dictionary of the Kentish Dialect*
John Pearson *The Life of Ian Fleming*
Rev. Montagu Pennington *Memoirs of the Life of Mrs. Elizabeth Carter*
Roy Philp *The Coast Blockade*
Sam Pockett *It's Cold In The Channel*
John Pollock *George Whitefield and the Great Awakening*
David Proctor *Music of the Sea*
Robert C. Ritchie *Captain Kidd and the War Against the Pirates*
A.H.W. Robinson *Marine Cartography in Britain*
N.A.M. Rodger *The Wooden World, An Anatomy of the Georgian Navy*
John Lewis Roget *Sketches of Deal, Walmer and Sandwich*
W. Clark Russell *Betwixt the Forelands*
Andrew Sargeant *The Life and Times of a Small House in Deal.*
Muriel V. Searle *John Ireland, the Man and his Music*
Robert Simper *Beach Boats of Britain*
James Simpsom *Eminent Men of Kent*
A.J. Smithers *Dornford Yates*
Robert Southey *Life of Nelson*
Earl Stanhope *History of England in the Reign of Queen Anne*
William Stanton *Journal of a Deal Pilot*
W.P.D. Stebbing *The Invader's Shore*
J. Harris Stone *The Piccadilly of the Sea - St. Margaret's Bay*
L.A.G. Strong *Flying Angel*
Christopher Sykes *Nancy, The Life of Lady Astor*
Arthur Tedder *The Navy of the Restoration*
Edward Thompson *Robert Bridges*
Rev. Canon C.F. Tonks, M.B.E. *The Walmer Churches*
Claire Tomalin *Mrs. Jordan's Profession*
Claire Tomalin *Samuel Pepys, The Unequalled Self*
Rev. T.S. Treanor *Heroes of the Goodwin Sands*
Rev. T.S. Treanor *Log of a Sky Pilot*
Rev. T.S. Treanor *The Cry From The Sea*
G.M. Trevelyan *England Under Queen Anne*
Sam Twining *My Cup of Tea*
Peter Ustinov *Dear me*
Ninette de Valois *Come Dance With Me*
Katherine Sorley Walker *Ninette de Valois*
Katherine D. Watson *Dr. Crippen*
Gabriel White *Edward Ardizzone*
George Whitefield *Journals*
Derek Wilson *The Astors*
Andrew Wilton *The Life and Work of J.M.W. Turner*
Norman Wisdom with William Hall *My Turn*

Richard Woodman and Jane Wilson *The Lighthouses of Trinity House*
Janet Robyn Worthington *Coopers and Customs Cutters: Worthingtons of Dover and Related Families, 1560- 1906*
Anne Wroe Perkin, *A Story of Deception*
Bill Whyman *Stone Alone*

Students of local history will always rely heavily on three excellent volumes: *'History of Deal'* by Stephen Pritchard (1864) *'History of Deal'* by John Laker' (1921) and *'Records of Walmer'* by Charles Elvin (1890). Tales of the renowned boatmen are chronicled in the Rev. T.S. Treanor's trilogy, the most famous of which is *'Heroes of the Goodwin Sands'* (1892). Stories of their heroic deeds are continued in George Bethel Bayley's *'Seamen of the Downs'* (1929). This readable account includes a rare interview with a Deal boatman, William 'Bonnie' Adams, Coxswain of the North Deal lifeboat, 'Charles Dibdin'. An exhilarating modern account of the Great Storm of 1703 appears in Martin Brayne's *'The Greatest Storm'* (2002).

There is a small army of local historians who constantly add fascinating details to our knowledge of the town's history. Among those who have been most generous regarding information are David Chamberlain, Julie Deller and the late David Collyer.

The author wishes to add a disclaimer to this present history. It is tempting for local historians to merely copy what has been previously recorded and there are two instances where I have done the same. The famous description of the Deal boatmen by Charles Dickens which appears in *'Household Words'* cannot be identified by 'The Dickens Society'. Nor can any of the references by Laker to the 'Annual Register' be located by myself or my researchers.
The unsourced snippets from Elizabeth Carter's letters are taken from several articles by a forgotten local historian, Barbara Collins.

The Sandwich, Deal, Dover and Canterbury stage coach
passing Dover Castle. Courtesy: Ivan Green collection.

ACKNOWLEDGEMENTS

Terry Bishop; Bodleian Library; Bonham's Auctioneers; British Broadcasting Corporation; British Library Newspapers; Rev W.J. Bromley, Rector of Stottesden; Buckingham Palace; Tom Burnham; Canterbury Cathedral Archives; Centre for Kentish Studies; Christie's Auctioneers; John Clapson; Leslie Coe; Rev. Seth Cooper, Vicar of Walmer; Christine Corner; L.W. Cozens; Sue Crabtree, Special Collections Librarian, Templeman Library, University of Kent at Canterbury; Cllr. Jim Cronk, His Worship the Mayor of Deal; Cutty Sark Trust; Daily Telegraph; Michael Davis; Deal Maritime Museum; Julie Deller; Department of Transport; Judith Doré; Dover District Council; East Kent Mercury; Family Records Office; Dr. Marc Feeney; Rev. Gary Gill; Captain Anthony Hackett; Susan Hare, Honorary Curator, Canterbury Cathedral Treasury; Peter Harris-Mayes; Rev. Canon Bruce Hawkins; Cllr. Pat Heath; John Hopper; Michael Hunt, Ramsgate Maritime Museum; Keith James LL.B.; David Jibb; Lynn King; Andrew Kirk, Assistant Curator, Theatre Museum; the late W.H. Lapthorne; Father Christopher Lindlaw; Alice and Mark Linington; London Metropolitan Archives; Ruth Loveridge; The Lowry Centre; Nick McConnell, Golden Hind Bookshop; Natasha McEnroe, Curator, Dr. Johnson's House, London; Alan Major; Roy Masini, Metropolitan Police Directorate of Information; Missions to Seafarers; National Army Museum; National Maritime Museum, Greenwich; National Museum of Photography; National Portait Gallery; Jacqueline O'Connell; Dr. Richard Palmer, Librarian and Archivist, Lambeth Palace Library; Bob Peacock; Brian Petch; Dr. Raymond Refauss, Librarian and Archivist, Church of Ireland Representative Church Body Library; David Robertson, Honorary Curator, Kent County Cricket Club; Royal Academy of Arts; Royal Thames Yacht Club; Sandwich Guildhall Museum Archive; Science Museum; Susan Shanks; Rev. Brian Sharp; Keith Skinner; The Stage; Simon Stait; Martin Tapsell; Tate Britain; Theatre Museum; Brian Thynne, Curator of Hydrography, National Maritime Museum; Trinity House; United Kingdom Hydrographic Office; University of Reading Library; Raymond Venables; Stephanie Thomson; Westminster City Library; Tracey Wahdan, Visitor Operations Director for English Heritage; Rowena Willard-Wright, Senior Curator, Dover Castle; Denise Willows, Winchester Cathedral; Dr. David Wright M.A., Ph.D.

The extract from 'The Noel Coward Diaries' edited by Graham Payn and Sheridan Morley is reprinted with the permission of Weidenfeld and Nicolson, an imprint of Orion Publishing Group.

The extract from 'Moonraker' by Ian Fleming (copyright Glidrose Publications Ltd 1955) is reprinted with the permission of Ian Fleming Publications Ltd.

E. W. Cooke's painting of the Rescue by the North Deal Lifeboat, 'Van Kook', is in a private collection. It is reproduced with the permission from John Munday's biography of E. W. Cooke published by The Antique Collectors' Club.

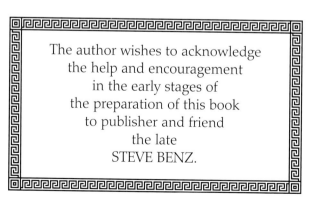

The author wishes to acknowledge
the help and encouragement
in the early stages of
the preparation of this book
to publisher and friend
the late
STEVE BENZ.

ABOUT THE AUTHOR

Gregory Holyoake is an actor, author and schoolteacher who lives in a seafront flat overlooking the Downs Anchorage at Deal. He trained as a schoolmaster at Culham College of Education, Oxfordshire, where he gained teaching certificates in English and Divinity. As an actor he trained at Rose Bruford College of Speech and Drama in Sidcup, Kent. He has been acting for thirty years in national tours, repertory, repertoire and pantomime. Gregory has been a freelance writer and photographer for nearly forty years. He has been a regular contributor to *'Country Life'*, *'Country Homes and Interiors'*, *'Illustrated London News'*, *'Heritage'*, *'This England'*, *'The Lady'* and *'Evening Standard'*. He began his journalistic career by writing for *'Young Oberver'* in *'The Observer Magazine'* where he often shared the page with *'Peanuts'*. For five years he was chief photo-journalist for the county magazine, *'Kent Life'*, when he became an authority on Kentish subjects. He recently published a photographic book on *'Scarecrows'* and he is currently researching the history of the real *'Dick Whittington'*.

Below - A young Gregory Holyoake (far left) with members of the Carter Avenue Gang outside his prefabricated home in Deal. The story of the author's childhood is told in 'The Prefab Kid - A Postwar Childhood in Kent' also by SB Publications.

The companion book to Deal All in the Downs is
Deal Sad Smuggling Town